Oracle Siebel Open UI Developer's Handbook

Duncan Ford, Alexander Hansal,
Kirk Leibert, Jan Peterson

Published in 2015 by P8tech, an imprint of Play Technologies (England) Limited

Copyright © Play Technologies (England) Limited

ISBN: 978-0-9929105-1-8

P8Tech
6 Woodside
Churnet View Road
Oakamoor
ST10 3AE

www.P8Tech.com

Foreword

A great work of software is as rare as a great work of art. That is why it is my honor to write an introduction for the latest extension of Siebel CRM into the world. Siebel Open UI promises a new era for Siebel and offers the people who work with it a new way of engaging with it. You are holding, in your hands, the key to that engagement.

Great works of software are deeply influential. Product marketing people often talk about *products*. Software sales people often talk about *solutions*. Great works of software change the nature of the code that follows. A great work of software transcends both those limits and offers something else – a new form of engagement with the world. Great works of software just don't just let people do things; it gives them a way to talk about and share what they did. It allows them to solve hard problems.

By all these measures, Siebel is a great work of software. Since Siebel Sales Enterprise was first introduced in 1995, the Siebel product line has expanded and forked off into dozens of applications and versions as varied as Siebel Marketing, Siebel Field Service, and even CRM OnDemand. Although very different in functionality, all these products were built on the same basic database structure and three-tiered architecture. Although Siebel Sales Enterprise set out to do something fairly basic, it consequently grew and changed over time.

Ultimately it provided a way for large groups of people to talk about, and think about, a very difficult problem – complex team sales. Before Siebel, sales people organized their work on business cards and little scraps of paper. Now CRM systems have become as central to business as ERP systems.

But perhaps its most valuable legacy is how Siebel has changed the lives of the people who work with it. Siebel technology created an ecosystem around it and provided an opportunity for many people to earn a livelihood; including myself. Very few people talk about how software can change the way people see the world. Thanks to Siebel technology, I see the world differently and I am not alone.

The authors have gone great lengths to create a book that is both comprehensive as well as informative. My hope and expectation is that after reading it, you will be able to do something meaningful professionally, personally, and for the world.

All the best,

Bruce Daley. Publisher, Siebel Hub

About the Authors

Duncan Ford is a veteran Siebel hacker, having worked in Education, Consulting, and Sales roles at Oracle. Outside of work, Duncan enjoys computer and tabletop games, plays the piano, and services the needs of four cats.

Alexander "@lex" Hansal enjoys tinkering with Siebel CRM and related technologies. He has been doing so since 2001. Alex believes in the power of sharing knowledge and publishes his findings on the Siebel Hub blog at http://siebelhub.com

Kirk Leibert lives in North Carolina with his wife, Tara (whom he wishes to thank for her tremendous hard work and support on this project), and five children. When not chasing customer demos as a Sales Consultant at Oracle, he enjoys spear fishing and hunting mammoth while simultaneously writing JavaScript renderers.

Jan Peterson works as a Customer Experience Solution Architect for Oracle Australia. Jan worked for Accenture and Siebel/Oracle in the past and has 10 years of CRM experience. During the course of his career he held various Consulting and Pre-Sales roles including configuration expert, technical architect and team lead. Jan holds a University diploma in computer science from the FSU Jena and an MBA from the La Salles University. He lives with his wife and daughter in Sydney, Australia.

Code

All the code in this book is available in a downloadable zip file.

Download the file from *www.P8tech.com/Siebel_Book.zip*

The file is password protected. The password is **polarbear**

Errata

Despite best efforts, mistakes can sometimes creep into books. If you spot a mistake, please feel free to email us at errata@p8tech.com (with the book title in the subject line). The errata page for the book is hosted at *www.P8tech.com/Siebel*

Table of Contents

Index

1

Introduction to Siebel Open UI

In December 2012, Oracle released Siebel CRM versions 8.1.1.9 and 8.2.2.2. These releases, also known as Innovation Pack 2012, made a new landmark user interface rendering technology, named **Open User Interface (Open UI),** available for the Siebel customer base.

Siebel Open UI is the first user interface rendering layer for Siebel CRM which supports all modern browsers on all device types and operating systems, be it desktop or laptop PCs, smartphones or tablets.

Beginning with versions 8.1.1.9 and 8.2.2.2, Oracle provides new functionality and features for Siebel CRM by means of Innovation Packs. This book is based on Innovation Packs 2013 and 2014.

This book will serve as your guide to Siebel Open UI by providing precise architectural insight, well-researched technical details, and hands-on examples.

This chapter covers the following topics

- Introducing Siebel Open UI
- Technologies used in Siebel Open UI
- Basic concepts for end users and administrators
- Siebel Mobile Applications

Introducing Siebel Open UI

When Siebel Systems Inc. introduced its first web-based enterprise applications in the late nineties, the dominant browser on corporate computers was Microsoft Internet Explorer. Other browsers such as Netscape Navigator only had a single-digit market share in the enterprise realm. Siebel CRM version 7.0, released in 2001, provided three ways of rendering the user interface in the browser:

- High-Interactivity (HI) client, using Microsoft's ActiveX technology, Java, JavaScript, and HTML
- Standard-Interactivity (SI) client, using only JavaScript and HTML

- Wireless client, using very simple HTML, WML or XML for mobile browsing

The ActiveX based client provided a superior user experience at the cost of only being supported by specific versions (and patches) of Microsoft Internet Explorer. The standard-interactivity and wireless clients were supported on other browsers as well but offered only a limited set of functionality at much lower comfort.

Over time the internet and browser market changed drastically. At the end of the first decade of the 21st century, three browsers dominated the internet with almost equal market share:

- Microsoft Internet Explorer
- Mozilla Firefox
- Google Chrome

In addition to new browsers which consistently surpassed the performance of older versions of Internet Explorer, a new generation of mobile devices emerged in the form of smartphones and tablets. Providing processing power and graphics resolutions previously reserved to workstation-class computers, these handheld devices revolutionized the way we access and provide information via the internet.

Also, at the end of the first decade, Oracle was under pressure from its customer base. Siebel CRM users found the lock-in to old (and unsecure) versions of Microsoft Internet Explorer unpalatable. They wanted to access Siebel CRM data in modern, more secure and faster browsers as well as on their new mobile devices.

Oracle listened to its customers and, after being announced in 2011, Siebel Open UI was released in 2012.

> As a matter of historical fact, there have been various attempts to modernize the Siebel user interface both by Siebel Systems and Oracle, such as the Web UI DDK which spawned from the Siebel CRM OnDemand project with IBM, or even a UI based on Adobe Flash which was never published.

In a nutshell, we can describe the key features of Siebel Open UI as follows:

- Based on open web standards such as HTML, JavaScript and CSS
- Supports all modern, standard-compliant browsers on any device type
- Keeps the well-known Siebel navigation pattern while introducing more modern usage paradigms
- Provides a safe migration path for existing customers and their customizations
- Implements a new Application Programming Interface (API) for extensibility
- Provides the user interface technology layer for desktop and mobile applications

The following screenshot shows the Siebel Call Center application in Open UI mode (Innovation Pack 2013), as an example for a desktop application (typically used on a desktop or laptop PC).

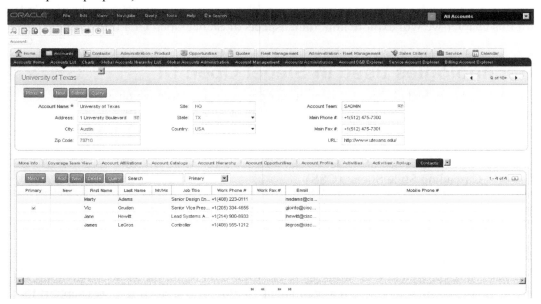

The next screenshot shows a Siebel Mobile Application - Financial Services Mobile - as rendered on a tablet device.

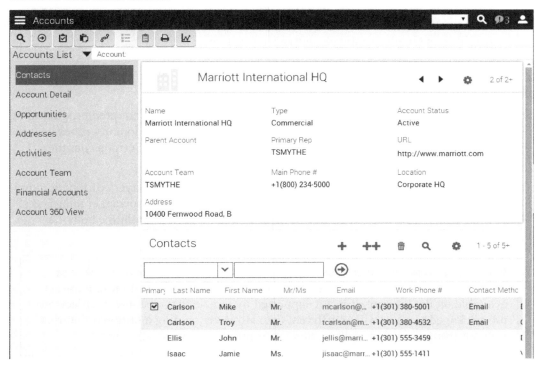

As we can discern from the above screenshot, Siebel Mobile Applications are optimized for mobile devices, displaying less data and providing a touch-enabled user experience. The Financial Services Mobile application is an example for the unified look and feel of desktop and mobile applications introduced with Innovation Pack 2014. In the remainder of this chapter we will explore important aspects of Siebel Open UI a little deeper.

Technologies used in Siebel Open UI

As stated above, Siebel Open UI is built on open web standards which are widely adopted by browser vendors and web developers. These standards are:

- Hypertext Markup Language (HTML)
- JavaScript
- Cascading Style Sheets (CSS)

Let's see how Siebel Open UI uses and supports these web standards.

HTML Support

As per the "Deployment Guide for Open UI" which can be found on My Oracle Support (http://support.oracle.com) as document 1499842.1, Open UI requires support for HTML5 as a minimum. Browsers which are not capable of rendering HTML5 are not considered suitable for Open UI deployments.

> Note that to access documents on *My Oracle Support* you must authenticate yourself as an Oracle employee, partner, or customer.

JavaScript Support

JavaScript is considered "the language of the web" and is a widely adopted programming language for browser-side logic. Siebel's Open UI client-side functionality relies heavily on JavaScript, thus any browser must provide full support for JavaScript as per the ECMA-262 standard.

JavaScript is used by Oracle and custom developers to provide all layers of functionality in the Siebel Open UI client. Any JavaScript-based library, with a special emphasis on **jQuery** (which is the library of choice by Oracle) can be used to optimize both the coding process and the user experience.

> Each Siebel version comes pre-packaged with specific versions of JavaScript libraries such as jQuery. While there might be newer versions of these libraries available on the internet, it is not supported by Oracle that customers replace any pre-packaged version with a different one. However, adding additional libraries sourced from the web or self-written is a supported customization practice.

CSS Support

Cascading Style Sheets are the standard way of providing layout and formatting for content displayed in browsers. The minimum version required by Open UI is 2.1 for Innovation Pack 2013 and CSS version 3 is the minimum requirement for Innovation Pack 2014.

> Information and training on web technologies such as HTML, JavaScript, jQuery and CSS can be found aplenty on the internet. Here are some resources to give you a start.
>
> jQuery: http://jquery.com
>
> Tutorials on web technologies: http://webplatform.org
>
> Online documentation by the Mozilla Developer Network: https://developer.mozilla.org

Please note that this book does *not* teach you the aforementioned web technologies. Medium to expert-level skills in web development are highly recommended should you intend to customize Siebel Open UI.

Other Standards Supported by Open UI

In addition to the web standards described above, Siebel Open UI supports the following standards:

- Web Accessibility Initiative - Accessible Rich Internet Applications (WAI-ARIA)
- Web Content Accessibility Guidelines (WCAG) 2.0 and Section 508
- Java Specification Request (JSR) 286
- Web Services for Remote Portlets (WSRP) 2.0

The aim of **WAI-ARIA** is to provide a standard for making web applications accessible for impaired users and those who use screen readers to access their applications. As per the documentation, Oracle supports the World Wide Web Consortium (W3C) initiative "where possible".

WAI-ARIA standardizes keyboard navigation and provides "landmarks" as HTML attributes in the web page which can be interpreted by screen-reading software supporting the standard.

More information about WAI-ARIA can be found at http://www.w3.org/WAI.

WCAG 2.0 is a collection of W3C recommendations to make web content more accessible for people with disabilities, and in general.

More information about WCAG 2.0 can be found at http://www.w3.org/TR/WCAG20.

In order to provide information about what accessibility features are supported by which product version, Oracle publishes its Voluntary Product Accessibility Templates (VPATs) for all its applications at
http://www.oracle.com/us/corporate/accessibility/vpats/index.html.

JSR 286 is the current version of the Java portlet specification and describes portlet programming models to support displaying an application's web content in another web application.

More information about JSR 286 can be found at
http://en.wikipedia.org/wiki/JSR-286.

WSRP is a network protocol standard for communication with portlets.

More information about WSRP can be found at
http://en.wikipedia.org/wiki/Web_Services_for_Remote_Portlets

Becoming a Siebel Open UI Developer

The typical veteran Siebel developer will feel a bit intimidated by the amount of web standards presented above. In order to successfully contribute to a Siebel Open UI project, developers must become fluent with web languages such as JavaScript, HTML and CSS and also familiarize themselves with quasi-standard JavaScript libraries such as jQuery.

Once this stage is reached, developers benefit from a rich application programming interface (API) and clear three-layer structure (data access, business logic, presentation) which comes as part of Siebel Open UI.

It is also foreseen that Open UI development will see a veteran Siebel developer paired with a veteran web developer. Oracle University recommends that Open UI training be attended by both types of developers in order to accelerate their ability to work together on Open UI projects.

The upcoming chapters will cover more details on the architecture and programming interfaces of Open UI.

Basic Concepts for End Users and Administrators

In the following section we will explore some Open UI specific features which differ in one way or another from the user experience in traditional High-Interactivity applications to which most Siebel users are familiar from their daily work. The features are categorized as follows:

- Browser Features
- Usability Enhancements
- Changed Navigation Patterns
- User Preferences
- Applet Features
- Notifications
- Updated Look and Feel
- Unsupported Features

Browser Features

Because it is based on open web standards, native browser features such as zoom can be used much easier with Siebel Open UI than with other Siebel client interfaces.

Browser Zoom

With most browsers, you can simply use the *CTRL* key in conjunction with the mouse wheel or the + or - keys to zoom in and out. This makes it easy to adjust the Siebel client to your viewing preferences.

Browser Print

Using the native browser print features with Siebel web clients might be a bit controversial as you can only print what you see on the screen. The following screenshot illustrates the dilemma.

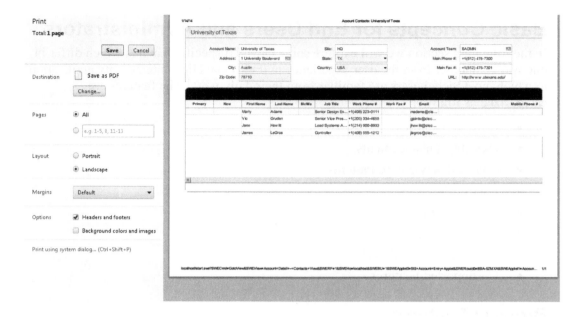

The screenshot shows the Google Chrome print dialog for a Siebel view. As can be seen, some of the data is truncated. Also, printing a list applet will always be limited to the currently visible records and columns.

As an alternative to native browser printing, end users can either rely on **Siebel Quick Print** or **Siebel Reports** which are fully Open UI-enabled. As these components are unchanged with Open UI we will not cover them in the remainder of this book.

Page Refresh

At any point in time, we can refresh a page by using the browser's refresh button. However, we have to keep in mind that we could also just submit a query to refresh the data displayed. Keep in mind that Siebel CRM is an enterprise CRM application delivered as a web site. Because of the 'heavy lifting' done by the Siebel Server in the background, the features, functions and capabilities provided by Siebel CRM are beyond the typical scope and range of a 'regular' web page.

Bookmarks

With Siebel Open UI, it is possible to bookmark any view using native browser functionality. The ability to bookmark individual records is still available as pre-defined functionality from the applet menu.

Resizing Text Areas

Most modern browsers interpret the `<textarea>` element of a page's HTML and provide a handle in the lower right corner to resize the text box using mouse gestures as shown in the screenshot below .

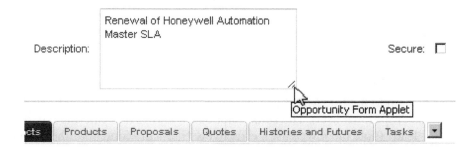

As indicated above, this is a browser feature and works on all text areas defined in applets without any further configuration. It must be noted that not all browsers support this functionality.

Logging Out

While the ActiveX-driven High-Interactivity client allowed users to end a session by simply closing the browser, be aware that this is not the case in Open UI as modern browsers do not offer an appropriate close browser event. To ensure that the session is closed properly on the server, we should therefore use the Log Out command in the File menu.

Usability Enhancements

Siebel Open UI introduces a lot of new usability features which provide a richer user experience. The following examples illustrate the most important changes.

Site Map Filter

A new search box on top of the Site Map allows end users to simply enter any part of text they are looking for. The content of the Site Map is filtered as soon as we type the third character. The following screenshot shows the Site Map after entering the text "mani" (in lowercase) in the search box. Subsequently, only views which have a name that contains the search term are displayed.

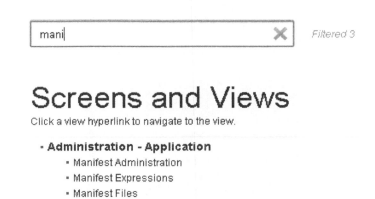

9

Site map search is a useful enhancement, especially for users with access to a large number of views.

Drop-Down List Filter

In a similar fashion to the Site Map filter, end users can now work with static pick lists (also known as drop-down lists). The screenshot below shows that entering a part of the text, such as "lead" (note the lowercase), effectively filters the content of the drop-down list.

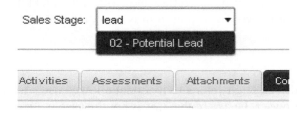

The drop-down list filter feature allows users to work more efficiently with static pick lists.

Common Controls

Siebel Open UI provides an updated look and feel for the most common controls such as the calculator or the date and time picker. The next screenshot shows the latter as an example.

As we will discuss in more detail in upcoming chapters, developers will benefit from the high configurability regarding both functionality and style of the enhanced controls.

Changed Navigation Patterns

While Oracle engineering strived to maintain most navigational aspects of the well-established High-Interactivity client, they made some changes to traditionally used patterns such as the following.

- Shuttle Applets (not available until Innovation Pack 2014)
- Right mouse click and double click (not available)
- Side menu (Innovation Pack 2014 or higher)
- Lock and sort of list columns (Innovation Pack 2014 or higher)

Shuttle Applets

When it comes to associating records in a many-to-many relationship, end users can use Multi-Value Fields. In early Siebel versions, a single list applet - the **MVG Applet** - opened, displaying the records which were associated with the parent record. Clicking a button in the MVG applet opened the **Associate Applet** which allowed end users to select existing records.

In version 7.5.3, the **Shuttle Applet** was introduced which combined both the MVG and the Associate Applet in a single pop-up window.

With Siebel Open UI, we observe that what goes around comes around. In Innovation Pack 2013 or earlier, the standard behavior of Multi-Value Fields in the new client is again based on the display of single lists instead of both lists side by side.

The following screenshot shows the **Address MVG Applet** in Siebel Open UI Innovation Pack 2013.

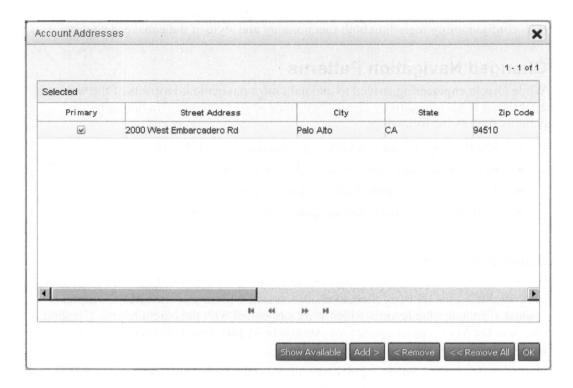

Clicking the Show Available button will toggle to the Associate Applet, but both applets are not shown side by side.

In Innovation Pack 2014, the Shuttle Applet functionality is fully functional again.

Right Mouse Click and Double Click

In contrast to the High Interactivity client, using the right mouse button does not open the applet menu in Siebel Open UI. Instead the browser context menu is opened as it would on any normal web site.

To open the applet menu, we have to explicitly click the Menu button on the applet header or use the *CTRL+SHIFT+M* keyboard shortcut.

Side Menu

In addition to tree and tab navigation (see the section on theme selection below), Innovation Pack 2014 introduced a new navigation pattern using a slide-in menu, also known as side menu or 'hamburger' menu. The following screenshot shows the new side menu.

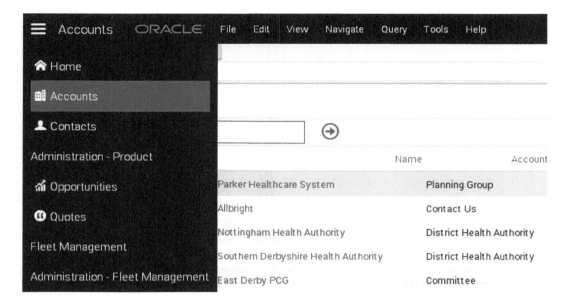

The side menu flips in from the left when the user clicks or taps the 'hamburger' icon (three horizontal bars) and allows for screen selection.

Lock and Sort of List Columns

Another change in navigation patterns is found with locking (freezing) and sorting columns in list applets. Beginning with IP 2014, end users are now presented with a menu when they click or tap a list column header. The menu options are to lock (or unlock) a list column or sort the data.

User Preferences

Many of the new features introduced with Siebel Open UI can be personalized. This means that end users can modify settings on the User Preferences screen to change the behavior or look and feel of the application. In this section, we will discuss the most important new features in the area of personalization introduced with Siebel Open UI.

Selecting Themes

One of the major enhancements that Open UI brings is the ability to create themes - sets of style sheets which are registered under a common name. We will discuss themes in great detail in chapter 8.

When a theme is registered, end users can select it using drop-down lists in the Behavior view of the User Preferences screen as shown in the following screenshot.

Chapter 1

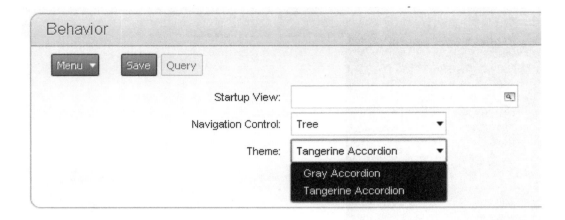

As of Innovation Pack 2013, Oracle provides four predefined themes for desktop applications - two tab-based and two tree-based - as well as one predefined theme for mobile applications.

- Gray Tab: a high-contrast theme with screen tab navigation
- Tangerine Tab: a lighter theme with screen tab navigation
- Gray Accordion: a high-contrast theme with left-hand screen navigation
- Tangerine Accordion: a lighter theme with left-hand screen navigation
- Siebel Mobile: a common theme for Siebel Mobile Applications

With Innovation Pack 2014, all applications - desktop or mobile - use the new 'Aurora' theme which supports tab-based, tree-based and side menu navigation.

After selecting Tree, Tab or Side Menu from the Navigation Control drop-down list, end users can select the desired theme in from the Theme drop-down list. Once the changes are saved, the browser can be simply refreshed, for example by pressing the *F5* key.

The following screenshot shows the predefined Tangerine Accordion theme in Innovation Pack 2013.

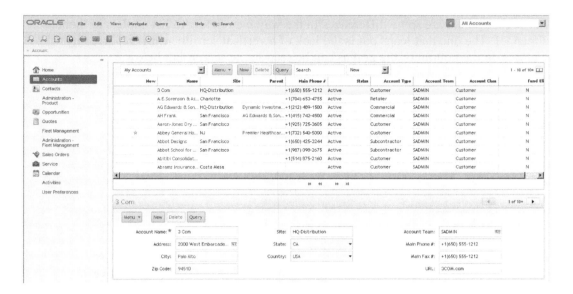

In addition to allowing end users to select their favorite theme, the Open UI framework allows switching themes dynamically, for example based on user profile attributes such as the country they work in.

This can be achieved through *Manifest Expressions*, which allow administrators to add conditional logic to select specific JavaScript files at runtime. You will learn more about Manifest Expressions in chapter 4.

Transition Effects

The Behavior applet also contains a Transition drop-down list which allows the user to select different transition effects (None, Slide In, Slide Left, Flip and Fade In).

While selecting None (the default) effectively turns transition effects off, the other settings result in a slide, flip or fade effect when the user navigates between views.

Applet Features

Siebel Open UI is built on top of the well-established logical user interface layer which provides screens, views, and applets. All standard applet types (list, form, tree, and chart as well as pick and MVG applets) are fully functional in Open UI. In the following we will discuss the differences between traditional clients and Open UI.

List Applets

While continuing to look and function in almost the same manner as they used to in the High-Interactivity client, list applets have undergone many changes. The technically obvious change is that they are no longer black-boxed ActiveX controls but use the **jQuery Grid** plugin to render a list of records.

As a result, there are some differences in the way we work with list applets in Siebel Open UI. The one that leaps out is the lack of a vertical scrollbar. It is replaced by buttons on the bottom of the grid as can be seen in the screenshot below.

The buttons serve the purpose of navigating between sets of records or between individual records.

Another change is that a search box is now included on the top of any list applet which exposes the Query Assistant button. In traditional Siebel clients this was only available in pick applets. By using the search box, end users can issue queries by entering the search term in the search box, selecting the column to query, and pressing *ENTER*. Where space is limited, the search bar is hidden and appears after the user clicks the magnifying glass icon on top of the applet.

Multiple File Attachments

Open UI enables end users to upload multiple attachments at once. This can be achieved either by simply dragging and dropping multiple files onto an attachment list applet or by selecting multiple files in the Open dialog which appears after clicking the New File button.

Drag and Drop Import

In Innovation Pack 2013 or higher, developers can add the following user properties (using Siebel Tools) to a list applet to enable the drag and drop import of data (e.g. from a spreadsheet).

- `ClientPMUserProp = EnableDragAndDropInList`
- `EnableDragAndDropInList = TRUE`

In case the `ClientPMUserProp` user property already has a value, we must use a comma as the separator. Alternatively, we can use a number suffix to create a sequence of user properties, such as `ClientPMUserProp1`, `ClientPMUserProp2` and so on.

After compiling these modifications, the list applet allows its records to be dragged (onto other applets) and accepts data dropped on it. For the latter to work correctly, the first row of the dataset must match the display names of the list applet columns you wish to import. Of course, all required fields must be filled and pick list values must match exactly. The screenshot below shows an example data set in Microsoft Excel.

	A	B	C	D	E
1	Last Name	First Name	Mr/Ms	Work Phone	Email
2	Ford	Duncan	Mr.	+44123456789	duncan@company.com
3	Hansal	Alexander	Mr.	+49123456789	alex@company.com
4	Leibert	Kirk	Mr.		kirk@company.com
5	Peterson	Jan	Mr.	+223456789	
6					

As can be seen in the screenshot, the user has already marked the data area and is ready to drag and drop it onto the Siebel list applet.

This feature can be useful in scenarios where business users receive smaller amounts of data in spreadsheets and wish to import them directly into Siebel CRM. You will learn more about this feature and other integration features of Siebel Open UI in chapter 16.

Collapsible Applets

Using another applet user property, `Default Applet Display Mode`, developers can control whether an applet should appear collapsed or expanded. In collapsed mode, only the applet header will be visible and a button allows the end user to expand the applet into full view.

The following screenshot shows the **Service Request Activity List Applet (CX sService)** which is used in the new Open UI based **Customer Experience (CX) Self Service** application.

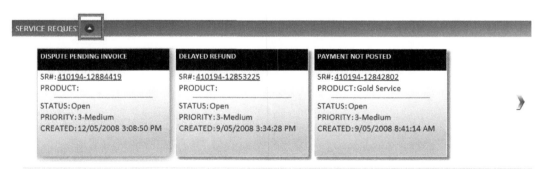

The applet is in expanded mode. By clicking the highlighted button, the user can collapse the applet.

> For more information about applet user properties, please refer to the book "Siebel CRM 8 Developer's Handbook" by Alexander Hansal or the Oracle Siebel documentation.

Tile/Card Visualization

As we can see in the above screenshot, a list applet can be configured to display records as tiles or cards. Beginning with IP 2013, this is part of the standard feature set and is enabled for selected applets, including the **Contact List Applet**, which is shown in the next screenshot.

End users can toggle between list and tile/card displays using buttons on the applet header. It is also possible to set the default display mode using the Visualization drop-down list in the Behavior view of the User Preferences screen.

Map Visualization

It is also possible to achieve the display of records on a map. In Innovation Pack 2013, the wiring for Google Maps is provided by Oracle but not implemented because of licensing issues.

With IP 2014, Oracle delivers a predefined renderer that uses Oracle's eLocation Services. The following screenshot shows the out-of-the-box map visualization for the Contact List Applet.

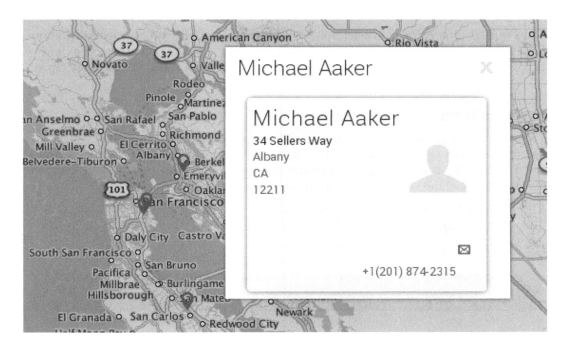

Contact records in the current query are displayed as pins on the map. In the screenshot, the user has clicked a pin and selected View Details to display a card with details about the contact.

Specialized Applets

On most occasions, simple list, form, or tree applets are used to access data in Siebel applications. However, some applications like Siebel Marketing make extended use of special applets such as Gantt diagrams or flow chart designers. These applets have been migrated by Oracle on an individual basis and Oracle announced their availability in the **Open UI Deployment Guide** which can be downloaded from My Oracle Support (http://support.oracle.com). At the time of writing almost every specialized applet is available within Open UI in Innovation Pack 2014.

The screenshot below shows the **Dispatch Board** applet in Open UI (IP 2013).

	Name	Service Region	Availability Status	Assignment Sco		2:00PM	3:00PM	4:00PM	5:00PM	6:00PM
Robert Hsu		NE Retail North					Field Repair			
Cary Mills		NE Retail North								
Darsha Patel		NE Retail North								
Nick Vance		NE Retail North						Appointment		

Select Service Region Assignment Score Calculate Distance Wireless Coverage (GMT-08:00) Pacific Time (US & Canada)

The Dispatch Board applet is used, for example, in the **Siebel Field Service** application and allows dispatching personnel to arrange activities in a service calendar using drag and drop. This is one example of a specialized applet which has been migrated to Open UI by Oracle.

Notifications

Experienced Siebel users are familiar with **Message Broadcast** functionality which provides a ticker-style message bar at the bottom of the Siebel application window. In Siebel Open UI, several changes and enhancements have been made to both the backend functionality and the way notifications are presented at the frontend.

The screenshot below shows the frontend which is now implemented as a notification icon on the top application banner. When the user clicks the icon, a list of messages is displayed.

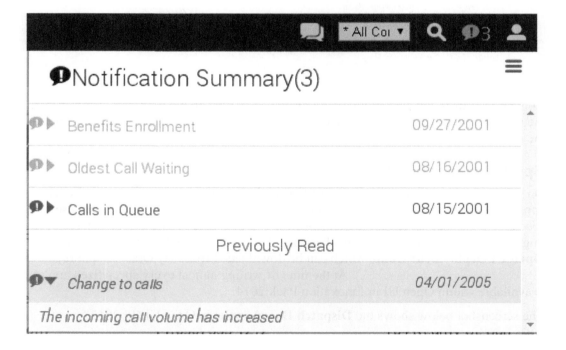

The icon counter displays the number of unread messages while the color is driven by the most urgent message. What cannot be shown in a screenshot is that the icon blinks when there is a message which has been marked as "Urgent with Alert".

When a user clicks a message, the message text is displayed and the message is marked as read. End users can also use a button to dismiss messages for which dismissal is allowed.

Updated Look and Feel

Many long-lived usability features of Siebel CRM have been refurbished during the development of Open UI. While backend functionality has stayed the same, changes in the look and feel are sometimes dramatic, as illustrated by the new notification summary described in the above section.

The following modules have undergone significant style changes in Open UI

- Task UI
- SmartScripts
- Product Configurator
- Calendar
- Report Panel
- Catalog Browser and Product Selection (Shopping Cart)
- Search and Find ("Binocular Search")
- iHelp (IP 2014 or higher)
- Communications Dashboard/Panel (IP 2014 or higher)

As an example, the screenshot below shows the new Communications Panel in Innovation Pack 2014.

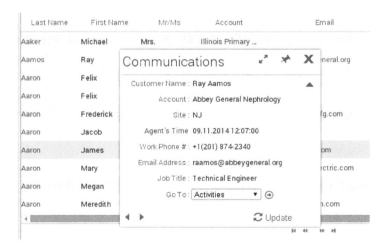

In contrast to the relatively static dashboard in previous versions, the new Communications Panel in IP 2014 can be used in floating mode (as shown in the screenshot) or docked to the application border.

Another example for updates regarding the look and feel of Siebel features is the report panel. While end users were presented with a pop-up dialog in traditional Siebel clients, Open UI renders the form to control report generation and scheduling on the left of the screen. In addition to the visual changes, end users can submit multiple reports instead of having to wait for a download.

When a report is generated, Open UI informs the end user with a message in the new notification area. The user can subsequently click on a link in the message to download the report.

Unsupported Features

Siebel Innovation Pack 2014 supports the majority of the original feature set of Siebel High-Interactivity applications in Open UI, such as iHelp or special purpose applets such as flowchart designers.

However, Oracle has announced a list of features to be implemented in later releases as well as a list of features which will not be supported in Siebel Open UI. Features which will not be available in Open UI include, for example, the Asset Dispatch Board and Parametric Product Search.

A complete list of features which are yet to be implemented is published by Oracle in the regularly updated document *"Siebel Open UI Deployment Guide"* which can be obtained via document Id 1499842.1 from My Oracle Support.

Customers are advised to review the latest version of this document as well as any other publications such as Statements of Direction (SOD) documents on a regular basis to stay up-to-date with Oracle's plans for migration of these features in future releases.

Siebel Mobile Applications

The technological implementation of Siebel Open UI by means of web standards such as JavaScript, HTML5 and CSS3 also opened the door for a new generation of mobile applications.

Historically, Siebel CRM has a solid track record in mobile computing. Since its inauguration in the mid-nineties it evolved around the needs of mobile users. Siebel Remote technology is used until today by thousands of traveling sales and service workers.

In addition to providing a fully functional Mobile Web Client for laptop users, Siebel has also been catering for handheld devices such as Personal Digital Assistants (PDAs) or the first generation of cell phones capable of rendering simple HTML or WML (Wireless Markup Language delivered via WAP protocol).

The revolution of mobile computing, triggered by the introduction of smart phones and tablets, also brought new operating systems, namely iOS from Apple and Android from Google and a new generation of devices with unprecedented computing power and graphic resolution.

It comes naturally that end users want to access their business data on these devices. Siebel Mobile Applications are a new family of Siebel applications introduced with version 8.1.1.9. Oracle ships the following mobile applications based on Open UI:

- Siebel Sales Mobile
- Siebel Service Mobile
- Siebel Pharma Mobile
- Siebel Consumer Goods Sales Mobile
- Financial Services Mobile (IP 2014 or higher)

The following screenshot shows the Siebel Sales Mobile Application's account list.

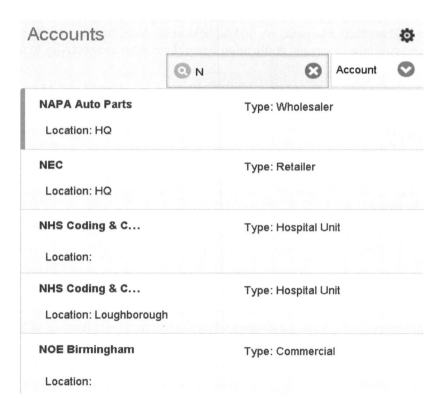

The screenshot shows the application on a smartphone in portrait orientation. The JavaScript libraries used to build the user interface layer - namely jQuery Mobile - and the underlying web templates and style sheets allow for a very dynamic user experience. It has to be noted that jQuery Mobile is no longer used in IP 2014 or higher. Instead all applications use a single rendering framework, providing even better support for 'design once, use everywhere' strategies.

Mobile applications are optimized for use on touch screen devices and use HTML5 to provide the look and feel of a native app. However they are still pure web clients and a browser and network connection is needed.

Besides the different look and feel, the underlying architecture for Siebel applications remains unchanged. Siebel developers still find themselves working with familiar object types such as applets, views and screens when they customize Siebel Mobile Applications.

Because of the youth and dynamics of the mobile application market, we can expect a lot of change in the way enterprise data is presented on mobile devices over the next few years.

Disconnected Mobile Applications

As of IP 2013, two mobile applications - Pharma and Service - are preconfigured by Oracle for disconnected operation. Administrators can specify which parts of the application - UI artifacts and data - should be held in the local browser storage so that end users can continue to use the application when there is no connectivity to the Siebel web server.

You will learn more about Siebel mobile applications in chapters 14 and 15.

Summary

In this chapter, we learned that Siebel Open UI is a new way of rendering the user interface for the Siebel Web Client. It is built on modern web standards such as HTML5, JavaScript and CSS3. Subsequently, Siebel users are no longer locked into specific (outdated) browsers.

Furthermore, Siebel Open UI allows developers to customize all aspects of the application and to deploy applications on multiple devices, including tablets and smartphones.

In this chapter, we discussed the out-of-the-box features and usability enhancements that Siebel Open UI introduces.

In the next chapter, we will have a closer look at the technical architecture of Siebel Open UI.

2

Siebel Open UI Architecture

This chapter describes the architectural concepts of Siebel Open UI. It introduces the differences to the 'traditional' Siebel UI and explains how Siebel Web Templates, the Siebel Web Engine, Manifests, JavaScript and Cascading Style Sheets work together to create the Open UI Framework.

This chapter is structured as follows.

- Open UI Architecture - The Big Picture
- Comparison of Traditional Siebel Web Clients and Open UI
- The JavaScript Framework of Open UI
- The Role of jQuery in Open UI

Open UI Architecture - The Big Picture

Understanding Siebel's overall web architecture is the key to understanding of the Open UI architecture because the former is the foundation for the latter. Let's examine the Open UI architecture piece by piece, starting with a diagram that lays out all the items we will discuss later in this chapter.

Siebel Open UI Architecture

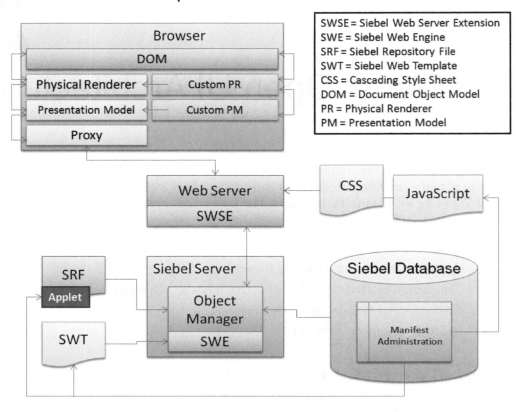

In this section, we will discuss the following architectural elements that have been created by Oracle or have undergone changes to make Open UI possible.

- Server-side Architecture
    - Manifest Administration Data
    - Object Manager with Siebel Web Engine (SWE)
    - Siebel Web Templates (SWT)
    - Web Server with Siebel Web Server Extension (SWSE)
- Client-side Architecture
    - The Proxy Layer
    - The Presentation Model (PM) Layer
    - The Physical Renderer (PR) Layer

Manifest Administration Data

With Innovation Pack 2013, new tables have been added to the Siebel database schema to hold manifest administration data for Siebel Open UI.

Manifests connect **user interface objects** such as applets or views to one or more **files** (to be downloaded by the browser, such as JavaScript files or style sheets) or **web templates** that are needed to provide the necessary client-side logic or rendering instructions for the object.

Manifest Expressions, created using Siebel Query Language, can be used to define the conditions when a certain set of files should be used for a given UI object.

The following diagram conveys the relationships between UI objects, Manifest Expressions, JavaScript files and web templates.

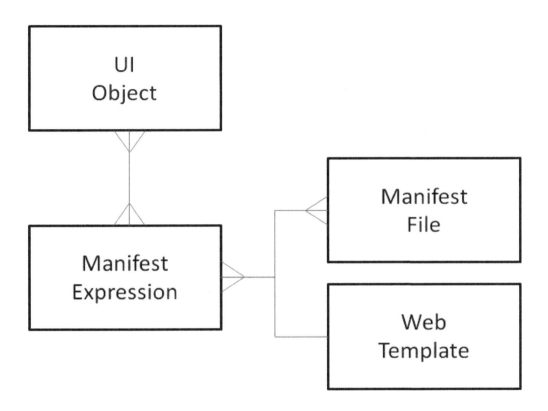

As can be seen in the above diagram, a UI object can be associated with multiple Manifest Expressions (which can be grouped and sequenced). When those expressions evaluate to 'true', the Open UI framework loads the Manifest Files associated with the expression (or group of expressions). In a similar manner, we can use Manifest Expressions to evaluate conditions when a certain web template definition is to be used for the UI object.

The screenshot below shows the Manifest Administration view in the Siebel Web Client.

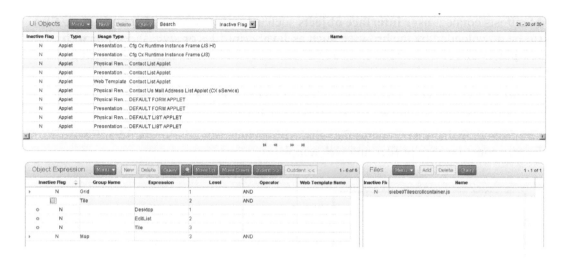

This view is situated in the Administration - Application screen and allows administrators to inspect and create associations between UI objects, expressions and files. In the screenshot we can see the evaluation logic for choosing the physical renderer for the Contact List Applet. In the lower half of the view, we can discern that when the application is in Desktop mode, the applet is in the EditList mode and the user has selected the Tile display, then the Tilescrollcontainer.js file will be loaded, resulting in the tile/card display we introduced in the previous chapter.

> In versions before IP 2013, manifests were administered using XML and text files in the OBJECTS folder on the Siebel Server. With IP 2013 and later, this has been replaced by the mechanism shown above. If you want to learn about the file-based manifest administration in versions before IP 2013, refer to appendix B at the end of this book.

In chapter 4, we will discuss the administrative tasks related to manifests in greater detail.

Object Manager with Siebel Web Engine

With the introduction of Open UI, the Siebel Web Engine (SWE), which is the 'rendering engine' inside an object manager, has been greatly enhanced so that it can provide another way of rendering Siebel data in a browser besides the traditional choices of High-Interactivity (HI), Standard-Interactivity (SI), or Wireless web clients.

Open UI is effectively switched on by means of a single component parameter, namely EnableOpenUI which, when set to TRUE together with the HighInteractivity parameter, turns the object manager into an **Open UI enabled object manager**.

Note that only applications that are enabled for High-Interactivity (HI) can be 'switched' to Open UI mode. It is not possible to turn a Standard-Interactivity (SI) application into an Open UI application, unless it can be rendered in High-Interactivity as well.

In an effort to modernize the decade-old SI applications, Oracle has started to rewrite applications such as **eService** or **Partner Portal** that are made available as new Open UI-based application definitions in the IP 2013 repository.

> Note that it is possible to run an Open UI enabled OM in parallel with a HI enabled OM. Both OMs can use the same SRF, database, and share any other components. This allows a flexible migration path from HI to Open UI by running both UI modes in parallel and gradually migrating customizations and users to Open UI.

Siebel Web Templates

Siebel Web Template (SWT) files have been around since the first web-based applications were published by Siebel Systems at the end of the nineties. They serve as templates for the Siebel Web Engine (SWE) and provide the 'skeleton' of HTML elements to be rendered in the browser and populated with data from the database.

In the age of Siebel Open UI, two significant differences can be found between the old and the new world.

- New folder structure
- Refurbished SWT files

New Folder Structure

Let's start with a look at the WEBTEMPL folder as it appears in Siebel 8.1.1.9 or higher:

The major difference between the new and older versions is the presence of the CUSTOM and OUIWEBTEMPL sub-directories. The WEBTEMPL folder still holds the SWT files for the traditional (HI and SI) web clients.

Customers who modified or created custom SWT files, even while still using HI or SI clients, are required to move all modified or custom files to the WEBTEMPL/CUSTOM folder during the upgrade process.

The OUIWEBTEMPL folder holds the SWT files created by Oracle for Open UI clients. All modified or custom files for Open UI must be placed in the OUIWEBTEMPL/CUSTOM folder.

When the SWE is in Open UI mode and needs to look up an SWT file, it first checks the OUIWEBTEMPL/CUSTOM folder. When the file is not found there, it uses the standard OUIWEBTEMPL folder. In case the file is not specialized for Open UI, the SWE falls back to the standard WEBTEMPL folder and tries to locate the file there.

Refurbished SWT files

The difference between Open UI and the traditional UI becomes very clear when we compare the two versions of the same SWT file, which we do in the following screenshot.

The screenshot shows the traditional version of the `CCFrameBanner.swt` file - the template for the menu-bearing, uppermost application banner - on the left and the Open UI version on the right.

In both files, the most prominent HTML element has been highlighted. In the traditional HI and SI world, `<table>` elements were used to provide the position information for other elements. For many years, this was a common practice of web developers to arrange page elements in the browser.

With the era of modern, JavaScript laden web applications, the `<table>` element lost much of its support by web developers. The new element of choice is the `<div>` element, which can be identified as the most prominent element in the Open UI version of the file in the previous screenshot.

The benefit of using `<div>` elements is that their content and position can be controlled much more easily at runtime using style sheets or JavaScript.

Web Server with Siebel Web Server Extension (SWSE)

As expected from any new web user interface framework, we find a lot of new folders and files in the `PUBLIC` directory of the Siebel Web Server Extension (SWSE). The screenshot below shows the new folder structure.

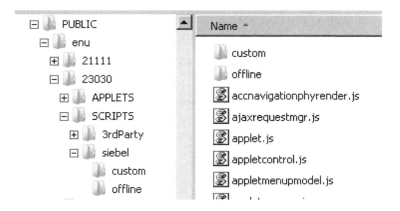

The above screenshot shows the sub-directory structure of the SWSE's PUBLIC folder. The file listing on the right shows a portion of the content of the new SCRIPTS/siebel sub-directory. In the next section, we will discuss the new sub-directories and their content.

> Note that for the sake of brevity and to accommodate different language packs and versions of Siebel CRM, we refer to the language specific directory (e.g. enu) as <Language> and the build specific directory (e.g. 23030) as <Build> in the remainder of this book.
>
> In an effort to increase the applicability of this book's information across operating systems, we use forward slashes (/) as the separator in directory paths.

JavaScript Files

The folders of interest for Open UI developers in terms of JavaScript are the following sub-directories of the PUBLIC/<Language>/<Build>/SCRIPTS folder.

/siebel: This folder contains the standard JavaScript files that make up the out-of-the-box Open UI framework. Files in this folder are developed by Oracle and **must not** be modified by any means. In order to minimize the impact on network bandwidth and maximize browser performance, most of the standard files are minified.

> **Minification** is the process of removing comments and unnecessary white space from code files. In addition, variable and function names are shortened and refactored. This is a common practice in web development and developers can choose from a variety of tools to minify (or un-minify) code files.

/3rdParty: This folder contains the as-delivered JavaScript libraries and packages developed by third parties. Examples are jQuery and various plug-ins such as *jqGrid* or *fullcalendar* among other libraries supporting special functionality in the Siebel Open UI client.

/siebel/custom: This is the folder where developers must upload all custom JavaScript files and third-party plug-ins. Subdirectories can be added as needed to this folder.

/siebel/offline: Files supporting disconnected mobile applications are found in this folder.

/siebel/samples: Since Innovation Pack 2014, this folder provides sample files that demonstrate customization scenarios.

Cascading Style Sheets (CSS)

The new CSS files for Open UI reside in the PUBLIC/<Language>/FILES folder together with the style sheets for the traditional HI and SI clients. In order to better understand which combination of files comprises a certain UI theme, we can have a glance at the standard theme.js file in the /siebel folder. The next screenshot shows a section of that file as of IP 2013.

```
/*...*/
var ua = navigator.userAgent;
var re = new RegExp("MSIE ([0-9]{1,}[.0-9]{0,})");
if (re.exec(ua) != null && parseFloat(RegExp.$1) <= 8) {...} else {...}

SiebelApp.ThemeManager.addTheme("GRAY_TAB",
    {css: {sb_theme: "files/theme-base.css",
           sc_theme: "files/theme-gray.css",
           sn_theme: "files/theme-nav-tab.css",
           sca_them: "files/theme-calendar.css",
           sd_theme: IE8inc}, objList: []}});
```

As we can see from the screenshot, the theme.js file contains JavaScript functions to register UI themes. The GRAY_TAB theme for instance consists of four files. Using the theme.js file as a reference makes it easier to identify the CSS files that are members of a UI theme.

> The previous screenshot was taken after undoing minification in order to make the content more readable.

We will discuss the modification and creation of UI themes in great detail in chapter 8.

Client-Side Architecture

Now we reach the layer where the Open UI JavaScript framework is put to work. The browser is responsible for loading, interpreting, and executing the HTML, JavaScript, images and CSS files received from the web server.

In stark contrast to previous Siebel web clients, Oracle engineering has taken great effort to create a sophisticated three-tiered framework that reminds us of the well-established **Model-View-Controller** (MVC) paradigm of modern application development. The layers that are formed by the JavaScript code delivered by Oracle are the following:

- The proxy layer
- The presentation model (PM) layer
- The physical renderer (PR) layer

In the following sections, we will discuss the architectural aspects of these layers from a high-level perspective. In chapters 5, 6 and 7 of this book, we will explore them in much more detail.

The Proxy Layer

A web application the size of Siebel CRM is much more than just a set of dynamically created HTML pages. Stemming from almost two decades of development, the Siebel user interface supports complex business processes that are not only carried out by human users in a (web) client but also through EAI interfaces of all kinds that communicate on the server level.

This requires strict separation of logic between the server and the client. As a result, many of the events in the browser must be propagated to the server and the server needs to send notifications and data back to the client.

For example, we can consider the seemingly simple task of data validation, let's say for an email address field: In a simple web application, the developer would usually write a piece of JavaScript code (executed by the browser) to validate the value the user enters as an email address and notify the user when the value is invalid.

In an application environment where it is common to update data through server-side interfaces, the validation logic cannot reside in the browser. Hence, Siebel CRM provides a business service layer on the server that allows for the processing of business logic. For the browser, this means that it needs to propagate the user entries to the server and display any notification that the server raises.

To handle this kind of interaction, the Siebel web clients have always implemented a proxy layer. For example, the High-Interactivity client relies on a substantial ActiveX framework that acts as a background mediator between the browser-side client and the server.

In Siebel Open UI, this background functionality has been completely rewritten in JavaScript. Many of the files residing in the `/siebel` folder contain code to implement the proxy functionality.

The Presentation Model (PM) Layer

Because separate layers are generally a good idea in modern application development, Siebel engineers at Oracle have established a layer which serves as an intermediary between the proxy layer and the actual (visual) user interface: the presentation model (PM) layer.

The purpose of the PM is to collect incoming data and metadata from the proxy and expose it to the physical renderer (PR). Likewise, it propagates event notifications from the physical layer to the proxy.

Presentation models are generic in the sense that they do not, in any way, determine the visual representation of the data. As we have seen with list applets in the previous chapter, we can drastically change the physical appearance of data - from a list of records to tiles or a map - by modifying just the renderer, not the presentation model.

The Physical Renderer (PR) Layer

The physical renderer (PR) is where data becomes pixels on the screen. In this set of JavaScript files, the focus is on how data is displayed. For example, a different physical renderer is required when we want to display a list of records as a carousel or an organization diagram.

A physical renderer can only 'talk' to the presentation model, using the methods exposed by the latter.

Event Flow in Open UI

To summarize our findings so far, we can inspect the following diagram.

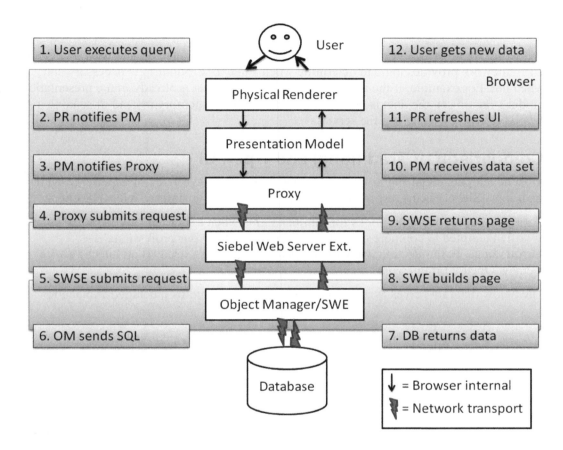

The above diagram depicts the event flow in the Open UI architecture. By looking at the typical end user process of a query, we can describe the resulting event flow as follows:

1. The user presses a key or clicks a button to execute the query.
2. The physical renderer (PR) recognizes the event and notifies the presentation model (PM).
3. The presentation model notifies the proxy.
4. The proxy generates and submits a request to the Siebel Web Server Extension (SWSE).
5. The SWSE forwards the request to the Object Manager (OM) session.
6. The OM generates an SQL query and submits it to the database.
7. The database returns the data set.
8. The Siebel Web Engine (SWE) builds the page and returns it to the SWSE.

9. The SWSE passes the page to the browser where the proxy picks it up.
10. The presentation model receives the new data set.
11. The physical renderer refreshes the user interface.
12. The user sees the new data.

While the above is a valid example of a full roundtrip to the database and back, the Open UI framework provides logic to determine when a network roundtrip is necessary and when not. For example, if the user navigates to a record that is already in the presentation model's record set, the data is retrieved from the browser memory instead of sending a - relatively costly - request to the server.

Comparison of Traditional and Open UI

Most developers preparing to work with Siebel Open UI have years of experience with traditional Siebel clients, especially the widely adopted High-Interactivity (HI) client.

Naturally, the human mind looks for familiar sights when exploring new terrain. Thus we are often tempted to compare the old and the new world in our professional surroundings. In this section, we will compare the ActiveX-based HI architecture with the new Open UI framework.

The below diagram serves as a starting point and is followed by a detailed explanation.

	High-Interactivity Architecture	Open UI Architecture
Browser (Client)	ActiveX Control	Physical Renderer
		Presentation Model
	ActiveX Proxy	Proxy
Web Server	ActiveX Components, Java Applets, CSS for formatting	JavaScript, CSS for format and position
Siebel Server	Web Templates using <table> element	Web Templates using <div> element
Database		Manifest Administration Data

As we can see in the above comparison chart, the High-Interactivity client relies on black-boxed ActiveX controls and an ActiveX proxy framework with almost no possibility of customizing style or behaviour.

In contrast, the client-side framework of Siebel Open UI provides an open, three-tiered framework and a full application programming interface (API) for customizations.

On the web server, the most striking difference between HI and Open UI is the content of the PUBLIC folder which, in case of HI, contains the various ActiveX controls, a host of Java applets and style sheets that serve the main purpose of providing basic formatting such as font family or colour.

In Open UI, the entire framework is written in JavaScript and CSS can be also used to position elements.

The JavaScript Framework of Open UI

In this section, we will have a closer look at the JavaScript framework of Siebel Open UI. As mentioned earlier, Open UI uses a mix of web technologies such as HTML, CSS and JavaScript.

While HTML and CSS are mostly used to take care of visual aspects of the user interface, the JavaScript framework of Open UI serves a deeper purpose of establishing the aforementioned three-layer architecture in the browser.

JavaScript Files Loaded by the Browser

An inspection of which JavaScript files are loaded is a good starting point for closer examination. The following screenshot shows a typical Open UI page in the HTML window of Mozilla Firebug.

As we can see, the HTML page loaded by the browser contains a large number of `<script>` elements that cause the browser to load the referenced JavaScript files either from its cache or from the web server.

The list of script references is created dynamically by the Siebel Web Engine (SWE) as it builds the page. The SWE gains its knowledge of which files to reference in a given HTML page by interpreting the manifest administration data. In addition, some files are loaded dynamically at runtime by means of the `require.js` framework which is integrated in Siebel Open UI. For more information about the `require.js` framework refer to `http://requirejs.org`.

The sequence of the file references is also of importance, as functions in one file will call other functions that must be already loaded into the browser's script engine.

The overall loading sequence of JavaScript files for a typical view in Open UI is as follows:

1. Third-party files (e.g. jQuery)
2. Utility functions and constants
3. Application environment proxy
4. View and business object proxy
5. Applet and business component proxy
6. Base presentation models and physical renderers
7. Specialized controls
8. HI framework files (for backward compatibility with traditional browser scripting)
9. Specialized presentation models
10. Specialized physical renderers
11. Custom scripts
12. Other third-party files

Many of these JavaScript files build what is known as the Open UI JavaScript API. For a detailed discussion of this API, refer to chapter 5.

The Structure of an Open UI JavaScript File

There are more than 150 JavaScript files shipped with Open UI in Innovation Pack 2013 (not counting the third-party code). With a few exceptions, most files share a similar structure which can be seen in the following screenshot.

```
if( typeof( SiebelAppFacade.ClientCtrlPModel ) === "undefined" ){

    SiebelJS.Namespace( 'SiebelAppFacade.ClientCtrlPModel' );
    //Module with its dependencies
    define("siebel/samples/clientctrlpmodel", [], function () {
    SiebelAppFacade.ClientCtrlPModel = ( function(){

        /*...*/
        function ClientCtrlPModel(proxy){...}

        /*...*/
        SiebelJS.Extend( ClientCtrlPModel, SiebelAppFacade.ListPresentationModel );

        ClientCtrlPModel.prototype.Init = function(){...};
```

The previous screenshot shows a section of a sample file (clientctrlpmodel.js). This file is provided with Innovation Pack 2014 as an example extension of the presentation model class for list applets. In the following section we will use this file to explore the typical structure of an Open UI JavaScript file.

But before we start, we have to talk about **classes** in JavaScript.

> While it might sound unusual to use the word 'class' in the context of JavaScript, we use it in this book for the sake of brevity. JavaScript per se is not an object-oriented language and has no `class` object. However, several techniques have evolved to use `function` and `prototype` definitions to create JavaScript objects that can be instantiated just like classes in object-oriented programming languages. For more information on this topic, refer to the article "Introduction to Object-Oriented JavaScript" on the Mozilla Developer Network. The article can be found at `https://developer.mozilla.org/en-US/docs/Web/JavaScript/Introduction_to_Object-Oriented_JavaScript`.

The structure of almost any Open UI JavaScript file (and any custom file that we intend to implement) is as follows:

1. Ensure that the class is loaded only once
2. Register the class
3. Define Dependencies
4. Extend an existing class (if necessary)
5. Implement functionality

In the following sections, we will use the aforementioned `clientctrlpmodel.js` file as an example to verify this structure.

Ensuring that the Class is loaded only once

Most Open UI JavaScript files use an `if` block like the following to determine whether the current class has already been defined and therefore is already loaded by the browser.

```
if(typeof (SiebelAppFacade.ClientCtrlPModel) === "undefined" )
{
    //remaining code
}
```

The code effectively ensures that any code within the `if` block is only executed in case the `SiebelAppFacade.ClientCtrlPModel` class is undefined.

Note that the comparison operator ("===") used in the above code snippet is known as an 'identity' operator and - in opposite to the usual 'equality' operator ("==") - does not execute type conversion.

Registering the Class

The first line within the `if` block of an Open UI framework file usually looks like the following:

```
SiebelJS.Namespace("SiebelAppFacade.ClientCtrlPModel");
```

The previous line invokes the Namespace method of the SiebelJS class (implemented in siebjs.js) to 'register' the new ClientCtrlPModel class in the application framework.

Note that SiebelAppFacade is the default namespace defined by Oracle.

Defining Dependencies

In the code example, we see the define function used next. This function is to be used in presentation model and physical renderer implementations to comply with the **Asynchronous Module Definition** (AMD) specification.

> AMD is an API for defining dependencies between JavaScript functions and is used by the require.js JavaScript framework, which itself is used in Open UI. You can learn more about AMD here:
> http://requirejs.org/docs/whyamd.html

The following is the define function as found in the clientctrlpmodel.js file:

```
define("siebel/samples/clientctrlpmodel", [], function () {
    //remaining code
      return "SiebelAppFacade.ClientCtrlPModel";
  });
```

The first parameter that must be passed to the define function is a string holding the reference name of the current file that is usually the relative folder path without the .js suffix. The reference name serves to identify the code within the define block.

The second parameter is a list of dependencies. In the previous example, there are no dependencies to resolve. To illustrate how dependencies are defined, the following is the beginning of the define function call of the physical renderer for the tile layout (TileLayoutPR.js):

```
define("siebel/TileLayoutPR", ["siebel/phyrenderer"]
```

The code in the TileLayoutPR.js file depends on code in the phyrenderer.js file, hence the latter is referenced in the second parameter.

The third parameter passed to the define function is the function body that expects the base and dependent files to be properly loaded.

The return value of the define function is the fully qualified name (Namespace.Class) of the new class as a string.

You can learn more about the define function in the require.js API documentation at http://requirejs.org/docs/api.html#define.

Extending Existing Classes

A 'class' (in JavaScript) can be defined as the return value of a function that calls the constructor of its super class. The class is registered as a sub class by using the SiebelJS.Extend function. The following code serves as an example for a regular programming pattern in Open UI.

```
SiebelAppFacade.ClientCtrlPModel= (function() {
    function ClientCtrlPModel (proxy) {
        SiebelAppFacade.ClientCtrlPModel.superclass.constructor.
call( this, proxy);
    }
    SiebelJS.Extend(ClientCtrlPModel,SiebelAppFacade.
ListPresentationModel);
    //code which defines the class' prototype functions
    return ClientCtrlPModel;
}());
```

The code defines the SiebelAppFacade.ClientCtrlPModel class as a function object, which is returned as the ClientCtrlPModel 'constructor' function.

The constructor function calls the constructor of the super class to ensure that any base functionality is loaded. Because we are looking at the code of a presentation model class, the current proxy object (proxy) is passed as an argument.

Any extension class must be contain a call to the SiebelJS.Extend function. In the previous example, the ClientCtrlPModel class extends the ListPresentationModel class, inheriting all its functionality.

The return value of the class function is the constructor function object.

Implementing Functionality

Wrapped tightly in the functions described above lays the actual implementation code or methods that define the functionality of the class.

Depending on the file we inspect, this can be a few humble lines to several thousands of lines of code.

In upcoming chapters of this book, we will provide hands-on coding examples for custom presentation models and physical renderers that will give you a greater understanding of the code than you can get from inspecting (minified and uncommented) pre-delivered files.

The Open UI JavaScript Framework: The Big Picture

To summarize our findings let's take a look at the following diagram:

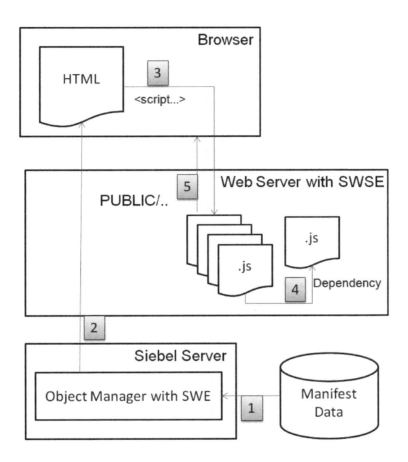

The JavaScript framework in Open UI consists of the following elements (the numbers in the below list reference the elements in the diagram).

- The Siebel Web Engine (SWE) that uses Manifest Data (1) to determine which JavaScript files need to be loaded by the browser for a given user interface object.

- The SWE also generates the page HTML with `<script>` references to the JavaScript files and passes it back to the web server (2).

- The browser interprets the HTML and starts loading the JavaScript files from its cache or from the web server (3).

- Dependencies, established using the `define` function (4), ensure that all JavaScript files are properly loaded (5).

The Role of jQuery in Open UI

Among other third-party JavaScript libraries, **jQuery** and its associated projects **jQuery UI** and **jQuery Mobile** (until IP 2013) play a vital role in Siebel Open UI.

> The jQuery project was founded in 2006 by John Resig. The goal of jQuery and similar libraries is to simplify JavaScript coding by providing easy-to-use functions. For example, only a single line of jQuery code is needed to make elements in the browser 'sortable', so that end users can rearrange them by drag and drop. In addition, jQuery equalizes browser specific interpretations of JavaScript, allowing developers to focus on the functionality of the code rather than dealing with the intricacies of individual browsers.
>
> More information about jQuery can be found at `http://jquery.com`.

jQuery has evolved into other projects such as jQuery UI, which focuses on user interface manipulation, and jQuery Mobile, which provides a framework for building rich mobile web applications which work on any browser and any device. The new Siebel Mobile Applications, for example, rely heavily on jQuery Mobile until IP 2013.

Additionally, there is a large developer community continuously creating jQuery plug-ins, which further enhance and extend the capabilities of the base library. For example, calendar applets in Open UI are rendered using the `fullcalendar` jQuery plug-in in IP 2013.

Oracle has chosen the three jQuery projects and a lot of plug-ins to implement much of the base functionality in Siebel Open UI.

Even though we could use any other technology that can be used in modern browsers to implement customizations, it is highly recommended to get a thorough understanding of jQuery and associated projects to ease the customization process.

As mentioned in previous sections of this book, customers can also use additional libraries and plug-ins but are not supposed to use other (higher or lower) versions of third-party libraries than those shipped with the product.

Summary

Siebel's Open UI architecture builds upon the well-established Siebel web architecture. As we have laid out in this chapter, the Siebel Web Engine and the SWT files have been enhanced to provide a modern foundation for a web user interface.

To manage the dependencies between UI objects and JavaScript or SWT files, Open UI introduces a new set of administrative data, namely manifests.

Built on solid web standards such as CSS and JavaScript, Open UI comes pre-defined with hundreds of new files on the web server. These files, when loaded in the browser, establish a three-tier architecture consisting of a proxy layer that handles the server communication, a presentation model layer that exposes the data obtained from the proxy, and a physical renderer layer that provides the visual aspects of Open UI.

All JavaScript provided by Oracle is written using a distinctive pattern, using modern web programming paradigms to ensure a consistent, open and extensible framework.

Besides as-delivered JavaScript from Oracle, Open UI also relies on third party libraries such as jQuery to deliver functionality.

In the following chapter, we will learn how to install or upgrade to a Siebel Innovation Pack and explore important administrative tasks related to Siebel Open UI.

3

Open UI Installation, Upgrade, and Setup

This chapter explains how to provision Siebel Open UI by covering the installation and upgrade process to Siebel Innovation Pack 2013 and higher. In addition, the administrative procedures for setting up Open UI-enabled object managers and administering manifests are laid out.

The chapter is structured as follows.

- Installing Siebel Innovation Packs
- Upgrading from Previous Versions of Siebel CRM
- Case Study: Enabling Open UI for Siebel Applications

Installing Siebel Innovation Packs

Open UI is a feature of modern Siebel CRM versions and cannot be 'installed', per se, by running a setup program. The path to Open UI is as follows:

- Install or upgrade to the latest Siebel CRM version
- Configure object managers to run in Open UI mode if necessary
- Migrate customizations (such as style sheets or browser scripts) if needed

In this and the following sections of this chapter we will lay out the detailed steps for each of these processes.

The question of installing a fresh Siebel environment or upgrading an existing one will be answered with 'upgrading' for the majority of Siebel projects as they have been using and customizing Siebel CRM for years already. For this reason, the focus in this chapter is on upgrade tasks.

Independent of starting from scratch or upgrading from a previous version, the new version of the software needs to be installed, so this part of the process is the same for any scenario.

> For details on the Siebel CRM architecture and the installation process, please refer to the book Siebel CRM 8 Installation and Management by Alexander Hansal or the Oracle Siebel Documentation.

The high-level process for installing the necessary Siebel CRM software version 8.1.1.11, or higher, to conduct a successful upgrade is as follows:

- Register at Oracle Software Delivery Cloud
- Download the installation archives
- Run the Siebel Network Image Creator
- Verify hardware and software requirements
- Verify or install prerequisite software
- Install and configure the Siebel Enterprise Server
- Install and configure the Siebel Web Server Extension
- Install and patch Siebel Tools

In the following sections we will explore some details of these steps. As stated above we will focus on upgrade-related steps rather than explaining the full installation and configuration process.

Registering at Oracle Software Delivery Cloud

Oracle makes most of its software packages available for download via the **Oracle Software Delivery Cloud**, also known as *Oracle E-Delivery*. The Oracle Software Delivery Cloud can be accessed at https://edelivery.oracle.com.

Before you can use the download site, you must register and agree to the terms and restrictions as well as the license agreement. Usually one day after registering, you are granted access and able to log in.

Once logged in, we find ourselves on the search page where we select Siebel CRM as the product pack and the platform such as Microsoft Windows x64 (64-bit). The search result is shown in the screenshot below.

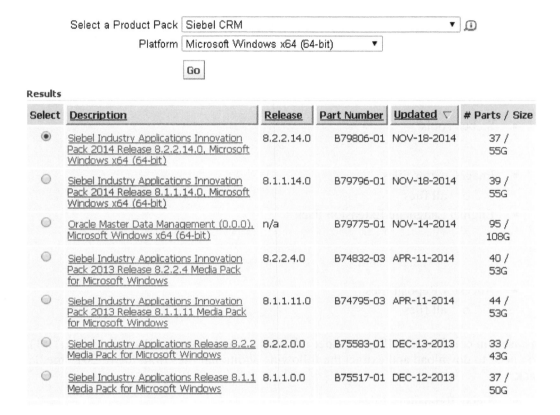

In the screenshot you can also see that the Siebel Industry Applications Innovation Pack 2014 media pack is selected (it was the latest release when this screenshot was taken). Depending on the time you read this, there might well be a newer innovation pack available. Clicking on the link will direct you to the download page.

Download the Installation Archives

To conduct an upgrade from a previous version of Siebel CRM to the latest innovation pack, we must download the installers shown in the following list which shows the `.jar` files to be extracted from the downloaded `.zip` archive. There will be more `.jar` files present which can be kept but the below list is the minimum number of `.jar` files.

Note that the list below is an example for Innovation Pack 2014 on Microsoft Windows and only refers to the English-American (ENU) language pack. If your environment runs on different operating systems and/or uses additional language packs or there is a newer innovation pack version, the file names will be different.

Innovation Pack Installers (8.1.1.14)

- Base Applications
  - o `SBA_8.1.1.14_Base_Windows_Siebel_Enterprise_Server.jar`
  - o `SBA_8.1.1.14_Base_Windows_Siebel_Web_Server_Extension.jar`
- Siebel Tools
  - o `SBA_8.1.1.14_Base_Windows_Siebel_Tools.jar`
  - o `SBA_8.1.1.14_enu_Windows_Siebel_Tools.jar`
- ImageCreator Files
  - o all files
- English Language Extension Pack
  - o `SBA_8.1.1.14_enu_Windows_Siebel_Enterprise_Server.jar`
  - o `SBA_8.1.1.14_enu_Windows_Siebel_Web_Server_Extension.jar`
- Ancestor Repositories
  - o all files

In case you consider installing an older release such as Innovation Pack 2013 (8.1.1.11), you need to download and extract the following additional files from the IP 2013 media pack.

- Siebel Repository Files
  - o `srf.zip`
- Siebel Tools
  - o `SBA_8.1.1.0_Base_Windows_Siebel_Tools.jar`
  - o `SBA_8.1.1.0_enu_Windows_Siebel_Tools.jar`

From the above lists we learn that in IP 2014, Siebel server software (**Siebel Enterprise Server** and **Siebel Web Server Extension**) and Siebel Tools is shipped as a single installer whereas the Siebel Tools installation for IP 2013 requires the base version plus the innovation pack. In a typical upgrade scenario you would already have Siebel Tools installed, so the base installers are probably not needed. They are listed here in case a fresh install is required.

The lists above do not mention the **Siebel Developer Web Client** because it is not inherently necessary to conduct an upgrade. However, you should download the installation archives for the Developer Web Client as well for later use.

Also it should be noted that Oracle ships the **Standard Repository Files (SRF)** (for IP 2013) and the **Standard Ancestor Repositories** (of all previous versions) separately. Both must be downloaded and subsequently used during the upgrade process.

All `.jar` files should be extracted from the downloaded `.zip` packages into a single folder together with the image creator files. It is recommended to use an *unzip* tool such as 7-zip.

The following screenshot shows the content of the folder after the extraction (IP 2014).

The next step is to extract the installers from the `.jar` files using the **Siebel Network Image Creator (snic)**.

Running the Siebel Network Image Creator

In order to generate the installer images, we need to execute the `snic.bat` (on Windows) or `snic.sh` (on UNIX/Linux) command line utility. This is accomplished by opening a command window and navigating to the folder which contains all the extracted files.

The Siebel Network Image Creator is written in Java, so it needs to access a **Java Runtime Environment (JRE)** or **Java Development Kit (JDK)**. It uses the `JAVA_HOME` environment variable to locate a JRE or JDK on the computer. In case the environment variable is not set on our machine, we must first set it using a command similar to the following:

```
set JAVA_HOME=C:\Program Files (x86)\Java\jre1.7.0_45
```

The above command sets the `JAVA_HOME` environment variable value to the path where the Java Runtime Environment is installed. The path may vary depending on the installation folder and Java version.

To invoke the Siebel Network Image Creator we execute the following command:

```
snic
```

This launches the graphical user interface (GUI) of the **Network Image Creator**. The following screenshot shows the Welcome page of the wizard.

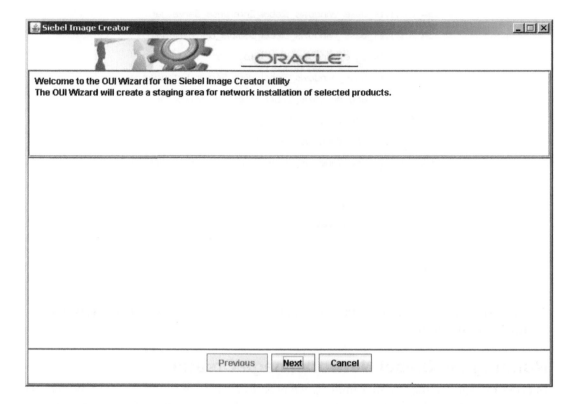

The following table describes the steps of the wizard and the necessary actions to create a new installation image for Innovation Pack 2014 on Microsoft Windows.

Step	Description	Tasks and Example Values
1	Start the Siebel Network Image Creator.	Run snic.bat on the command line.
2	The Welcome dialog is displayed.	Click Next
3	Select options.	Select the following: • Create a new image or add product(s) to an existing image Click Next

(Continued)

4	Specify a directory path.	**Example:** `C:\Siebel_Install_Image` Click Next
5	Select a platform	Select the following: • Windows Click Next
6	Select products	Select the following: • Siebel Enterprise Server • Siebel Tools • Siebel Web Server Extension Click Next
7	Specify languages	Select the following: • ENU – English (American) • Any other language(s) needed Click Next
8	Files are extracted	Wait until the file extraction is finished.
9	Extraction summary is displayed	Review the summary information. Click Finish

As a result of the above process, the directory specified in step 4 is created and contains subdirectories which hold the installation image files for the products specified in step 6.

Verify Hardware and Software Requirements

With new releases of standard software there are often changes regarding the requirements for hardware and auxiliary software such as the operating system or the database we want the software to install and run on.

Siebel CRM is no exception to this rule and Oracle publishes the software compatibility lists on its **My Oracle Support** portal under the Certifications tab. The following screenshot shows an excerpt of the search results for Siebel Application Server 8.1.1.11.0.

Certification Results	
Displaying Siebel Application Server 8.1.1.11.0 Certifications.	
View ▾	
Certified With	**Number of Releases / Versions**
▷ **Application Servers (3 Items)**	
▽ **Databases (1 Item)**	
PostgreSQL	1 Release (9.2.2+)
▽ **Desktop Applications, Browsers and Clients (4 Items)**	
IBM DB2 Client	1 Release (9.7)
Microsoft SQL Server Native Client	1 Release (0)
Microsoft Word	2 Releases (2010, 2007)
Oracle Database Client	4 Releases (11.2.0.4.0, 11.2.0.3.0, 11.2.0.2.0, 11.2.0.1.0)
▷ **Enterprise Applications (14 Items)**	
▷ **Management and Development Tools (5 Items)**	
▷ **Middleware (10 Items)**	
▽ **Operating Systems (5 Items)**	
HP-UX Itanium	2 Versions (11.31, 11.23)
IBM AIX on POWER Systems (64-bit)	2 Versions (7.1, 6.1)
Linux x86-64	5 Versions (SLES 10, Red Hat Enterprise Linux 6, Red Hat Enterprise Linux 5, Oracle Linux 6, Oracle Linux 5)
Microsoft Windows x64 (64-bit)	3 Versions (2012, 2008 R2, 2008)
Oracle Solaris on SPARC (64-bit)	2 Versions (11, 10)
▷ **Software Interoperability (7 Items)**	

For example, we can read from the certification list that Siebel (Application) Server 8.1.1.11.0 is supported and certified on Microsoft Windows 2012 Server 64-bit.

Verify or Install Prerequisite Software

If we upgrade by installing a fresh Siebel Enterprise, we must also ensure that the following third party prerequisite software is installed with the correct version.

- Operating system
- Relational Database Management System (RDBMS) server and client
- Web Server
- Java Development Kit (JDK)

Migrate the Siebel Enterprise Server

With an upgrade in mind, we need to install (or migrate to) the target version of the following Siebel server software.

- Siebel Server
- Siebel Database Server Utilities

All that is needed to conduct an upgrade are utilities and scripts situated in the installation folder of the database server utilities. However, these can only be installed on a machine where a Siebel server installation folder is present. So you typically install both of them in one go.

It is not necessary (nor possible at this point of the upgrade process) to configure and start a Siebel server against the database which will be upgraded, so the focus of this section is on the main installation steps, assuming that there is already an older Siebel server installation on the same machine.

However, we must keep in mind that the new environment will also be used for testing or it will even serve as the new development environment. This is why we must also quickly cover the steps to install Siebel server and the client software which is not immediately needed to conduct the upgrade, such as the web server extension or the developer web client.

With Innovation Pack 2013, Oracle introduced a refurbished Siebel server installer that is capable of conducting both a "New" and a "Migrate" installation. The former is usually chosen for a fresh installation or when the original Siebel server software was not installed using Oracle Universal Installer (versions before 8.1.1.8). The "Migrate" option is useful to upgrade existing instances to the latest release without the need to configure a new enterprise.

The following screenshot shows the Welcome page of the installer for Siebel Enterprise Servers.

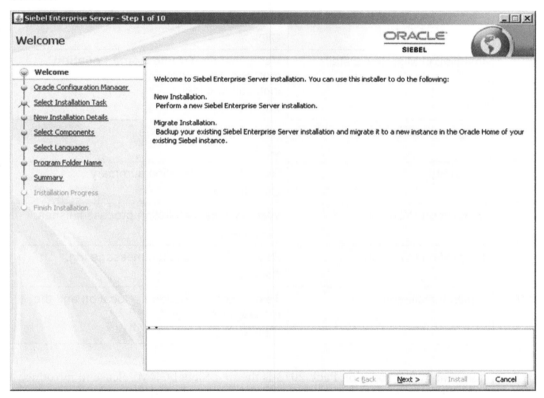

The installation wizard uses dialogues to collect information and extracts the software component files to the directories on disk. The following table provides the steps for installing Siebel Server and Siebel Database Server Utilities as a migration installation.

Step	Description	Tasks and Example Values
1	Start the Siebel Enterprise Server installer.	Run the `setup.bat` file in the `Siebel_Enterprise_Server\Disk1\install` folder of the installation image with administrative privileges.

(Continued)

2	The Welcome dialog is displayed.	Click Next
3	Configure Security Updates	Optionally, provide the My Oracle Support email address to receive security updates and initiate the configuration manager. Click Next Confirm the dialog if you have not provided an email address
4	Select Installation Task	Select the following: • Migrate Installation Click Next
5	Installation Migration Details	Verify that the **Oracle Home Location** matches the Siebel Enterprise Server installation folder. Click Next
6	Program Folder Name	Accept the default value Click Next
7	Summary	Review the installation summary Click Install
8	Installation Progress	Wait until the installation process finishes. Click Next
9	Installation Complete	Review the installation message log. Click Next
10	Finish Installation	Take a note of the log file location and the messages displayed. Click Close

As mentioned above, Innovation Pack 2013 is the first Siebel CRM release to introduce a full installer for a non-base version. As the above example scenario is a "Migrate" installation, the Siebel server software such as Gateway Name Server and Siebel Server(s) on the machine are technically upgraded to the latest release. However, we still need to upgrade the database for the enterprise to become fully operational again.

Install and Configure the Siebel Web Server Extension

From a technical standpoint, the Siebel Web Server Extension (SWSE) is not involved in the actual upgrade process. However, we might intend to conduct preliminary tests soon after the upgrade process completes, so it is a good idea to have Siebel web server ready on the latest version.

The "Migrate" installation for the SWSE works in a very similar manner to migrating the Siebel Enterprise server; it is not laid out in greater detail.

Apply the Latest Siebel Tools Patch (IP 2013)

Having the latest Siebel Tools release available on a Windows machine is a prerequisite for conducting the upgrade. In most cases, a prior version of Siebel Tools is already present, so we'll only discuss the patch installation to the latest innovation pack.

The following table lists the steps for applying a Siebel Tools patch.

Step	Description	Tasks and Example Values
1	Start the Siebel Tools patch installer.	Run the `setup.bat` file in the `Siebel_Tools\Disk1\install` folder of the installation image with administrative privileges.
2	The Welcome dialog is displayed.	Click Next
3	Select Oracle Home	Select the correct **Oracle Home** for the current Siebel Tools installation. Click Next
4	Installation Details	Click Install to start the installation
5	Installation Progress	Wait until the installer completes Click Exit

Install or Migrate Siebel Tools (IP 2014)

The new installer for Siebel Tools and Siebel Developer/Mobile Web Client in IP 2014 provides a "Migrate" or "New" install option just like the server installer. The following scenario describes a migration installation for Siebel Tools IP 2014.

Step	Description	Tasks and Example Values
1	Start the Oracle Universal Installer.	Double-click the `setup.bat` file in the `8.1.1.14\Windows\Client\Siebel_Tools \Disk1\install` folder with administrative privileges.
2	The Welcome dialog is displayed.	Click Next
3	Oracle Configuration Manager	Uncheck the option to receive security updates. Click Next Click Yes to confirm that you do not wish to receive security updates.
4	Installation Type	Select Migrate Installation. Click Next

(Continued)

5	Installation Details	Provide an Oracle Home name (or keep the default) Enter the client installation directory path. Example: `C:\Siebel\8.1\Tools_1` (default value). Click Next
6	Summary	Click Install
7	The installation process is displayed	Wait for the installation to finish
8	Success Message is displayed	Click Next
9	Finish	Click Close Click Yes to confirm

While the Siebel Developer Web Client is not directly needed to conduct the upgrade process, we should (of course) apply the available patch installers as well or install a new instance. The process for migrating or installing the Developer Web Client is practically the same as for Siebel Tools. For details on the installation of the Siebel Developer Web Client refer to appendix A of this book.

Copy the new Standard Siebel Repository File (IP 2013)

In IP 2013, it is recommended to replace the existing siebel_sia.srf file in the language specific OBJECTS directory of the Siebel Tools installation folder with the new standard SRF file which we have downloaded from Oracle's Software Delivery Cloud.

To do so, we extract the srf.zip file and navigate to the correct language specific sub-folder to copy the siebel_sia.srf file for the desired language pack (for Siebel Tools, this will probably be the ENU variant).

Next, we paste the file into the correct language-specific sub-folder of the OBJECTS directory of the Siebel Tools installation folder. It is okay to overwrite the existing file.

This step finalizes the migration installation of Siebel Enterprise server software, Siebel Web Server Extension and Siebel Tools. Depending on your project, additional steps might be necessary.

Upgrading from Previous Versions of Siebel CRM

Since version 8.1.1.10 / 8.2.2.3, Oracle no longer delivers repository changes via a loose compilation of Siebel Tools archive files (.sif) and data imports but via an automated process of merging the changes made by Oracle and the modifications of developers at the customer site into a new repository.

This technique is known as **repository merge** and is common to Siebel upgrades from major version 7.8 to a higher major version such as 8.1.1. For the first time in Siebel's history, reaching a patch level such as 8.1.1.11 is no longer considered a mere patch. In fact we must run a process called **Incremental Repository Merge** (IRM).

Beginning with Innovation Pack 2013, IRM is orchestrated by the **Siebel Upgrade Wizard**, which - as the name suggests - executes numerous tasks in their correct order to upgrade a Siebel database to a higher version. The Upgrade Wizard is a well-established tool and has served customers during thousands of major release upgrades. The following screenshot shows the Siebel Upgrade Wizard.

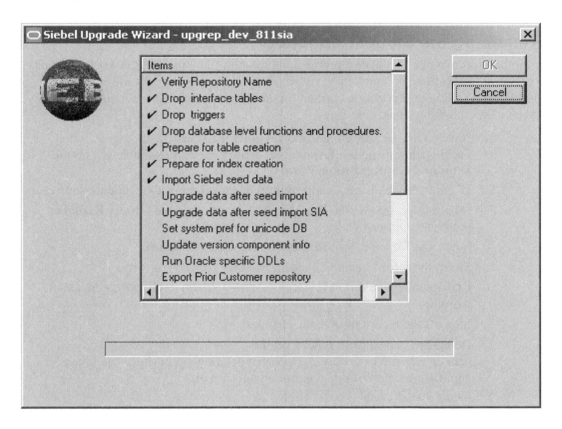

The upgrade process and IRM are described in the **Siebel Database Upgrade Guide** of the Siebel bookshelf.

The following is a list of the most important upgrade tasks:

1. Rename the Siebel Repository
2. Import Ancestor Repositories
3. Prepare Siebel Tools
4. Run the Database Configuration Wizard (upgrep)
5. Launch the Siebel Upgrade Wizard (upgrep)
6. Backup the database and execute database statistic packages
7. Continue the Siebel Upgrade Wizard (Siebel Tools tasks)

8. Analyze and resolve merge conflicts
9. Run the Database Configuration Wizard (upgphys)
10. Create a log summary
11. Compile a new Siebel Repository File
12. Apply post-upgrade configurations

In the remainder of this section, we will discuss the details of each step.

Renaming the Siebel Repository

In order to prepare the Siebel development database for the upgrade, the existing Siebel Repository needs to be renamed to `Prior Customer Repository`. In addition, we should delete all other repositories present in the development database. To do so, we execute the following steps.

1. If necessary, export all repositories other than `Siebel Repository` to backup files, using the **Export Repository** process available within the **Database Configuration Wizard**.
2. Login to Siebel Tools, connecting to the development server data source.
3. If necessary, expose the **Repository** object type in the **Object Explorer** (using the Options dialog).
4. Select the Repository object type in the **Object Explorer**.
5. Select the record named `Siebel Repository`.
6. Change the name to `Prior Customer Repository`, observing the exact wording.
7. Step off the record to save the changes.
8. Delete any repositories other than the `Prior Customer Repository` (a backup was made in step 1). Note that deleting a repository can take a significant length of time, approximately 1 hour.
9. Close Siebel Tools.

In newer versions of Siebel CRM, this step can be omitted as the repository is renamed automatically. However, deleting excess repositories is still a manual task (as described in step 8 above).

Importing Ancestor Repositories

As mentioned above, Oracle makes ancestor repositories available as a separate download package. After downloading and extracting the package we find a folder structure with utility scripts and the repository backup files (`.dat`).

In order to verify and copy the files to the appropriate directory in the **Database Server Utilities** installation folder, Oracle provides a command line utility named `copydat.bat` (or `.sh` for UNIX/Linux).

The `copydat` utility must be executed at the command prompt as follows (example for Windows operating systems).

```
copydat.bat SES_HOME d:\TEMP\anc.log
```

`SES_HOME` must be replaced with the actual path to the Siebel Enterprise server installation root directory. The second parameter is the path to a log file.

The screenshot below shows the output of the `copydat` utility on a Windows command shell.

As the utility does not simply copy files, but also verifies the CRC checksums, the process of importing the ancestor repository backup files takes a while.

Preparing Siebel Tools

Siebel Tools will be invoked several times in the IRM process. It is necessary to prepare some parameters in the Siebel Tools configuration file (`tools.cfg`) as instructed in the documentation.

The following procedure guides us through the process of preparing Siebel Tools.

1. Navigate to the Siebel Tools installation folder and open the language specific subfolder of the BIN directory (usually ENU).
2. Open the `tools.cfg` file with a text editor.

3. Set the following parameters:
   - `ServerDbODBCDataSource = SSD  default instance`
   - `SymStrPrefix = SBL_`
   - `EnableToolsConstrain = FALSE`
   - `DockRepositoryName = Prior Customer Repository`
4. Save and close the `tools.cfg` file

Running the Database Configuration Wizard (upgrep)

The following table lists the steps for executing the **Siebel Database Configuration Wizard** to collect parameters for the **Siebel Upgrade Wizard**. The example scenario details an upgrade to Innovation Pack 2013 on a Windows operating system using an Oracle database server.

Step	Description	Tasks and Example Values
1	Start the Database Configuration Wizard.	Launch the Database Configuration Utility from the Windows Start menu.
2	Siebel Server Directory	Example Value: • `D:\siebel\ses\siebsrvr` Click Next
3	Database Server Utilities Directory	Example Value: • `D:\siebel\ses\dbsrvr` Click Next
4	RDBMS Platform	Select the following: • Oracle Database Enterprise Edition Click Next
5	Siebel Database Operation	Select the following: • Upgrade Database Click Next
6	Environment Type	Select the following: • Development Click Next
7	Upgrade Options	Select the following: • Upgrade Siebel Database Schema (upgrep) Click Next

(Continued)

8	Siebel Industry Application	Select the following • Siebel Industry Application Click Next Note: Select Siebel Horizontal Application if you upgrade from the non-vertical repository.
9	Current Siebel Version	Select the following • v8_1_1SIA_to_v8_1_1_9SIA Click Next Note: Ensure you select the correct current version depending on your project
10	Siebel Tools Installation Directory	Example Value: • `D:\siebel\tools` Click Next
11	Siebel Tools Data Source Name	Example Value: • `ServerDataSrc` Click Next
12	Database Encoding	Select the following: • UNICODE Database Click Next
13	ODBC Data Source Name	Example Value: • `Siebel_DSN` Click Next Note: Enter the exact name of the Enterprise ODBC data source.
14	Database User Name	Example Value: • `SADMIN` Click Next
15	Database Password	Example Value: • `Fz7ugnR$` Click Next
16	Database Table Owner	Example Value: • `SIEBEL` Click Next
17	Database Table Owner Password	Example Value: • `oLt32$th` Click Next

(Continued)

18	Index Table Space Name	Example Value: • `siebelindex` Click Next
19	Table Space Name	Example Value: • `siebeldata` Click Next
20	Database Server OS	Select the following: • Windows Click Next
21	Oracle Parallel Index	Select the following: • Does not use the Oracle Parallel Indexing option Click Next
22	Security Group ID / Grantee	Example Value: • `SSE_ROLE` Click Next
23	Log Output Directory	Example Value: • `upgrep_dev_811sia` Click Next
24	Select runupg option	Select the following: • Yes apply configuration changes now Click Next
25	Summary	Review the summary information Click Next
26	Siebel Upgrade Wizard starts	Click OK
27	Siebel Upgrade Wizard executes steps	Wait until Siebel Upgrade Wizard prompts for manual steps.

Launching the Siebel Upgrade Wizard (upgrep)

As indicated above, the Siebel Upgrade Wizard is launched by the Database Configuration Wizard automatically when we select the option to do so. This only works on Microsoft Windows.

In case we execute the upgrade process on UNIX or Linux operating systems, or in case we need to launch the Siebel Upgrade Wizard manually on Windows, we can do so by issuing the following command:

```
SES_HOME\siebsrvr\BIN\siebupg /m master_upgrep_dev_811sia.ucf
```

The above is an example of how to invoke the Siebel Upgrade Wizard from the command line. The /m switch is followed by the path to the upgrade configuration file (.ucf) which has been created by the Database Upgrade Wizard.

If the upgrade process has been interrupted due to an error, we must resolve the problem and restart the upgrade wizard using the above command. The wizard will continue with the steps it has not yet completed.

Backing up the Database and Executing Database Statistics Packages

One step of the upgrade process actually has to be carried out manually. The upgrade wizard will stop and display the following dialog.

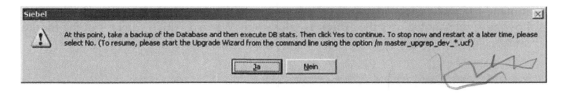

The dialog instructs us to take a backup of the database and then execute "DB stats" (database statistics packages). After doing so, we click Yes to continue. Alternatively, we can click No and stop the wizard, having to launch it manually after carrying out the manual tasks.

As instructed, we should use any preferred technique to take a backup of the database.

In order to execute the database statistics packages we can issue the following command against the database (the below example is for Oracle database; a **sysdba** account must be used to run the command):

```
EXEC DBMS_STATS.gather_schema_stats (ownname => 'SIEBEL',
cascade
=>true,estimate_percent => dbms_stats.auto_sample_size);
```

In the above example command, 'SIEBEL' is the name of the table owner, which is usually the preferred table owner name for Siebel databases.

Oracle also makes a database statistics script available for its customers on the My Oracle Support portal. It can be found on document 781927.1 for download. We can run the downloaded script file as an alternative to the above command.

In addition to backing up the database and executing the statistics packages, we should also prepare the database for a higher number of open cursors. The following command is an example, for the Oracle database, and has to be executed by a **sysdba** account:

```
alter system set open_cursors=1000 scope=spfile;
```

Finally, we shut down and restart the database.

Continuing the Siebel Upgrade Wizard (Siebel Tools)

After its re-launch, the Siebel Upgrade Wizard continues to execute the upgrade steps. The remaining steps are mostly executed by Siebel Tools. When we run the process on a Windows machine with Siebel Tools installed (the preferred option), Siebel Tools is invoked automatically.

The first task is a batch compilation of the "New Siebel Repository" (i.e. the new standard repository) into a temporary file which will subsequently replace the siebel_sia.srf file currently used by Siebel Tools. This is done to ensure that Siebel Tools uses the most recent repository file before executing the incremental merge.

After the siebel_sia.srf file for Siebel Tools is replaced, the upgrade wizard issues a command to invoke Siebel Tools for the Incremental Repository Merge (IRM). The following screenshot shows the **IPack Deployment Wizard** which carries out the merge in Siebel Tools.

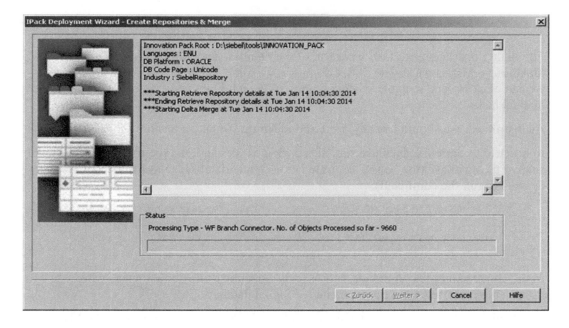

The merge process is inherently lengthy and can take 12 or more hours depending on the memory available to Siebel Tools and the connection to the server's database.

During the merge process, the two paths of modification - new features introduced by Oracle and customizations - are merged into a "New Customer Repository" which will become the new "Siebel Repository" once the upgrade is complete.

Depending on how many versions are crossed and (even more) depending on the number of customizations, the merge process will encounter conflicts which must be resolved before the upgrade can be completed.

Analyzing and Resolving Merge Conflicts

Once the incremental repository merge is complete, we must analyze and subsequently resolve the merge conflicts. This task requires skills and experience we can only gather from conducting upgrades. If we find ourselves in a chicken-or-egg situation, having to conduct an upgrade process without experience, it might be worthwhile considering external resources such as consultants with a solid experience in Siebel upgrades.

Siebel Tools provides specialized views and a hierarchical merge report to assist us with identifying critical conflicts. The following screenshot shows the **Hierarchical Merge Report** in Siebel Tools.

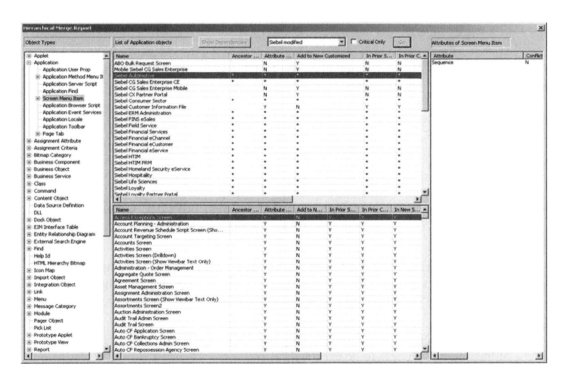

To invoke the Hierarchical Merge Report, we must follow these steps.

1. Login to Siebel Tools, connecting to the server database.
2. In the menu bar, navigate to Screens > Application Upgrader > Application Upgrade Objects List.
3. Right-click the record representing the IRM and select Hierarchy Reports.

As an alternative to using the graphical user interface options provided by Siebel Tools to analyze the merge data, we can also use anything from simple SQL queries to business intelligence tools (when available) to inspect the raw data in the database.

The following tables contain the merged data.

- `S_MERGE_LOG_OBJ`: Differences at the object level (e.g. Applet or List Column)
- `S_MERGE_LOG_ATTR`: Differences at the property level (e.g. Search Specification).

Conflicts can range from anything like minor differences in properties to renamed or deleted (obsoleted) object definitions which - when referenced in earlier versions, for example within a custom script - can cause errors at runtime.

Resolving conflicts should be taken seriously and tested diligently. This effort is typically measured in weeks rather than in hours.

Once we have finished the task of analyzing and resolving merge conflicts, we must launch Siebel Tools once more, invoking the **IPack Deployment Wizard** using a command similar to the following:

```
TOOLS_HOME\bin\siebdev.exe /u SADMIN /p Fz7ugnR$ /d
"ServerDataSrc" /c "TOOLS_HOME\BIN\ENU\tools.cfg" /l ENU
/iPackmode /IRM UpgDeltaMerge
```

The above command launches Siebel Tools (`siebdev.exe`), logging in as `SADMIN`, connecting to the server database. The `/iPackmode` and `/IRM UpgDeltaMerge` parameters are necessary to invoke the IPack Deployment Wizard at Siebel Tools startup. Note that `TOOLS_HOME` must be replaced with the actual path to the Siebel Tools installation folder.

The IPack Deployment Wizard prompts that the delta merge has been completed and displays a check box labeled Conflict resolution completed. By checking the box and clicking Finish, we confirm that the task of analyzing and resolving merge conflicts has been completed.

As a result of this action, the upgrade history table is updated which allows the final steps of the upgrade process to be executed.

Running the Database Configuration Wizard (upgphys)

The **Upgrade Custom Database Schema (upgphys)** process is a set of tasks executed by the Siebel Upgrade Wizard to finalize the upgrade of a development server database. To run this process we launch the Database Configuration Wizard and provide parameters as shown in the table below (example for Oracle database on Microsoft Windows).

Step	Description	Tasks and Example Values
1	Start the Database Configuration Wizard.	Launch the Database Configuration Utility from the Windows Start menu.
2	Siebel Server Directory	Example Value: • `D:\siebel\ses\siebsrvr` Click Next
3	Database Server Utilities Directory	Example Value: • `D:\siebel\ses\dbsrvr` Click Next
4	RDBMS Platform	Select the following: • Oracle Database Enterprise Edition Click Next
5	Siebel Database Operation	Select the following: • Upgrade Database Click Next
6	Environment Type	Select the following: • Development Click Next
7	Upgrade Options	Select the following: • Upgrade Custom Database Schema (upgphys) Click Next
8	Siebel Industry Application	Select the following • Siebel Industry Application Click Next Note: Select Siebel Horizontal Application if you upgrade from the non-vertical repository.
9	Current Siebel Version	Select the following • v8_1_1SIA_to_v8_1_1_9SIA Click Next Note: Ensure you select the correct version depending on your project

(Continued)

10	Database Encoding	Select the following: • UNICODE Database Click Next
11	ODBC Data Source Name	Example Value: • Siebel_DSN Click Next Note: Enter the exact name of the Enterprise ODBC data source.
12	Database User Name	Example Value: • SADMIN Click Next
13	Database Password	Example Value: • Fz7ugnR$ Click Next
14	Database Table Owner	Example Value: • SIEBEL Click Next
15	Database Table Owner Password	Example Value: • oLt32§th Click Next
16	Index Table Space Name	Example Value: • siebelindex Click Next
17	Table Space Name	Example Value: • siebeldata Click Next
18	Database Server OS	Select the following: • Windows Click Next
19	Oracle Parallel Index	Select the following: • Does not use the Oracle Parallel Indexing option Click Next

(Continued)

20	Security Group ID / Grantee	Example Value: • `SSE_ROLE` Click Next
21	Log Output Directory	Example Value: • `upgphys_dev_811sia` Click Next
22	Select runupg option	Select the following: • Yes apply configuration changes now Click Next
23	Summary	Review the summary information Click Next
24	Siebel Upgrade Wizard starts	Click OK
25	Siebel Upgrade Wizard executes steps	Wait until Siebel Upgrade Wizard completes.

After the Siebel Upgrade Wizard has completed, we should launch Siebel Tools and verify that a new repository named `Siebel Repository` exists and that it contains our customizations as well as new Oracle features for the latest release.

The other repositories, used during the merge, are removed during the Upgrade Custom Database Schema (upgphys) process.

> For customers who have already been using (and customizing) Siebel Open UI in versions 8.1.1.9 / 8.2.2.2 or 8.1.1.10 / 8.2.2.3, it is important to understand this process also includes a step which migrates the manifest data from the XML files (used in those older versions) to the new database tables introduced in IP 2013.

Creating a Log Summary

Because of the large number of intricate tasks the upgrade wizard executes (or rather "orchestrates"), we should safeguard all log files to identify erroneous steps later. To accomplish this, we can simply make a backup copy of the subdirectories (named for example `upgphys_dev_811_sia`) which the upgrade wizard creates in the Siebel server's log folder.

In addition, we should employ the **Log Parser** utility to create an easily readable set of HTML files which serve as a summary of the process activity.

To invoke the log parser, we run a command similar to the following.

```
SES_HOME\ses\siebsrvr\bin\logparse /S SES_HOME /G ENU /R
upgrep_dev_811sia
```

The above command - `SES_HOME` must be replaced with the path to the actual Siebel Enterprise Server installation directory - executes the `logparse` command line utility. The parameters passed are the current home directory of the Siebel Enterprise Server (`/S`), the language (`/G`) and the name of the folder containing the files generated by the Siebel Upgrade Wizard (`/R`).

The log parser works for every process executed by the Upgrade Wizard, including database upgrades (such as described in this chapter) but also database utilities such as exporting and importing repositories or Siebel database installations.

The following screenshot shows the Steps/Errors Summary HTML page generated by the log parser utility.

Steps/Errors Summary   Back to main page

This table contains a summary of all the steps in the process upgrep_dev_811sia and displays any errors that may have occurred in each step.

For steps of type 'File Execute' that have more than 8 errors, a hyperlink to the errors is displayed instead.
(Please note that this value can be set using the /E option of this utility)

Each step has two possible statuses. They are:

- Complete   This step is complete. But you still should review the log files for errors that must be resolved.
- Incomplete   This step has failed, causing the upgrade/install process to stop. You need to examine the errors, fix the problem, and restart the process.

Each error has two possible severities. They are:

- L   The severity of this error is low as it did not cause the process run to fail. Any errors listed are unacceptable and should be investigated further.
- H   The severity of this error is high as it caused the process being run to fail. This is an unacceptable error. You must correct the problem and rerun the process.

Step	Name	Start Time	End Time	Net Cost	Parallel	Interrupted	Status
0	Verify Repository Name	2014-01-15 11:45:22	2014-01-15 11:45:25	00h:00m:03s			Complete
1	Drop interface tables	2014-01-15 11:45:25	2014-01-15 11:46:20	00h:00m:55s			Complete
2	Drop triggers	2014-01-15 11:46:21	2014-01-15 11:46:22	00h:00m:01s			Complete
3	Drop database level functions and procedures.	2014-01-15 11:46:22	2014-01-15 11:46:24	00h:00m:02s			Complete
4	Prepare for table creation	2014-01-15 11:46:24	2014-01-15 11:46:26	00h:00m:02s			Complete
6		2014-01-15 11:46:26	2014-01-15 11:53:19	00h:06m:53s			Complete
7	Prepare for index creation	2014-01-15 11:53:19	2014-01-15 11:53:21	00h:00m:02s			Complete
9		2014-01-15 11:53:21	2014-01-15 12:03:22	00h:10m:01s			Complete
11		2014-01-15 12:03:22	2014-01-15 12:11:58	00h:08m:36s			Complete
12	Import Siebel seed data	2014-01-15 12:11:58	2014-01-15 12:21:20	00h:17m:58s	☑		Complete

The summary files allow us to examine execution timings, commands executed and errors generated.

It is recommended to always generate the HTML summary before taking the full backup of the log files.

Compiling a new Siebel Repository File

The new `Siebel Repository` generated by IRM and the (optional) conflict resolution steps must be compiled into a new custom **Siebel Repository File** (SRF). To do so, we run a full compile as usual.

The resulting SRF must be placed on all development workstations and servers to make all new features and customizations fully available.

Applying Post-upgrade Configurations

Depending on the original Siebel CRM version we started from, there might be a considerable number of additional configuration tasks waiting to be completed before we can make full use of our Siebel environment and before we can start upgrading the test and production environments.

The following is a list of issues which typically need to be addressed during an upgrade to IP 2013 or later. The list is not complete. Depending on the project specifics, fewer or more steps might be required.

Please consider the following list with extra care when your project includes customizations in these areas.

- Clib functions in eScript
- EAI File Transport
- Intensive use of 'traditional' browser script
- Custom ActiveX controls
- Apply IP 2014 API changes to Open UI customizations

Server scripts which require access to the file system will fail due to access restrictions

This issue affects any custom script which uses `Clib` file access methods such as `Clib.fopen` in Siebel **eScript**. A new system preference named `Allow File System Access` must be set to `TRUE` to re-enable file access. Apart from this quick resolution, it might be worthwhile to explore other, more secure, options to access the file system of server machines from scripts.

EAI File Transport security restrictions will cause file operations to fail

Many Enterprise Application Integration (EAI) interfaces developed by Oracle or customers rely on the **EAI File Transport** business service. For the sake of higher file system security, a new server parameter named `EAIFileTransportFolders` has been made available in version 8.1.1.10.

This parameter must be set to a path or semicolon-separated list of paths which are suitable targets for the EAI File Transport business service.

For Siebel Tools or the Developer Web Client an entry similar to the following must be added to the configuration (`.cfg`) file to enable file system access for the EAI File Transport business service.

```
[EAIFileTransportConfigSubsys]
EAIFileTransportFolders = D:\temp;C:\temp
```

Usually the `[EAIFileTransportConfigSubsys]` profile does not exist in an as-delivered `.cfg` file, so it has to be added.

Traditional Browser Script might not execute in Open UI clients

Several problems and bugs have been reported by customers regarding the execution of 'traditional' browser scripts in Open UI clients. This relates to browser scripts authored in Siebel Tools with the traditional High-Interactivity client (and Microsoft Internet Explorer) in mind.

Developers and architects should be aware of the following common problems which might occur when a traditional browser script executes in an Open UI environment.

Code which runs in Internet Explorer might not execute in other browsers

This can be due to a missing semicolon at the end of a line of code which older IE versions accept but other browsers such as Google Chrome refuse to execute. Another reason might be that the developer explicitly or implicitly expected the code to be executed in IE and referenced ActiveX-related methods available only in IE.

The SetProfileAttr() function fails because of security restrictions

For security reasons, Oracle has disabled the `SetProfileAttr` method in browser scripts by default since version 8.1.1.10 / 8.2.2.3. To re-enable the method, we can set the `EditProfileAttr` server parameter to `TRUE`.

However, Oracle does not support using the `SetProfileAttr` method in Open UI, so it is advisable to explore other ways of setting profile attributes. One way of doing this could be via a server-side business service which is invoked from the browser script.

Write operations to business components from browser script are restricted

Another security feature, namely the ability to prevent access to business component data and methods from external scripts (including browser scripts) has been implemented by Oracle in 8.1.1.9 in the form of a new server parameter named `BusCompAccessLevel` and new business component user properties (`DirectUIAccess` and `DirectUIAccessFieldList`).

The `BusCompAccessLevel` parameter accepts the following values:

- `None`: No direct operations on business components are allowed
- `Readonly`: Only queries (read operations) are allowed (this is the default value)

- `All`: Read and write operations on business components are allowed

Developers wishing to continue to use the business component access functions in newer versions must use this parameter and the new user properties according to the documentation, which can be found at `http://docs.oracle.com/cd/E14004_01/books/Secur/Secur_AccessControl32.html`.

Traditional browser script methods might not execute due to bugs

Several bugs have been reported (and might well be resolved by the time you read this) regarding the execution of traditional browser scripts in Open UI. While Open UI is officially backward compatible, the mix of the old browser script API and the new Open UI framework poses a lot of challenges for developers.

Developers and architects are encouraged to check the My Oracle Support portal frequently for updates on Siebel Open UI and to install the latest patch sets which are provided by Oracle on a monthly basis.

Custom ActiveX controls must be migrated to Open UI

As a matter of fact, Siebel Open UI is designed to operate in all browsers, regardless of device or form factor. As such, the framework utilizes JavaScript instead of ActiveX, which is only available in Microsoft Internet Explorer.

Customers who wish to take full advantage of the browser independence that comes with Open UI are encouraged to replace all ActiveX related customizations with JavaScript.

Applying IP 2014 API changes to Open UI customizations

In case you are upgrading to Innovation Pack 2014 or higher and have already implemented custom Open UI scripts, you should consider migrating custom code that was created for version IP 2013 or earlier to conform to the API changes introduced in IP 2014.

On rare occasions, custom Open UI scripts from earlier versions could not work as expected in IP 2014 due to changes in the Document Object Model (DOM) such as obsolete or renamed elements or class names. The same is relevant for custom style rules that might not match the selectors any more in IP 2014.

Please refer to this book's chapters that deal with the Open UI API, CSS themes and scripting techniques for details on the enhancements and features introduced with IP 2014.

In addition you should review the *Post-Upgrade Configuration Tasks* chapter in the *Configuring Siebel Open UI* guide in the Siebel bookshelf. You can find this chapter at `http://docs.oracle.com/cd/E58886_01/books/config_open_ui/appendix_c_post_upgrade.html`.

Case Study: Enabling Open UI for a Siebel Application

Once we are able to start up the Siebel servers and login to the application (probably still in its original mode of High-Interactivity), we can start creating object managers which run the same application in Open UI mode.

A 'side-by-side' scenario is recommended practice and should be done instead of simply 'switching' the original application to Open UI. During the first stages of the migration project, the option of comparing the old and new world is something that we really do not want to miss.

In addition, we might want to provide developers with shortcuts to invoke the Developer Web Client or Siebel Tools in Open UI mode.

The following list describes the steps necessary to create an Open UI-enabled object manager in a Siebel server environment. Note that starting with IP 2014, the installer has an option to activate Open UI by default, so the following steps are only necessary for upgrades from earlier versions or if you want to set up an Open UI enabled object manager from scratch.

Siebel Server Configuration Tasks

The following procedure describes how to create a new component definition for an Open UI-enabled object manager.

1. Login to the Siebel Web Client as administrator.
2. Navigate to Administration - Server Configuration > Component Definitions.
3. Create a new component definition record and provide valid values for the following fields:

Field	Example Value
Name	Call Center Object Manager (ENU) - Open UI
Alias	SCCObjMgr_OUI_enu
Component Type	Application Object Manager
Component Group	Siebel Call Center
Description	Evaluation OM for Open UI

4. Save the record by pressing *CTRL+S*.
5. If the record no longer has focus, use a query to retrieve the new record again.

6. In the Component Parameters list, find and set the following parameters (Example values are for a Siebel Call Center application in American English):

Parameter	Description	Example Value
EnableOpenUI	Enables Open UI	True
HighInteractivity	Enables High Interactivity	True
Application Name	The name of the application as in the Siebel Repository	Siebel Universal Agent
Application Splashtext	The text to display on the login screen	Siebel Call Center Open UI
Application Title	The text to display in the browser title	Siebel Call Center Open UI
OM - Configuration File	Path to the configuration file	uagent.cfg
Locale Code	The locale to use for data formatting	ENU
Maximum Tasks	Maximum number of sessions	100
ListRowStyle	Must be set for compatibility	Siebel List
AppletSelectStyle	Must be set for compatibility	Applet Select
EAI File Transport Folder List	List of folders for file export or import	d:\siebel;c:\siebfile
Application Repository File (Click the Advanced button to see this parameter)	Name of the SRF file	siebel_sia.srf
DefaultNavigation (IP 2014 or higher)	Sets the default navigation style (side, tab or tree)	NAVIGATION_SIDE

7. Click Activate in the component definition list to activate the new component definition.
8. Log out of the application.
9. Stop and restart the Siebel Server services which run the component group.

Siebel Web Server Extension (SWSE) Configuration Tasks

The following procedure describes how to add a new virtual directory to the Siebel web server that points to the new object manager.

1. Open the SWSE configuration file (eapps.cfg). This file is found in the BIN folder of the SWSE installation folder on the web server machine.

2. Locate the section for the original application (e.g. `[/callcenter_enu]`)
3. Copy the entire section and paste it below the original
4. Rename the new section (e.g. `[/cctest_oui]`)
5. In the `ConnectString` parameter of the new section, replace the reference to the original object manager (after the last slash) with the alias name of the new object manager (e.g. `SCCObjMgr_OUI_enu`)
6. Save and close the `eapps.cfg` file
7. On the SWSE machine, run a command similar to the following to create a new virtual directory for the new application:

```
SWSE_HOME\bin\metabaseedit.exe cctest_oui
SWSE_HOME\BIN\ENU\eapps.mtb
```

In the above command, `SWSE_HOME` should be replaced with the actual path to the SWSE installation folder. The above command is for Microsoft Windows.

8. Restart the web server

To test the new object manager we navigate to the new URL (e.g. `http://localhost/cctest_oui`) in a browser of our choice. The Open UI login page should be displayed as shown in the screenshot below.

ORACLE®
Siebel Customer Relationship Management

Siebel Call Center Open UI Innovation Pack 2013

User ID

Password

☐ Remember my User ID

LOGIN

Accessibility

Now we can log in and start using the application in Open UI mode.

Case Study: Desktop Shortcuts for Developer Web Client or Siebel Tools

In order to use the Siebel Developer Web Client or Siebel Tools in Open UI mode, we must modify the appropriate configuration (`.cfg`) files and add or edit the `EnableOpenUI` parameter to the `[InfraUIFramework]` section.

It is advisable to copy an existing configuration file, rename it (e.g. to `uagent_oui.cfg`) and modify the copy as mentioned above. Using the new configuration file, we can create desktop shortcuts which allow us to access the application in Open UI mode.

The Siebel Developer Web client uses the system default browser when no other browser is specified at start up. In case we want to produce shortcuts which open in a specific browser we can use the **/b** command line switch.

The following is an example for a desktop shortcut command which launches the Siebel Call Center Developer Web Client in Mozilla Firefox.

```
D:\sea\client\BIN\siebel.exe /c
d:\sea\client\bin\ENU\uagent_oui.cfg /b "D:\Program Files
(x86)\Mozilla Firefox\firefox.exe"
```

By using shortcuts, as described above, we can provide quick access to frequently used applications in different browsers for evaluation or testing purposes.

Summary

In order to get the most recent version of Siebel Open UI, we must either install or upgrade to the latest Siebel CRM release. In this chapter we described the installation and upgrade processes in great detail.

The upgrade process includes the **Incremental Repository Merge** which produces a new custom repository. Project team members and project leaders must recognize the challenge that depending on how much time was invested in customizing Siebel CRM, more or less effort has to be made to resolve conflicts and configure the application to become operational again after the merge.

Once the application is operational, we can start setting up object managers in Open UI mode for evaluation and testing. In addition we learned in this chapter how to set up shortcuts for the Siebel Developer Web Client and Siebel Tools.

In the next chapter, we will discover the administrative tasks around Open UI manifests.

4

Manifest Administration

While Siebel Open UI provides us with great flexibility and extensibility using JavaScript, the challenge lies in 'registering' the right piece of code with the correct user interface object. In this chapter, we will learn how to use Manifest Administration views to accomplish this task.

The chapter is structured as follows:

- Review: Open UI Manifests
- Manifest Files
- Manifest Expressions
- Manifest Administration

Review: Open UI Manifests

As discussed in chapter 2, the purpose of Siebel Open UI manifest data is to connect user interface objects such as applets, views or navigation elements with files that the browser loads at runtime such as JavaScript files or style sheets. In addition, we can use the manifest administration to specify which web template definition (in the repository) shall be used by the SWE to generate the HTML code for an applet or view.

Administrators can use **Manifest Expressions** for conditional logic that will define under what circumstances a specific web template or set of files should be loaded.

Three new views in the Siebel Web Client have been introduced in IP 2013 to administer manifest data, replacing the XML files which have been used in 8.1.1.10 / 8.2.2.4 and earlier. For information about the manifest XML files, refer to Appendix B at the end of this book.

The next screenshot shows the Manifest Administration view of the Administration - Application screen in the Siebel Web Client.

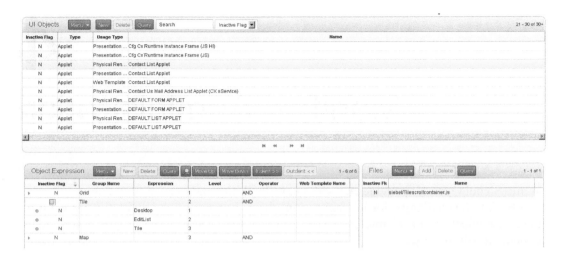

This view allows administrators to inspect and create associations between UI objects, expressions and files. In the screenshot, we can see the evaluation logic for choosing the physical renderer for the **Contact List Applet**. In the lower half of the view, we can see that when the application is in Desktop mode and the applet is in EditList mode and the user has selected Tile display, the `Tilescrollcontainer.js` file will be loaded, resulting in the tile display we introduced in chapter 1.

Manifest Files

Every file that we want to associate with a user interface object must be registered first. This is accomplished in the Manifest Files view of the Administration - Application screen, which is shown in the next screenshot.

In a fresh, out-of-the-box Siebel environment we only find the as-delivered files from Oracle and third parties registered in this view. Whenever we want to use a custom file, we must register it in the above list. This procedure is discussed in the following case study.

While most of the files that we would find (or register as custom files) in the Manifest Files list would contain JavaScript code, there is no limitation on the type of file. As of IP 2014, CSS files are registered for standard or custom themes and we could also register any other file type that could be loaded by a browser. The only condition we have to fulfill is that the file is available in the respective subdirectory of the `PUBLIC/<Language>` folder of the Siebel Developer Web Client or Siebel Web Server Extension.

It is also possible to register files - for example style sheets - that reside on different web servers by using the full URL path.

Case Study: Registering a Custom JavaScript File

With the goal of providing a hands-on scenario, this chapter includes case study sections. In this first case study, we will learn how to register a custom file. Because we have not yet learned how to create a custom JavaScript file, we will be using an empty file, having to keep in mind that the scenario will not be applicable for a real-life project because the file actually only contains a comment line.

To register a custom file, we follow the process described below.

1. Open a text editor and create a file with the following content.

```
/* This is a test file. */
console.log("Test file loaded");
```

The above code will write the message "Test file loaded" to the browser's JavaScript console. As mentioned above, this is for demonstration purposes only. We will learn to create more useful custom JavaScript files and how to register them in upcoming chapters.

2. Save this file as `TestFile.js` to the `/siebel/custom` folder, which is located in the `PUBLIC` directory of either Siebel Developer Web Client or SWSE. Below is a full example path to the folder reserved for custom Open UI JavaScript files.

```
D:\siebel\client\PUBLIC\enu\23030\SCRIPTS\siebel\custom
```

The above is an example for a Windows installation of the Siebel Developer Web Client. Depending on your specific installation and product version, the exact folder path, especially the language subdirectory (`enu` in the above example) and the build subdirectory (`23030`) may vary.

3. In the Siebel Web Client, navigate to the Administration - Application screen, Manifest Files view.
4. Create a new record in the Files list.

5. Enter the relative path (using forward slashes) to the custom file, obeying exact typing. Preferably, copy and paste the names. The following is an example entry for a custom file named `TestFile.js`.

   `siebel/custom/TestFile.js`

6. Save the record.

As we can see, registering custom files is quite straightforward. Once the file is registered we can use it in the Manifest Administration view.

Manifest Expressions

Introduced as a new feature in IP 2013, **Manifest Expressions** allow administrators to encapsulate conditional logic to evaluate whether a specific set of files should be downloaded or used for a given user interface object.

Manifest expressions are administered in the Manifest Expressions view of the Administration - Application screen. The following screenshot shows this view.

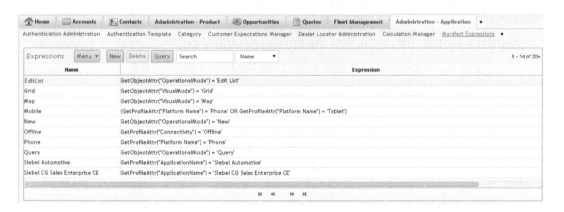

As we can see, manifest expressions have a name - such as Edit List for the first record in the screenshot - and an expression which is formulated in **Siebel Query Language**. The first record visible, in the screenshot, has the following expression:

`GetObjectAttr("OperationalMode") = 'Edit List'`

The above expression uses the `GetObjectAttr` method to get the value of the `OperationalMode` attribute. The expression will evaluate to `TRUE` when the value matches the string `Edit List`. This expression is intended to be used exclusively with applets, as they can have multiple modes, including `Edit List`. The previous expression enables us to evaluate whether a list applet is currently displayed in `Edit List` mode.

A quick inventory of the as-delivered expressions shows that Oracle engineering focused on using object or profile attributes. The following is a list of popular methods used in manifest expressions:

Method used in manifest expression	Description
`GetObjectAttr("OperationalMode")`	Used with applets to evaluate the current display mode (e.g. "Edit List").
`GetObjectAttr("VisualMode")`	Used with applets to evaluate the current visual mode (e.g. "Tile").
`GetProfileAttr("ApplicationName")`	Used to determine the current application's name.
`GetProfileAttr("Platform Name")`	Used to determine the platform (*Desktop*, *Tablet* or *Phone*) in IP 2013.
`GetProfileAttr("Device")`	Replaces the "Platform Name" attribute (above) in IP 2014.
`GetProfileAttr("Connectivity")`	Used to determine whether a mobile application is in offline or online mode.
`LookupName()`	Retrieves the Language-Independent Code (LIC) of a list of values entry. Used with themes in IP 2014 or higher.
`Preference ("Behavior", "DefaultTheme")`	Returns the current value of a user preference setting (The default theme in the example). Used with themes in IP 2014 or higher.

The as-delivered manifest expressions must not be modified but can be reused by administrators in the Manifest Administration view. It is also possible to create custom expressions as shown in the following case study.

Case Study: Creating Custom Manifest Expressions

Using the Manifest Expressions view, we can create custom expressions if needed. The following is an example procedure that guides us through the process of creating a custom manifest expression for evaluating the value of a **system preference**. In our sample scenario, a system preference is used as a switch between standard and custom behavior of the application. This would allow administrators to 'reset' the application to the standard by disabling all Open UI customizations at once by means of setting a system preference value to TRUE or FALSE.

1. Navigate to the Administration - Application screen, Manifest Expressions view.

2. In the Expressions list, create a new record with the following values:

Column	Example value
Name	OUIBOOK Show Customizations
Expression	SystemPreference("OUIBOOK Show Customizations") = 'TRUE'

The above expression will evaluate to TRUE when the value of the OUIBOOK Show Customizations system preference is 'TRUE'. Otherwise, the expression will evaluate to FALSE. The SystemPreference method is one of the many methods supported by the Siebel Query Language.

While these are the minimum required steps to create a manifest expression, we should complete the scenario by creating the system preference. The following procedure guides us through this process.

3. Navigate to the Administration - Application screen, System Preferences view.

4. Create a new record with the following values:

Column	Example value
System Preference Name	OUIBOOK Show Customizations
System Preference Value	TRUE

The author's experiments have shown that manifest expressions can be created using standard Siebel Query Language syntax. However, there seems to be a limitation to which Siebel Query Language functions are supported. In the above case study we demonstrated the use of the SystemPreference function, which has been confirmed to work in IP 2013 and IP 2014.

Other functions of the Siebel Query Language are described in the Oracle Siebel documentation at the URL below but not all of them might operate well within manifest expressions.

The reference documentation for the Siebel Query Language can be found at

http://docs.oracle.com/cd/E14004_01/books/ToolsDevRef/operators_conditions11.html

---

Manifest Administration

The actual association of user interface objects such as applets or views with files and (optionally) expressions takes place in the Manifest Administration view of the Administration - Application screen.

This view consists of three applets, which we will explore in greater detail in the remainder of this chapter:

- UI Objects list
- Object Expression list
- Files list

The UI Objects List

The upper list applet of the Manifest Administration view allows administrators to work with records representing user interface objects. Data provided by Oracle ("seed data") is write-protected. It is however possible to add new custom entries. The following screenshot shows the UI Objects list applet.

UI Objects	Menu ▾	New	Delete	Query	Search		Inactive Flag ▾
Inactive Flag	**Type**		**Usage Type**				
N	Applet		Presentation Model		▾ eCalendar Monthly Applet Without Employee		
N	Applet		Physical Renderer		eService Social Media Links(Nav Links)		
N	Applet		Physical Renderer		eService Transaction Links(Nav Links)		
N	Applet		Physical Renderer		Service Request Detail Applet		
Y	Applet		Presentation Model		Service Request Detail Applet		
N	Application		Common		PLATFORM DEPENDENT		
N	Applet		Physical Renderer		Opportunity Form Applet - Child		
N	Applet		Presentation Model		Opportunity Form Applet - Child		
N	Applet		Physical Renderer		JPE Relationship Hierarchy Flat List Applet		
N	Navigation		Physical Renderer		NAVIGATION_TAB		

The following table describes the columns of the UI Objects list applet.

Column	Example Value	Description
Inactive Flag	N	Controls whether the UI object record is active (value = "N") or inactive (value = "Y").
Type	Applet	The type of the UI object represented by the record. (See below for an explanation of possible values)

(Continued)

Usage Type	Physical Renderer	The category or Open UI framework layer referenced by the object. (See below for an explanation of possible values)
Name	Contact List Applet	The name of the UI object as in the Siebel Repository. Generic entries use reserved names such as "*PLATFORM DEPENDENT*".

The Type column can have the following values:

Applet: UI object records with this type represent applets. Generic entries exist to represent groups of applets such as the entry named DEFAULT FORM APPLET.

Application: Used to define sets of files which must always be loaded or which should only be loaded for a specific combination of application and platform. As an example, the screenshot below shows the as-delivered application entry named PLATFORM DEPENDENT in the Manifest Administration view.

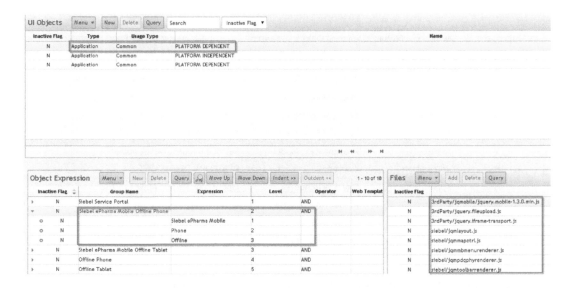

In the previous screenshot, four records in the Object Expression list at the lower left of the view are highlighted to illustrate the concept of platform dependency. The expression group named Siebel ePharma Mobile Offline Phone combines three expressions (using a logical AND operator) to determine whether the current application is Siebel ePharma Mobile, running on a phone device and is currently in offline mode. In case these three conditions evaluate to TRUE, the Open UI framework loads the list of JavaScript files (partially visible in the Files list at the bottom right corner of the view).

The PLATFORM DEPENDENT entry for the application type object also contains other expression groups for variations of applet/device combinations.

Control: Not currently used in the as-delivered application. It could potentially be used to load custom files for individual controls.

Menu: Not currently used in the as-delivered application. It could potentially be used to load custom files for menus.

Navigation: Used to support the navigational elements of the application, such as screens (tab or tree style) or the launch pad of mobile applications (in IP 2013 or earlier).

Toolbar: Not currently used in the as-delivered application. It could potentially be used to customize toolbars.

View: Used to associate specialized presentation models and physical renderers with views. Support for view objects has been added in patch set 8.1.1.11.3.

The Usage Type column can have the following values:

Common: Used in conjunction with the Application type to define file sets to be loaded when the application is initialized.

Theme: Used in conjunction with the Application type. This usage type provides an alternative way to register style sheets with the application. Starting with Innovation Pack 2014, this is used to associate the out-of-the-box themes with the application. For more information about themes and how to customize them, refer to chapter 8.

Presentation Model: Used in conjunction with common UI objects such as applets or views to define the presentational model files to be loaded when the object is initialized.

Physical Renderer: Used to define the physical renderer files to be loaded when common UI objects such as applets or views are initialized.

Web Template: Used to define conditions for using a specific web template for a given user interface object (applet or view). The term *web template* refers to the repository object associated with the applet or view which refers to a web template file (`.swt`) external to the repository.

Resources: The *Resources* usage type can be used to refer to any type of file that can be loaded by a browser. For example, the invoice printing option of the Siebel Service Mobile application uses a *Resources* entry to associate an HTML template file with a view.

Default Objects

The as-delivered list of UI objects contains various entries using reserved, generic names such as the aforementioned PLATFORM DEPENDENT. The following table explains the default objects:

Name	Description
DEFAULT FORM APPLET	Default presentation model and physical renderer for form applets.
DEFAULT LIST APPLET	Default presentation model and physical renderer for list applets.

(Continued)

DEFAULT TREE APPLET	Default presentation model and physical renderer for tree applets.
DEFAULT VIEW	Default presentation model and physical renderer for views.
NAVIGATION_TAB	Default physical renderer for navigation elements such as screen tabs or view tabs.
NAVIGATION CONTROL	Default presentation model for navigation elements.
NAVIGATION_BUTTON_PHONE and NAVIGATION_BUTTON_TABLET	Default physical renderer for navigation buttons in mobile applications. (Not used in IP 2014)
NAVIGATION_LAUNCHPAD_PHONE and NAVIGATION_LAUNCHPAD_TABLET	Default physical renderer for the launch pad-style site map in mobile applications. (Not used in IP 2014)
NAVIGATION_TREE	Default physical renderer for tree-style navigation.
NAVIGATION_SIDE	(IP 2014 or higher): Default physical renderer for the side menu navigation option.
PLATFORM DEPENDENT	Common files to be loaded dependent on application and device type.
PLATFORM INDEPENDENT	Common files to be loaded always.

As we will discuss later in this book, it might become necessary to "override" these default entries. To do so, we can copy an existing entry and use the copy to load custom files.

The Object Expression List

Using the Object Expression list applet in the bottom left corner of the Manifest Administration view, administrators can define simple or complex (grouped) expressions that allow the Open UI framework to determine under what circumstances a set of files (associated with the group or single entry) should be loaded.

To illustrate this concept, we will have a look at three examples:

- Single (ungrouped) expressions
- Grouped expressions
- Expressions for web templates

Single (ungrouped) Expressions

The following screenshot shows the content of the Object Expression list applet for the default physical renderer for list applets in Innovation Pack 2013.

	Object Expression	Menu ▼	New	Delete	Query 🔍	Move Up	Move Down	
	Inactive Flag ⬍	**Group Name**		**Expression**			**Level**	
○	N		Phone				1	
○	N		Tablet				2	
○	N		Desktop				3	

To locate this entry, we must execute a query in the UI Objects list using the following search criteria:

- Usage Type = "Physical Renderer"
- Name = "DEFAULT LIST APPLET"

As we can see in the previous screenshot, there are three expression entries (Phone, Tablet and Desktop). The Level field defines the order in which the expressions are evaluated. Such entries are considered 'single' because they do not belong to an expression group. With each entry, one or more files are associated (not visible in the screenshot).

For example, the file associated with the Desktop expression (which evaluates to `true` when the application is in desktop mode) is `siebel/jqgridrenderer.js`, which is the standard physical renderer responsible for displaying list applets in desktop applications such as Siebel Call Center.

Grouped Expressions

When more than one condition must be satisfied to load a specific file or a list of files, we can create **expression groups**.

The following screenshot shows the Object Expression list for the physical renderer of the `Contact List Applet`.

	Object Expression	Menu ▼	New	Delete	Query 🔍	Move Up	Move Down	Indent >>	Outdent
	Inactive Flag ⬍	**Group Name**		**Expression**		**Level**		**Operator**	
▶	N	Grid				1		AND	
▼	N	Tile				2		AND	
○	N		Desktop			1			
○	N		EditList			2			
○	N		Tile			3			
▶	N	Map				3		AND	

The list contains three groups named Grid, Tile and Map. The Tile group is expanded and we can see that it contains three expressions (Desktop, EditList and Tile). The Operator value for the Tile group is set to AND, indicating that all expressions in this group must evaluate to `true` to satisfy the condition and load the files associated with the group (not visible in the screenshot). Subsequently, the Tile group defines the following logical statement: "If the current application is in desktop mode AND the applet is in Edit List mode AND the applet is in Tile display mode".

The file associated with the Tile group is specifically used to render records in list applets as tiles.

Expressions for web templates

As indicated earlier, we can also use manifest expressions to determine when to use a specific web template for a user interface object. The as-delivered entry for the `Contact List Applet` for the *Web Template* usage type is a good example.

The following screenshot shows Siebel Tools displaying the list of **Applet Web Templates** defined for the `Contact List Applet` in the Siebel Repository.

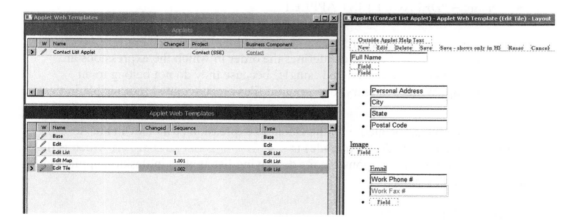

There are five web templates defined for the applet, the selected record at the bottom of the list is named Edit Tile. For illustrative purposes, the screenshot also shows the **Applet Editor** (on the right) with the Edit Tile template loaded. As we can discern from the screenshot, the Edit Tile layout is radically different from a typical list applet and shows several list columns of the applet arranged in a single stack.

> In order to enable Siebel Tools to use the new SWT files in the `OUIWEBTEMPL` folder, we must add the `EnableOpenUI` parameter (set to `TRUE`) to the `[InfraUIFramework]` section of the `tools.cfg` file.

The Edit Tile and Edit Map web templates are reserved for the special scenario that occurs when a user switches the Contact List Applet into *Tile (Card)* or *Map* display mode. The manifest administration entry for the applet uses the expressions shown in the screenshot below to determine the applet display mode and the associated web template.

| Object Expression | Menu ▼ | New | Delete | Query 🔍 | Move Up | Move Do |

Inactive Flag	Group Name	Expression	Level	Operator	Web Template Name
☐	Tile		1	AND	Edit Tile
N		Desktop	1		
N		EditList	2		
N		Tile	3		
Y	Map		2	AND	Edit Map
Y		Desktop	1		
Y		EditList	2		
Y		Map	3		

In the screenshot we can see two expression groups named Tile and Map. Instead of one or more JavaScript files in the Files applet (not visible in the screenshot), there is a single web template associated with each group directly in the Object Expressions list. For example, when the expressions in the Tile group evaluate to `true`, the Open UI framework uses the `Edit Tile` template to render the applet. The name of the web template must match exactly the name of the *Applet Web Template* entry in the Siebel Repository.

Associating File lists with UI objects without expressions

If we wish to associate one or more files with a user interface object *without evaluating any conditions*, we still must add a single record to the Object Expression list. This record has no field values except for the Level field, which is mandatory and should have a value of 1.

The Files List

The Files list applet at the bottom right of the Manifest Administration view is used - as indicated earlier - to provide a list of files which are associated with either a single expression or an expression group.

The following screenshot shows the Files list applet displaying the list of JavaScript files associated with the PLATFORM INDEPENDENT entry in the UI Objects list.

Files	Menu ▼	Add	Delete	Query	
Inactive Flag					**Name**
N		3rdParty/jquery.cookie.js			
N		3rdParty/jquery.livequery.js			
N		postload.js			
N		preload.js			
N		siebel/appletmenupmodel.js			
N		siebel/appmenupm.js			
N		siebel/msgbrdcstpm.js			
N		siebel/pdqpmodel.js			
N		siebel/perf.js			
N		siebel/toolbarpmodel.js			

Visible in the above screenshot are some of the JavaScript files which will always be loaded regardless of application or device because they are associated with the PLATFORM_INDEPENDENT entry on the Application type (not visible in the screenshot).

Working with the file list is easy because we can add files that were previously registered in the Manifest Files view. The Inactive Flag can be used to deactivate certain file entries (setting the flag to Y) and subsequently prevent them from being loaded.

In IP 2014 and higher, there is also a Sequence column (not shown in the screenshot) which allows administrators to set the order in which the files will be loaded.

Case Study: Associating a custom JavaScript file with an applet

In continuation of this chapter's case studies, we will now bring together the custom JavaScript file we registered in the first case study and the expression we created in the second case study. For the sake of demonstration we will use the as-delivered Service Request Detail Applet as the target object.

To associate the applet with a custom JavaScript file, using an expression, we execute the following steps.

1. Log in to the Siebel application as an administrator
2. Navigate to the Administration - Application screen, Manifest Administration view
3. In the UI Objects list, create a new record with the following values:

Column	Example value
Type	Applet
Usage Type	Physical Renderer
Name	Service Request Detail Applet

4. In the Object Expression list, create a new record with the following values:

Column	Example value
Expression	OUIBOOK Show Customizations
Level	1

5. In the Files list applet, click the Add button.
6. In the Files pick applet, locate the record for the siebel/custom/TestFile.js file.
7. Select the file and click OK.
8. Log out of the application and log back in. This is necessary to allow the object manager to load the manifest data.
9. Navigate to the *My Service Request* view (this view contains the *Service Request Detail Applet*).
10. Open the browser's developer tools and navigate to the list of source files (e.g. "Sources" in Google Chrome).
11. Expand the source tree and verify that the *TestFile.js* file is loaded.

12. Navigate to the browser's JavaScript console and verify that the message "Test file loaded" is displayed.

It is a recommended practice to verify that the manifest files are properly loaded. This ensures correctness of the manifest administration data. In case the files are not loaded by the browser, we should review the manifest settings thoroughly. For instance, wrong spelling or casing of file names is a typical cause of error. In addition, most browsers do not load JavaScript files which contain script that is syntactically wrong.

As indicated at the beginning of the case study, the scenario is solely for demonstration because the JavaScript file does not contain valid Open UI code. In case you wish to avoid problems with this configuration, return to the Manifest Administration view set the Inactive flag for the UI object you created in the previous case study to Y.

Summary

Manifest administration views are a powerful feature that allows administrators to manage the relationships between user interface objects and files to be downloaded by the browser. To apply conditional logic, we can re-use or create manifest expressions using Siebel Query Language.

In addition, we can instruct the Open UI framework to load specific web templates for a given UI object under certain conditions.

In the next chapter, we will explore the Siebel Open UI JavaScript framework.

5

The Siebel Open UI JavaScript Framework

Before we set out to add custom JavaScript code to our Siebel Open UI implementation, we must thoroughly understand the as-delivered framework and the application programming interface (API) developed by Oracle. In addition, we should strive to act responsibly and avoid unnecessary code as much as possible.

In this chapter we will undertake a detailed exploration of the Open UI JavaScript framework and the API as well as provide reasons when to script and when not to script.

The chapter is structured as follows.

- Open UI JavaScript Framework Overview
- Classes and Methods of the Proxy Layer
- Scripting Considerations

Open UI JavaScript Framework Overview

In regard to what we have already learned about the Open UI JavaScript framework in previous chapters, we can draw the following diagram of the browser-side Open UI JavaScript framework.

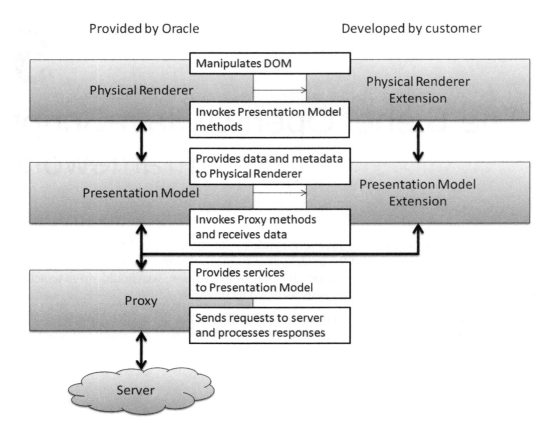

From the above diagram we can derive the following facts.

- The JavaScript files loaded by the browser at runtime contain classes and methods that comprise a complex, yet open and extensible framework.

- The framework is organized in three tiers, namely the **proxy**, **presentation model** and **physical renderer** layer.

- The purpose of the proxy layer is to act as a communication layer between the presentation model layer and the server. It also provides the base classes that represent the primary Siebel objects such as the application, business components, applets, and so forth.

- The presentation model (PM) layer stands between the proxy and the physical renderer tier and serves the purpose of defining a logical abstraction layer to hold data and metadata and provide this information to the physical renderer. The PM also communicates with the proxy.

- The physical renderer (PR) layer's responsibility is to implement the visualization of data on the screen by constructing user interface objects such as applets and populating them with data. The PR is the only layer in the framework that manipulates the browser's **Document Object Model**

(DOM). In addition, the PR invokes the PM in case of any event or data manipulation incurred by the end user.

- The PM and PR layers provide an extensibility API. The proxy layer cannot be extended or customized.

The diagram presented above emphasizes the three tier architecture of the Open UI JavaScript framework as well as the fact that customers can only create extensions to the Presentation Model layer and Physical Renderer layer but not the Proxy layer.

In this chapter we will discuss the classes and methods contributing to the Siebel Open UI API which are exposed by the proxy layer.

The subsequent two chapters will cover details on the API for presentation model and physical renderer classes.

Classes and Methods of the Proxy Layer

The Siebel Open UI proxy layer is a collection of JavaScript files that establishes the foundation of the framework as well as a communication channel to the server-side logic.

Of the hundreds of JavaScript files located in the `PUBLIC/<Language>/<Build>/SCRIPTS` folder and its subdirectories, approximately four-dozen files contain the JavaScript code to establish the proxy layer in the browser.

Given the fact that these files are plain text files - albeit minified - it is possible to inspect them and gain insight into the intricacies of the proxy functionality. However, Oracle only supports Open UI customizations that make use of the classes and methods described in the official documentation. While it makes sense to explore the most prominent proxy files for educational purposes, we strongly advise against exploiting the code for "hacks" or even modifying the as-delivered files.

At any time, we can use the browser developer tool to inspect the `<head>` section of the HTML page that is loaded by the browser for any given view of a Siebel application.

The HTML header section contains references to style sheets (.css files) and script files (using the `<script>` element). The following screenshot shows the Elements tab of **Google Chrome Developer Tools** after logging in to Siebel Call Center IP 2013 in Open UI mode.

The previous screenshot shows the beginning of the list of `<script>` elements, each of which either contains inline code or a reference to a file located on the web server. The browser will load and execute the JavaScript code in those files in the sequence defined by the list.

The following table describes some of the JavaScript files that establish the proxy layer.

File Name	Description
swecommon.js	Functions used by Siebel Web Engine (SWE)
swemessages.js	Message text definitions
jsPropset.js	Property set functions
siebjs.js	Basic framework functions such as `SiebelJS.Log`
utils.js	Collection of utility functions
loadindicator.js	Manages display of "busy" icon
siebelconstants.js	Definition of constants
ajaxrequestmgr.js	Manages AJAX requests
contentloader.js	Manages view loading process
applicationenv.js	Provides application environment functions
cmdmgr.js	Handles command accelerators (keyboard shortcuts)
componentmgr.js	Framework for components
component.js	Generic components such as applet and view
applicationcontext.js	The application "shadow" object

(Continued)

errorObject.js	Error message handling
service.js	Business service and property set handling
notifyobject.js	Notification handler
sweTimer.js	Performance measurement
view.js	View proxy
busobj.js	Business Object proxy
applet.js	Applet proxy (form applet)
listapplet.js	List Applet proxy
buscomp.js	Business Component proxy
bcfield.js	Business Component field proxy
appletcontrol.js	Applet control proxy
menu.js	Applet menu proxy
controlbuilder.js	Manages special controls such as pick or MVG fields.
StyleFlipper.js	Theme Manager (see chapter 8)
localeobject.js	Localization management

While the list is not complete, we can conclude that the proxy layer - and the remainder of the Open UI JavaScript framework - is built using a truly modular approach. Most of the files contain JavaScript "class" definitions and establish the service layer for the presentation model and the API.

In the following section, we will discuss the most important JavaScript classes and their methods. Note that this chapter and the other chapters in this book only describe objects that are documented by Oracle and therefore supported when used in custom JavaScript code.

> For a comprehensive description of the scope of support provided by Oracle for requests related to Open UI customizations, refer to Oracle Support Document 1513378.1 (*Scope of Service for Siebel Configuration and Scripting - Siebel Open UI*). The document can be found at
> https://support.oracle.com/epmos/faces/DocumentDisplay?id=1513378.1
>
> (A valid Oracle Support account is required to view this document)

JavaScript Classes of the Proxy Layer

The following table describes the most prominent JavaScript classes of the proxy layer of Siebel Open UI.

Name	Description
SiebelJS	Provides basic framework functions for class extension and logging.
SiebelApp.S_App	Represents "the application" and provides core application logic such as business service instantiation.
SiebelApp.Utils	Container for utility functions.
SiebelApp.ThemeManager	Manages registration of themes in IP 2013 and earlier (see Chapter 8).
SiebelApp.Constants	Provides access to constant values.
SiebelApp.S_App.LocaleObject	Allows access to locale specific values and settings.
SiebelAppFacade.ComponentMgr	Manages component construction, destruction and location.
SiebelAppFacade.Component	The generic component class.
SiebelApp.S_App.View	The view object
SiebelApp.S_App.BusObj	The business object
SiebelApp.S_App.Applet	The applet object (base class)
SiebelApp.S_App.ListApplet	Extension class for list applets
SiebelApp.S_App.BusComp	The business component object
SiebelApp.S_App.BCField	The business component field object
SiebelApp.S_App.AppletControl	The applet control object

Class names in Siebel Open UI are (mostly) in the form of *"Namespace"."Class"*. As can be seen in the previous table, SiebelApp and SiebelAppFacade are two important namespace definitions. SiebelApp serves as the global namespace while SiebelAppFacade is a child of SiebelApp and is typically used for extensions, including custom ones.

In the following section, we will describe the most prominent methods of the following classes:

- SiebelJS
- Application
- Constants

- Utils
- Component
- Component Manager
- Locale Object
- Applet
- List Applet
- Applet Control
- Business Component
- Business Component Field
- View
- Business Object

In addition to a description for each class, we will also provide short but meaningful code examples that demonstrate how to use the most prominent class methods.

> Note that the code examples in this chapter are of purely educational nature and should not be applied to an existing Siebel environment. This chapter serves as a reference, so when you work through the upcoming chapters of this book (which provide fully functional code examples), feel encouraged to come back to this chapter for a deeper explanation of the methods used in the example code.

The SiebelJS Class and its Methods

Defined in the file `siebjs.js`, the `SiebelJS` class provides the following methods:

- `SiebelJS.Namespace`
- `SiebelJS.Extend`
- `SiebelJS.Dependency`
- `SiebelJS.Log`

Let us look at each method in greater detail.

SiebelJS.Namespace

The `SiebelJS.Namespace` method is used by any other class to register itself as an object that is part of the framework. The `Namespace` method adds the object passed by its name to the `SiebelApp` namespace as a new empty JavaScript object.

The following example code demonstrates how to use the `SiebelJS.Namespace` method:

```
SiebelJS.Namespace("SiebelAppFacade.CustomPR");
```

The line of code is typically found at the beginning of any class definition file, be it out-of-the-box or custom. In the example, the string `SiebelAppFacade.CustomPR` is passed to the Namespace method. As a result, CustomPR (a custom physical renderer class) will be added to the SiebelAppFacade namespace as an object.

When we implement custom extension classes, we must always use the SiebelJS.Namespace method to add the new object to the framework.

SiebelJS.Extend

Similar to the Namespace method, the SiebelJS.Extend method is used in many other class definition files. Its purpose is to provide the necessary code that allows developers creating a JavaScript function to inherit another function's prototype, making the latter a **superclass** of the former.

The SiebelJS.Extend method takes two function objects as arguments and is typically used as per following code example:

```
function CustomPR(){
  SiebelAppFacade.CustomPR.superclass.constructor
    .apply(this,arguments);
}
SiebelJS.Extend(CustomPR, SiebelAppFacade.PhysicalRenderer);
```

In the previous example, CustomPR is a function that will hold the implementation of a custom physical renderer extension. The function itself does nothing but call its superclass' constructor.

By using the SiebelJS.Extend method as shown in the previous example, we pass the new CustomPR function definition as the first argument and an already existing function object (SiebelAppFacade.PhyiscalRenderer in the example) as the second argument.

As a result, the CustomPR function's prototype will contain all prototype methods defined for its SiebelAppFacade.PhysicalRenderer superclass, allowing the developer to use or override the superclass' functions in the CustomPR implementation.

SiebelJS.Dependency

The SiebelJS.Dependency method takes a class name as a string input argument and returns the object representing that class. It is used mainly to obtain references to global classes such as SiebelApp.Utils, SiebelApp.Constants or SiebelApp.S_App (the global "application" class). For more information on these classes refer to the following sections in this chapter.

The following code example shows a typical usage scenario for SiebelJS.Dependency:

```
var consts  = SiebelJS.Dependency("SiebelApp.Constants");
```

The example code assigns a reference to the SiebelApp.Constants class to the variable consts. The developer can now use the consts variable as shorthand for the SiebelApp.Constants class.

SiebelJS.Log

In typical JavaScript development scenarios, developers want to be able to introspect and watch certain variables and objects during their lifecycle as the code is executed. In the web developer community, it is common practice to use the JavaScript `console` object and its various functions - such as `console.log` - to print messages to the browser's console.

While in theory this practice is applicable to the Open UI JavaScript code as well, we are advised to use the built-in `SiebelJS.Log` method instead of direct calls to `console.log`. The reason for this is that `SiebelJS.Log` acts as a wrapper for the `console.log` function, preventing issues that arise in browsers such as Microsoft Internet Explorer. Older versions of Internet Explorer only allow calls to `console.log` when they are in debug mode.

The following is a typical call to `SiebelJS.Log`:

```
SiebelJS.Log("Custom function reached");
```

The line of code will result in the text `Custom function reached` to appear in the browser's JavaScript console.

> If you are eager to see the code examples in a more realistic context, read on. In the next chapter, we will start creating our own custom extension classes.

The Siebel Application Class and its Methods

As mentioned earlier, the Open UI framework provides global classes such as `SiebelApp.S_App`. This object is referred to as the "Application Class" and implements global functionality in the form of methods we can call within our custom JavaScript implementation. The core functionality of the application class is defined in the file `applicationcontext.js`.

The following table describes some important methods of the `SiebelApp.S_App` class.

Method Name	Description
GetActiveBusObj	Returns a reference to the currently active business object instance.
GetActiveView	Returns a reference to the currently active view object instance.
GetAppletControlInstance	Returns a new applet control object instance that can be added to an applet object.
GetAppName (similar to GetName)	Returns the name of the application definition in the Siebel Repository, for example "Siebel Universal Agent".
GetAppTitle	Returns the title of the application, for example "Siebel Call Center".
GetAppPropertySet	Returns the current application property set.

(Continued)

GetDirection	Returns "RTL" when the application is configured for "right-to-left" reading mode (e.g. for Arabic) and null when the application is not configured for "right-to-left" reading mode.
GetPageURL	Returns the current application base URL such as "http://webserver/callcenter_enu/start.swe".
GetProfileAttr	Returns the value of a profile attribute.
GetService	Returns an object representing the business service passed as an argument.
GotoView	Navigates to a view.
IsExtendedKeyBoard	Returns true if extended keyboard shortcuts are available.
IsMobileApplication	Returns true when the current application is a Siebel Mobile application. When the return value is false, the application is a desktop application.
LogOff	Executes the LogOff method, ending the current session.
NewPropertySet	Returns a new empty property set instance.
uiStatus	Allows controlling the busy or free state of the user interface.

The seasoned Siebel developer might miss the SetProfileAttr method in the previous list. As per the Oracle documentation, Open UI does not support this method. For existing HI implementations, customers can set the EditProfileAttr server parameter to TRUE for a short-term workaround. In the long term, setting profile attributes should only be done in server side script, for example, by calling a business service method.

For a complete listing of supported methods of the SiebelApp.S_App class, refer to the *Configuring Siebel Open UI* guide in the Siebel bookshelf.

Let's explore examples that describe how to use some of the methods provided by the SiebelApp.S_App class. The following scenarios are typical for an Open UI customization project.

- Accessing the Active View and its Applets
- Working with Business Services and Property Sets

Accessing the Active View and its Applets

The GetActiveView method of the SiebelApp.S_App class is useful when we need to obtain references on the following objects:

- The current view
- The applets within the current view
- The controls and/or list columns of each applet in the current view
- The business component associated with each applet in the current view

The following code example illustrates how to use the GetActiveView method:

```
var oView = SiebelApp.S_App.GetActiveView();
var sViewName = oView.GetName();
var oAppletMap = oView.GetAppletMap();
SiebelJS.Log("View '" + sViewName
    + "' contains the following applets:");
for (applet in oAppletMap){
  SiebelJS.Log(applet);
}
```

The code does the following:

- Instantiate the variable oView as the current view object.
- Use the GetName method of the view object to get the current view's name.
- Use the GetAppletMap method of the view object to get a collection of object references to each applet within the current view, i.e. the "applet map".
- Use the SiebelJS.Log method to print the name of the current view to the browser console.
- Iterate through the applet map and print the name of each applet to the browser console.

While the previous code accomplishes nothing more than printing information on the console, we learn that it is easy to access the currently active view and its related objects.

For more information about the methods available for views, applets and business components, refer to the respective sections in this chapter.

Working with Business Services and Property Sets

Understanding how to invoke business services in the context of a Siebel application is a vital topic. It is a recommended practice to encapsulate common business logic into server-side business service methods. Business services can be invoked in many ways on the server environment, for example, as a step in a workflow process. Let's learn how to invoke business service methods and work with property sets in the Open UI JavaScript environment.

> As this book focuses solely on browser-side scripting for Siebel Open UI, you might want to find more information about how to create custom business services in the book "Oracle Siebel CRM Developer's Handbook" by Alexander Hansal or the Oracle Siebel documentation.

Whenever we want to invoke a method of a server-resident business service from browser-side code in Siebel applications, we have to follow this procedure:

1. Instantiate the business service
2. Create and populate the input property set
3. Invoke the business service method
4. Parse the output property set (optional)

In Siebel Open UI it is possible to invoke a business service method in two ways:

- **Synchronous**: The calling process (and the user) has to wait until the method execution is finished.

- **Asynchronous**: The calling process (and the user) can proceed and a callback function will be invoked once the method execution is finished.

In this section, we will learn how to use both ways of invocation, starting with an example for synchronous invocation.

The following code example demonstrates how to use the GetService method of the application class and invoke a server side business service in synchronous mode. The example uses the as-delivered *Workflow Process Manager* business service, which is used to run a sample workflow process (also part of the Siebel standard repository). This workflow process navigates to another view and hence is a good example for a synchronous process.

```
var oSvc = SiebelApp.S_App.GetService(
    "Workflow Process Manager");
var iPS = SiebelApp.S_App.NewPropertySet();
var oPS;
iPS.SetProperty("ProcessName","Account - New Quote");
iPS.SetProperty("RowId",oApplet.GetBusComp().
GetFieldValue("Id"));
if(oSvc){
  oPS = oSvc.InvokeMethod("RunProcess", iPS);
  SiebelJS.Log(oPS);
}
```

The example code accomplishes the following:

- Assign the oSvc variable an object instance referencing the *Workflow Process Manager* business service. Note that every server side business service, be it delivered by Oracle or custom written, must be registered with the application object in the Siebel Repository using the `ClientBusinessServiceN` user property.

- Use the `NewPropertySet` method of the application class to create a new empty property set named `iPS` to submit input arguments.

- Declare the `oPS` variable to hold the output property set.

- Set properties in the input property set. Which input properties to set depends on the implementation of the business service method we want to call. In our example, we specify the name of the workflow process to run (the as-delivered `Account - New Quote` process, for example) using the `ProcessName` input argument and the `ROW_ID` of the primary record by retrieving the value of the `Id` field from the current applet's business component. Note that the code example does not include the code necessary to instantiate the `oApplet` variable.

- If the `oSvc` variable is successfully instantiated, invoke the **RunProcess** method of the Workflow Process Manager business service. The `oPS` variable will contain the output property set returned from the server.

- For testing purposes, write the `oPS` object to the console.

In our second code example, we will demonstrate how to invoke a business service method in **asynchronous** mode. Since Innovation Pack 2013, it is possible (albeit not required) to pass a configuration object to the `InvokeMethod` method of a business service. The configuration object must specify whether the method invocation should be carried out synchronously or asynchronously. A callback function must be specified as part of the configuration object, which will be invoked after the server has finished executing the business service method.

> The following example invokes the `Query` method of the as-delivered `EAI Siebel Adapter` business service. To learn more about the EAI Siebel Adapter business service, refer to the Oracle Siebel documentation for Enterprise Application Integration.

```javascript
var oSvc = SiebelApp.S_App.GetService("EAI Siebel Adapter");
var iPS = SiebelApp.S_App.NewPropertySet();
var oPS;
iPS.SetProperty("OutputIntObjectName",
    "Internal Account Interface");
iPS.SetProperty("SearchSpec","[Account.Name] LIKE 'A*'");
if(oSvc){
  var config = {};
  config.async = true; //make asynchronous request
  config.scope = this;
  config.selfbusy = true; //don't mask UI
  config.cb = function(){
```

```
    oPS = arguments[2];
    if (oPS!== null){
      SiebelJS.Log("Record count: " + oPS.GetChild(0)
          .GetProperty("NumOutputObjects"));
    }
  }
  oSvc.InvokeMethod("Query", iPS, config);
}
```

The example code accomplishes the following:

- Instantiate the variable `oSvc` as a reference to the `EAI Siebel Adapter` business service.

- Instantiate the `iPS` variable as the input property set.

- Declare the `oPS` variable to hold the output property set.

- Populate the input property set with two arguments specific to the `Query` method of `EAI Siebel Adapter`.

- Test whether the `oSvc` variable is an object.

- Create a new object named `config`.

- Set the `async` property of the `config` object to `true` to define an asynchronous call.

- Set the `scope` property to the current object (`this`).

- Set the `selfbusy` property to `true` to avoid the UI being "masked" with the busy icon (spinning wheel icon).

- Define the callback (`cb`) function that will be invoked when the server has executed the business service method. In the callback function, we can apply the third element (using index `[2]`) in the arguments array to the `oPS` variable. As an example, we use the `GetChild` method to access the first child (`0`) of the output property set, and use the `GetProperty` method to obtain the value of the property named `NumOutputObjects`, which we write to the browser console.

- Invoke the `Query` method of the business service, passing the input property set and the `config` object.

The seasoned Siebel developer will recognize a lot of methods such as `GetService` or `GetProperty` from other Siebel scripting languages such as *eScript*. It is good to know that for business services and property sets, the well-established methods are available in the Open UI API as well.

The Constants Class and its Methods

In this and other chapters of this book, we repeatedly refer to the *Configuring Siebel Open UI* guide in the Siebel bookshelf. This document contains not only theoretical information but also practical code examples.

In many of these code examples, we find references to the `SiebelApp.Constants` class in the form of the following code line:

```
var consts = SiebelJS.Dependency("SiebelApp.Constants");
```

This code initializes the `consts` variable as an object that references the `Constants` class. This class is defined in the as-delivered `siebelconstants.js` file. The main purpose of the `Constants` class is to set and get constant values that are used within the Open UI framework.

The class has the following main methods:

- set
- get

The set Method

As an example for the `set` method, the `siebelconstants.js` file contains the following line:

```
SiebelApp.Constants.set("SWE_APPLET_PM_PS", "apm");
```

This line sets the value of the constant named `SWE_APPLET_PM_PS` to `apm`. This specific constant defines the type of the property set which holds the presentation model properties for an applet (more information on presentation models and property sets will be provided in Chapters 6 and 7).

The get Method

Open UI developers - both at Oracle and at customer sites - are encouraged to use the `get` method as a simple lookup function to get the current value of a constant instead of using the actual values. This is because in future releases, or in other language packs, the values could be different.

It is a recommended practice to use the `SiebelJS.Dependency` method as shown earlier to obtain an object reference to the `Constants` class in our custom code and use the `get` method of the `Constants` class as in the following example:

```
var sPSType = consts.get("SWE_APPLET_PM_PS");
```

The line of sample code initializes the `sPSType` variable with the value of the `SWE_APPLET_PM_PS` constant. The value of the variable will be `apm` once the line has been executed.

The Utils Class and its Methods

In some of the code examples in the *Configuring Siebel Open UI* guide, we find references to the `SiebelApp.Utils` class. This class is defined in the as-delivered `utils.js` file and defines a great variety of utility methods that are used by Oracle engineering.

The only method that is exposed in the Siebel bookshelf is the `IsEmpty` method.

The IsEmpty Method

The `IsEmpty` method returns `true` or `false` depending whether the input argument is undefined or an empty string. The `Utils` class and its `IsEmpty` method can be used as in the following example:

```
var utils = SiebelJS.Dependency("SiebelApp.Utils");
var sTest;
if (utils.IsEmpty(sTest)){
   SiebelJS.Log("sTest is empty");
}
```

The example code does the following.

- Initialize the `utils` variable as a reference to the `SiebelApp.Utils` class.
- Declare a variable named `sTest`.
- Test if the `sTest` variable is empty using the `IsEmpty` method of the `utils` object.
- Print a message to the browser console if the variable is empty.

Because the variable `sTest` is declared but has not been explicitly initialized, the `IsEmpty` method will return `true` and the message sTest is empty will be printed to the browser console.

While the `SiebelApp.Utils` class contains significantly more methods than the one described in this section, they are not documented by Oracle and hence we must refrain from using them in custom JavaScript code.

However, the general idea of creating a utility class is an inspiring one. Being the resourceful developers that we are, we should strongly consider creating a library class for reusable methods in our project.

The Component Class and its Methods

The Siebel Open UI framework maintains a hierarchical structure of user interface components. A component can, for example, be an applet that is part of a view. In the Open UI component model, the view is the parent component of the applet and the applet is a child component of the view.

The as-delivered `SiebelAppFacade.Component` class represents user interface components such as views and applets in Open UI. The following table describes the methods of the Component class.

Method	Description
Component	The main constructor that returns a component object.
GetChildren	Returns an array containing all children of a component, for example all applets within a view.
GetParent	Returns a component object representing the parent object of the component. When the component has no parent, the method returns `null`.
GetSiblings	Returns an array containing all components on the same level within the hierarchy, for example the other applet(s) in the same view.
GetPM	Returns the presentation model of the component object.
GetPR	Returns the physical renderer of the component object.
Setup	Invokes the `Setup` method of the component object.

Show	Instantiates the physical renderer (PR) of the component if necessary and invokes the following PR methods in the sequence stated:
	`ShowUI`
	`BindEvents`
	`BindData`

The purpose of the Component class is to provide an abstract object layer for instantiating user interface artefacts such as applets. For example, when a user clicks the select icon in a field that uses a pick list, the pick applet is constructed as a component and its `Show` method is invoked. This ensures that all physical renderer methods are invoked and the pick applet appears on the screen.

It can be expected that custom developers will not need to use the low-level Component class and its methods directly because custom presentation models and physical renderers will always provide enough context to work with the current view or its applets.

For a code example how the Component class and its methods can be used, refer to the next section.

The Component Manager Class and its Methods

The `SiebelAppFacade.ComponentMgr` class provides methods to obtain and work with components. The following table describes the methods exposed by the `Component Manager` class.

Method	Description
FindComponent	Takes the name of a component (applet or view) and returns the component instance.
MakeComponent	Creates and inserts a new component in the current component hierarchy below the parent component passed as the first argument. The `Setup` method of the component's presentation model will be invoked and receives the property set passed as the second argument.
DeleteComponent	Removes the component object passed as an argument from the component hierarchy and invokes the `EndLife` method of this component.
Show	Invokes the `Show` method of the component passed as the input argument.
DisplayTree	Prints the current component hierarchy on the browser console.

Similarly to the `Component` class, custom developers will usually not need to use the `Component Manager` class and its methods. Under certain circumstances, however, we can benefit from the easy access to objects when our code is outside the context of a presentation model or physical renderer. This could be the case in utility functions or functions which are called as part of a `postload` or `preload` event listener. For more information on event listeners in Siebel Open UI, refer to Chapter 10.

The following example code demonstrates how the `Component` and `Component Manager` class and their methods can be used in custom code:

```
var oAppletComp = SiebelAppFacade.ComponentMgr
    .FindComponent("SIS Account List Applet");
var oAppletSiblings = oAppletComp.GetSiblings();
SiebelJS.Log("First sibling PM: "
    + oAppletSiblings[0].GetPM().GetPMName());
var oViewComp = oAppletComp.GetParent();
var oViewChildComps = oViewComp.GetChildren();
SiebelJS.Log("Number of applets: " + oViewChildComps.length);
```

The sample code does the following:

- Instantiate the `oAppletComp` variable as a component object representing the `SIS Account List Applet`. Note that the `FindComponent` method returns `null` in case the object is not found in the active component hierarchy.

- Instantiate the `oAppletSiblings` variable as an array containing components each of which represents an applet other than the `SIS Account List Applet` which is a child of the current view.

- Print the name of the presentation model that the first sibling applet currently uses to the browser console.

- Instantiate the `oViewComp` variable using the `GetParent` method of the applet component object. The variable will be a reference to the view component object.

- Use the `GetChildren` method of the `view` component to retrieve an array containing one component object for each applet.

- Print the number of applets - the array's length - to the browser console.

The Locale Object Class and its Methods

The `SiebelApp.S_App.LocaleObject` class is a collection of methods that can prove useful in multi-language or multi-locale environments. Because Siebel CRM supports multiple languages and locales, code that operates on data types such as **date**, **number** or **currency** must be crafted in a way that makes it locale-agnostic.

The following table describes the most prominent methods of the Locale Object class.

Method	Description
FormattedToString	Converts a string representing a locale-specific value such as "24.10.2014" (German date) to a string representing the currently active locale, for example "10/24/2014" (English-American date).
StringToFormatted	Converts a string representing a value in the currently active locale to a locale-specific representation. For example "10/24/2014" will be converted to "24.10.2014" when the format mask is "DD.MM.YYYY".
GetDateFormat	Returns a string representing the date format of the client machine's regional settings, e.g. "M/D/YYYY" for an English-American locale or "DD.MM.YYYY" for a German locale.
GetDayOfWeek	Takes a number between 0 and 6 as the first argument. Returns the full name of the corresponding day in the machine's locale when the second argument is 0. Using 1 or 2 as the second parameter yields a shortened version. For example, `GetDayOfWeek(3,1)` will return "Wed" for Wednesday. The function refers to Sunday (0) as the first day of the week.

(Continued)

`GetDispCurrencyDecimal`	Returns the decimal separator of the machine's locale. For example a dot (".") with English-American locale settings. This and other functions starting with "GetDisp" are useful to obtain the localized separator characters for various data types. For a complete list, refer to the *Configuring Siebel Open UI* guide in the Siebel bookshelf
`GetFuncCurrCode`	Returns the three-letter code of the application's default currency, e.g. "USD".
`GetLocalString`	Returns the translated value for a given message key. Messages are defined in the `swemessages_<Language>.js` files.
`GetTimeFormat`	Returns the time format used in the client machine locale. For example "h:mm:ss p" for an English-American locale or "HH:mm:ss" for a German locale.
`GetTimeZoneName`	Returns the name of the time zone used for the current user as defined in the user preferences.

The following example code shows a potential use case for the Locale Object class:

```
var sNumberSeparator = SiebelApp.S_App.LocaleObject
    .GetDispNumberSeparator();
//create new regular expression
//to identify all $,% and number separator characters
var regExp = new RegExp( "[\\$\\%\\"
    + sNumberSeparator + "]","g");
//test with localized string
var sVal = "$ 430.000,00";
sVal = sVal.replace(regExp,"");
var nVal = parseFloat(sVal);
```

The code does the following:

- Instantiate a variable named `sNumberSeparator` with the character used to separate numbers (also known as "thousands separator") in the current user's locale. In a German locale, the value of the variable would be a dot character (".").

- Create a new regular expression object to match all dollar, percentage and thousands separator characters. More information about regular expressions can be found at `http://en.wikipedia.org/wiki/Regular_expression`.

- Instantiate a test variable named `sVal` with a value of `$ 430.000,00`, which is four hundred thirty thousand dollars in a German locale. Note that the dot character is used to separate the thousands and a comma is used as the decimal separator.

- Use the `replace` method to apply the regular expression object against the `sVal` variable . The value of `sVal` after this line is `430000,00`.
- Use the `parseFloat` method to convert the string representation of the value to a number. The value of the `nVal` variable will be `430000`. Note that the `parseFloat` method ignores everything after a non-number, so the conversion rounds down the result.

The code example supports a scenario where we obtain a formatted, localized string and have to convert it safely to a number for further computation. The code would work for any locale because it uses the `GetDispNumberSeparator` method of the Locale Object class to determine the thousands separator character that is currently in use.

The Applet Class and its Methods

When working with applet objects, the methods described in the following table can be used by developers.

Method	Description
GetControls	Returns an object which contains one AppletControl object for each active control in the applet.
GetName	Returns the name of the applet as registered in the Siebel repository.
GetBusComp	Returns an object representing the applet's business component.
GetFullId	Returns the element id which is used to identify the applet in the browser's document object model (DOM). An example return value is "S_A2".
GetRecordSet	Returns an array of objects. Each object represents a record in the current record set for the applet and contains the fields and their values.
GetRawRecordSet	Returns a similar array as GetRecordSet albeit including the Id field (ROW_ID) and unformatted values.
GetSelection	Returns the index number (0...n) of the currently selected record in the record set.
GetPModel	Returns the presentation model instance for the applet.

We will be able to explore fully functional code examples that use the methods described in subsequent chapters of this book.

The List Applet Class and its Methods

While the methods listed in the previous section apply to all applet types, list applets expose somewhat more specialized methods that are described in the following table.

Method	Description
GetListOfColumns	Returns an object where each member is an applet control object representing one column of the list applet.
GetListPrefs	Returns a string which represents the available and visible list columns and their current width as per user preferences.
GetRowsSelectedArray	Returns an array of Boolean values. True represents a selected record index while false denotes an unselected record.

As mentioned, the subsequent chapters will provide real-life code examples of how to use methods provided by the applet classes.

The Applet Control Class and its Methods

Each control within an applet is represented as a JavaScript object that exposes a variety of methods. The following table describes some of the most important methods of the applet control class.

Method	Description
GetCaseSensitive	Returns "1" if the field is case sensitive (for queries) and "0" if the field is not case sensitive.
GetDisplayName	Returns the display name (label) of the control which is displayed in the UI to the user.
GetFieldName	Returns the name of the business component field associated with the control.
GetHeight	Returns the height of the control in pixels.
GetWidth	Returns the width of the control in pixels.
GetInputName	Returns the value of the name attribute for the control in the DOM, for example "s_2_1_181_0". Used to address the element for example in a jQuery selector in IP 2013 or earlier. In IP 2014 or higher, we can use the plug-in wrapper API to address DOM elements (see chapter 7).
GetMaxSize	Returns the maximum number of characters a user can enter in the control.
GetMethodName	Returns the name of the method invoked by the (button) control.

(Continued)

`GetPMPropSet`	Returns the property set for the control. See further for an example how to obtain the property set for a control.
`GetPopupType`	Returns the type of popup associated with the control, for example "Mvg" for a Multi-Value Group applet.
`GetPrompt`	Returns the index number of the prompt text associated with the control, for example "821". The index number must be used with the `LookupStringCache` method of the `SiebelApp.S_App` class to obtain the localized text.
`GetUIType`	Returns a string representing the type of control, for example "JText" for a text box control.
`IsCalc`	Returns `true` if the control is exposing a calculated business component field, `false` if not.
`IsEditEnabled`	Returns "1" if the control is editable. Returns null if the control is read-only.

The Business Component Class and its Methods

Unlike in traditional Siebel CRM implementations, direct access to the business component layer, especially from 'unsafe' places such as a browser-side script, is something we should refrain from. The Open UI API for presentation models - to be introduced in the next chapter - provides various ways to interact with data and it is usually not necessary to invoke business component methods directly.

However, there are various `Get` methods that - when implemented responsibly - can prove useful for navigating the current record set. Some of these methods are described in the following table.

Method	Description
`GetFieldMap`	Returns an object collection where each element represents a field of the current business component. Only fields which are exposed in the UI are available through this method.
`GetFieldValue`	Returns the unformatted value for a field passed as the input argument.
`GetIdValue`	Returns the `ROW_ID` value of the current record.

The Business Component Field Class and its Methods

Each field of a business component exposed in Open UI is a JavaScript object. The following table lists some of the more prominent methods of the business component field class.

Method	Description
GetDataType	Returns a string defining the data type of the field, for example "text".
GetLength	Returns the logical length of the field, for example "100".
IsCalc	Returns "1" if the field is a calculated field, null if not.
IsRequired	Returns "1" if the field is a required field, null if not.

The View Class and its Methods

As we have seen in the earlier code examples, it is fairly easy to get a handle on the currently active view and its applets. The view class itself provides many useful methods, some of which are described in the following table.

Method	Description
GetAppletMap	Returns a collection of applet objects which are used in the current view.
GetApplet	Takes the name of an applet and returns the corresponding applet object if the applet is present in the current view.
GetActiveApplet	Returns an object representing the currently active applet.
GetName	Returns the name of the view as stored in the Siebel repository.

The Business Object Class and its Methods

The business object class offers a small amount of methods that are explained in the next table.

Method	Description
GetBCMap	Returns a collection of business component objects. Only business components which have already been instantiated in the current business object are returned.
GetBCArray	Returns the list of currently instantiated business components as an array.
GetBusCompByName	Takes the name of a business component and returns the corresponding object if the business component is currently instantiated in the business object.
GetName	Returns the name of the business object as stored in the Siebel repository.

Scripting Considerations

In the previous sections of this chapter we explored many JavaScript objects and methods exposed by the Open UI framework. They form the application programming interface (API) for browser-side scripting in Siebel Open UI. Compared to previous traditional web clients of Siebel CRM, Open UI offers architects and programmers a lot more choice if they wish to implement requirements (and how). But with choice comes great responsibility.

As a responsible member of a Siebel CRM implementation project team, it is important to understand that while we can accomplish a lot by writing browser-side code and using the provided APIs of Siebel Open UI and third-party libraries, we are always standing on the brink of failure.

This is because we should not only consider code that does not work a failure (which is obvious enough), but also code which is haphazardly soldered together and causes more harm than good, be it during maintenance or during upgrades to future Siebel versions.

In order to avoid such pernicious code we should always keep in mind the following rules.

- With large-scale enterprise software frameworks such as Siebel CRM, always consider browser-side coding as the last resort. For example, you do not even need a single line of code to create an entire view with applets and link the buttons on those applets to server-side logic.

- Do not make browser-side scripting an end in itself, producing unnecessary code for the sake (or joy) of coding. In other words: Do not reinvent the wheel.

- If you decide to use browser-side code to implement requirements, verify that at least one of the following statements applies.

- o It is required to manipulate the state of elements within the browser's DOM, such as changing the background color of fields or hiding buttons and it is not feasible to do this on the server level.
- o It is required to enter into a dialogue with the end user that accomplishes more than displaying an information or error message and it cannot be accomplished using server-side functionality such as the Siebel Unified Messaging Framework (UMF).
- o It is required to receive or submit data from (or to) other client-side applications such as Microsoft Office or other web based applications and there is no way of doing that on the server side.
- o It is necessary to collect data within the browser which is inaccessible to the server-side code. In this case, collect the data in a browser-side script and submit it to a server-side business service as soon as possible.

To further illustrate the statements, let us visualize the Siebel CRM enterprise architecture as in the following diagram:

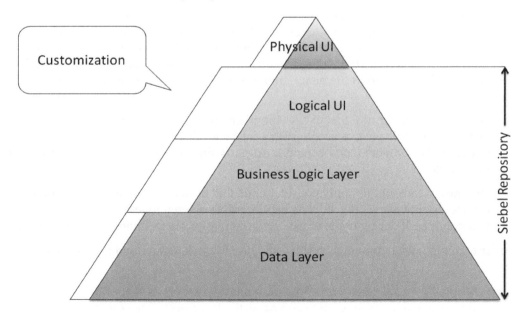

In the diagram we depict the Siebel architecture as a pyramid. On the bottom of the pyramid is the solid foundation we find in the physical Siebel database schema. Customization on this layer is purely additive in nature, which means that custom developers can use Siebel Tools to create new column and table definitions but cannot modify existing objects in this layer.

Building on top of the data layer is the business logic layer with business components and business services providing the vast array of server-side processing logic. Custom developers can extend and modify this layer.

The logical UI layer is known for providing metadata about screens, views and applets and the way they access data. However, most aspects of the visual appearance of those objects are not defined in the Siebel repository but outside of it.

All the layers mentioned before form a firm foundation for the physical user interface which simply consumes the metadata provided by the lower layers. As we can see from the diagram, customization on this layer is kept to a minimum.

The previous diagram represents the well-established approach to Siebel customization. As we can see, objects on a lower layer support objects on the upper layers and there is no danger of customizations 'hanging in the air'.

Let us imagine a customization scenario where only the physical user interface layer would be used to implement requirements, as in the following diagram.

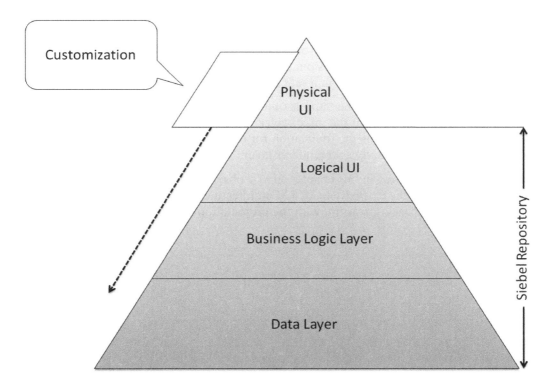

As we can see, applying too many customizations in the physical UI layer without supporting objects in the lower layers would find them in a situation similar to an avalanche or landslide – there would be a constant danger of falling down. This danger becomes manifest in Siebel CRM implementation projects when browser-script based customizations no longer work as expected or where they cause a high level of effort in their maintenance.

As we mentioned on previous occasions, this book focuses on Siebel Open UI and the power of its API. Hence we will see a lot of code in the upcoming chapters. But let us never forget that Siebel CRM is built on a multi-tier architecture, which we should not neglect in our efforts to implement customer requirements.

The level of effort (and the cost for development and maintenance) of customizations is different depending on the layer we customize. For example, it is much cheaper to use an as-delivered administrative tool such as Data Validation Manager to accomplish validation tasks than to write a browser script to do the same thing.

Likewise, using well-established declarative techniques in Siebel Tools (for example, generating a new applet definition) is less effortful than using script code to accomplish a data display in the browser.

Even when we resort to browser scripting (because of one of the reasons mentioned previously), it can still be more cost effective to use simple CSS rules in a style sheet than to write JavaScript methods to modify the appearance of elements in the browser.

Summary

The Siebel Open UI JavaScript framework provides a vast and powerful application programming interface (API) that custom developers can use to write browser-side extensions to the Siebel web client in a safe manner.

In this chapter, we enumerated the various objects (classes) and the methods provided by the Open UI API on the level of the proxy layer. While the proxy layer, per se, cannot be modified or extended, it forms the foundation for the upper client-side layers, namely the presentation model and the physical renderer layer.

With the knowledge gained in this chapter and by observing the ground rules for safe customizations across the entire Siebel CRM architecture, we can now venture into real-life customization scenarios, starting with the presentation model layer in the next chapter.

6
Creating a Custom Presentation Model

Now that we are comfortable with the architecture and the Application Programming Interface (API) of Siebel Open UI, we can start to design and implement custom JavaScript extensions to fulfill user interface requirements. In this chapter, we will discover the following topics:

- Setting up the development environment
- Using a presentation model template
- Methods of the Presentation Model class
- Case Study: Creating a custom presentation model for an applet

Setting up the Development Environment

Because most of the actual implementation work in Siebel Open UI is done outside of Siebel Tools, developers must choose their tools and utilities wisely. The following is a list of software tools we would typically need in addition to the usual local Siebel development environment to be able to implement Open UI customizations efficiently:

- Code editor for JavaScript, HTML, and CSS
- Image editor
- Utilities for validating and minifying code
- Browsers and plug-ins

Code Editor for JavaScript, HTML, and CSS

Before starting to produce code extensions for Siebel Open UI in earnest, we should evaluate and choose among the various code editors and integrated development environments (IDEs) on the market.

It is out of the scope of this book to provide a market overview or even a concrete recommendation of a single product. Some developers might be happy - and productive - with a somewhat old-fashioned text editor while others might find it preferable to use the latest IDE and download skins for it from the internet.

Independent of our final choice, we should however select an editor that fulfils at least the following minimum requirements:

- Support for web standards (JavaScript, HTML, CSS)
- Syntax highlighting
- Method listing
- Code completion
- Registration of additional libraries
- Reformatting (un-minifying) of code
- Regular updates

The list might not be complete when you have more specific needs. For example, in larger projects, integration with version controls systems might become a necessity.

Image Editor

In one way or another, you will have to view, modify or create image files for Siebel Open UI. Professional graphics designers are, of course, well equipped for these tasks and the average Siebel developer should familiarize her- or himself with one of the many tools available.

Utilities for Validating and Minifying Code

Before we check in code or deploy it to production servers, we must be able to conduct at least a minimum of well-grounded quality assurance. There is an abundant offering of web-based and locally installed tools available that allow developers to identify code flaws or deprecated methods.

As a rule of thumb, we should keep the size of code files (that the browser must download) small. One of the established ways in the JavaScript coding community to achieve this is by "minifying" JavaScript and CSS files before they are uploaded to the web server.

The minification process strips all comments and white space, such as tab stops or line breaks, from the code. In addition, it refactors the code so that variable names and function names are shortened.

As an example of a popular JavaScript utility capable of minifying, the following screenshot shows the **Google Closure Compiler** with some sample code.

The Google Closure Compiler can be accessed via the web at `http://closure-compiler.appspot.com`. It can also be downloaded as a Java command line application for local use.

The result of minimization is a much smaller file, which is still readable by the browser but - even after "un-minifying" - loses a lot of its original meaning for the human eye. Therefore it is important to keep a working copy of the development files in a safe place.

Browsers and Plug-ins

Web developers are well aware of the features and performance of the latest versions of the major browsers. In a Siebel Open UI project, there might be a very strict regimen on end user devices and - for the sake of keeping the cost of testing to a minimum - the supported browser/device combinations made available to the end user community are limited.

Developers can, however, benefit from the rich development tools - either built-in or available as browser plug-ins - of modern browsers such as Google Chrome or Mozilla Firefox. And while these browsers might not be used by end users, developers can increase their productivity by using these feature-rich products to conduct unit tests and debugging.

As an example of a built-in development tool, the following screenshot shows the Siebel Open UI application in the 3D View window of Mozilla Waterfox, the 64bit variant of Firefox.

This specific feature of Mozilla's development tool allows developers to quickly identify DOM elements by adding depth to the usually two-dimensional user interface.

It goes without saying that when developers use different browsers than end users, the final product must still be tested in all supported browser/device combinations before it is deployed to production.

Using a Presentation Model Template

As has been laid out in previous chapters, the Open UI JavaScript framework establishes a strict coding environment. Adhering to the intrinsic rules of this framework is paramount to succeeding in a complex enterprise-class customization project.

Extension classes for presentation models, physical renderers and other building blocks of the Open UI framework must follow a coding convention we can describe as a 'scaffold'. In the construction industry, a scaffold shields workers from hazards, allowing them to access all work areas quickly and focus on their tasks. Likewise, in the software industry, we use scaffolds to establish a secure groundwork for development.

The following code example serves as a template for a presentation model extension class. This code is provided with the file named PMTemplate.js, which is available for download with this book.

```
if(typeof(SiebelAppFacade.PMTemplate) === "undefined"){
  SiebelJS.Namespace("SiebelAppFacade.PMTemplate");
  define("siebel/custom/PMTemplate", [], function(){
```

```
SiebelAppFacade.PMTemplate = (function(){
  function PMTemplate(proxy){
    SiebelAppFacade.PMTemplate.superclass
      .constructor.apply(this,arguments);
  }
  //extend PM for form applets
  SiebelJS.Extend(PMTemplate,
      SiebelAppFacade.PresentationModel);
  //extend PM for list applets
  //SiebelJS.Extend(PMTemplate,
      //SiebelAppFacade.ListPresentationModel);

  PMTemplate.prototype.Init = function(){
    SiebelAppFacade.PMTemplate.superclass.Init
      .apply(this,arguments);
    SiebelJS.Log("Custom PM " + this.GetPMName()
      + ": Init method reached.");
    //implement Init method here
  };

  PMTemplate.prototype.Setup = function(propSet){
    SiebelAppFacade.PMTemplate.superclass.Setup
      .apply(this, arguments);
    SiebelJS.Log("Custom PM " + this.GetPMName()
      + ": Setup method reached.");
    //implement Setup method here
  };

  //implement custom functions here
  return PMTemplate;
}());
  return "SiebelAppFacade.PMTemplate";
});
}
```

For a detailed explanation of what the code template accomplishes, refer to the remainder of this chapter.

To use the example template code as a starting point for a custom presentation model, we can follow the steps in the following procedure.

1. Using a suitable editor, create a new, empty file.
2. Save the file to the PUBLIC/<Language>/<Build>/SCRIPTS /siebel/custom folder, using a file name convention. For example save the file as OpptyFormPM.js, indicating that the file contains a custom presentation model for an opportunity form applet. Presentation model files should always have a suffix 'PM'.
3. Copy and paste the template code into the new file.

4. Replace all occurrences of '`PMTemplate`' with the file name (without the `.js` extension) you chose in step 2. For example, use '`OpptyFormPM`' as the new text. While this is not a technical necessity, adhering to this practice will ensure that you use unique and standardized names for your custom classes.

5. Save the file.

Another way of getting started quickly is to use Duncan Ford's online Code Template Generator for Open UI. It can be accessed at `http://tiny.cc/prpm-code-generator`.

While we could now get started with implementing the custom functionality of the new extension class, it is recommended practice to register the new file immediately in the manifest administration in order to ensure that everything works as expected. The following procedure describes how to register the new presentation model extension with an applet for testing purposes:

1. Log in to the Siebel Developer Web Client with an administrative user account.

2. Navigate to the Administration - Application screen, Manifest Files view.

3. In the Files list, create a new record.

4. Enter the relative path to the new file, for example:
   `siebel/custom/OpptyFormPM.js`

5. Navigate to the Manifest Administration view.

6. In the UI Objects list, create a new record with the following values:

Column	Value
Type	Applet
Usage Type	Presentation Model
Name	Opportunity Form Applet - Child

Note : In your particular Siebel CRM environment, a similar record might already exist. In this case, query for the record, select it and continue with step 8.

7. In the Object Expression list, create a new record with the following values:

Column	Value
Expression	`Desktop` (use the Pick List)
Level (required)	`1`

Note: Using the `Desktop` expression prevents the file from being loaded on mobile devices. If you are implementing an extension class that should be loaded independent of the platform, the Expression field can be left empty.

8. In the Files list, click the Add button and associate the file you registered in step 4.

9. Log out of the application.

10. Log in to the application again.

11. Navigate to the Opportunities screen, My Opportunities view.

12. Open the browser's developer tools. For example, in Google Chrome press *F12*.

13. Open the JavaScript console.

14. Verify that the console messages appear as implemented in the template file, similar to `Custom PM Opportunity Form Applet - Child_PM: Init method reached.`

Alternatively, or in addition to the previous steps, you might also want to use the Sources tab of the browser's developer tool to verify the presence of the custom file.

Once we complete the previous procedure, we can start implementing the custom presentation model. But before we do so, we have to understand the methods of a presentation model class.

Methods of the Presentation Model Class

The `PresentationModel` class, which is part of the Open UI core framework developed by Oracle, is well documented in the Oracle Siebel documentation. While it is not the intention of the authors of this book to replicate the documentation, we will discuss the most important methods of the `PresentationModel` class in this section.

The methods we will discuss are the following:

- AddProperty, SetProperty and Get
- AddMethod and ExecuteMethod
- Init and Setup
- OnControlEvent and AttachEventHandler
- AttachPMBinding
- AttachPostProxyExecuteBinding and AttachPreProxyExecuteBinding
- AddValidator

For a complete listing and description of all available methods of the PresentationModel class, refer to the *Siebel Open UI Configuration Guide* in the Siebel bookshelf.

The AddProperty, SetProperty and Get Methods

The Siebel Open UI framework uses **properties** to store and share information. Properties are globally available JavaScript objects and can store anything from a simple string to a collection of objects such as the current record set. The PresentationModel class provides three methods to work with properties:

- **AddProperty**: Adds a new property to the presentation model and sets its value.
- **SetProperty**: Sets the value of a property. When the property does not exist, it will be created.
- **Get**: Returns the value of a property

The following is an example that shows how to use these methods.

```
this.AddProperty("BookTitle","Siebel Open UI");
var bTitle = this.Get("BookTitle");
this.SetProperty("BookTitle", bTitle
    + " Developers Handbook");
SiebelJS.Log(this.Get("BookTitle"));
```

The first line in the example adds a new property named BookTitle to the presentation model and sets its value to Siebel Open UI.

The second line uses the Get method to retrieve the current value of the BookTitle property and assign it to the bTitle variable.

The call to SetProperty in the third line overwrites the value of the BookTitle property with 'Siebel Open UI Developers Handbook' (the result of the string concatenation).

The fourth line writes the value of the BookTitle property to the browser console.

The value stored in a property is not limited to a string. When working with applets, developers can use the Get method to access important core Open UI properties from the presentation model and many of these will return complex objects. The most prominent of these core properties are described in the following table.

Property	Description
GetControls	Returns an object array where each object represents a control on the current applet. This includes hidden controls as well as controls configured to appear in 'More' mode.
GetRecordSet	Returns an object array where each object represents a record in the applet's current record set. Data in the record set is formatted according to the client locale settings. Note that the record set will most often contain only a subset of the full results from the data source (business component).
GetRawRecordSet	Identical to GetRecordSet albeit the data is not formatted. In addition, the raw record set also contains system fields such as the Id field.
GetFullId	Returns the DOM element Id of the current applet's container, e.g. 'S_A1'.
GetMode	Returns the current applet mode, e.g. 'Base'
GetPlaceholder	Returns the Id used as the 'placeholder' in the DOM, for example 's_1_1'. The placeholder Id is used in the element's child objects.
GetListOfColumns	(List applets only) Returns an object array where each object corresponds to a column in the list applet.
GetSelection	Returns the index of the currently selected record.
GetBusComp	Returns an object representing the applet's business component.
GetNumRows	Returns the number of rows of the applet's current record set.
GetRowsSelectedArray	(List applets only) Returns an array representing the current record set. Selected records have a value of 'true' while unselected records have a value of 'false'.

For a full listing of properties available in presentation models for applets, refer to the *Siebel Open UI Configuration Guide* in the Siebel bookshelf.

The AddMethod and ExecuteMethod Methods

Every method - or function - we define as part of our custom presentation model must be registered using the AddMethod method and executed using the ExecuteMethod method.

The AddMethod method has the following syntax:

```
this.AddMethod("Method",NewMethodDefinition (arg,argN),
    {sequence:value, override:value, scope:value});
```

The first parameter is the name of the method that will be added to the presentation model. If a method with the same name already exists, the framework evaluates the `sequence` and `override` arguments to determine the execution order of the existing method and the new method definition.

The second parameter is the new method definition with (optional) input arguments. It can be either a function signature or a direct function call.

The third parameter is an object providing the following arguments:

- **sequence**: When set to `true` and a method with the same name already exists and the `override` argument is set to `false`, the new method definition will be invoked **before** the existing method. When set to `false` (the default value) and a method with the same name already exists and the `override` argument is set to `false`, the new method definition will be invoked **after** the existing method.

- **override**: When set to `true`, the Open UI framework will not invoke any method that already exists but invoke the new method definition instead. When set to `false` (the default value), any existing method will be invoked according to the value of the `sequence` argument.

- **scope**: Defines the scope of the new method definition. The default is the current presentation model (`this`).

The following code snippet shows an example implementation of the `AddMethod` method.

```
this.AddMethod("ShowSelection", PostShowSelection,
    {sequence:false, scope:this});
```

The code adds the `ShowSelection` method to the presentation model. If the `ShowSelection` method is already defined in the framework - which is the case for this specific example - the `PostShowSelection` method will be invoked after the existing method because the `sequence` argument is set to `false`.

> Note that we use the key word '`Post`' as the prefix for the new function name to indicate that it will be invoked after the original method. Likewise we should use '`Pre`' as the name prefix when the `sequence` argument is set to `true`. By following this naming convention, we ensure that our code is understandable.

The `ShowSelection` method is one of many documented Open UI framework methods and is invoked every time a different record is selected. For a list of the most important framework methods, refer to the end of this section.

The `PostShowSelection` method could be implemented as follows:

```
function PostShowSelection(){
    SiebelJS.Log("After ShowSelection");
}
```

The code is a simple example and the only thing it does is print the text `After ShowSelection` to the browser console. In real life, we would use this custom method to implement any business logic we would like to see executed after a record is selected.

The `ExecuteMethod` method must be used to execute a method within a presentation model, be it as-delivered or custom. The syntax of the `ExecuteMethod` method is as follows:

```
this.ExecuteMethod("MethodName", arg1, argN);
```

The first parameter is a string referencing the method to be executed. It must have been previously registered using the `AddMethod` method.

If necessary, arguments that follow the first parameter will be passed to the method. The `ExecuteMethod` method returns the output of the method it executes.

The following is an example for using the `ExecuteMethod` method:

```
var sValue = this.ExecuteMethod("GetFieldValue", oControl);
```

The sample code initializes a variable named `sValue` with the return value of the `GetFieldValue` method, which is executed against an applet control object passed as `oControl`.

Siebel Open UI Framework Methods

As indicated earlier, the Open UI framework provides a number of pre-built methods such as the aforementioned `ShowSelection` method.

The following table describes the most important framework methods:

Method	Parameter(s)	Description
CanInvokeMethod	Name of a method	Determines whether a method can be invoked in the current situation or not. Returns `true` when the method can be invoked and `false` when it cannot.
CanUpdate	Name of a control	Determines whether a control can be updated. Returns `true` when the control can be updated and `false` when it cannot.
FieldChange	Control object and current value	Invoked when a field value changes and the field loses focus.
GetFieldValue	Control object and value	Invoked when the framework prepares the UI.
InvokeMethod	Name of a method and arguments (if any)	Used to invoke methods, for example on the applet or business component level.

(Continued)

LeaveField	Control object, value, flag	Invoked when a control loses focus. The flag indicates whether to keep focus (`true`) or not (`false`).
PostExecute	Method name, input property set, output property set, object.	Invoked after a method invocation returns (from the server).
ShowSelection	No parameters	Invoked when a record other than the current one gets selected.
CellChange	Row Id, control object, value	(List applets only) Invoked when a grid cell has changed.

For a complete list of available methods for presentation models, refer to the *Configuring Siebel Open UI* guide in the Siebel bookshelf.

The Init and Setup Methods

The `Init` and `Setup` methods of a presentation model should always be implemented in a custom extension class.

The `Init` method is invoked by the Open UI framework when the presentation model is initialized. It can be seen as a container for all other method invocations, such as `AddProperty` or `AddMethod`.

Developers are obliged to call the superclass' `Init` method before any other code.

The minimum implementation of the `Init` method is as follows.

```
PMTemplate.prototype.Init = function(){
  SiebelAppFacade.PMTemplate.superclass.Init
    .apply(this,arguments);
  //implement Init method here
};
```

The code example shows an implementation of the `Init` method for the `PMTemplate` class. The first line in the function body applies the `Init` method of the super class of `PMTemplate`.

> JavaScript supports different ways to invoke a function, namely `call` and `apply`. The difference between these two methods is that `apply` passes arguments as an array (a single object), while `call` passes the parameters one by one. For more information about the `call` and `apply` methods, refer to the JavaScript documentation libraries on the internet such as the **Mozilla Developer Network (MDN)**. Information about the function object can be found, for example, at https://developer.mozilla.org/en-US/docs/Web/JavaScript/Reference/Global_Objects/Function.

The `Setup` method of a presentation model must be implemented whenever developers want to read or modify the current property set. This property set is passed to the presentation model from the proxy layer and contains system properties as well as user properties for the current object.

As is the case with the `Init` method, the first line of the `Setup` method should invoke the super class' `Setup` method. However there is no obligation to do that.

The following is an example implementation of the `Setup` method:

```
PMTemplate.prototype.Setup = function(propSet){
  SiebelAppFacade.PMTemplate.superclass.Setup
     .apply(this,arguments);
  var apm = propSet.GetChildByType(
  consts.get("SWE_APPLET_PM_PS"));
  //implement remainder of Setup method here
};
```

The code example demonstrates how to use the `Setup` method of a custom presentation model. The first line calls the `Setup` method of the super class of the custom `PMTemplate` class.

The second line demonstrates how to access one of the child property sets that are contained within the property set passed to the presentation model. The value passed to the `GetChildByType` method is derived from a predefined constant named `SWE_APPLET_PM_PS`, which denotes the type of property set used to hold an applet presentation model's user properties. System constants are defined in the as-delivered `siebconstants.js` file. It is recommended to use the constants defined by Oracle whenever possible to avoid issues during patches and/or upgrades to future versions of Siebel CRM.

If it is not the developer's intention to work with the presentation model property set, the `Setup` method can be omitted.

The OnControlEvent and AttachEventHandler Methods

Whenever we want to send custom events such as a click on an object from the physical renderer to the presentation model, we must do so by using the `OnControlEvent` method. While this method is defined in the `PresentationModel` class, it is usually called from within a physical renderer.

The `AttachEventHandler` method must be used to specify a method (registered via `AddMethod`) that will be invoked when the custom event is received by the presentation model.

The following code is an example of how to use the `AttachEventHandler` method within the `Init` method of a custom presentation model:

```
this.AddMethod("getAccountInfo",getAccountInfo,
    {sequence:false, scope:this});
this.AttachEventHandler("GET_ACCT_INFO","getAccountInfo");
```

```
function getAccountInfo(args){
  //implement event handler here
}
```

The first line of code calls the `AddMethod` method to register the custom `getAccountInfo` function.

The second line registers the `getAccountInfo` method as the function to be invoked when the event named `GET_ACCT_INFO` is received.

The remaining code in the previous example implements the `getAccountInfo` function. For example, we can imagine invoking a server side business service such as *Workflow Process Manager* to obtain account data that must be displayed when a user clicks the label of the Account field in a form applet. For an implementation of this example, refer to chapter 11.

To invoke the `GET_ACCT_INFO` event, we would typically add code like the following to the physical renderer's `BindEvents` method:

```
var myPM = this.GetPM();
var accLabel = $("#Account2_Label");
var args = "";
accLabel.click(function(e){
   myPM.OnControlEvent("GET_ACCT_INFO",args);
   //remaining code in physical renderer
});
```

The example code does the following:

- Initialize a variable named `myPM` as the current presentation model using the physical renderer's `GetPM` function.
- Set the `accLabel` variable as a jQuery collection representing a form applet label using the id value (`#`) of the element representing the label in the DOM.
- Set the `args` variable to an empty string.
- Use the jQuery `click` handler to specify a function to be executed when a user clicks the label.
- In the click handler function, we use the presentation model's `OnControlEvent` method to trigger the `GET_ACCT_INFO` event.

Note that beginning with IP 2014, we can use the Event Helper object to implement an event handler. For more details on physical renderer implementations refer to the next chapter of this book.

The AttachPMBinding Method

Similar to the `OnControlEvent` method, the `AttachPMBinding` method is primarily used in physical renderer code. The purpose of this method is to register a 'binding' between an existing property or function and a local physical renderer method. When the property is modified or the function is invoked, the PR method will be executed.

The syntax of the `AttachPMBinding` method is as follows (the example shows the physical renderer code):

```
this.GetPM().AttachPMBinding("Property or function",
function, {scope});
```

The first parameter is the name of a property or function. When the property is modified from anywhere within the framework or the function is executed, the method specified as the second parameter will be invoked. The scope argument must be used to define the scope of that method.

Because the code is part of a physical renderer, we must use the `GetPM` method to obtain the presentation model object.

The following is a code example from a physical renderer:

```
this.GetPM().AttachPMBinding("SE_Progress",
UpdateProgressBar, {scope: this});
```

The code, specified as part of the physical renderer's constructor function, will register the `UpdateProgressBar` function to be invoked every time the `SE_Progress` property is modified.

It should be noted that the `BasePR` class, which is the base physical renderer class (extended by most other physical renderers), also exposes an `AttachPMBinding` method that simply forwards the call to the presentation model's `AttachPMBinding` method. So using `this.AttachPMBinding` in a physical renderer would also work.

The AttachPostProxyExecuteBinding and AttachPreProxyExecuteBinding Methods

The `AttachPostProxyExecuteBinding` and `AttachPreProxyExecuteBinding` methods are used to register a function with framework methods such as `NewRecord` or `WriteRecord`. When the framework method is invoked, the registered function will be executed.

As the name suggests, the 'Post' variant will execute the registered function **after** the proxy layer returns the method invocation and the 'Pre' variant will do the same **before** the method is sent to the proxy layer.

The syntax of both methods is the same. The following example shows the 'Pre' variant:

```
this.AttachPreProxyExecuteBinding("NewRecord",
function(methodName, inputPS, outputPS){
  SiebelJS.Log("Before " + methodName);
});
```

The example will write a message to the browser console every time the NewRecord method is invoked. This will happen *before* the method is actually sent to the proxy layer.

Instead of a specific method name we can also pass the string ALL as the first parameter. This will cause the registered function to be executed every time a framework method is invoked - independent of the name of the method.

The AddValidator Method

Introduced in IP 2014, the AddValidator method allows us to intercept an event and 'validate' it with a function. When the validation function returns true, the event flow continues, when it returns false, the framework stops running the event handlers.

The following code shows an example usage scenario for the AddValidator method.

```
this.AddValidator(
SiebelApp.Constants.get("PHYEVENT_COLUMN_BLUR"),
function(row, ctrl,val){
    if (val == "*"){
        alert("Asterisk detected!");
        return false;
    }
    else{ return true;}});
```

The example code registers a validator function in the current presentation model for the blur event on a list column (PHYEVENT_COLUMN_BLUR). The validation function will be invoked every time the event occurs - when the column loses focus - and will be passed the current row index, the control object and the current value.

In the example code, an alert is generated when the value is an asterisk (*). In that case the return value of false will prohibit any further events from being executed.

Case Study: Creating a Custom Presentation Model for an Applet

With the knowledge gained in the previous sections of this chapter, we can now set out to implement our first simplistic, but operational, customization for Siebel Open UI, consisting of a custom presentation model (discussed in this chapter) and a custom physical renderer (discussed in the next chapter).

Before we begin, let us have a look at the case study scenario.

Introducing the Case Study Scenario

Our fictitious customer uses Siebel Call Center with Open UI. They asked us to provide a proof-of-concept (POC) to demonstrate the possibilities of browser-side customization in Siebel Open UI.

The customer wants to improve the process of capturing opportunities by providing a visual cue for the completeness of a record. In a first set of meetings, we agreed on implementing a color-coded progress bar on top of the form applet that end users utilize to enter opportunity data.

Because this requirement can only be met by browser-side code, the team of Open UI developers has been tasked with implementing the prototype. The team has decided to implement the event handling and logic in a custom presentation model and to take care of the user interface manipulation in a custom physical renderer.

In this part of the case study, we will implement the custom presentation model and associate it with the **Opportunity Form Applet - Child** applet (a standard applet used in various views of the Opportunities screen).

The high-level process of creating a custom presentation model for an applet is as follows:

1. Create a new custom presentation model extension.
2. Register the extension with the applet.
3. Implement the business logic.
4. Test the custom code.

In the following sections, we will provide detailed procedures to implement the first part of this case study. The code files provided with this chapter of the book include a complete example file (`OpptyFormPM.js`), which represents the implementation of this chapter's case study.

Creating a New Custom Presentation Model Extension

Starting with the presentation model template we introduced earlier in this chapter, we can quickly produce a working presentation model extension class. The following procedure guides us through the necessary steps:

1. Using a suitable JavaScript editor, open the file that contains the presentation model template.
2. Use the editor's 'Save As…' functionality to save the file under a new name to the `PUBLIC/<Language>/<Build>/SCRIPTS /siebel/custom` folder of the Siebel Developer Web Client. For example, use `OpptyFormPM.js` as the file name.
3. In the new file, replace all occurrences of '`PMTemplate`' with '`OpptyFormPM`' (the same string you used as the file name, without the `.js` extension).
4. Verify that the `Init` and `Setup` methods are present and contain a call to `SiebelJS.Log`. If you use the template presented at the beginning of this chapter, these lines should be present. If they are not, ensure that the `Init` and `Setup` methods look like the following:

```
OpptyFormPM.prototype.Init = function(){
  SiebelAppFacade.OpptyFormPM.superclass.Init
      .apply(this,arguments);
  SiebelJS.Log("Custom PM " + this.GetPMName()
      + ": Init method reached.");
  //implement Init method here
};

OpptyFormPM.prototype.Setup = function(propSet){
  SiebelAppFacade.OpptyFormPM.superclass.Setup
      .apply(this, arguments);
  SiebelJS.Log("Custom PM " + this.GetPMName()
      + ": Setup method reached.");
  //implement Setup method here
};
```

5. Save the file and compare it with the following screenshot.

```
if(typeof(SiebelAppFacade.OpptyFormPM) === "undefined"){
    SiebelJS.Namespace("SiebelAppFacade.OpptyFormPM");
    define("siebel/custom/OpptyFormPM", [], function(){
        SiebelAppFacade.OpptyFormPM = (function(){
            var consts = SiebelJS.Dependency("SiebelApp.Constants");
            function OpptyFormPM(){
                SiebelAppFacade.OpptyFormPM.superclass.constructor.apply(this,arguments);
            }
            SiebelJS.Extend(OpptyFormPM, SiebelAppFacade.PresentationModel);
            OpptyFormPM.prototype.Init = function(){
                SiebelAppFacade.OpptyFormPM.superclass.Init.apply(this,arguments);
                SiebelJS.Log("Custom PM " + this.GetPMName() + ": Init method reached.");
                //implement Init method here
            };
            OpptyFormPM.prototype.Setup = function(propSet){
                SiebelAppFacade.OpptyFormPM.superclass.Setup.apply(this, arguments);
                SiebelJS.Log("Custom PM " + this.GetPMName() + ": Setup method reached.");
                //implement Setup method here
            };

            //implement custom functions here
            return OpptyFormPM;
        }());
        return "SiebelAppFacade.OpptyFormPM";
    });
}
```

The screenshot shows the new OpptyFormPM.js file after the steps described in this part of the case study.

Registering the Extension with the Applet

Our new file does not do much apart from printing messages to the browser console. However, we should administer the manifest data early in the process to ensure that the file can be properly loaded by the Open UI framework.

The following procedure describes the steps necessary to register the custom presentation model file with the **Opportunity Form Applet - Child** applet:

1. Log in to the Siebel Developer Web Client with an administrative user account.
2. Navigate to the Administration - Application screen, Manifest Files view.
3. In the Files list, create a new record.
4. Enter the relative path to the new file, for example:
   `siebel/custom/OpptyFormPM.js`
5. Navigate to the Manifest Administration view.
6. In the UI Objects list, create a new record with the following values:

Column	Value
Type	Applet
Usage Type	Presentation Model
Name	Opportunity Form Applet - Child

Note: Depending on your environment, a similar record might already exist. In this case, query for the record, select it, and continue with step 8.

7. In the Object Expression list, create a new record with the following values:

Column	Value
Expression	Desktop (use the Pick List)
Level	1

8. In the Files list, click the Add button and associate the file you registered in step 4.

While the previous steps are sufficient to complete the manifest administration, we should always verify that the new custom file is successfully loaded. The following procedure describes the testing process:

9. Log out of the application.
10. Log in to the application again.

11. Navigate to the Opportunities screen, My Opportunities view.

12. Open the browser's developer tools. For example, in Google Chrome press *F12*.

13. Open the JavaScript console.

14. Verify that two messages appear in the console (one for the Init method, one for the Setup method), similar to 'Custom PM Opportunity Form Applet - Child_PM: Init method reached'.

15. Alternatively, or in addition to the previous steps, you might also want to use the Sources tab of the browser's developer tool to verify that the browser has loaded the custom file.

The following screenshot shows the Google Chrome developer tool after the steps described earlier.

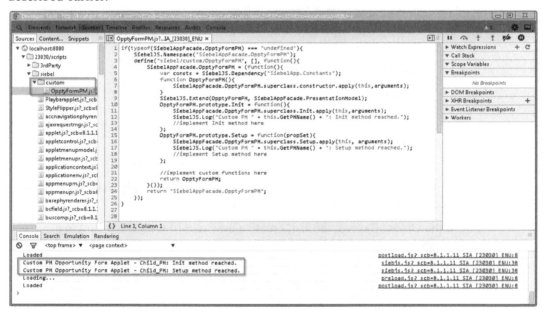

In the bottom area of the screen, the two console messages are visible (highlighted). In the explorer section on the left, the custom folder has been opened and the custom OpptyFormPM.js file is visible and opened in the viewer area.

Implementing the Business Logic

Now that the new custom file is successfully loaded by the Open UI framework, we can start to implement the necessary business logic. For the sake of simplicity, we assume that the file is opened in a JavaScript editor while the application is running. By directly editing the file, we can simply save our changes and refresh the browser cache to test them.

As we recall, the requirement is to display a progress bar indicating the completeness of an opportunity record. The business logic of this requirement can be described as follows:

- Declare a property to store the completeness level (0 to 100) of a record.

- Implement a custom 'compute' function to calculate the completeness level. For a simple prototype it seems sufficient to calculate the share of populated controls in the applet against the total control count.

- Ensure that the Open UI framework invokes the custom function every time a control value has changed or a different record is selected. Attentive readers of this book might already have the `FieldChange` and `ShowSelection` methods in mind.

The next procedure explains how to implement the business logic just described.

1. In the custom `OpptyFormPM.js` file, locate the last line of code within the `Init` method.

2. Create a new line within the `Init` method after the last line and add the following code:

```
this.AddProperty("C_Progress",0);
this.AddMethod("ComputeProgress", ComputeProgress, {sequence :
false, scope : this});
this.AddMethod("ShowSelection",PostShowSelection, {sequence :
false, scope : this});
this.AddMethod("FieldChange", PostFieldChange, {sequence :
false, scope: this});
```

The first line in the code example uses the `AddProperty` method to add a new property named `C_Progress` (the 'C' is used to denote a custom property) and initialize it with a value of zero.

The second line registers the `ComputeProgress` method with the Open UI framework, using the `AddMethod` method.

The `AddMethod` method is deployed twice more to register custom functions (`PostShowSelection` and `PostFieldChange`) to be invoked after the framework methods `ShowSelection` and `FieldChange` respectively.

3. Save your changes.

4. In the code, locate the comment '`//implement custom functions here`'. This comment is part of the template presented earlier in this chapter. If the comment is not present, locate the closing bracket of the `Setup` method.

5. After the comment or the closing bracket of the `Setup` method, add the following code:

```
function ComputeProgress(){
    SiebelJS.Log("ComputeProgress method reached.");
```

```
}
function PostShowSelection(){
    this.ExecuteMethod("ComputeProgress");
}
function PostFieldChange(){
    this.ExecuteMethod("ComputeProgress");
}
```

The code example includes three function declarations, one for each method we registered earlier in the `Init` method.

At this point, the only line of code in the `ComputeProgress` method writes a message to the browser console, so we can confirm that the custom method is invoked properly.

The only line of code we write in the `PostShowSelection` and `PostFieldChange` methods uses the `ExecuteMethod` method to invoke the `ComputeProgress` function. Thus we ensure that our main custom function is invoked when the record selection changes or when the value of any of the current applet's controls changes.

6. Next we set out to implement the desired functionality of computing the completeness of the current record in the `ComputeProgress` function. The follow code shows one of probably many approaches of how to accomplish this. Refer to the comments in the listing and the text thereafter for explanations.

```
function ComputeProgress(){
  var nProgress = 0; //level of completeness
  var nTotalControls = 0; //counter
  var nNonEmptyControls = 0; //counter for populated controls
  var arrControls = this.Get("GetControls");
  var sFieldValue = "";   //field value
  var sControlName, oControl, sFieldName;

  for (sControlName in arrControls){  //parse controls array
    if(arrControls.hasOwnProperty(sControlName)){
      oControl = arrControls[sControlName];
      //get the BC field name
      sFieldName = oControl.GetFieldName();
      if (sFieldName != ""){ //if it is a true input field
        nTotalControls++;    //increase total control count
        sFieldValue = this.ExecuteMethod("GetFieldValue",
        oControl);  //get field value
        if (sFieldValue != ""){ //if field is populated
          nNonEmptyControls++;  //increase count
        }
      }
    }
  } //end for-in
  //compute percentage of populated against all input controls
  //removing 1 for the applet title control
  nProgress = (nNonEmptyControls - 1) /
```

```
        (nTotalControls - 1) * 100;
    //and write to property
    this.SetProperty("C_Progress", nProgress);
    SiebelJS.Log("Progress: " + nProgress + "%");
}
```

The code listing shows the complete ComputeProgress function. The code functionality is described below.

The first lines are declarations of the following variables.

Variable	Description
nProgress	The computed level of completeness (0 - 100)
nTotalControls	Counter for all input controls on the current applet.
nNonEmptyControls	Counter for populated input controls.
arrControls	Object array representing the current applet's control set.
sFieldValue	To hold the field value of a control.
sControlName	To hold the name of a control.
oControl	The control object.
sFieldName	To hold the control's field name.

Note that in this educational code example, we are using a naming convention for variables, using the first part of the variable name to describe its data type. For example the nProgress variable is a number. In your project, you should define and agree upon coding and naming conventions early to avoid confusion and misunderstandings.

To populate the arrControls variable, we use the Get method to retrieve the object array stored in the GetControls property. This array contains all controls that are present in the current applet's web layout (including hidden controls).

The for-in loop iterates through the array of control objects. The first if statement if(arrControls.hasOwnProperty(sControlName)) uses the JavaScript hasOwnProperty method to filter out any array members that might have been inherited (for more information about the hasOwnProperty method, refer to the Mozilla Developer Network at https://developer.mozilla.org/en-US/docs/Web/JavaScript/Reference/Global_Objects/Object/hasOwnProperty)

Within the first if block, we obtain the current control object as oControl and use the GetFieldName method of the *Control Object* class to get the current field value as sFieldName.

Now we can test whether the control exposes a 'real' field, which means it is a typical applet input control - associated with a business component field and not a button or other object. We accomplish this using another `if` block: `if(sFieldName != "")`.

If the control is associated with a field, we increase the `nTotalControls` variable by one and execute the `GetFieldValue` method against the control to get the field value.

The final `if` block checks whether the current control's value is not empty, which means it is actually populated.

If the field is populated, we increase the `nNonEmptyControls` variable by one, effectively counting the non-empty input controls.

Once the `for-in` loop has completed, we can now compute the share of populated controls against the total number of 'real' input controls using this formula:
`nProgress = (nNonEmptyControls - 1) / (nTotalControls - 1) * 100`.

The formula subtracts one from both counters to remove the applet title control from the equation. The applet title control is used to display a field value (typically the Name field) in the applet header and cannot be edited by the user.

The formula divides the number of non-empty controls by the number of user-editable input controls and multiplies the result by 100 to achieve a percentage representation within a range from 0 to 100.

The line `this.SetProperty("C_Progress", nProgress)` sets the `C_Progress` property value to the computed value.

Finally we use the `SiebelJS.Log` method to write the computed value to the browser console for tracing and debugging purposes.

Testing the Custom Code

When developing custom Open UI code such as the one we just created, it is worth keeping the Developer Web Client running while editing the JavaScript file directly. After changing the code in the editor, switch to the browser and delete the cache (either selectively or entirely). Then reload the page, which is typically facilitated by the **F5** key. The browser's developer tools allow you to introspect and debug your code.

The following is an example procedure for testing code changes described in this case study in Google Chrome. We assume that the Siebel application is running and already displays the view we want to test.

1. Ensure that the custom code is syntactically correct and save the file.
2. In Google Chrome, press *CTRL+SHIFT+DEL* to open the Clear Browsing Data dialog in the Settings tab.
3. Select the timeframe for deletion using the dropdown list on top of the dialog.
4. Select (at a minimum) the Cached images and files checkbox.
5. Click the Clear browsing data button.

As an alternative to these steps for clearing the browser cache, you might want to install one of the various browser extensions which allow for the deletion of the browser cache at the click of a button or with a simple keyboard shortcut. Note that Google Chrome automatically clears the cache when the refresh button is clicked while the developer tools are open. In addition you can right-click or hold-click the refresh button to get a menu of options for the reload process while the browser is in debug mode.

6. Refresh the page by pressing *F5*.
7. Press *F12* to open Google Chrome's developer tools.
8. Navigate to the JavaScript console.
9. Verify that the log messages appear. This confirms that the custom presentation model is executed successfully.

As explained at the beginning of this case study, we will cover the process of creating a custom physical renderer in the next chapter. The role of the renderer in this scenario will be to actually display and update the progress bar within the form applet.

Summary

In this chapter we learned how to extend the as-delivered Presentation Model class to implement custom extensions for client side logic.

We introduced the requirements for a development environment and discussed the methods and properties implemented in the `PresentationModel` class provided by Oracle.

In this chapter's case study - the first of two parts - we created a custom presentation model extension class which captures the logic of calculating the completeness of a record by computing the ratio between populated and empty fields in an applet.

In the next chapter, we will discuss the methods of the standard physical renderer class and complete the case study scenario by implementing a custom physical renderer extension.

7

Creating a Custom Physical Renderer

More often than writing presentation model extensions (as introduced in the previous chapter), we have to implement customizations that affect the visual representation of data and elements in the Siebel Open UI client. In this chapter, we will continue our journey through the plains of Open UI customization and learn how to create custom physical renderer extensions. The chapter will be structured as follows:

- Using a physical renderer template
- Methods of the Physical Renderer class
- About the Plug-in Wrapper and Plug-in Builder classes
- Case Study: Creating a custom physical renderer for a form applet
- Case Study: Creating a default physical renderer for list applets

Using a Physical Renderer Template

Since the structure of an Open UI extension class has been laid out in previous chapters, we can go ahead and have a look at a template for a physical renderer. As we will see, the overall code structure is very similar to what we have already learned in Chapter 6.

In the following code example, we define a template for a typical physical renderer extension. This code is available as part of the code files that come with this book. Refer to the file PRTemplate.js:

```
if(typeof(SiebelAppFacade.PRTemplate) === "undefined"){
  SiebelJS.Namespace("SiebelAppFacade.PRTemplate");
  define("siebel/custom/PRTemplate", ["siebel/phyrenderer"],
  function(){
    SiebelAppFacade.PRTemplate = (function(){
      var PM;
      var PRName = "";
      function PRTemplate(pm){
        SiebelAppFacade.PRTemplate.superclass.constructor
            .apply(this,arguments);
      }
```

```
      //Extend form applet renderer
      SiebelJS.Extend(PRTemplate,
          SiebelAppFacade.PhysicalRenderer);
      //Extend list applet renderer
      //SiebelJS.Extend(PRTemplate,
          //SiebelAppFacade.JQGridRenderer);
      PRTemplate.prototype.Init = function() {
        SiebelAppFacade.PRTemplate.superclass.Init
            .apply(this, arguments);
        PM = this.GetPM();
        PRName = PM.Get("GetName") + "_PRTemplate";
        SiebelJS.Log("Custom PR " + PRName
            + ": Init method reached.");
        //implement bindings (PM.AttachPMBinding) here
      };

      PRTemplate.prototype.ShowUI = function(){
        SiebelAppFacade.PRTemplate.superclass.ShowUI
            .apply(this, arguments);
        SiebelJS.Log("Custom PR " + PRName
            + ": ShowUI method reached.");
        //implement ShowUI method here
      };

      PRTemplate.prototype.BindEvents = function(){
        SiebelAppFacade.PRTemplate.superclass.BindEvents
            .apply(this, arguments);
        SiebelJS.Log("Custom PR " + PRName
            + ": BindEvents method reached.");
        //implement BindEvents method here
      };

      PRTemplate.prototype.BindData = function(bRefresh){
        SiebelAppFacade.PRTemplate.superclass.BindData
            .call(this, bRefresh);
        SiebelJS.Log("Custom PR " + PRName
            + ": BindData method reached.");
        //implement BindData method here
      };
      //implement custom functions here
      return PRTemplate;
    }());
    return "SiebelAppFacade.PRTemplate";
  });
}
```

As we can discern from the code example, the overall scaffold is the same as for any other applet-related extension class. However, we must be careful in choosing the super class as there are different base renderers for different types of applets or other user interface elements. In addition, a physical renderer implements different methods such as `ShowUI` or `BindData`. We will learn more about these methods later in this chapter.

The following table describes the most important as-delivered physical renderer classes, which we can extend to create a custom physical renderer.

Class Name	Description	Super Class	File
BasePR	Base renderer class.		Basephyrenderer.js
PhysicalRenderer	Base class for form applets.	BasePR	phyrenderer.js
JQGridRenderer	Base class for list applets.	PhysicalRenderer	jqgridrenderer.js
AccNavigationPhyRenderer	Renders navigation elements such as screen tabs.		accnavigationphyrenderer.js
AppletMenuPR	Applet menu renderer	BasePR	appletmenupr.js
DashboardPhyRenderer	Renders the CTI dashboard	PhysicalRenderer	Dashboardprenderer.js
FlowChartRenderer	Renderer for flow chart designer.	PhysicalRenderer	flowchartrenderer.js
GanttRenderer	Base renderer for Gantt diagrams.	PhysicalRenderer	ganttrenderer.js
fsDispatchBoardRenderer	Field Service Dispatch Board.	GanttRenderer	Fsdispatchboardrenderer.js
JQFullCalRenderer (IP 2013 and earlier)	Renderer for calendar applets.	PhysicalRenderer	Jqfullcalrenderer.js

(Continued)

JQMFormRenderer (IP 2013 and earlier)	Form applet renderer for mobile applications.	BasePR	jqmformrenderer. js
JQMGridRenderer (IP 2013 and earlier)	List applet renderer for mobile applications.	JQMScrollContainer	jqmgridrenderer. js
JQMScrollContainer (IP 2013 and earlier)	Renderer for infinite scrolling lists in mobile applications.	JQMFormRenderer	Jqmscroll container.js
MsgBrdCstPhyRenderer	Renderer for message broadcast (notification) control.		msgbrdcstpr.js
NavigationRenderer	Base navigation renderer		Navigation renderer.js
SmartScriptRenderer	Base renderer for SmartScripts.	PhysicalRenderer	Smartscript renderer.js
TaskPhyRenderer	Base renderer for Task UI.	BasePR	taskprenderer.js
TileLayoutPR	Renderer for tile layout.	PhysicalRenderer	tilelayoutpr.js
ToolbarRenderer	Renders application toolbars.	BasePR	toolbarrenderer. js
TreeAppletPR	Tree applet renderer.	BasePR	Treeappletphy renderer.js
ViewPR	Base view renderer	BasePR	viewcmp.js

The previous information has been derived by introspecting the as-delivered JavaScript files in the /siebel folder. In this chapter and its case study section, we focus on extending the PhysicalRenderer class. Nonetheless, the information in this chapter should apply to all renderer classes.

Similar to what we learned in the previous chapter, the following procedure should be followed to start a new physical renderer extension project:

1. Using a suitable editor, create a new, empty file.

2. Save the file to the `PUBLIC/<Language>/<Build>/SCRIPTS /siebel/custom` folder, using a convenient file name convention. For example save the file as `OpptyFormPR.js`. Physical renderer files should always have the suffix 'PR'.

3. Copy and paste the template code into the new file.

4. Replace all occurrences of `PRTemplate` with the file name (without the `.js` extension) you chose in step 2. For example, use `OpptyFormPR` as the new text.

5. Save the file.

6. Register the new file in the manifest using the Physical Renderer type and verify that it is properly loaded. For more details on how to do this, refer to the previous chapter or this chapter's case study.

As an alternative approach, you can peruse Duncan Ford's Open UI PR/PM Code Template Generator online at `http://tiny.cc/prpm-code-generator` to generate PR (or PM) templates.

Before we set out to implement the functionality of our custom renderer, we must understand the methods of the Physical Renderer classes.

Methods of the Physical Renderer Class

Building on the `BasePR` class, the `PhysicalRenderer` class provides the methods necessary to construct applets and bind them to their presentation model. In the following sections, we will describe the most important physical renderer methods in detail.

The methods we will discuss are the following:

- Init
- ShowUI
- BindEvents
- BindData
- GetPM
- EndLife

For a complete listing and description of all available methods of the `PhysicalRenderer` class, refer to the *Siebel Open UI Configuration Guide* in the Siebel bookshelf.

The Init Method

The Init method of the BasePR class that is inherited by the PhysicalRenderer class defines the following base renderer methods:

- ShowUI
- BindData
- BindEvents
- AttachPMBinding (see the next note)
- EndLife

The AttachPMBinding method of the physical renderer class is merely a shortcut to the presentation model's AttachPMBinding method. Thus, the following two lines of PR code yield the same result:

```
this.GetPM().AttachPMBinding(property, function, arguments);

this.AttachPMBinding(property,function,arguments);
```

Note that the only difference between the two lines of code is that the first uses the GetPM method to obtain the presentation model instance while the second does not.

While it is not necessary to implement a physical renderer's Init method, it can be considered good practice. In a custom physical renderer extension, the Init method is the ideal place to initialize variables that will be used in other functions and to attach local methods to properties using the aforementioned AttachPMBinding method.

The ShowUI method

The first method to be executed after the Init method in a physical renderer is the ShowUI method. This method constructs the user interface elements (the controls) for the applet. At this stage the applet and its controls are visible but not associated with any data.

The following screenshot shows the Account Entry Applet in the Chrome debugger while code execution is halted after the ShowUI method.

As we can see in the screenshot, the UI construction is finished but no data is visible.

The `ShowUI` method of a physical renderer is often overridden in custom extensions to achieve the goal of manipulating, adding, or removing user interface elements. For example, we can use it to place additional controls such as a progress bar on a form applet.

The BindEvents Method

After the `ShowUI` method, the `BindEvents` method registers the event handlers for specific controls. If our customization requires specific handling of events such as mouse clicks, the `BindEvents` method is the right place for the respective JavaScript implementation.

The BindData Method

Called after `BindEvents`, the purpose of the `BindData` method is to populate the applet controls with the actual data. To accomplish this, the `PhysicalRenderer` class does the following:

1. The `BindData` method invokes the `ShowSelection` method.
2. The `ShowSelection` method gets the current control set from the presentation model's `GetControls` property.
3. The `ShowSelection` method invokes the `ShowControlValue` method for each control in the current control set.
4. The `ShowControlValue` method obtains the field value for each control, using the `GetFormattedFieldValue` method of the control object and populates the control by calling the `EnableControl` and `SetControlValue` methods.

The `BindData` method must be overridden whenever we wish to fill the visual elements with data. This can be anything in the way of displaying data as text or applying a more visual representation such as a bar chart.

The GetPM Method

A physical renderer can 'get' a reference to its presentation model by invoking the `GetPM` method. Via the returned object reference, we can invoke presentation model methods such as `Get` or `SetProperty` to obtain or modify the value of a property.

The following code is a typical example of using the `GetPM` method within a physical renderer class:

```
var myPM = this.GetPM();
var sAppletId = myPM.Get("GetFullId");
var oControlSet = myPM.Get("GetControls");
```

The code instantiates the `myPM` variable with the current presentation model reference. Then it uses the `myPM` object to invoke the `Get` method in order to obtain the values of two properties, namely `GetFullId` and `GetControls`.

The EndLife Method

The `EndLife` method is reached when a physical renderer is no longer needed, which typically happens when the user navigates to a different view.

Code that is placed in this method will be invoked at the end of the physical renderer's life cycle. This is usually done to accomplish 'clean-up' tasks.

About the Plug-in Wrapper and Plug-in Builder Classes

Siebel CRM Innovation Pack 2014 introduced new renderer classes, namely the Plug-in Wrapper (PW) and Plug-in Builder classes. This is an aspect of architectural changes that will probably lead to a more modular structure of Siebel Open UI in future releases.

A Plug-in Wrapper is a renderer class that controls the behaviour and visual appearance of individual applet controls. Beginning with IP 2014, Oracle provides several standard plug-in wrappers for native applet controls such as text fields, buttons, check boxes or more advanced elements such as calculator controls or date pickers.

The Plug-in Builder class supports the Plug-in Wrapper architecture by providing an abstraction layer between the physical renderer of the applet and its controls. It allows attaching a plug-in wrapper class to a physical control under given conditions which can be evaluated at runtime. For example, a check-box control could become a 'flip-switch' when a touch screen is detected.

> Please note that the information in this section is applicable only to Innovation Pack 2014 or higher.

Methods of the Plug-in Wrapper Class

The Plug-in Wrapper base class (`BasePW`) provides the following methods.

- ShowUI and BindEvents
- GetEl
- GetValue and SetValue
- SetState

For a complete listing and description of all available methods of the Plug-in Wrapper class, refer to the *Siebel Open UI Configuration Guide for Innovation Pack 2014* in the Siebel bookshelf.

In chapter 12 of this book we will introduce a complete example for a custom plug-in wrapper.

The ShowUI and BindEvents Methods

The ShowUI and BindEvent methods of the Plug-in Wrapper class serve the same purpose as discussed above for the Physical Renderer class. In the ShowUI method, we ensure that the visual appearance of the control is implemented. In the BindEvents methods we take care of the event handling.

The GetEl Method

The GetEl ("Get Element") method simplifies locating the DOM element for a given control. The following is an example implementation of the GetEl method within a custom plug-in wrapper.

```
var elem = this.GetEl();
var name = elem.attr("name");
var newSlider = $("<div id='slider" + name + "'></div>");
```

The example code does the following:

- Instantiate a variable named elem as the jQuery object for the current control, using the GetEl method.
- Use the jQuery attr method to retrieve the value of the name attribute for the DOM element representing the control.
- Create a variable named newSlider as a jQuery object that represents a \<div\> element. The id attribute of the \<div\> element is the result of concatenating slider with the value of the current control's name attribute.

The GetValue and SetValue Methods

The GetValue method of a plug-in wrapper returns the current value of the control. If multiple instances of the same control exist, an index number can be passed as an argument.

The SetValue method is invoked when the value of the control associated with the plug-in wrapper is changed. It takes the new value as the first argument and an index number as an optional second argument. The index argument is required when there are multiple instances of the control. The SetValue method is typically overridden such as in the following code example.

```
SliderPW.prototype.SetValue = function (value, index) {
  SiebelAppFacade.SliderPW.superclass.SetValue
      .call(this, value, index);
  //set the slider value
  $("#slider" + name).slider('value',Number(value));
};
```

The above code example accomplishes the following.

- Implement an override of the `SetValue` method of the base class of the custom `SliderPW` class (this class implements a jQuery Slider widget).
- Call the superclass' `SetValue` method.
- Set the value of the slider widget to the value passed to the `SetValue` method.

The SetState Method

The `SetState` method is used to change the state of a control that is associated with the plug-in wrapper. The method receives three arguments, namely state, flag and index. The state argument can have one of the following values.

- EDITABLE
- ENABLE
- SHOW
- FOCUS

The `SetState` method can be overridden when we want to implement code that is executed when the framework changes a control's state. The `flag` argument will be `true` when the current state of the control should be reversed. For example, when a control that is editable should become read-only or vice-versa, the `SetState` method will be invoked with a `state` value of `EDITABLE` and a `flag` value of `true`.

The following example code shows how to use the SetState method.

```
var oSecFlg = oControlSet["Secure2"];
var oSecFlgPW = this.GetUIWrapper(oSecFlg); //get PW
oSecFlgPW.SetState(consts.get("SHOW"), true); //hide control
```

The code in the previous example accomplishes the following:

- Instantiate the `oSecFlg` variable as a reference to the `Secure2` control from the current control set.
- Use the `GetUIWrapper` method (see below) to obtain the plug-in wrapper instance for the control.
- Call the `SetState` method, passing the value of the `SHOW` constant and `true`, thus hiding the control.

We can imagine the `SetState` method as shorthand that can be used to write more streamlined code rather than to call the individual jQuery methods.

Methods of the Plug-in Builder Class

The Plug-in Builder class supports the Plug-in Wrapper class with the following methods.

- AttachPW
- GetUIWrapper
- GetHoByName

The AttachPW Method

When we want to implement a custom plug-in wrapper (PW), we must use the AttachPW method of the Plug-in Builder class to attach the custom PW class to a control **type**. We also define a function that must return true or false depending on whether conditions for attaching the custom PW are met or not.

The following code example demonstrates how to use the AttachPW method.

```
var cbctrl = SiebelApp.Constants.get("SWE_CTRL_CHECKBOX");
SiebelApp.S_App.PluginBuilder.AttachPW(cbctrl,SiebelAppFacade
    .CustomCheckPW, function (control, objName) {
        return SiebelAppFacade.DecisionManager.IsTouch();
});
```

The example code does the following.

- Instantiate a variable cbctrl with the value of the constant named SWE_CTRL_CHECKBOX. This constant defines the internal type for check box controls.

- Invoke the AttachPW method of the PluginBuilder class and pass the cbctrl variable, the custom PW class (CustomCheckPW) and a function definition to evaluate conditions. The condition function can use the current control and object (i.e. applet) as they are passed as arguments.

- In the example, the return value of the condition function is what the IsTouch method of the DecisionManager class returns. In case the current device is touch-enabled, the return value would be true, otherwise it would be false.

Only when the condition function returns true will the custom PW actually be attached to the control type.

The following table describes some of the control types that can be used with the AttachPW method. The base class for each type of control is indicated as well. This base class must be extended in order to create a custom plug-in wrapper.

Constant Name	Base Class	Description
SWE_CTRL_TEXT	FieldPW	Generic field
SWE_CTRL_COMBOBOX	DropDownPW	Drop down menu
SWE_CTRL_CHECKBOX	CheckBoxPW	Check box

(Continued)

SWE_CTRL_TEXTAREA	FieldPW	Text area
SWE_CTRL_DATE_PICK	DatePW	Date picker
SWE_CTRL_DATE_TIME_PICK	DatePW	Date picker with time
SWE_CTRL_RADIO	PhysicalRenderer	Radio button
SWE_CTRL_FILE	FilePW	File browser
SWE_CTRL_LABEL	LinkPW	Label
SWE_CTRL_MVG	FieldPW	Multi-Value Group

The constant values must be fetched using the get method of the SiebelApp.Constants class as in the following example.

```
var consts = SiebelJS.Dependency("SiebelApp.Constants");
var cbctrl = consts.get("SWE_CTRL_CHECKBOX");
```

The above code instantiates the consts variable as shorthand for the SiebelApp.Constants class and stores the current value of the SWE_CTRL_CHECKBOX constant in the cbctrl variable.

For a complete list of control types that can be used to customize Siebel Open UI, refer to the *Configuring Siebel Open UI* guide in the Oracle Siebel documentation.

The GetUIWrapper Method

The GetUIWrapper method is available through the physical renderer but actually implemented by the Plug-in Builder class. It returns the plug-in wrapper instance of a control object (passed as the input argument). The following example code shows how to use the GetUIWrapper method.

```
var ctrlEl = this.GetUIWrapper(control).GetEl();
```

The above example code calls the GetUIWrapper method within the current physical renderer and passes a control object. It also invokes the GetEl method of the wrapper to retrieve the DOM element of the control object and store it in the ctrlEl variable.

The GetHoByName Method

The GetHoByName method ("**Get H**elper object **By Name**") returns an instance of the Event Helper class which is used to define event handlers on controls that are constructed in the browser using JavaScript. The Event Helper class allows us to streamline the binding of controls to browser events (such as click or mousedown). In the following section, we discuss how to use the Event Helper class.

Using the Event Helper Class

The following example code demonstrates how to use the Event Helper class in Innovation Pack 2014 and beyond to implement a click event handler on a control label.

```
OpptyFormPR.prototype.BindEvents = function(){
  var accLabel = $("#Account2_Label");
  var eventHelper = SiebelApp.S_App.PluginBuilder
      .GetHoByName("EventHelper"); //get the Event Helper
  if (eventHelper && accLabel.length) { //if they exist
    eventHelper.Manage(accLabel, "click", { ctx:this },
        OnClickMoreInfo); //call EH Manage for click event
  }
  SiebelAppFacade.OpptyFormPR.superclass
      .BindEvents.call(this);
};

function OnClickMoreInfo(e){
  //called on click event by event helper
  //code to call PM control event goes here
}
```

The example code accomplishes the following:

- Implement the BindEvents method of a custom physical renderer (OpptyFormPR).

- Retrieve the jQuery object representation of the account label.

- Instantiate the eventHelper variable as an instance of the generic EventHelper helper object, using the GetHoByName method of the PluginBuilder class.

- Verify that the eventHelper and accLabel variables are instantiated

- Use the Manage method of the event helper object to define an event handler function (OnClickMoreInfo) for the click event on the account label (accLabel).

The code also shows the body of the OnClickMoreInfo function which is invoked when the user clicks on the account label.

The Manage method is the only documented method of the Event Helper class. For a complete example that uses the code shown above, refer to Chapter 11.

Case Study: Creating a Custom Physical Renderer for an Applet

In continuation of the previous chapter's case study, we will now learn how to create and register a custom physical renderer extension for a form applet.

We recall that our fictitious customer requires a color-coded progress bar on top of the form applet that the end users utilize to enter opportunity data.

In the previous case study, we already implemented the necessary business logic in a custom presentation model that computes the completeness of a record by comparing the number of populated fields against the total number of fields in the applet. The completeness is expressed as a value between 0 and 100 and stored in a property.

With the knowledge gained about physical renderer methods, we can now build the custom code so that a progress bar is actually placed on the form applet and updated whenever the property holding the level of completeness is modified.

The process of creating a custom physical renderer for a specific applet is basically the same as for a presentation model and consists of the following steps.

- Create a new custom physical renderer extension
- Register the extension with the applet
- Implement the code to visualize the data
- Test the custom code

In the following, we will provide step-by-step instructions on how to implement the second part of this case study.

A sample file (OpptyFormPR.js) is provided with this chapter's code archive.

Creating a New Custom Physical Renderer Extension

Starting with the template we introduced earlier in this chapter, we can quickly produce a working physical renderer extension class. The following procedure describes how to accomplish this.

1. Using a suitable JavaScript editor, open the file that contains the physical renderer template.
2. Use the editor's 'Save As...' functionality to save the file under a new name to the /siebel/custom folder of the Siebel Developer Web Client. For example use OpptyFormPR.js as the file name.
3. In the new file, replace all occurrences of 'PRTemplate' with 'OpptyFormPR' (the same string you used as the file name, without the .js extension).
4. Verify that prototypes for the physical renderer methods are present and contain a call to SiebelJS.Log. If you use the template presented at the beginning of this chapter, this code should be present. If they are not, ensure that the Init and ShowUI methods look like the following.

```
OpptyFormPR.prototype.Init = function(){
  SiebelAppFacade.OpptyFormPR.superclass.Init
    .apply(this, arguments);
  PM = this.GetPM();
```

```
  PRName = PM.Get("GetName") + "_OpptyFormPR";
  SiebelJS.Log("Custom PR " + PRName
      + ": Init method reached.");
  //implement bindings (PM.AttachPMBinding) here
};

OpptyFormPR.prototype.ShowUI = function(){
  SiebelAppFacade.OpptyFormPR.superclass.ShowUI
      .apply(this, arguments);
  SiebelJS.Log("Custom PR " + PRName
      + ": ShowUI method reached.");
  //implement ShowUI method here
};
```

Note that the SiebelJS.Log calls use a variable named PRName to display the current applet name in the browser console. The template code provided with this chapter uses the GetName property and concatenates its value with 'OpptyFormPR' as can be seen in the next screenshot.

---

5. Save the file and compare it with the following screenshot.

```
if(typeof(SiebelAppFacade.OpptyFormPR) === "undefined"){
    SiebelJS.Namespace("SiebelAppFacade.OpptyFormPR");
    define("siebel/custom/OpptyFormPR", ["siebel/phyrenderer"], function(){
        SiebelAppFacade.OpptyFormPR = (function(){
            var PM;
            var PRName = "";
            function OpptyFormPR(pm){
            SiebelAppFacade.OpptyFormPR.superclass.constructor.apply(this,arguments);}
            //Extend form applet renderer
            SiebelJS.Extend(OpptyFormPR, SiebelAppFacade.PhysicalRenderer);
            //Extend list applet renderer
            //SiebelJS.Extend(OpptyFormPR, SiebelAppFacade.JQGridRenderer);
            OpptyFormPR.prototype.Init = function() {
                SiebelAppFacade.OpptyFormPR.superclass.Init.apply(this, arguments);
                PM = this.GetPM();
                PRName = PM.Get("GetName") + "_OpptyFormPR";
                SiebelJS.Log("Custom PR " + PRName + ": Init method reached.");
                //implement bindings (PM.AttachPMBinding) here
            };
            OpptyFormPR.prototype.ShowUI = function(){
                SiebelAppFacade.OpptyFormPR.superclass.ShowUI.apply(this, arguments);
                SiebelJS.Log("Custom PR " + PRName + ": ShowUI method reached.");
                //implement ShowUI method here
            };
            OpptyFormPR.prototype.BindEvents = function(){
                SiebelAppFacade.OpptyFormPR.superclass.BindEvents.apply(this, arguments);
                SiebelJS.Log("Custom PR " + PRName + ": BindEvents method reached.");
                //implement BindEvents method here
            };
            OpptyFormPR.prototype.BindData = function(bRefresh){
                SiebelAppFacade.OpptyFormPR.superclass.BindData.call(this, bRefresh);
                SiebelJS.Log("Custom PR " + PRName + ": BindData method reached.");
                //implement BindData method here
            };
            //implement custom functions here
            return OpptyFormPR;
        }());
        return "SiebelAppFacade.OpptyFormPR";
    });
}
```

The screenshot shows the new OpptyFormPR.js file after performing the steps described in this part of the case study.

Registering the Extension with the Applet

Again, we start with a file that does nothing other than write a line to the browser console when a method is reached. Before we set out to write more code, we register the file in the manifest administration views.

The following procedure describes the steps to register the custom physical renderer file with the applet named Opportunity Form Applet - Child.

1. Log in to the Siebel Developer Web Client with an administrative user account.

2. Navigate to the Administration - Application screen, Manifest Files view.

3. In the Files list, create a new record.

4. Enter the relative path to the new file, for example: `siebel/custom/OpptyFormPR.js`.

5. Navigate to the Manifest Administration view.

6. In the UI Objects list, create a new record with the following values:

Column	Value
Type	Applet
Usage Type	Physical Renderer
Name	Opportunity Form Applet - Child

Note: Depending on your Siebel environment, a similar record might already exist. In this case, query for the record, select it and continue with step 8.

7. In the Object Expression list, create a new record with the following values:

Column	Value
Expression	Desktop (use the Pick List)
Level	1

8. In the Files list, click the Add button and associate the file you registered in step 4.

While these steps are sufficient to complete the manifest administration, we should always verify that the new custom file is successfully loaded. The following procedure describes the testing process.

9. Log out of the application.

10. Log in to the application again.

11. Navigate to the Opportunities screen, My Opportunities view.

12. Open the browser's JavaScript console.

13. Verify that messages appear in the console (one for each method), similar to 'Custom PR Opportunity Form Applet - Child_OpptyFormPR: Init method reached.'

14. Additionally, you might want to verify the presence of the custom file in the Sources tab of the developer tool.

This completes the process of creating a boilerplate physical renderer extension and registering it with an applet. In the next section, we will implement the code that displays and updates the progress bar as per our fictitious requirement.

Implementing the Physical Renderer Code

The steps required to display a progress bar can be laid out as follows:

- Attach a custom function to the property that is populated by the presentation model.
- Insert a `<div>` element after the applet title and apply the **jQuery Progressbar** widget.
- Implement the custom function to apply updates to the progress bar widget.
- For a complete prototype, add code to manipulate the progress bar background color depending on the completeness level.

The following procedure provides the steps to implement this code design:

1. In the custom `OpptyFormPR.js` file, locate the last line of code within the `Init` method.

2. Create a new line within the `Init` method and add the following code:

```
this.AttachPMBinding("C_Progress", UpdateProgressbar,
    {scope: this});
```

As described earlier in this chapter, the `AttachPMBinding` method is, in fact, a presentation model method. However, the same method is implemented in the `BasePR` class, which is the super class of the `PhysicalRenderer` class that we extend. We use the `AttachPMBinding` method to bind the custom `UpdateProgressbar` function to the `C_Progress` property. Recall that this property is created and updated by the presentation model we implemented in the first part of this case study in the previous chapter. Subsequently, the custom `UpdateProgressbar` function will be executed each time the value of the `C_Progress` property changes.

3. Save your changes.
4. Locate the prototype for the `ShowUI` method.
5. Add the following code before the closing bracket of the `ShowUI` method:

```
//show progressbar
var oControlSet = PM.Get("GetControls");
//get the applet title control object
var oTitle = oControlSet["Opportunity Name Title"];
var sTitleId = oTitle.GetInputName(); //get the s_x_y_z Id
var sProgressbarOptions = {value:0}; //set progressbar options
var pbarloc = $("#" + sTitleId);  //select the title control

//create an empty div after the label
```

```
pbarloc.after("<div id='PBAR'></div>");
//convert the empty div to a progressbar
$("#PBAR").progressbar(sProgressbarOptions);
```

This code does the following:

- Obtain the current control set using the presentation model's `Get` method to get the value of the `GetControls` property.

- Obtain a reference to the control object representing the applet title. For the applet in our example, the name of the control is '`Opportunity Name Title`'.

- Get the element id of the applet title using the `GetInputName` method of the control object.

- Set the initial progress bar value to zero. The options for the progressbar widget are documented on the jQueryUI API page at `http://api.jqueryui.com/progressbar`.

- Use the jQuery selector function to address the applet title as a jQuery object.

- Use the jQuery `after` method to add HTML code after the title object. The HTML code creates an empty `<div>` element with an `id` value of '`PBAR`'.

- Address the new `PBAR` element and apply the `progressbar` widget function, passing the initial options.

6. To test the code written so far, comment out the line that calls the `AttachPMBinding` method in the `Init` function. This is necessary to avoid an error message because the custom `UpdateProgressbar` function is not yet implemented.

7. Save your changes.

8. Empty the browser cache and reload the page in the Siebel web client.

9. Compare your work to the following screenshot.

The screenshot shows the `Opportunity Form Applet - Child` applet in the My Opportunities view after the changes made so far to the custom physical renderer code.

The empty progress bar is visible below the applet title. Note that there is no custom style applied, resulting in the default layout of the widget.

If no progress bar is visible at this stage, this might be related to the fact that the style sheet for jQuery UI not being loaded in Siebel versions higher than IP 2013. Adding the following CSS rules to a custom style sheet rectifies the problem.

```css
.ui-progressbar{
    height: 2em;
    border: solid darkgrey 1px;
    display: inline-block;
    padding: 0px!important;
    width: 400px;
    height: 10px;
}
.ui-progressbar-value{
    display: block!important;
    height: 100%;
}
```

For more information on CSS and custom style sheets in Siebel Open UI, refer to the next chapter. To continue this case study in IP 2014 or higher without creating a custom style sheet, add the above CSS rules to the end of the as-delivered `theme-aurora.css` file but ensure that you move the code to a custom style sheet once you have implemented it.

To continue with the progress bar implementation, we carry out the following steps.

10. In the JavaScript file, un-comment the line you commented out in step 6.

11. Locate the comment '`//implement custom functions here`'. This comment is part of the template presented earlier in this chapter. If the comment is not present, locate the closing bracket of the last prototype method.

12. Add the following code:

```javascript
function UpdateProgressbar(){
var val = parseInt(PM.Get("C_Progress"));  //get value from PM
$("#PBAR").progressbar("value", val); //set the value of PBAR

//red-amber-green depending on value
var color;

//below val = 50, green will be 0-100, above 100
var g = val <= 50 ? val*2 : 100;

//below val = 50, red will be 100, above 100 - 0
var r = val > 50 ? 200 - (val*2) : 100;

//color in rgb % style e.g. "rgb(40%,100%,0%)"
color = "rgb(" + r + "%," + g + "%,0%)";
```

```
$(".ui-progressbar .ui-progressbar-
value").css("background",color); //apply color
}
```

The previous example code is a prototype implementation of the `UpdateProgressbar` function. The function accomplishes the following:

- Get the value of the `C_Progress` property via the presentation model and convert it to a full integer using the `parseInt` method.

- Address the `progressbar` widget that was created in the `ShowUI` method and set its value according to the property.

- Adjust the background color of the progress bar depending on the current level of completeness. A low value will result in a reddish background, medium values will render an amber background and higher values will result in a green background. This part of the code is experimental and the author is aware of the fact that the example might not fulfill accessibility requirements such as for colorblind users. The background color and other style aspects of the `progressbar` widget could well be accomplished using external style sheets. We will learn how to create custom style sheets for Siebel Open UI later in this book.

With the above code in place, we are now ready to test it in the Siebel web client.

Testing the Custom Code

The following procedure guides us through the process of testing our custom physical renderer. As with the first part of this case study, we assume the Siebel Developer Web Client is running and connected to the Siebel Sample Database while we edit the JavaScript file.

1. Ensure that the custom code is syntactically correct and save the file.
2. Clear the browser cache and reload the page.
3. Navigate to the My Opportunities view. Create a test record if necessary.
4. Observe that the form applet shows a colorized progress bar below the title.
5. In the form applet, clear the Revenue field and use the **TAB** key to leave the field.
6. Observe that the progress bar shrinks. The background color of the progress bar should change according to its length.
7. In the list applet select a different record and observe that the progress bar is updated when the newly selected record has a different number of populated fields.

The next screenshot shows the opportunity form applet after the modifications described in the case study.

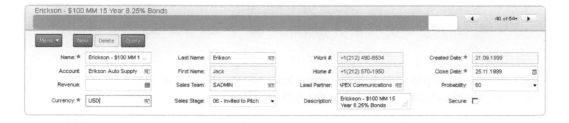

The sample record in the screenshot has all but one of its fields populated; hence the progress bar is green and almost completely filled.

This test proves that our code is fully functional and concludes our two-part case study.

Let's now explore a more complex (and closer to real life) example of a physical renderer for list applets.

Case Study: Creating a Default Physical Renderer for List Applets

The imaginative requirement for this case study is that our customer wants to apply **conditional formatting** to certain columns in list applets. The aim is to modify a cell's background color depending on the current field value.

For example, the background color of cells in the *Probability* column that displays the probability for an opportunity as a value between 0% and 100% should be red for values below 80% and green for values above that threshold.

The customer also wishes that the threshold value should be available for modification by the end user at runtime.

In addition, the extension should be applicable to any list applet. Our architect has pointed out that we can use the DEFAULT LIST APPLET UI object in the manifest administration to associate custom extension classes with all list applets.

To control which columns of an applet should be subject to conditional formatting, the architect proposes to store the business component field names for the respective columns in **applet user properties,** which are passed on to the presentation model. So in fact, our case study requirement will need both a presentation model extension (to retrieve the applet user properties) as well as a physical renderer extension for list applets (to apply the conditional format).

In short, we will implement the following as a prototype:

- Applet user properties
- Presentation model extension to get user properties
- Physical renderer extension that
    - Gets the user properties from the presentation model
    - Identifies the columns to be formatted in the current list applet

    o   Provides a dialog for the end user to enter a target value

    o   Alters the background color of grid cells according to their value

The code files provided with this chapter include a sample implementation of the presentation model (ConditionalFormatListPM.js) and physical renderer file (ConditionalFormatListPR.js).

Creating Applet User Properties for Presentation Models

Earlier in this book we introduced the ClientPMUserProp applet user property. It can be used to define a list of user properties that will actually be passed to property sets that are available in the presentation model layer.

For our case study example we will need two applet user properties. The first holds a list of names of business component fields that will be eligible for conditional formatting when the applet displays a corresponding list column. The second user property will be used to hold the default threshold values for the initial colorization for each individual field.

The following procedure guides us through the process of creating the necessary user properties for a test applet, namely the Opportunity List Applet:

1. If necessary, log in to Siebel Tools.
2. Navigate to the definition of the Opportunity List Applet and check out the object or project.
3. Navigate to the list of Applet User Properties for the applet.
4. Create three new user property records as follows:

Name	Value
ClientPMUserProp	CF Field List, CF Threshold List
CF Field List	Primary Revenue Amount, Primary Revenue Win Probability
CF Threshold List	500000,50

Note that when the ClientPMUserProp record is already present, we can either extend its value by adding the new values after a comma or use a sequenced user property strategy by creating entries named ClientPMUserProp1, ClientPMUserProp2 and so forth.

The names of the custom user properties ('CF Field List' and 'CF Threshold List') are chosen deliberately and can be different in your specific implementation.

The value of the CF Field List user property is a comma separated list of business component field names. The field names must correspond to existing fields in the applet's business component and are case sensitive. In addition, the fields must be exposed as list columns on the applet.

The value of the `CF Threshold List` user property is a comma separated list of numbers that will be used as the default threshold value for the conditional format. The first entry in the list corresponds to the first field in the `CF Field List` user property and so on.

5. Compile the applet
6. Check in the object or project

The previous procedure can be repeated for other list applets if needed, using appropriate names of **numeric** business component fields as values for the `CF Field List` user property.

The procedure also demonstrates how easy it is to add a set of custom user properties for an applet that can be picked up in the presentation model.

Creating a Custom Presentation Model Extension for List Applets

As we are already familiar with the fundamental steps for creating a custom presentation model extension, this part of our case study will not go into details for every step. The next procedure outlines the steps to create a presentation model that picks up the applet user properties and makes them available to the physical renderer:

1. Use the presentation model template discussed in the previous chapter to create a new custom JavaScript file.
2. Locate the line `SiebelJS.Extend(PMTemplate, SiebelAppFacade.PresentationModel);` and comment it out.
3. Locate the line `SiebelJS.Extend(PMTemplate, SiebelAppFacade.ListPresentationModel);` and remove the comment for that line.

The previous steps assume that you are using the template provided with this book. If the line `SiebelJS.Extend(PMTemplate, SiebelAppFacade.ListPresentationModel);` is not present, ensure that it is added before the `Init` method and that all other lines calling `SiebelJS.Extend` are commented out. We must extend the `ListPresentationModel` class because we are creating a custom presentation model class for list applets.

4. Replace all occurrences of `PMTemplate` with the name of the new object, for example `ConditionalFormatListPM`.
5. Save the file in the `/siebel/custom` folder using the object name as the file name, for example `ConditionalFormatListPM.js`.
6. In the Siebel Web Client, navigate to the Administration - Application screen, Manifest Files view and register the new file.

7. Navigate to the Manifest Administration view and create a new entry for the test applet as follows.

Column	Value
Type	Applet
Usage Type	Presentation Model
Name	Opportunity List Applet

8. In the Object Expression list create a new record and set the Level to 1.
9. In the Files list, add the file reference you created in step 6.

> Note that for the first development and testing cycle, we register the custom JavaScript file with a single applet instead of a default entry. This is a recommended practice to avoid inadvertently wreaking havoc to all list applets should our code contain errors. Once the code is sufficiently tested, we will replace the single applet registration with a default entry for all list applets.

10. Log out and log in to the application.
11. Navigate to the My Opportunities view.
12. Open the browser's developer tool and verify that the new custom file is loaded.

Now that we have created and registered a custom presentation model extension file, we can start implementing the functionality to retrieve the values of applet user properties.

The following procedure guides us through the necessary steps for this implementation:

1. Open the ConditionalFormatListPM.js file in the editor.
2. Verify that the following line (from the template) exists:
   ```
   var consts = SiebelJS.Dependency("SiebelApp.Constants");
   ```
3. If the previous line is not present, add it before the line function ConditionalFormatListPM(proxy){

> Using a shorthand (consts) to SiebelApp.Constants to access constants defined by Oracle engineering is a recommended practice to avoid issues should Oracle decide to change naming strategies in future releases.

4. Locate the comment //implement Setup method here.
5. After the comment (within the Setup method body), add the following code:
```
var apm = propSet.GetChildByType(
    consts.get("SWE_APPLET_PM_PS"));
```

```
this.SetProperty("CF Field List",
    apm.GetProperty("CF Field List"));
this.SetProperty("CF Threshold List",
    apm.GetProperty("CF Threshold List"));
```

The previous code does the following:

- Access the current property set (passed to the presentation model's `Setup` method) and retrieve the child property set representing the applet presentation model (`apm`), using the constant name '`SWE_APPLET_PM_PS`' (Applet Presentation Model Property Set).

- Use the `GetProperty` method to access the two applet user properties by their name and store their values in two presentation model properties, so they can be accessed easily by the physical renderer.

6. Save the file and compare your changes with the following screenshot:

```
if(typeof(SiebelAppFacade.ConditionalFormatListPM) === "undefined"){
    SiebelJS.Namespace("SiebelAppFacade.ConditionalFormatListPM");
    define("siebel/custom/ConditionalFormatListPM", [], function(){
        SiebelAppFacade.ConditionalFormatListPM = (function(){
            //get constants
            var consts = SiebelJS.Dependency("SiebelApp.Constants");
            function ConditionalFormatListPM(proxy){
                SiebelAppFacade.ConditionalFormatListPM.superclass.constructor.apply(this,arguments);
            }
            //extend list PM
            SiebelJS.Extend(ConditionalFormatListPM, SiebelAppFacade.ListPresentationModel);
            ConditionalFormatListPM.prototype.Init = function(){
                SiebelAppFacade.ConditionalFormatListPM.superclass.Init.apply(this,arguments);
                SiebelJS.Log("Custom PM " + this.GetPMName() + ": Init method reached.");
                //implement Init method here
            };
            ConditionalFormatListPM.prototype.Setup = function(propSet){
                SiebelAppFacade.ConditionalFormatListPM.superclass.Setup.apply(this, arguments);
                SiebelJS.Log("Custom PM " + this.GetPMName() + ": Setup method reached.");
                //implement Setup method here
                var apm = propSet.GetChildByType(consts.get("SWE_APPLET_PM_PS"));  //get applet PM property set (apm)
                //get value of applet user props
                this.SetProperty("CF Field List", apm.GetProperty("CF Field List"));
                this.SetProperty("CF Threshold List", apm.GetProperty("CF Threshold List"));
            };

            //implement custom functions here
            return ConditionalFormatListPM;
        }());
        return "SiebelAppFacade.ConditionalFormatListPM";
    });
}
```

The previous procedure completes the implementation of a custom presentation model extension for list applets to fulfill the requirements of this case study. The presentation model effectively retrieves the custom applet user properties and makes them available to the physical renderer, which we will implement in the following section.

Creating a Custom Physical Renderer for List Applets

As per our requirements, the physical renderer should implement the following functionality:

- Retrieve the applet user properties
- Locate the column(s) in the list applet
- Handle the user interaction
- Alter the background color of grid cells

In the following steps, we will provide guidance on how to accomplish these requirements.

The next procedure guides us through the steps to create the initial physical renderer file and register it:

1. Use the physical renderer template discussed in this chapter to create a new custom JavaScript file.

2. Locate the line `SiebelJS.Extend(PRTemplate, SiebelAppFacade.PhysicalRenderer);` and comment it out.

3. Locate the line `SiebelJS.Extend(PRTemplate, SiebelAppFacade.JQGridRenderer);` and remove the comment for that line.

The previous steps assume that you are using the template provided with this book. If the line `SiebelJS.Extend(PRTemplate, SiebelAppFacade.JQGridRenderer);` is not present, ensure that it is added before the `Init` method and that all other lines calling `SiebelJS.Extend` are commented out. `JQGridRenderer` is the as-delivered physical renderer class for list applets and we must extend this class rather than the `PhysicalRenderer` class because we are implementing a custom physical renderer for list applets rather than form applets.

---

4. Replace all occurrences of `PRTemplate` with the name of the new object, e.g. `ConditionalFormatListPR`.

5. Save the file in the `/siebel/custom` folder using the object name as the file name, e.g. `ConditionalFormatListPR.js`.

6. In the Siebel Web Client, navigate to the Administration - Application screen, Manifest Files view and register the new file.

7. Navigate to the Manifest Administration view and create a new entry for the test applet as follows.

Column	Value
Type	Applet
Usage Type	Physical Renderer
Name	Opportunity List Applet

8. In the Object Expression list create a new record and set the Level to 1.

9. In the Files list, add the file reference you created in step 6.

10. Log out and log in to the application.

11. Navigate to the My Opportunities view.

12. Open the browser's developer tool and verify that the new custom file is loaded.

After completing the previous procedure, we have successfully created and registered a base file, which we will now extend to implement the specific requirements.

The following procedure describes the necessary code additions:

1. Open the ConditionalFormatListPR.js file in the editor.

2. Locate the comment line //implement BindData method here.

3. After the comment - but within the BindData method - add the following code:

```
var sColName;
//get list of fields
var sCFFieldList = PM.Get("CF Field List");
//get list of desired values
var sCFThresholdList = PM.Get("CF Threshold List");
if (sCFFieldList){ //if fields are defined
  //split strings to arrays
  var arrCFFields = sCFFieldList.split(",");
  var arrCFThresholds = sCFThresholdList.split(",");
  var oColumns = this.GetColumnHelper().GetColMap();

  for (var i = 0; i < arrCFFields.length; i++){
    //for each field passed by user prop
    for (sColName in oColumns){
      //for each list column
      if (oColumns[sColName] == arrCFFields[i]){
        //when field is exposed by column
        //call CF function, pass column name and desired value
        this.ConditionalFormat(sColName,arrCFThresholds[i]);
      }
      else {//do nothing
```

```
        }
      }
    }
  }
  else{
    SiebelJS.Log("No fields defined for formatting.")
  }
```

The code accomplishes the following:

- Declare a variable `sColName` to hold the name of an individual column.

- Initialize the `sCFFieldList` and `sCFThresholdList` variables with the values of the `CF Field List` and `CF Threshold List` user properties respectively by using the PM's `Get` method.

- Verify that a list of fields is actually defined for the applet. If so, the code continues. If not, the `else` block is reached and a console message is logged, indicating that the applet has no fields defined for conditional formatting.

- Split the comma separated lists into arrays using the `split` function.

- Use the `GetColMap` method of the object returned by the `GetColumnHelper` method to initialize the `oColumns` variable as a list of columns and their respective business component field names.

> Note that the `GetColumnHelper` and the `GetColMap` methods are specific to physical renderers for list applets and are not officially documented. Hence, we should use them with caution. The `GetColMap` method returns an object list where each entry represents a (currently visible) column in the list applet and its associated business component field. The column is referenced by its placeholder name (for example `Primary_Revenue_Amount`), while the business component field name is exactly the same as defined in the Siebel repository.

- Iterate through the array of fields passed by the `CF Field List` user property.

- For each field, a second loop iterates through the column list represented by the `oColumns` variable and tries to locate a column associated with that field.

- When a column is found, the `ConditionalFormat` method (to be implemented later) is invoked and the name of the column as well as the accompanying threshold value, are passed as arguments.

The previous code snippet deals with retrieving the values of the applet user properties and locating the columns corresponding to the fields specified in the `CF Field List` user property.

The following procedure describes how to implement the custom `ConditionalFormat` method that implements the user interaction and color management:

1. In the `ConditionalFormatListPR.js` file, locate the comment `//implement custom functions here`.

2. After the comment, add the following code:

```
ConditionalFormatListPR.prototype.ConditionalFormat =
function(column, highval){
  var oRecordSet = PM.Get("GetRecordSet");
  var sPlaceholder = PM.Get("GetPlaceholder");
  var applet = $("#" + sPlaceholder);
  var record, row_id, header, row, cell;
  var color_a, color_b, g, r;
  var sVal = "";  //field value as string
  var nVal = 0;    //field value as number
  var nShare = 0;  //share of field value in %
  var sHeaderHTML = "";  //column header HTML
  //image file to use for column header icon
  var sHeaderImage = "collab_ts_active_new.gif";

  //get column map
  var oColumns = this.GetColumnHelper().GetColMap();
  var sFieldName = oColumns[column]; //get field name
  header = $("#jqgh_" + sPlaceholder + "_" + column);
  that = this; //for click function
  if (!highval) {highval = 100;}  //default for desired value
  header.click(function(e) {
    //add click event handler to column header
    if(e.ctrlKey) { //when CTRL key is pressed at click
      //prevent event "bubbling"
      e.stopImmediatePropagation();
      highval = prompt("Please enter target value");
      //invoke CF function
      that.ConditionalFormat(column, highval);
    }
  });
  sHeaderHTML = header.html(); //get column header HTML
  if (sHeaderHTML.indexOf(sHeaderImage) < 0){
    //if header has no icon
    sHeaderHTML += "<img src='images/" + sHeaderImage + "'>";
    //append image reference for icon
    header.html(sHeaderHTML); //replace header HTML
    header.parent().attr("title","CTRL+click to set target"
        + "value for conditional formatting");  //tooltip
  }
  for (record in oRecordSet) { //for each record in list
    row_id = Number(record)+1; //calculate "row id" 1,2,3..)
    row =  applet.find("tr[id=" + row_id + "]");//current row
    cell = row.find("td[id*=" + column + "]"); //select cell
    sVal = oRecordSet[record][sFieldName];
    //remove characters from string (watch locales!)
    if(sVal){sVal = sVal.replace(/[\$\,\%]+/g,"");}
    else{sVal = "0";} //default to zero
    nVal = parseFloat(sVal); //get as float
```

```
    nShare = nVal*100/highval;  //calculate share

    g = nShare/2 < 50 ? nShare*2 : 100;  //calculate green
    r = nShare/2 >= 50 ? 200 - (nShare*2) : 100;  //red
    color_a = "rgba(" + r + "%," + g + "%,0%,1)";
    color_b = "rgba(100%,100%,100%,1)";  //white
    //fallback on solid background for browsers
    //that can't do linear gradient
    cell.css("background",color_a);
    //Chrome example for linear gradient,
    //for Mozilla use moz-linear-gradient
    cell.css("background","-webkit-linear-gradient(left,"
        + color_a + " 0," + color_b + nShare + "%)")
  }
};
```

The code in the previous example listing does the following:

- Get the current record set from the GetRecordSet property, which contains all records currently visible in the list applet.
- Get the applet placeholder that will be used to identify the applet and its child elements.
- Initialize the applet variable as a jQuery collection, using the applet placeholder to identify the applet.
- Declare various variables to be used later.
- Get the column map for the applet.
- Retrieve the business component field name for the current column.
- Access the column header using jQuery. Note that the element id of column headers for list applets follows a pattern like 'jqgh_' + 'Applet Placeholder' + '_Column Name' (where 'jqgh' stands for 'jQuery grid header').
- Use the jQuery click event handler to specify a function that is executed when the end user clicks the column header. This function uses the event object to determine whether the CTRL key has been pressed while clicking. If this is the case, the click event handler function uses the stopImmediatePropagation method to prevent the click event from 'bubbling up', which means attracting other event handlers.
- For demonstration purposes, a simple prompt dialog is used to solicit the new target value from the end user. This could be replaced by a more suitable jQuery dialog in a real production setting. Finally, the click event handler function invokes the ConditionalFormat method (recursively) to refresh the formatting.
- By adding an image (<img>) tag to the existing column header HTML code, the function effectively provides a visual cue to the end user that the column and its header have a special purpose. The example code also modifies the

`title` attribute to produce a tooltip message, which the browser displays when the mouse cursor hovers over the column header.

Because of the educational nature of the code and for the sake of brevity, the message texts are hard coded. In a realistic project scenario we should strive to look up the messages from a library of translatable messages such as **Symbolic Strings** or separate JavaScript files.

In the final `for-in` loop, we iterate through the current record set and do the following for each record:

- Retrieve the 'pseudo' row identifier (1,2,3 and so forth).
- Select the current row using the jQuery `find` method.
- Select the grid cell for the column.
- Retrieve the cell's value, which is actually the formatted and localized value.
- Use the `replace` function to remove characters like `$`, `%` or commas from the value string. Again, the code presented here is educational and only takes an English-American locale into account. To handle the formatting of field values in other locales, it is recommended to peruse the `LocaleObject` class (discussed in Chapter 5).
- Convert the string to a floating point number using the `parseFloat` function.
- Calculate the share of the current value as a percentage of the target (threshold) value.
- Calculate the green and red color components for the current share. The algorithm increases the green value until the share reaches 50% and then reduces the red value. This results in a red/amber/green color gradient.
- Use the calculated color to set the background of the cell. For compatibility reasons the example code shows how to set a solid background as well as use the vendor specific linear-gradient CSS rules.

To test the code, we must - as always - complete the following steps:

1. Save the JavaScript file.
2. Empty the browser cache and reload the page.
3. If necessary, navigate to the My Opportunities view.
4. Verify that the Probability % and the Revenue column in the list applet are colorized.
5. Verify that the headers of the colorized columns display a special icon.
6. Verify that by holding the **CTRL** key while clicking the column header, a prompt is displayed.
7. Enter a test value in the prompt.
8. Click OK or press the **ENTER** key.

9. Verify that the background color of the cells changes according to the target value.

The following screenshot shows the Opportunity List Applet after implementing this case study.

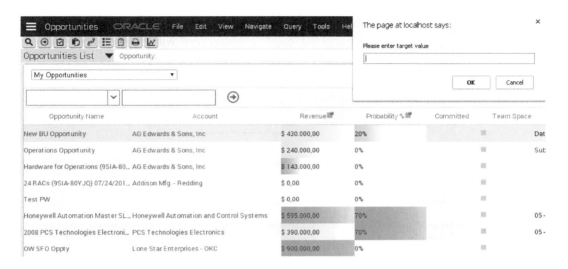

The Probability % and Revenue columns are conditionally formatted and their header displays a special icon. The screenshot also shows the prompt that is displayed when one of the column headers is clicked while the **CTRL** key is pressed.

Applying Default Customizations

So far we used a single test applet to verify that our code works as expected. For customizations that should be applied to all applets (or other UI objects) of the same type, we can use the *default entries* in the Manifest Administration view.

The following procedure describes how to register the example presentation model and physical renderer created in this case study for all list applets:

1. If necessary, log in to the Siebel Web Client using an administrative account.

2. Navigate to the Administration - Application screen, Manifest Administration view.

3. In the UI Objects list, execute a query to locate any records used for testing, for example query for objects where *Name = Opportunity List Applet*.

4. Deactivate the test entries by setting the Inactive Flag column to Y.

5. Execute another query for objects with a name of DEFAULT LIST APPLET.

183

6. When the query returns only two read-only records, these are the seed records delivered by Oracle, one for the default presentation model for list applets, the other for the default physical renderer. Depending on the environment you work in, the query could also return custom 'override' records for this default entry.

7. If only the read-only seed records are displayed, copy both records.

8. Select the new custom record for the default presentation model.

9. In the Object Expression list, create a new record with the following values.

Column	Value
Expression	Desktop (Use the pick list)
Level	1

10. In the Files list, click the Add button and select the custom presentation model, for example `siebel/custom/ConditionalFormatListPM.js`.

11. Repeat steps 8 to 10 for the custom UI object record representing the default physical renderer. In the Files list choose the custom physical renderer file, for example
`siebel/custom/ConditionalFormatListPR.js`.

12. Log out and log in again to the application.

13. Navigate to the My Opportunities view to verify that the list applet is displayed correctly and the customizations are applied.

When using the default UI objects such as DEFAULT LIST APPLET in the Manifest Administration view, we must do so with extreme caution because even the slightest error in the administrative data or the custom code could render *all* list applets in the application unusable, including the list applets in the Manifest Administration view. Hence, we would be unable to undo our changes administratively.

If we find ourselves in this undesirable situation and suspect the custom code to be the culprit, we must use the High-Interactivity (HI) client to navigate to the Manifest Administration view and deactivate or delete the custom entries.

Summary

In this and the previous chapter, we have learned to create a combination of a custom presentation model and a custom physical renderer to implement the business logic and visual behaviour as requested by a fictitious customer. This chapter and its case studies focused on the physical renderer methods and we explored two scenarios - for form and list applets - and how to change the way data is displayed in the user interface.

In the next chapter, we will explore themes and style sheets for Siebel Open UI.

8

Style Sheets and Themes

One of the major differences between the traditional Siebel web user interfaces and Open UI is the ability to gain more precise control over the look and feel of the application by using Cascading Style Sheets (CSS). In this chapter, we will discover the role of CSS in Open UI and provide hands-on examples for creating custom themes.

The following topics will be discussed in this chapter:

- CSS and Open UI
- The Open UI Themes API
- Register Style Sheets
- Pre-built themes
- Case study: Creating a custom theme
- Case study: Defining the appearance of UI elements in CSS
- Case study: Registering a global custom CSS file in the manifest
- Case study: Switching themes using JavaScript

Because of significant architectural differences between Innovation Pack 2013 or earlier and IP 2014 and the fact that this book attempts to describe both versions, pay special attention when working through this chapter as some of the content only applies to a specific version (either IP 2013 or IP 2014 but not both). We have added information in the respective sections and their titles to make you aware of the version specific content.

CSS and Open UI

Much of the 'openness' of Siebel Open UI results from the effort Oracle has taken to rebuild the UI infrastructure. Namely, web templates (SWT files) have been enhanced and rewritten to use modern web development patterns. One example of this is the replacement of HTML tables with `<DIV>` elements.

Unlike the static `<TABLE>` element, a `<DIV>` element can be controlled easily using Cascading Style Sheets (CSS) and JavaScript.

In addition to these elementary changes, Oracle engineering also removed static formatting instructions or style sheet references from the SWT files, enabling greater dynamic alteration to the UI using CSS.

Like many other modern web applications, Siebel CRM uses CSS to apply formatting and positioning directives to the UI elements rendered by the browser. Oracle has created completely new style sheets from scratch and delivers **standard themes** out of the box with Siebel versions that support Open UI.

An Open UI theme is a collection of style sheets that - when applied by the browser - result in the homogenous appearance of the application. We will discuss the standard themes in an upcoming section of this chapter.

Customers can extend standard themes or create their own custom themes in order to modify the application's look and feel. This applies to desktop applications as well as to new Siebel Mobile Applications for smartphones and tablets.

To successfully create and maintain Open UI themes, a solid understanding of CSS is a necessity. It is not within this book's scope to teach CSS but there are a wide variety of tutorials available on the internet to acquaint oneself with this web standard. For example, we can find online tutorials and API references for CSS and other web standards on WebPlatform.org at `http://docs.webplatform.org/wiki/css`.

The Open UI Themes API

The Siebel Open UI framework allows JavaScript developers to dynamically work with themes using the `SiebelApp.ThemeManager` class. This class has the following methods that are important for our work with Open UI themes:

- addTheme
- addResource
- getTheme
- getActiveTheme
- flipTheme

> The `ThemeManager` class has been deprecated in Innovation Pack 2014. The information in this section applies only to IP 2013 or earlier. As of IP 2014, themes are managed in the manifest administration. For detailed information on how to work with themes in IP 2014, refer to subsequent sections of this chapter.

In the following sections, we will explain the purpose of each method of the `ThemeManager` class and provide code examples to illustrate how to use it.

Understanding the addTheme Method

The addTheme method of the ThemeManager class is used to register a collection of style sheets under a common name - the 'theme'. When we inspect the as-delivered siebel/theme.js file in IP 2013 or earlier, we find that Oracle uses the addTheme method to register the four standard desktop themes delivered with IP 2013. As we will see, in an upcoming section of this chapter, customers are encouraged to use the same approach to register custom themes.

The following code is a snippet from the standard siebel/theme.js file and illustrates how to use the addTheme method:

```
SiebelApp.ThemeManager.addTheme(
"GRAY_TAB", {
  css: {
    sb_theme: "files/theme-base.css",
    sc_theme: "files/theme-gray.css",
    sn_theme: "files/theme-nav-tab.css",
    sca_them: "files/theme-calendar.css",
    sd_theme: IE8inc
  },
  objList: []
});
```

As can be seen in the code listing, the addTheme method takes two parameters. The first parameter of type string ("GRAY_TAB" in the previous example) is the **common name** for the theme.

The second parameter is an object list named css that contains references to the CSS files. The entries in this list are pairs of identifiers (for example 'sb_theme') and individual file references. The latter are relative paths to the CSS files (for example "files/theme-base.css" in the previous listing) to their location in the PUBLIC folder of the Siebel Web Server Extension.

The objList element has no documented use at the time of writing.

The following table describes some of the identifiers used by Oracle in the as-delivered theme.js file and the sequence in which the CSS files are loaded for desktop applications:

Identifier	Description	Sequence
sb_theme	Specifies the **base** layout	1
sc_theme	Specifies the **color** scheme	2
sn_theme	**Navigation**-specific style rules	3
sca_them	Specific styles for **calendar** applets	4
other entries	Specific style sheets for Internet Explorer or tree navigation	n/a

For each of the first four identifiers in the previous list, a placeholder has been reserved for customers. The name of this placeholder is identified by inserting the letter 'e' (as in 'extension') after the first two characters of the standard identifier name. For example, a custom CSS file registered with the identifier sce_theme will be loaded **after** the as-delivered sc_theme. By adhering to this naming convention, customers can ensure that custom style sheets are loaded in the correct sequence.

However, customers are free to use any unique identifier and define the loading sequence as they desire in the addTheme method.

For more information about the sequence that the Open UI framework applies when loading style sheets, refer to the Oracle Siebel documentation at http://docs.oracle.com/cd/E14004_01/books/config_open_ui/customizing_app lets_and_layouts8.html.

Using the addTheme method in custom JavaScript files is the officially supported method to register custom themes in Innovation Pack 2013 or earlier. As mentioned earlier, there have been significant architectural changes in IP 2014 where the only method to register custom themes is by using views in the Manifest Administration screen. We will learn how to register custom themes using both the JavaScript method and the manifest method later in this chapter.

Understanding the addResource Method

The addResource method of the ThemeManager class is intended for customer use and allows for a custom style sheet to be added to an existing theme at runtime. The following is an example for using the addResource method in a custom JavaScript file:

```
SiebelApp.ThemeManager.addResource(
"GRAY_TAB", {
  css : {
    "sce_theme" : "files/custom/custom-blue.css"
  }
});
```

The previous example code adds the custom-blue.css file (stored in the PUBLIC/<Language>/files/custom folder) to the existing GRAY_TAB theme using sce_theme as the identifier.

The addResource method is especially useful when we want to add CSS rules to one or more existing themes rather than creating a new theme.

Understanding the getTheme Method

The getTheme method takes the name of a theme that has been defined using the addTheme method as the input parameter and returns an object containing the theme's definition. The following example code shows a usage scenario for the getTheme method:

```
var oGrayTabTheme =
SiebelApp.ThemeManager.getTheme("GRAY_TAB");
SiebelJS.Log(oGrayTabTheme);
```

The previous line of code assigns the return value of the getTheme method to the oGrayTabTheme variable and prints the value of the variable to the browser's JavaScript console.

The following screenshot shows the output of the previous code on the console.

```
▼ Object {css: Object, objList: Array[0], reqJs: Array[0], firstLoad: false}
   ▼ css: Object
      colorbox: "files/custom/colorbox.css"
      global: "files/custom/custom-global.css"
      sb theme: "files/theme-base.css"
      sc theme: "files/theme-gray.css"
      sca_them: "files/theme-calendar.css"
      sd theme: ""
      sn theme: "files/theme-nav-tab.css"
    ▶ __proto__: Object
   firstLoad: false
 ▶ objList: Array[0]
 ▶ reqJs: Array[0]
 ▶   proto   : Object
```

The object returned by the getTheme method contains - among other items - an object named css that enumerates the style sheets currently associated with the theme.

Using the getTheme method, as shown earlier, is a recommended approach when it comes to creating custom themes in IP 2013 or earlier. Instead of listing the individual files of a 'base' theme, we can inherit the current base theme without having to repeat the full file listing for the base theme.

We will see a real-life example for the getTheme method later in this chapter.

Understanding the getActiveTheme Method

The getActiveTheme method of the ThemeManager class returns the common name of the theme that is currently loaded.

The following code snippet illustrates how the getActiveTheme method can be used.

```
var curTheme = SiebelApp.ThemeManager.getActiveTheme();
```

When the previous line is executed, the value of the variable named curTheme will be the common name of the active theme. For example, the return value could be GRAY_TAB.

The getActiveTheme method is useful to identify the currently active theme and use this information for making decisions in the remaining code.

Understanding the flipTheme method

While end users can select a theme manually at runtime using the Behavior view in the User Preferences screen, it might become a necessity to switch from one theme to the other programmatically. This is accomplished by calling the flipTheme method.

The following line of example code demonstrates the use of this method.

```
SiebelApp.ThemeManager.flipTheme("GRAY_TAB");
```

Using the flipTheme method in a custom JavaScript function, developers can control when to switch to a specific theme. For instance, a toolbar button could be created to switch between a 'Tree' or 'Tab' display. Later in this chapter, we will show how to use the flipTheme method in a case study.

Registering Style Sheets

When it comes to loading custom or third-party style sheets in Siebel Open UI, developers must use one of the following techniques depending on the Siebel CRM version:

- **IP 2013** or earlier: Use the ThemeManager class in a **custom JavaScript file**.
- **IP 2014** or later: Register style sheets directly with UI objects in the **manifest administration** views.

In the following, we will give you an overview of these two approaches. Later in this chapter, we will conduct case studies to show both methods in action.

Using the ThemeManager Class in Custom JavaScript (IP 2013 or earlier)

In order to define custom themes or extend existing themes using JavaScript in IP 2013 or earlier, developers must create a custom JavaScript file. In that file, methods of the ThemeManager class - such as the aforementioned addTheme or addResource methods - are invoked to register custom or third-party style sheets with custom or existing themes. The case study "Creating a Custom Theme in IP 2013" will guide you through this process.

The custom JavaScript file will have to be registered in the manifest at the **Application** object level using the '**Common**' usage type.

Using custom JavaScript code to register style sheets has been supported since version 8.1.1.9 / 8.2.2.2 and is the only supported method in versions before Innovation Pack 2014.

Registering Style Sheets in the Manifest Administration (IP 2014 or later)

Starting with Innovation Pack 2014, style sheets can only be registered with user interface objects in the manifest administration views using the **Theme** usage type.

This allows developers to implement scenarios like the following without having to write JavaScript code:

- Use a different style sheet for certain views or applets.
- Use style sheets depending on conditional expressions.
- Apply 'skinning' strategies to control the look and feel of customer or partner facing applications.

The obvious benefit of using the manifest rather than custom JavaScript is the easier maintenance of administrative data. The process of registering files with the manifest is also less error prone than writing custom code.

To register style sheets in the manifest, developers must create entries in the UI Objects list of the Manifest Administration view specifying Theme as the Usage Type.

The following screenshot shows the Manifest Administration view in IP 2014 with two example entries that use the Theme usage type.

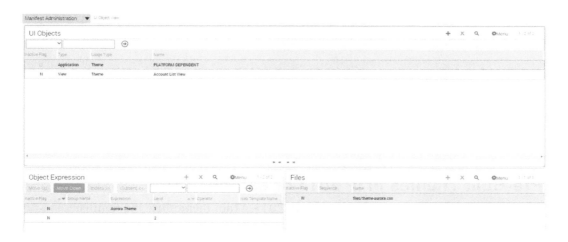

In the screenshot, we can see the first entry in the UI Objects list being highlighted. It defines the themes to be loaded for the entire application and is named PLATFORM DEPENDENT. This entry uses an expression (Aurora Theme) to determine whether the *Aurora* theme is selected as the default theme in the user preferences. In the Files list we can see that one CSS file will be loaded when the expression evaluates to *true*. The second expression is empty and applies when there is no specific theme selected by the user, thus it defines the 'default' theme.

The second UI object in the previous screenshot is defining a special theme for the Account List View and is actually a custom entry.

Pre-Built Themes

As indicated earlier in this book, Oracle delivers the following standard Open UI themes with Siebel CRM in IP 2013 or earlier:

- Four themes for desktop applications:
  o Gray Tab
  o Tangerine Tab
  o Gray Accordion
  o Tangerine Accordion
- One theme for mobile applications:
  o Mobile Theme

With Innovation Pack 2014 and the adoption of responsive web design, Oracle has deprecated the IP 2013 themes and the only pre-built theme shipped with IP 2014 ("Aurora") is the same for desktop and mobile devices. The Aurora theme supports the following types of navigation:

- Tab navigation

- Tree navigation

- Side Menu navigation (new in IP 2014)

A 'Side Menu' is a popup menu initially designed for devices with smaller viewports such as tablets or smartphones. This type of navigation is often referred to as 'Hamburger Menu', which refers to the icon typically used for this menu with three horizontal dashes (reminding vaguely of the popular fast food dish).

In the following we will discuss the pre-built themes for both versions in greater detail.

Pre-Built Themes in IP 2013 or earlier

Among the desktop themes shipped with IP 2013, 'Tab' themes use the familiar navigation pattern of showing screen tabs horizontally on top of the application window while the 'Accordion' themes - also referred to as 'Tree navigation' - implement a collapsible tree on the left side of the application window.

'Gray' and 'Tangerine' refer to the basic colors for the respective theme.

The following screenshot shows the Siebel Call Center desktop application (IP 2013) using the *Tangerine Accordion* theme.

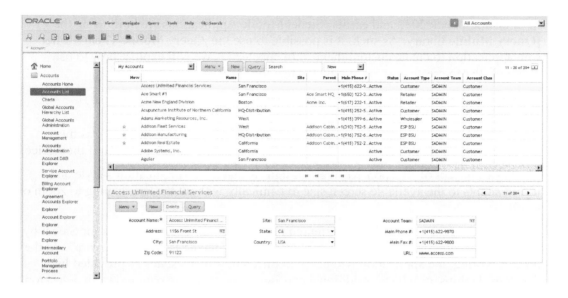

End users can choose their preferred theme in the Behavior view of the User Preferences screen. In addition, we could use the flipTheme method to switch themes programmatically, for example depending on the user's organization.

The next screenshot shows the **Siebel Mobile Sales** application (IP 2013) with the standard mobile theme as it appears on a tablet.

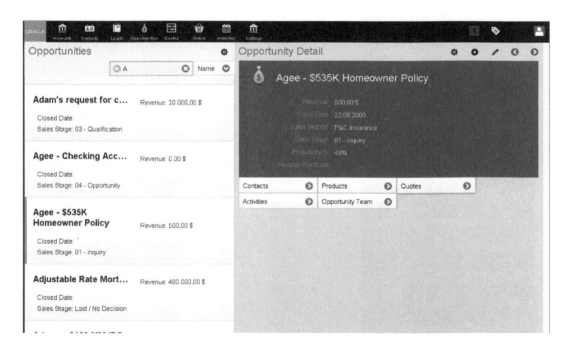

Oracle ships only one standard theme for mobile applications in IP 2013.

In Innovation Pack 2013 and earlier, Siebel Mobile Applications are built using the **jQuery Mobile** library. As such, it is possible to use the jQuery Mobile ThemeRoller web application to create custom themes. In chapter 15, we will explore how to use ThemeRoller to create custom mobile themes for IP 2013.

Pre-Built Themes in IP 2014

One of the most significant architectural changes in Innovation Pack 2014 was the introduction of a single responsive design for all applications, independent of the device.

The basic concept of 'Responsive Web Design' is that a web application's style and layout adapts to the available screen size dynamically without the user having to zoom or scroll.

Starting with IP 2014, Oracle implemented responsive web design patterns for Siebel by providing a single theme that fits all applications. This theme is named "Aurora". At the time of writing, the application will adapt to different screen estates as provided by desktops, laptops, or tablets. Additional configuration would be required to fit a desktop application onto a smartphone though. Oracle has announced plans to enhance the responsive web design pattern in future versions.

The following screenshot shows the Siebel Call Center application in IP 2014 on a laptop using the Aurora theme with 'Side Menu' navigation pattern.

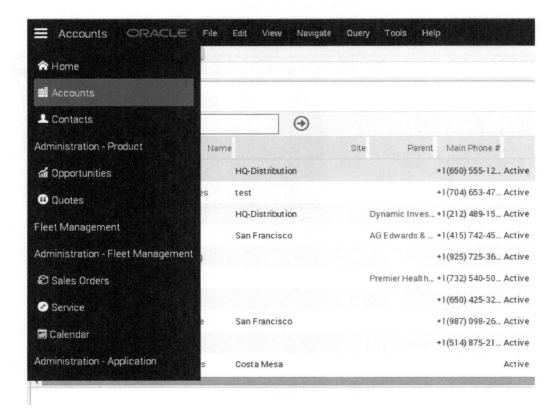

In the previous screenshot, the side menu is currently open, displaying the screens. The default state of the menu is hidden and the user has to click or tap the 'hamburger icon' to open the menu.

If we access the same application using a mobile device such as a tablet, the layout, position and font sizes will automatically adjust to the screen size and device orientation (landscape or portrait).

The following screenshot shows the Siebel Call Center application using a viewport typically provided by a tablet in portrait mode.

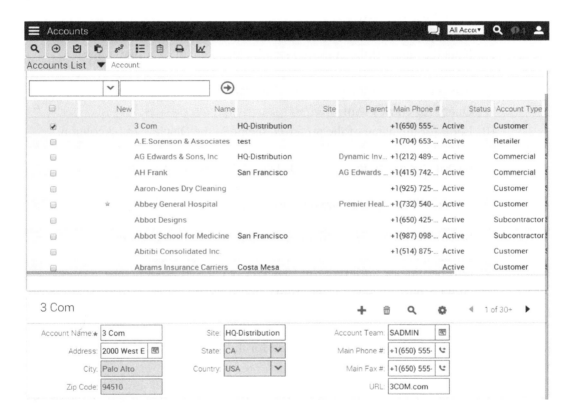

By comparing the previous two screenshots, we can see that the logo and menu are no longer displayed on a smaller screen which is a result of the browser applying different styles depending on the screen width. In chapter 15 we will introduce customization techniques for mobile applications that honor the responsive web design of IP 2014.

Identifying standard CSS files in IP 2013

When setting out to work on a custom theme it is advisable to start from a standard theme that matches the desired final look and feel most closely. Identifying the CSS files used for a standard theme is crucial for understanding the Open UI style sheets.

The following procedure demonstrates how to identify the CSS files of a standard theme in Innovation Pack 2013:

1. Log in to a Siebel web application as an administrator.
2. Navigate to the User Preferences screen, Behavior view
3. In the Navigation Control field, select the preferred navigation pattern ('Tree' or 'Tab').
4. In the Theme field, select the preferred standard theme that you would like to use as a starting point for a custom theme.
5. Click the Save button
6. Press *F5* to reload the page. The new theme should be applied.
7. Note the name of the preferred standard theme (for example 'Gray Tab').
8. Navigate to the Administration - Data screen, List of Values view.
9. Query for entries with Type = 'OUI_THEME_SELECTION'.
10. Look for the name of the preferred theme in the Display Value column.
11. Note the value of the Language-Independent Code column for the same record (for example GRAY_TAB). This is the internal code used in the standard theme.js file.
12. Using a File Explorer, navigate to the PUBLIC/<Language>/<Build>/SCRIPTS/siebel folder of either the Siebel Developer Web Client or the Siebel Web Server Extension.
13. Locate and open the theme.js file in a text editor capable of reformatting or 'un-minifying' JavaScript code. If possible, use the text editor's functionality to 'un-minify' the code.
14. Locate the name of the preferred theme (for example GRAY_TAB) in the theme.js file.
15. Inspect the list of CSS files loaded for the theme in the addTheme method.

Following the previous procedure ensures that we have the complete list of standard CSS files for a given Open UI theme as provided by Oracle.

Identifying Standard CSS Files in IP 2014

Because the registration of style sheets has moved into the manifest administration with IP 2014, the process of identifying standard CSS files in this version (and above) is different.

The following procedure describes how to identify standard CSS files in IP 2014 and higher:

1. Repeat steps 1 to 11 in the previous (IP 2013) procedure to identify the Language-Independent Code (LIC) value for the standard theme you

want to use as the basis for customization. For example, you might identify AURORA_THEME as the LIC for the *Aurora* standard theme.

2. Navigate to the Administration - Application screen, Manifest Administration view.

3. Use a query to locate the following seed data record:

Column	Value
Type	Application
Usage Type	Theme
Name	PLATFORM DEPENDENT

4. In the Object Expression list, identify and select the record that uses an expression to identify the theme selected by the user. For example, you will find one entry using the Aurora Theme expression.

5. In the Files list, inspect the list of files (it might be only one file) that contribute to the standard theme. For example, you will identify the theme-aurora.css file as the standard CSS file for the *Aurora* theme.

6. To verify that the LIC identified in step 1 matches the standard theme, navigate to the Manifest Expressions view and query for the expression found in step 4. Inspect the expression and verify that it contains the LIC value.

Like many other standard files, the theme-aurora.css file is minified. Oracle provides an uncompressed version of the file in the same folder.

In the following case studies, we will describe the steps to create a custom theme based on a pre-built theme.

Case Study: Creating and Registering a Custom Theme

Custom themes are a way of building upon the pre-defined set of as-delivered style sheets while maintaining a state of high upgradeability. This case study guides us through the process of creating and registering a custom Open UI theme using JavaScript.

The high-level process of creating a custom theme is as follows:

1. Create a custom CSS file

2. Create and register a custom theme.js file (IP 2013 or earlier)

3. Register a custom CSS file (IP 2014 or later)

4. Register the custom theme in the List of Values administration

Depending on the Siebel CRM version you are using, only steps 2 or 3 of the previous process may apply. In the following we will provide guidance for each of the previous steps in detail.

Creating a Custom CSS File

The following procedure describes how to create a custom CSS file to hold all custom style rules and overrides. Note that the file is empty at the beginning, except for a simple test rule. We will provide further CSS examples later in this chapter.

1. Use a text editor to create a new file and name it appropriately (for example `mystyle.css`).

2. For testing purposes add the following CSS code to the new file:

```
/* Custom Logo */
.siebui-logo,
#_sweclient #_sweappmenu .siebui-logo {
    background-image: url('../../images/ebus_reversed.gif');
    width: 160px;
    height:50px;
    background-repeat: no-repeat;
}
```

The previous CSS rule replaces the standard Oracle logo (displayed as the background image of a `<div>` element using the `siebui-logo` class on the left side of the application menu) with a different image displaying the text 'powered by Siebel eBusiness'. The `ebus_reversed.gif` image file is delivered with the standard set of images and is referenced here to serve as a test case to evaluate whether the custom CSS file is properly loaded.

3. Save the `mystyle.css` file to the following folder path (SWSE or Developer Web Client).
   `/PUBLIC/<Language>/files/custom`

Note: Create the `custom` folder as a sub-directory of the `files` folder if it does not already exist.

> While CSS files can be edited with any simple text editor, it is advisable to use an Integrated Development Environment (IDE) or web editor that is capable of syntax highlighting, auto completion, and syntax checking for CSS.

Creating and Registering a Custom theme.js File (IP 2013)

The following procedure demonstrates how to create and register a custom `theme.js` file in Innovation Pack 2013. For information on how to register a custom theme in IP 2014 or higher, refer to the next section.

1. Create a new JavaScript file and save it in the `siebel/custom` folder as `theme.js`

Note that the name of the custom JavaScript file can be chosen at will, it is not necessary to name it `theme.js`.

2. Add the following code to the new file:

```
SiebelApp.ThemeManager.addTheme(
  "OUI_BOOK", JSON.parse(JSON.stringify(
      SiebelApp.ThemeManager.getTheme("GRAY_TAB")))
);

SiebelApp.ThemeManager.addResource(
  "OUI_BOOK",
  {
    css : {
      "custom": "files/custom/mystyle.css"
    }
  }
);
```

The previous code uses the `addTheme` method of the `ThemeManager` class to add the custom theme `OUI_BOOK` to the current list of themes (instead of `OUI_BOOK` you can, of course, use any common name except the ones already used by Siebel standard themes). The `getTheme` method is used to retrieve the current definition of the `GRAY_TAB` theme, which is the starting point in this example. By using the `getTheme` method we ensure that our custom JavaScript always refers to the correct list of files that the as-delivered theme defines.

In order to avoid modifying the original theme (`GRAY_TAB`) we have to convert the object returned by the `getTheme` method to a string and re-parse it into an object using the `JSON.stringify` and `JSON.parse` functions. More information about the JSON object and its methods can be found at `https://developer.mozilla.org/en-US/docs/Web/JavaScript/Reference/Global_Objects/JSON`.

After defining the new theme, we use the `addResource` method to add a reference to our custom `mystyle.css` file to the new `OUI_BOOK` theme.

The following screenshot shows the custom `theme.js` file after the aforementioned changes.

```
SiebelApp.ThemeManager.addTheme (
    "OUI_BOOK", JSON.parse(JSON.stringify(SiebelApp.ThemeManager.getTheme("GRAY_TAB")))
);

SiebelApp.ThemeManager.addResource(
    "OUI_BOOK",
    {
        css : {
            "custom": "files/custom/mystyle.css"
        }
    }
);
```

The previous screenshot shows the custom `theme.js` file after the modifications explained in the procedure so far. Depending on your implementation project, the code can be different.

    3.   Save the custom `theme.js` file.

This chapter's code archive contains an example file (`theme.js`) with the previous code.

Like every other custom JavaScript file, the custom `theme.js` file must be registered in the Manifest Administration views to ensure it is loaded at the right time. The following procedure describes the steps for registering the file and associating it with the correct UI object:

    1.   Log in to the Siebel Web Client as an administrator.

    2.   Navigate to the Administration - Application screen, Manifest Files view.

    3.   In the Files list, create a new record and enter the following in the Name column.

```
siebel/custom/theme.js
```

    4.   Navigate to the Manifest Administration view.

    5.   In the UI Objects list, execute a query using the following values:

        •   Type = Application

        •   Usage Type = Common

        •   Name = PLATFORM_DEPENDENT

In an out-of-the-box installation, there is one record returned, which is read-only because it is part of the Oracle seed data set. In an already customized environment, we might find a second custom record with the same values. That record will be editable.

    6.   If only the seed data record is displayed, use the Copy Record command to copy the record and select the new copy.

    7.   If there is already a custom record, select it and continue with step 9.

    8.   In the Object Expression list, create a new record with the following values:

Column	Value
Expression	Desktop (Note: use the pick list)
Level	1

9. In the Files list, click the Add button and select the newly registered file from the Files pick list (for example siebel/custom/theme.js).

The previous procedure is necessary to register the custom theme.js file as a manifest file and associate it with the **Application** object type. By using the **Desktop** expression, we ensure that the custom theme.js file is only loaded when the Siebel application is in desktop mode so our custom theme does not interfere with mobile applications.

Registering a Custom CSS File (IP 2014 and later)

If your project is using Siebel CRM Innovation Pack 2014 or later, you must follow the procedure described in this section to register custom CSS files in the manifest administration. This also applies if you are migrating from earlier versions to IP 2014.

1. Navigate to the Administration - Application screen, Manifest Files view.

2. In the Files list, create a new record and add a reference to the new custom style sheet in the Name column such as the following.
   files/custom/mystyle.css

3. Navigate to the Manifest Expressions view.

4. Create a new record with the following values.

Column	Value
Name	OUI Book Theme
Expression	LookupName (OUI_THEME_SELECTION, Preference ("Behavior", "DefaultTheme")) = "OUI_BOOK"

In the previous expression, the LookupName function returns the Language Independent Code (LIC) value for the theme currently saved in the user preferences. In case the return value matches the string "OUI_BOOK" (which means that the user has selected the OUI Book Theme as the preferred theme), the expression will evaluate to true.

5. Navigate to the Manifest Administration view.

6. In the UI Objects list, execute a query using the following values:
   - Type = Application
   - Usage Type = Theme
   - Name = PLATFORM_DEPENDENT

In an out-of-the-box installation, there is one record returned that is read-only because it is part of the Oracle seed data set. In an already customized environment, we might find a second custom record with the same values. That record will be editable.

7. If only the seed data record is displayed, use the Copy Record command to copy the record and select the new copy.

8. If there is already a custom record, select it and continue with step 10.

9. In the Object Expression list, create a new record with the following values:

Column	Value
Expression	OUI Book Theme (Note: use the pick list)
Level	1

10. In the Files list, use the Add button to associate files in the following sequence (adjust the value of the Sequence field if necessary).

Sequence	File Name
1	files/theme-aurora.css
2	files/custom/mystyle.css

Note that we have to include the standard CSS file first because the custom CSS file only contains overrides.

Registering the Custom Theme in the List of Values Administration

To enable end users to select the custom theme in the Behavior view of the User Preferences screen, we must register the custom theme in the List of Values administration view. The following procedure guides us through this process:

1. If necessary, log in to the Siebel application as an administrator.

2. Navigate to the Administration - Data screen, List of Values view.

3. In the List of Values list, execute a query with the following search criteria: Type = 'OUI_THEME_SELECTION'

4. Locate and select the record for the standard theme from which you started (e.g. with a Display Value of 'Gray Tab').

5. Use the Copy Record command to copy the selected record.

6. In the new record, set the following fields:

Column	Value
Display Value	`Open UI Book`
Language Independent Code	`OUI_BOOK`

Note that the value of the Language Independent Code column must match exactly the name of the custom theme as it is referenced in the custom `theme.js` file (IP 2013) or the manifest expression (IP 2014). The display value can be chosen at will.

7. Click the Clear Cache button to reload the List of Values cache.

8. Log out of the application.

9. Log in to the application again.

10. Navigate to Tools > User Preferences.

11. Navigate to the Behavior view.

12. Open the dropdown list for the Theme field and verify that the new custom theme appears. Note that you might have to change the value in the Navigation Control field first depending on the base standard theme you chose as a starting point for the custom theme.

13. Click the Save button.

14. Press the *F5* key to reload the browser page.

15. Verify that the Oracle logo in the top left corner of the application is replaced with the Siebel emblem (according to the test rule we entered in the custom `mystyle.css` file).

The following screenshot shows the Behavior view and the test logo displayed in the top left corner in IP 2013 (Gray Tab theme).

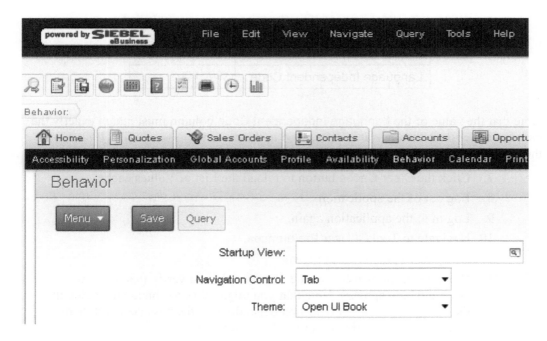

The previous procedure concludes the process of creating and registering a custom style sheet. Now we are ready to add CSS rules to the `custom.css` file as needed to change the look and feel of the application.

In the following case studies we will explore the process of identifying the CSS classes for a given UI element and we will provide styling examples.

Case Study: Defining the Appearance of UI Elements in CSS

Before we start adding CSS rules to our custom style sheet we must understand the process of identifying the CSS class (or classes) associated with a given user interface element. The following procedure explains how to accomplish this:

1. If necessary, log in to the Siebel application.
2. Navigate to a view that displays the object types you want to modify.
3. Right-click the user interface element that you wish to modify and select Inspect Element from the context menu. Note: This applies to Mozilla Firefox and Google Chrome browsers. For other browsers, the procedure might be different. For example, to inspect the application top banner, right-click in the lower area of the application banner as shown in the next screenshot.

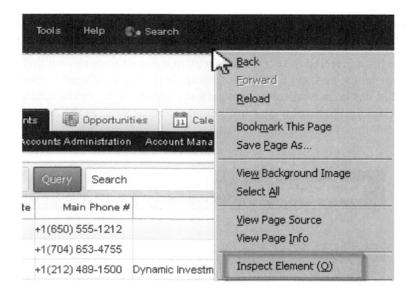

The previous screenshot shows the context menu of Mozilla Firefox after right-clicking in the lower area of the application banner. The Inspect Element menu command is highlighted.

After clicking the Inspect Element command, the browser's developer tool opens and displays the page's source code with the selected element highlighted. The following screenshot shows the result of inspecting the application top banner in Mozilla Firefox.

In the screenshot, we have highlighted the `<div>` element that represents the application top banner. In the Rules panel on the right hand side of the developer tool, the currently active CSS rules for the element are displayed. The rule that applies to the application banner is named `#_sweappmenu > div`, which denotes a `<div>` element that is a child of another element with an id of `_sweappmenu`.

Note: In case the exact element has not been selected, it might be necessary to use the code inspector to select the element manually by clicking it in the source code view.

To ensure we have selected the correct element, and to experiment with different CSS styles, we can change and add CSS rules directly in the browser's developer tool. The next screenshot has been taken after changing the default style for the application banner to a dark blue background color by simply typing in `darkblue` as the new value of the background color.

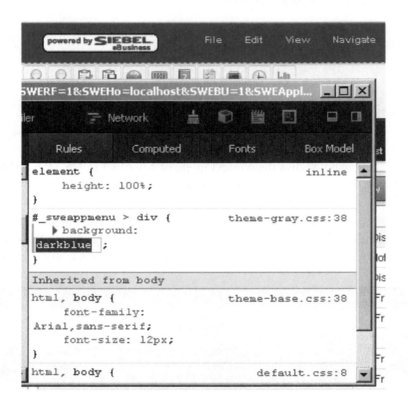

As we can see, the browser applies the style changes made in the Rules window immediately. Note that these changes are not permanent. By refreshing the browser page (by pressing *F5*), the style is read again from the `.css` file. In the previous example we used a common color name (`darkblue`), which is understood by most modern browsers. We can define colors in CSS files in many different ways. The most common is to use the RGB (red - green - blue) color scheme with hexadecimal representations of the three color channels. For example, a value of `#00008B` would result in the same dark blue color.

Once we are satisfied with the selection, we can create an identical entry for the CSS rule in our custom style sheet. Some browsers such as Google Chrome allow the modified rule to be copied directly from the rule inspector. If copying is not an option, we could open the standard `.css` file, locate the respective entry and copy it. Of course, we can also type the new rule manually but for complex rules, this is time consuming and error prone.

In continuation of our example, we add the following CSS rule to the custom `mystyle.css` file:

```
/* Application Top Banner */
#_sweappmenu > div,
#_sweappmenu {
    background: darkblue;
}
```

In the previous code, the first line is a comment, enclosed in `/* */` to provide inline documentation. A CSS rule identifies the object using a CSS selector (`#_sweappmenu > div` in the example) and specifies the style instructions as name/value pairs within curly brackets. While an exact selector like `#_sweappmenu > div` serves the purpose for this example, it can be beneficial to include more common selectors such as `#_sweappmenu` in a comma separated list. This ensures that our custom style sheet covers more ground and supports light variations in the DOM that might occur in future versions of Siebel Open UI.

In the previous example, the only style instruction is to set the `background` color to `darkblue`.

To test our changes, we can now clear the browser cache and reload the page.

In the following case studies we will introduce various CSS examples to illustrate how to create a rich custom theme by applying style directives to different elements of the Open UI application. A complete example file (`mystyle.css`) is available with this chapter's code archive.

Case Study: Customizing General Colors and Fonts

One of the most obvious reasons for creating custom style sheets would likely be that end users and application developers want Siebel applications to conform to company style guides and corporate identity policies.

In the following we will provide examples for CSS style rules that control the overall look and feel of a Siebel desktop application.

Setting global font family, size and application background

By applying the following rules to the `<body>` element and by using the asterisk (*) selector that matches all elements, we can control the font family, font size and other global aspects of an application's look and feel such as the background color or image:

```
/*Global Look and Feel */
body {
    background: lightblue;
    font-size: 1.1em!important;
}
```

```
*{
    font-family: verdana, sans-serif!important;
}
```

In the previous example, we set the background color of the `<body>` element to a light blue. The font size will be determined by taking the default size and multiplying it by 1.1.

> The `!important` directive forces the browser to accept the rule even if it has been specified as 'important' in other style sheets. Using the `!important` directive should only be considered a last resort. In Siebel Open UI, several rules in standard style sheets use this directive.
>
> The `em` unit denotes a relative measurement of font sizes in browsers. You can also specify fixed font sizes using units of measures such as `pt` (points), `px` (pixels), `cm` (centimetres) or `in` (inches).

The global font family as per the previous example will be `verdana`. If the browser cannot locate this font, it will apply a `sans-serif` default font.

Controlling the Look and Feel of Hyperlinks

In Siebel CRM, hyperlinks - or 'drilldowns' - are a widely used navigation mechanism. Technically, they are HTML anchor elements and we can control their look and feel by using CSS rules like in the following example:

```
/*Hyperlinks and Drilldowns*/
a a:visited a:active,
.drilldown {
    color: blue!important;
    text-decoration: none;
}
a:hover{
    text-decoration: underline;
}
```

The previous rules set the color of hyperlinked text to blue and suppress any text decoration (e.g. underlining the text) for visited and active hyperlinks. Using the `a:hover` directive, we ensure that a different style - underlined text in the example - is used when the mouse cursor hovers over the text.

Applying Style Rules to Navigation Elements

Navigation elements such as screen tabs, view tabs, or menus (at the application and applet level) are implemented in Siebel Open UI using specialized classes. By overriding the style rules for these classes we can control the look and feel of those elements.

The following example style rules illustrate how to achieve a custom style for screen tabs and the second navigation level also known as aggregate categories or aggregate views:

```
/*Screen Tabs*/
#s_sctrl #s_sctrl_tabScreen.ui-tabs ul.ui-tabs-nav li a{
    border-radius: 0;
}
#s_sctrl #s_sctrl_tabScreen.ui-tabs ul.ui-tabs-nav li.ui-
state-hover a,
#s_sctrl #s_sctrl_tabScreen.ui-tabs ul.ui-tabs-nav li.ui-tabs-
active a{
    background: darkblue;
    border-radius: 0;
}
/*First and second level navigation*/
#s_sctrl div.ui-tabs, #s_sctrl div.ui-tabs ul.ui-tabs-nav,
#s_sctrl div.ui-tabs ul.ui-tabs-nav li,
#s_sctrl #s_sctrl_tabView.siebui-empty-tabs, #s_sctrl
#s_sctrl_tabView{
    border-radius: 0;
    background: lightblue;
}
/*Second level navigation*/
#s_sctrl #s_sctrl_tabView.ui-tabs ul.ui-tabs-nav li a,
#s_sctrl #s_sctrl_tabView.ui-tabs ul.ui-tabs-nav li a:hover,
#s_sctrl #s_sctrl_tabView.ui-tabs ul.ui-tabs-nav li.ui-tabs-
active a{
    color: black;
    background: lightblue;
    border: none;
}
```

The previous example's rules set the background and foreground colors for screen tabs and second level navigation links under the various states such as being the active tab or being hovered over (or not).

In addition, we provide a rule to override the border radius to zero, resulting in a 'flat' look and feel.

The next set of style rules controls the third and fourth level navigation elements, namely view tabs and view links:

```
/*View Tabs (third level navigation)*/
#s_vctrl_div ul.dynatree-container > li > span > a,
#s_vctrl_div #s_vctrl_div_tabScreen.ui-tabs ul.ui-tabs-nav li
a {
    border-radius: 0;
}
.siebui-subview-navs .siebui-nav-tabScreen.ui-tabs ul.ui-tabs-
nav li.ui-state-hover a,
.siebui-subview-navs .siebui-nav-tabScreen.ui-tabs ul.ui-tabs-
nav li.ui-tabs-active a{
```

```
      background: darkblue;
      border-radius: 0;
}
/*4th level navigation*/
.siebui-subview-navs .siebui-nav-tabView.ui-tabs ul.ui-tabs-
nav li.ui-tabs-active a,
.siebui-subview-navs .siebui-nav-tabView.ui-tabs ul.ui-tabs-
nav li a:hover
{
      background: darkblue;
      border-radius: 0;
}
```

As with the first and second level navigation, we aim for a darker background style for active or hovered elements and set the border radius to zero.

The following CSS rules control the various menus and dropdown lists in Siebel CRM desktop applications:

```
/*LOVs and Menus*/
#s_vctrl_div ul.dynatree-container ul a:hover,
#s_vctrl_div ul.dynatree-container ul a:focus,
#s_vctrl_div ul.dynatree-container ul a:active,
.bannerDiv a:hover,
.bannerDiv a:focus,
.bannerDiv a:active,
.ui-autocomplete.ui-menu a.ui-state-focus,
.siebui-appletmenu .siebui-appletmenu-item a.ui-state-hover,
.siebui-appletmenu .siebui-appletmenu-item a.ui-state-focus,
.siebui-appletmenu .siebui-appletmenu-item a.ui-state-active,
.ui-menubar .ui-menubar-item a.ui-state-hover,
.ui-menubar .ui-menubar-item a.ui-state-focus,
.ui-menubar .ui-menubar-item a.ui-state-active {
      color: white;
      background: darkblue;
}
.ui-menu,
 .ui-menu .ui-menu-item a {
      background-color: darkgray;
      border-color: darkgray;
      border-radius: 0;
 }
.ui-menu .ui-menu-item a.ui-state-disabled {
      opacity: 1;
      background: lightgray;
      color: darkgray;
}
```

The settings in the previous example rules result in a dark gray background for menus and a dark blue background with white text color for selected menu items. Disabled menu items will have a light gray background.

The following screenshot shows the Siebel Call Center application (IP 2013) with a custom style sheet that implements the examples shown in this chapter so far.

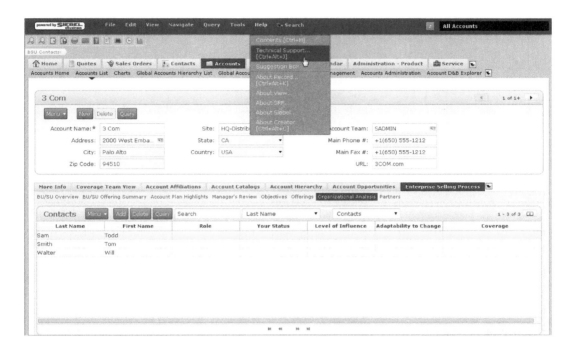

As is the nature with complex enterprise applications, there would be many more elements to customize. For the sake of brevity, we have provided a simplistic scenario.

Case Study: Applying Custom Style Rules to Applets

Applets are the most prominent elements of the Siebel user interface. They convey data and functionality to the end user. It is therefore important to be able to control the look and feel of applets.

In this case study, we will explore real-life examples for customizing the style of applets in Siebel Open UI.

Applet Buttons, Titles and Backgrounds

Each applet has a title bar, buttons and a data area. The following example CSS rules show how we can apply custom styles to these components.

Highlighting the Selected Applet

We can use CSS rules like the following to highlight the currently selected applet so that it visually stands out from the other applets in the view:

```
/*Applet Borders (selected)*/
div.Selected,
.siebui-applet.siebui-active{
    border: solid darkblue;
    border-radius: 0;
    border-width: 2px;
    box-shadow: none
}
/*Applet Title Bar (selected)*/
div.Selected tr.AppletButtons,
.siebui-catalog-search div.Selected .AppletButtons,
.siebui-applet.siebui-active .siebui-applet-header{
    background: lightblue;
    color: black;
    text-shadow: none;
    border-radius: 0px;
}
```

The CSS rules will result in a 2 pixel wide dark blue border and a solid light blue title bar background for a selected applet.

Controlling the Look and Feel of Applet Buttons with Innovation Pack 2013 or earlier

The following is an example of how to apply a style override to applet buttons in Innovation Pack 2013:

```
/*Applet Buttons IP 2013*/
.appletButton,
.AppletMenu span.miniBtnUIC>button{
    background: dodgerblue;
    color: white;
    text-shadow: none;
    border-radius: 0px;
}
```

The previous CSS rule applies to button controls on list and form applets as well as pick applets.

Controlling Buttons and Icons with Innovation Pack 2014

With the theme changes that come with IP 2014, it might become necessary to use different CSS rules than for previous versions. The following is an example CSS rule for IP 2014:

```
/*Applet Buttons IP 2014*/
.siebui-applet .AppletButtons button,
.siebui-applet .siebui-applet-buttons button{
```

```
        background: white;
        color: dodgerblue;
}
```

The previous CSS rule sets the background color for applet buttons to white and the text color to dodgerblue.

The new standard theme in IP 2014 supports icons to be displayed on applet buttons rather than the button caption text. This is accomplished by Oracle by shipping a new standard font (oracle.ttf) with the application. This font is specified as the 'oracle' font family in the standard CSS files. The font files are located in the PUBLIC/FONTS directory on the Siebel web server, so the browser can download them at runtime.

The following example CSS rule overrides the icon for the query button (a magnifying glass) to a different icon (a magnifying glass within a box):

```
.siebui-icon-newquery::before {
  content: "\e683";
}
```

The previous example CSS rule uses the ::before pseudo-element to address objects with a class named siebui-icon-newquery - the class used for the query button. The ::before - and ::after - pseudo-elements must be used in conjunction with the content property to define an element's content. The content value is specified in hexadecimal code as \e674. More information about the content CSS property can be found on the Mozilla Developer Network at https://developer.mozilla.org/en-US/docs/Web/CSS/content.

Inspecting the *oracle* font - for example with the *Insert Symbol* functionality of Microsoft Word - allows us to find the hexadecimal codes for all symbols in the font. The following screenshot shows the *oracle* font symbols in MS Word.

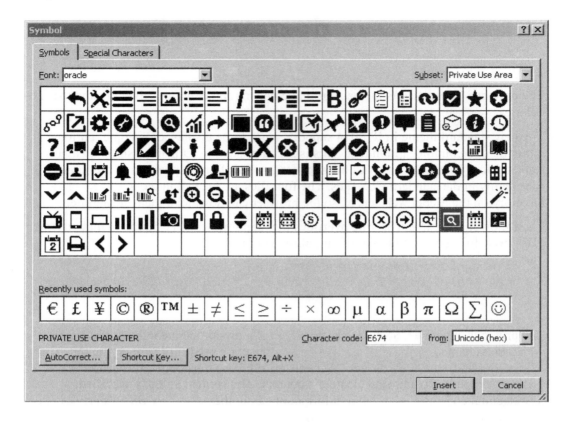

In order to view the font in programs such as MS Word, it must be installed locally on the machine.

In some customization scenarios it might become necessary to use custom or third-party fonts that can be registered in custom style sheets like in the following example:

```
@font-face {
    font-family: 'ouibook';
    src: url(../fonts/custom/ouibook.ttf);
}
```

The previous CSS rule will register the ouibook font family and instruct the browser to download the ouibook.ttf file from the PUBLIC/FONTS/custom folder on the Siebel web server. The previous example only illustrates the concept and the ouibook.ttf file is non-existent.

In addition, we might want to consider using open source fonts such as Font Awesome (http://fortawesome.github.io/Font-Awesome).

Setting the Background Color for Form Applets

The background of form applets sets the stage for the data controls. It is important to choose a distinct color or background image. The following is an example CSS rule to set the form applet background to a soft white tone:

214

```
/*Applet Background*/
.AppletBack,
.AppletHIFormBorder {
    background: whitesmoke;
    border-radius: 0px;
}
```

Instead of solid colors, we could also use image files by providing the following value to the background argument. The value of the `background` property would have the following syntax:

```
url(path to image file)
```

Another alternative to solid colors are gradient definitions like the following example:

```
linear-gradient(to top,#ccc 0%,#fff 70%)
```

The previous example would result in a gradient color fill from grey (`#ccc`) to white (`#fff`) with full white fill beginning at 70% from the bottom.

The drawback of using gradient fills is that not all browsers implement this feature alike and it is likely that the result will look different depending on the browser. Using a background image for complex backgrounds might seem a safe solution, but introduces the cost of downloading an additional file. In addition, images do not scale well in responsive web design. Hence, we should resort to flat colors whenever possible.

Highlighting Selected Records in List Applets

The currently selected records are typically highlighted in Siebel list applets using a distinct color. The following example CSS rule shows us how to control the highlight color:

```
/*Selected Record Highlight*/
.ui-jqgrid .ui-jqgrid-btable .ui-state-highlight td {
    background-color: #fff95b !important;;
}
```

The previous rule sets the currently active record highlighted to a yellow background.

Case Study: Positioning and Removing UI Elements

While most CSS rules will revolve around controlling the visual style of objects such as colors and sizes, we also need to be able to control the location of elements in the browser window or to remove them completely because we do not need them.

In this case study we will explore CSS examples for Siebel Open UI that allow us to understand how to fulfil these requirements.

Setting the Location of UI Elements

The location of global user interface elements such as the logo or the toolbar can be adjusted with CSS rules similar to the following:

```
/*  Position toolbar to the right */
.siebui-button-toolbar{
    float: right;
    z-index: 1;
    position: relative;
}
```

The previous CSS rule will result in a positioning of the application toolbar to the right side of the application window. The z-index property can be used for better control of the element's position in the graphical z-axis, which can be imagined as a third dimension in addition to the width and height of an element. A higher z-index will result in an element to be shown on top of other elements.

The main application containers in Siebel Open UI are implemented as <div> elements with the following values for their name and id attributes:

- _sweclient: The overall parent container for the web client

- _sweappmenu: Contains the top banner with the application menu

- _swethreadbar: The thread bar

- _swescrnbar: The container for screen tabs and navigation links

- _swecontent: The content container that acts as parent for the various panels such as Task Pane, Dashboard or the Report Panel.

- _sweview: Represents the view and is the parent container for applets

The toolbar is implemented as a <div> element with the class siebui-button-toolbar.

Each of the aforementioned container elements can be individually controlled in their appearance, size, and location using CSS just like any other UI element.

Hiding UI Elements

There might be various reasons to hide specific user interface elements. For example, their presence could distract the user. The following example CSS rules use the display property to hide the thread bar and the placeholder for non-rendering standard interactivity applets that are shown in IP 2013:

```
/* Hide Threadbar and SI Applet Message */
#_swethreadbar,
.AppletBlock{
    display: none;
}
```

Setting the `display` property to `none` effectively removes the element as can be seen in the following screenshot, which shows the Siebel Call Center application with all of the aforementioned style changes.

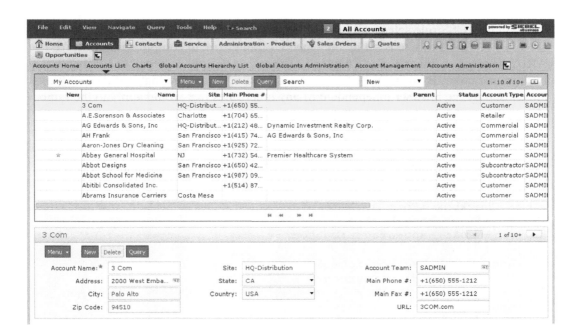

As a result of the custom style sheet, the application uses a blue color scheme and does not display a thread bar. In addition, the toolbar is located at the right side of the application.

Case Study: Implementing Special Style Requirements

Apart from defining the overall visual appearance of the Siebel Open UI web client, we can also define more complex CSS rules for controlling the appearance of user interface elements based on certain conditions. For example, we might want to highlight required fields in form applets to stand out from the other fields.

In the following case study, we will explore some example style rules that demonstrate how easily this can be achieved using CSS.

Highlighting Required Fields

The following example CSS rule allows us to specify the appearance of required fields in form applets:

```
/* Highlight Required Fields*/
input[aria-required="true"],
div.mceGridField input.siebui-ctrl-mvg[aria-required="true"],
input[aria-required="true"][readonly="readonly"] {
```

```
        border-color: red!important;
        background: lightcoral!important;
        font-weight: bold;
}
```

The previous CSS rule selects all `input` elements that have the `aria-required` attribute set to `true`. This attribute is set by the Open UI framework to comply with the WAI-ARIA standard as illustrated in Chapter 1. The style rule applies a red border and background color. By using the `!important` directive, we ensure that that these settings are chosen by the browser independent of any other rules that would apply to the same elements.

Controlling the Appearance of Checkboxes

The following example CSS rule allows us to control the visual appearance of check boxes on form applets:

```
/* Checkbox (Form Applets) */
input[type=checkbox] {
    -webkit-appearance:button;
}
input[type=checkbox]:checked {
    background: darkgreen;
}
input[type=checkbox]:hover {
    background: lightgray;
}
```

The `-webkit-appearance` property is currently only interpreted (as intended) by Google Chrome and Apple Safari; other browsers will not obey the rule at the time of writing. By specifying `button` as the appearance we can use different colors, or images such as a checkmark icon, as the background for different states of the input element. The previous example specifies a dark green background for the checked state of a check box and a light gray background for the hover state.

Setting Alternating Row Colors

To make list applets easier to read, we can specify two different colors and alternate them as can be seen in the following screenshot.

The previous screenshot shows the SIS Account List Applet after applying a custom style rule similar to the next CSS example. Note that in IP 2014, the standard *Aurora* theme specifies alternating row colors for list applets out of the box.

```
/* Alternating row colors */
.ui-jqgrid .ui-jqgrid-btable tr:nth-child(even) td {
    background-color: lightblue;
}
.ui-jqgrid .ui-jqgrid-btable tr:nth-child(odd) td {
    background-color: aliceblue;
}
```

The previous example rule uses the nth-child CSS selector and results in a light blue background for even (second, fourth, etc.) grid rows and a darker shade of blue for odd (first, third and so forth) grid rows.

Case Study: Registering a Global Custom CSS file in the Manifest

If you intend to create multiple custom themes, it might become cumbersome to maintain all individual CSS files, especially when they contain rules that should apply globally across all themes. For example, you might have implemented custom tooltips (see Chapter 12 for an example implementation) and wish that the style of these tooltips remains consistent across standard and custom themes.

One possible approach for this scenario is to register a 'global' custom CSS file for all themes. Because of the architectural differences between IP 2013 and IP 2014, the implementation is different. In IP 2013 we will have to use a custom JavaScript file to call the addResource method of the ThemeManager class, while in IP 2014 we will have to register the global custom CSS file in the manifest administration views.

The following scenario is based on IP 2014 and guides us through the process of registering a custom CSS file with the application object in order to implement a style sheet that is applied independent of the selected theme:

1. Create a new (empty) file named `custom-global.css` (for example) and save it in the `PUBLIC/<Language>/files/custom` folder.

2. Log in to the Siebel Web Client as an administrator.

3. Navigate to the Administration - Application screen, Manifest Files view.

4. In the Files list, create a new record and enter the following in the Name column.
   ```
   files/custom/custom-global.css
   ```

5. Navigate to the Manifest Administration view.

6. In the UI Objects list, execute a query using the following values:
   - Type = Application
   - Usage Type = Theme
   - Name = PLATFORM_DEPENDENT

In an out-of-the-box installation, there is one record returned, which is read-only because it is part of the Oracle seed data set. In an already customized environment, we might find a second custom record with the same values. That record will be editable.

7. If only the seed data record is displayed, use the Copy Record command to copy the record and select the new copy.

8. If there is already a custom record, select it and continue with step 9.

9. In the Object Expression list, create a new record with the following values for each theme (standard or custom) you are using. Note that there might be existing entries. Just create the entries you need.

Column	Value
Expression	(Use the pick list to select the expression for the theme). For example, select 'Aurora Theme'
Level	(Choose the next highest number in the sequence). For example, enter 2.

10. Add one more expression record keeping the Expression column empty and just set the Level field to the next highest value. This will be the 'default' expression in case no theme is selected in the user preferences.

The following screenshot shows the Object Expression list applet with example records.

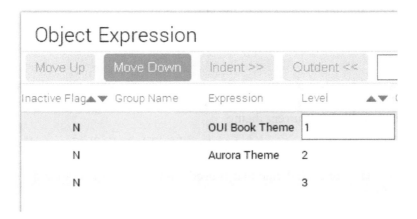

The first record in the previous screenshot represents the custom 'OUI Book Theme', the second represents the standard 'Aurora Theme' and the third record represents the 'default' entry.

11. Repeat the following steps for each entry in the Object Expression list:
    o   Select the record in the Object Expression list applet.
    o   In the Files list, click the Add button and select the CSS file for the theme represented by the expression.
    o   Set the Sequence in increments of 1.
    o   Add any other CSS files specific to the theme.
    o   As the last file, select the custom global CSS file you registered in step 4. Set the Sequence field to the next value in the sequence.
    o   For the 'default' expression, choose one of the CSS files you are using in standard or custom themes.

The following screenshot shows the Files list applet for the expression representing the standard 'Aurora Theme'.

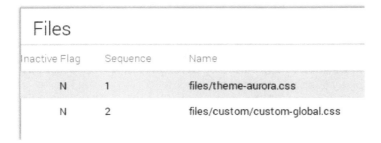

In the previous screenshot, the first file in the sequence is the standard theme-aurora.css file. The second (and last) file is the custom-global.css file.

12. Log out and log back in to the application.

13. Open the browser's developer tools and verify that the custom-global.css file is loaded.

We have now registered an empty custom-global.css file with every theme for the application. In upcoming chapters we will use this file to hold CSS rules that should be applied independent of the current theme.

If you would like to implement a global custom CSS file in IP 2013 or earlier, you would have to modify the custom theme.js file and use the addResource method of the ThemeManager class for each theme that is used within your project to add the custom-global.css file.

Case Study: Switching Themes using JavaScript

One of the benefits of the ThemeManager class is that it allows full programmatic control over the set of style sheets being loaded by the browser. To illustrate this, the following example case study guides us through a scenario during which we will use the flipTheme method to 'flip' to the theme a user has just currently selected in the form applet in the Behavior view of the User Preferences screen. To accomplish this, we will create a custom presentation model and physical renderer for the **User Profile Behaviour Applet**.

As usual, the complete example code is available with this chapter's code archive (InstantStyleFlipPM.js and InstantStyleFlipPR.js).

The instructions in the following case study are simplified for the sake of brevity. If you need more information on how to create custom presentation model and physical renderer files, refer to Chapter 6 and 7 respectively.

1. Create a new JavaScript file named InstantStyleFlipPM.js (preferably as a copy of a presentation model template file) and save it to the siebel/custom folder. This is our new custom presentation model file.

2. If you use a template, ensure that all occurrences of PMTemplate are replaced with InstantStyleFlipPM.

3. Implement the presentation model's Init method as follows:

```
InstantStyleFlipPM.prototype.Init = function(){
  SiebelAppFacade.InstantStyleFlipPM.superclass.Init
      .apply(this,arguments);
  this.AddProperty("StartupThemeChange",""); //theme field
  this.AddProperty("StartupNavCtrlChange",""); //nav field
  this.AddMethod("FieldChange", PostFieldChange,
      {sequence : false, scope: this } );
};
```

The previous code establishes two presentation model properties (StartupThemeChange and StartupNavCtrlChange) to hold the values of the Navigation Control and Theme fields respectively.

In addition we register the PostFieldChange function to be invoked after the FieldChange framework method.

4. Implement the PostFieldChange function as follows:

```
function PostFieldChange(control,value){
//invoked after each field change
  switch (control.GetName()){
    case "StartupTheme":
      this.SetProperty("StartupThemeChange",value);
      break;
    case "StartupNavCtrl":
      this.SetProperty("StartupNavCtrlChange",value);
      break;
  }
}
```

The previous example code identifies the control that has been changed by its name and sets one of the two properties to the new value.

5. Use a template to create the custom physical renderer file as InstantStyleFlipPR.js and save it to the siebel/custom folder.

6. Implement the physical renderer's Init method as follows:

```
InstantStyleFlipPR.prototype.Init = function() {
  SiebelAppFacade.InstantStyleFlipPR.superclass.Init
      .apply(this,arguments);
  var PM = this.GetPM();
  PM.AttachPMBinding("StartupThemeChange",FlipTheme,
      {scope: this});
  PM.AttachPMBinding("StartupNavCtrlChange",NavCtrlChange,
      {scope: this});
}
```

The previous code attaches the FlipTheme function to the StartupThemeChange property and the NavCtrlChange function to the StartupNavCtrlChange property. As a result, the PR functions will be invoked whenever the respective property is modified by the PM.

7. Implement the custom FlipTheme and NavCtrlChange functions as follows:

```
function FlipTheme(){
  //get new Theme name
  var newTheme = this.GetPM().Get("StartupThemeChange");
  if (newTheme != ""){
    SiebelApp.ThemeManager.flipTheme(newTheme.toUpperCase()
```

```
      .split(" ").join("_"));
  if (navCtrlChanged){
    //user selected new Navigation Control value
    this.GetPM()
    //save record
    .ExecuteMethod("InvokeMethod","WriteRecord");
    document.location = document.location; //force refresh
  }
 }
}

function NavCtrlChange(){
  navCtrlChanged = true;
}
```

The FlipTheme function gets the value of the StartupThemeChange property and if this value is not empty, invokes the flipTheme method of the ThemeManager class. The value passed to the flipTheme method is computed as the result of a split and join operation against the displayed field value. For example, a field value of "Gray Tab" would become "GRAY_TAB" after the operation. For as-delivered themes, this conversion produces a valid Language Independent Code entry (in the List of Values) for the respective theme that is the required input for the flipTheme method. In a real-life scenario, it is required to lookup the language independent code using a server-side business service to avoid problems that could arise if the language independent code in the LOV is not an uppercase version of the display value. The previous code is kept short for the sake of brevity and demonstration.

In case the user changed the Navigation Control field, for example from "Tab" to "Tree" the FlipTheme function ensures that the current record is saved by invoking the WriteRecord method and enforces a page refresh by re-setting the document location.

The NavCtrlChange function simply sets the navCtrlChanged variable (evaluated in the FlipTheme function) to true to indicate that the user has changed the value of the Navigation Control field.

8. Save your changes.

9. Register the new custom presentation model and physical renderer file with the **User Profile Behavior Applet** in the manifest administration views. Refer to Chapter 7 for detailed instructions on how to register custom JavaScript files against user interface objects.

10. Re-login to the application and clear the browser cache.

11. Navigate to Tools > User Preferences > Behavior.

12. Set the Navigation Control field to Tab (if not already set).

13. Set the Theme field the a different as-delivered tab theme. For example if the current value is Gray Tab, select Tangerine Tab.

14. Notice that as soon as you set the field value, the new theme is immediately applied.

This simplified - and a bit challenging - case study demonstrates that it is possible to influence the current theme programmatically from custom JavaScript code.

Note: The previous case study example only applies to Innovation Pack 2013 and earlier. As of IP 2014, the ThemeManager class is no longer exposed.

Summary

Siebel Open UI truly stands up to its name because of its ability to use cascading style sheets for fine-grained control over the visual aspects of the user interface.

In this chapter we learned how to register custom themes with the Open UI JavaScript framework. In various case studies we provided examples of how to apply custom styles to user interface elements from the logo to individual applet controls.

This chapter also introduced us to the concept of registering style sheets in the manifest administration views and how to flip themes programmatically.

In the next chapter, we will learn how to customize non-applet user interface objects such as navigation elements and views.

9

Customizing Other User Interface Objects

In the previous chapters of this book, we learned how to create custom extension classes for presentation models and physical renderers for applets. While applets are the most prominent user interface objects, the Siebel Open UI API also provides extensibility for other objects that make up the Siebel client, such as views or navigation tabs. This chapter introduces case studies through which you will learn how to customize the following UI objects:

- Screen and View Tabs
- Views

Customizing Screen and View Tabs

It is an established standard that end users navigate between screens and views in the Siebel client using tabs or links. In the following case studies we will learn how to customize screen and view tabs, as well as other aspects of navigation within the Siebel client. The main business reason for putting effort into the customization of navigational UI elements is that end users should be able to find their way through the maze of screens and views as effortlessly and efficiently as possible.

In this section, we will provide step-by-step instructions for the following case study scenarios:

- Creating extension classes for navigational elements
- Sorting the drop-down menu for screens and views
- Sortable screen tabs

The first scenario forms the foundation for the other two in terms of creating a custom extension class for the out-of-the-box navigation physical renderer class.

Case Study: Creating Extension Classes for Navigational Elements

As indicated earlier, customizing user interface elements (other than applets) follows the same principles of creating custom classes that extend standard presentation models and physical renderers for respective elements.

The base physical renderer class for navigation tabs on all levels (screen, screen link, view) is `SiebelAppFacade.AccNavigationPhyRenderer`. For the sake of brevity we will refer to this class as 'navigation renderer' from now on.

In Chapter 7, we learned how to create a custom physical renderer extension and the task of creating one for the navigation renderer is no different. The following procedure guides us through the steps needed to create a custom extension class for the navigation renderer:

1. Copy the physical renderer template file provided with this book (`PRTemplate.js`) and save it in the `/siebel/custom` folder using a convenient name, for example `CustomNavigationPR.js`.

2. Open the new file with a suitable editor.

3. Replace all occurrences of `PRTemplate` with the custom name, for example `CustomNavigationPR`.

4. Ensure that the `define` method is implemented as follows:

```
define ("siebel/custom/CustomNavigationPR",
["siebel/accnavigationphyrender"], function () {
```

If you use the template code provided with this book, you might just need to uncomment the previous line in the code and comment the other call to the `define` method. The code line defines the dependency of the new extension class to the as-delivered `accnavigationphyrender.js` file, which contains the code for the navigation renderer class.

5. Ensure that the line calling the `SiebelJS.Extend` method reads like this:

```
SiebelJS.Extend(CustomNavigationPR,
    SiebelAppFacade.AccNavigationPhyRenderer);
```

The line defines the `CustomNavigationPR` class as an extension class of the `SiebelAppFacade.AccNavigationPhyRenderer` class. If you use the template provided with this book, ensure that all other calls to `SiebelJS.Extend` are removed or commented out.

6. Save the file and compare your work with the following screenshot.

```
if(typeof(SiebelAppFacade.CustomNavigationPR) === "undefined"){
    SiebelJS.Namespace("SiebelAppFacade.CustomNavigationPR");
    define ("siebel/custom/CustomNavigationPR", ["siebel/accnavigationphyrender"], function () {
        SiebelAppFacade.CustomNavigationPR = (function(){
            //var consts = SiebelJS.Dependency("SiebelApp.Constants");
            var PM;
            var PRName = "";
            function CustomNavigationPR(pm){
            SiebelAppFacade.CustomNavigationPR.superclass.constructor.apply(this,arguments);}
            SiebelJS.Extend(CustomNavigationPR, SiebelAppFacade.AccNavigationPhyRenderer);
            CustomNavigationPR.prototype.Init = function() {
                SiebelAppFacade.CustomNavigationPR.superclass.Init.apply(this, arguments);
                PM = this.GetPM();
                PRName = PM.GetPMName() + "_CustomNavigationPR";
                SiebelJS.Log("Custom PR " + PRName + ": Init method reached.");
                //implement bindings (PM.AttachPMBinding) here
            };
            CustomNavigationPR.prototype.ShowUI = function(){
                SiebelAppFacade.CustomNavigationPR.superclass.ShowUI.apply(this, arguments);
                SiebelJS.Log("Custom PR " + PRName + ": ShowUI method reached.");
                //implement ShowUI method here
            };
            CustomNavigationPR.prototype.BindEvents = function(){
                SiebelAppFacade.CustomNavigationPR.superclass.BindEvents.apply(this, arguments);
                SiebelJS.Log("Custom PR " + PRName + ": BindEvents method reached.");
                //implement BindEvents method here
            };
            CustomNavigationPR.prototype.BindData = function(bRefresh){
                SiebelAppFacade.CustomNavigationPR.superclass.BindData.call(this, bRefresh);
                SiebelJS.Log("Custom PR " + PRName + ": BindData method reached.");
                //implement BindData method here
            };
            //implement custom functions here
            return CustomNavigationPR;
        }());
        return "SiebelAppFacade.CustomNavigationPR";
    });
}
```

The screenshot shows the CustomNavigationPR.js file after the modifications just described. Some comments have been removed for improved readability.

The following steps describe how to register the new custom file with the NAVIGATION_TAB user interface object, which defines the presentation model and physical renderer files for tab-based navigation.

7. Log in to the Siebel Developer Web Client with an administrative user account.

8. Navigate to the Administration - Application screen, Manifest Files view.

9. In the Files list, create a new record.

10. Enter the relative path to the new file, for example:
    siebel/custom/CustomNavigationPR.js

11. Navigate to the Manifest Administration view.

12. In the UI Objects list, execute a query with the following field values:
```
Type = Navigation
Usage Type = Physical Renderer
Name = NAVIGATION_TAB
```

The NAVIGATION_TAB entry in the manifest administration tables represents the UI object for tab-based navigation elements within desktop clients. There are other elements for the *Navigation* type provided as seed data that represent, for example, the physical renderer for tree-based navigation within desktop clients or navigation renderers for mobile applications (in IP 2013 or earlier) that run on smartphones or tablets.

As of IP 2014, we will also find the new NAVIGATION_SIDE entry that represents the side-bar menu navigation. In addition, the special navigation renderers for mobile applications are deprecated in IP 2014.

---

13. If the query returns only one record that is read-only, *copy* this record to create a customizable entry. If the query returns two records, select the one that is writeable, as this is a custom record that has been previously created in your database.

14. In the Object Expression list, create a new record with the following values:

Column	Value
Expression	Desktop (use the Pick List)
Level	1

15. In the Files list, click the Add button and associate the file you registered in step 10.

16. Log out of the application.

17. Log in to the application again.

18. Open the browser's JavaScript console.

19. Verify that log messages appear in the console similar to Custom PR NavigationDetailObject_PM_CustomNavigationPR: BindData method reached.

This completes the process of creating and registering a custom extension class for the navigation renderer. Once we have verified that the custom class is loaded correctly, we can begin to implement navigation-specific customizations.

The following case study scenario shows us how to sort the text in drop-down menus for tab navigation elements.

Case Study: Sorting the Drop-down Menu for Screens and Views

When the Siebel Open UI client is displayed using a theme for tab navigation, all tabs are displayed horizontally. In case there are more tabs than can be displayed on the screen - due to the limitations of the screen or window width - a drop-down menu is automatically generated at the right of the navigation bar, allowing the user to reach the navigation items that cannot be displayed in a single row of tabs or links.

By default, this drop-down menu is not sorted alphabetically as can be seen in the following screenshot.

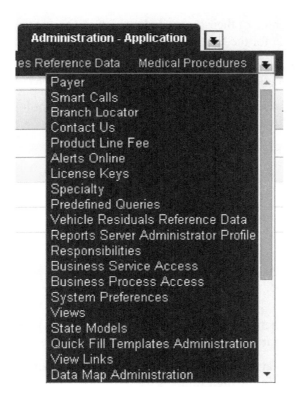

The screenshot shows the drop-down menu for second level navigation links on the Administration - Application screen. The links are sorted as per the screen view sequence defined in the Siebel repository but not alphabetically.

In the following case study scenario, we will add code to the custom extension class we created, earlier, in order to apply alphabetical sorting to the entries in screen- or view-level drop-down menus. The next procedure describes the necessary steps to implement this behaviour. As usual, a complete example file (`CustomNavigationPR.js`) is provided with this chapter's code archive.

1. Open the `CustomNavigationPR.js` file with a suitable editor.

2. Add a new line at the end of the `BindData` method and add the following code:

```
$('#j_s_vctrl_div_tabScreen option')
    .sort(NASort).appendTo('#j_s_vctrl_div_tabScreen');
$('#j_s_sctrl_tabScreen option')
    .sort(NASort).appendTo('#j_s_sctrl_tabScreen');
$('#j_s_sctrl_tabView option')
    .sort(NASort).appendTo('#j_s_sctrl_tabView');
```

The above code uses the jQuery selector function (`$`) to select the entries (`option`) in the drop-down menus generated for first, second, and third level navigation. The menus can be isolated using the value of their `id` attribute which is, for example, `j_s_sctrl_tabScreen` for the first level screen bar.

After selecting the menu options, the code calls the JavaScript `sort` method passing the name of a compare function (to be implemented in the next step).

The resulting sorted list is then appended to the respective drop-down menu using the jQuery `appendTo` method.

3. Place the cursor before the line `return CustomNavigationPR;` and add a new line.

4. Implement the compare function as follows:

```
function NASort(a, b) {
    return (a.innerHTML > b.innerHTML) ? 1 : -1;
}
```

The function implements a **JavaScript comparison function** as per the documentation of the array sort method, which can be found at `https://developer.mozilla.org/en-US/docs/Web/JavaScript/Reference/Global_Objects/Array/sort`.

A valid comparison function returns `1` if the first parameter (`a`) is higher up in the sort order than the second parameter (`b`) and returns `-1` if otherwise.

We use the `innerHTML` attribute of the elements because they are passed as HTML elements similar to the following example:

```
<option value="tabScreen10">Addresses</option>
```

The `innerHTML` attribute value for the previous example HTML `<option>` element would be 'Addresses'.

5. Save the file.

6. Empty the browser cache and reload the current page in the Siebel Open UI client.

7. If necessary, use the Behavior view in the User Preferences screen to switch to a theme that supports tab navigation.

8. Navigate to the Administration - Application screen.
9. Open the drop-down menu for the second level navigation links and verify that the menu items are sorted alphabetically.

The following screenshot shows the results of the previous custom code.

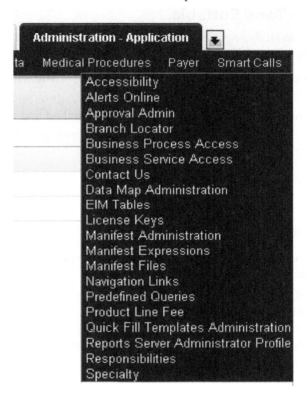

As can be seen in the screenshot, the items in the drop-down menu for the second level navigation bar of the Administration - Application screen are sorted alphabetically.

Case Study: Sortable Screen Tabs

The presence of jQuery libraries in Siebel Open UI makes it easy for developers to implement sophisticated usage scenarios. For example, end users might find it useful to arrange screen tabs with drag and drop gestures instead of having to use the as-delivered Tab Layout view on the User Preferences screen.

The implementation process can be broken down into the following high-level steps.

- Make the screen tabs sortable.
- Define temporary storage of the screen tab layout using a browser cookie.
- Implement a custom server-side business service method to store the screen tab layout permanently in the Siebel database.

- Invoke the custom business service method.

The following case study scenarios will guide us through the steps to implement this functionality.

Making Screen Tabs Sortable

In this part of the case study, we will use the jQuery sortable widget to enable sortable screen tabs. The implementation steps are as follows:

1. If necessary, open the `CustomNavigationPR.js` file with a suitable editor.
2. Add a new line at the end of the `BindData` method and add the following code:

```
//sortable screen tabs
var jqscr = $("#s_sctrl_tabScreen li").parent();
jqscr.sortable({ snap: true });
//axis: "x" could be used as well
```

The code implements the following:

- Initialize a variable `jqscr` as a jQuery object representing the DOM element that contains all screen tabs.
- Apply the jQuery UI `sortable` widget to the jQuery selection. The `snap` option enables 'snap-in' behaviour when moving the tab. The `axis` option is mentioned in the comment and would restrain the way the user is able to move the element, for example only on the horizontal (x) axis.

> More information about the jQuery UI sortable widget can be found at
> http://jqueryui.com/sortable.

With the previous lines of code, it is now possible to arrange screen tabs with drag and drop. However, the arrangement is lost every time the navigation elements are re-drawn, which happens every time a user navigates to a new view. Following an iterative approach, our case study includes test steps such as the following.

3. Save the file.
4. Empty the browser cache and reload the current page in the Siebel Open UI client.
5. If necessary, use the Behavior view in the User Preferences screen to switch to a theme that supports tab navigation.
6. Try to drag a screen tab to a different location. Observe that all screen tabs can be arranged using drag and drop.

7. Navigate to a different view and observe that the order of screen tabs reverts back to the default and your arrangement from step 6 is lost (this is expected behaviour at this point).

At this point, the screen tabs are sortable but the changes made by the user are not permanent. In the second part of this case study, we will implement temporary storage of the screen tab layout using a browser cookie.

Storing Screen Tab Layout using a Browser Cookie

In order to store the tab order temporarily, we can use a browser cookie. In the following steps, we will add code to read and verify the cookie and apply the tab order stored in the cookie to the screen tabs.

1. Return to the code editor.
2. Add the following lines of code after the code you entered in step 2 of the previous procedure.

```
var arrTabs = new Array();
var sTabText = "";
var sCookieName = "OUIBOOK_TABLAYOUT";
var sCookieValue = jQuery.cookie(sCookieName); //get cookie
var i = 0;

if (sCookieValue){ //if cookie is set
  arrTabs = sCookieValue.split(","); //create array
  for (i = 0; i < arrTabs.length ; i++){ //parse array
    $("#s_sctrl_tabScreen li").each(function( index ) {
      //for each screen tab
      sTabText = $(this).text(); //get screen tab caption
      if (sTabText == arrTabs[i]){
        //if caption matches current array item
        $(this).insertAt(i,jqscr); //insert tab
      }
    });
  }
}

jqscr.on("sortstop", function (event, ui){
//event handler when user releases tab
  $("#s_sctrl_tabScreen li").each(function( index ) {
    //get current tab array
    arrTabs[index] = $(this).text();
  });
  sCookieValue = arrTabs.toString();
  jQuery.cookie(sCookieName, sCookieValue, {expires:365});
});
```

The code accomplishes the following:

- Initialize several variables to be used later.
- Use the jQuery `cookie` method to retrieve the value of the cookie named `OUIBOOK_TABLAYOU`' and store it in the `sCookieValue` variable.
- Verify that the `sCookieValue` variable is not empty.
- Use the `split` method to populate the `arrTabs` array with the individual screen tabs stored in the cookie string.
- Implement a `for` loop to iterate through the `arrTabs` array.
  - For each currently visible screen tab, get its caption text.
  - Compare the caption text with the current array item.
  - If there is a match, call the `insertAt` extension function (see below for the implementation of this function) to insert the current tab at the index position, thus restoring the screen tab order from the sequence stored in the cookie.
- Implement the `sortstop` event handler function, which is invoked whenever a user stops the sorting process by dropping an element.
  - In the `sortstop` event handler function, read the current array of screen tabs and store it as a string in the cookie.

The previous implementation ensures that the screen tab sequence is stored in a cookie whenever the user rearranges the tabs by drag and drop. Furthermore, the sequence is restored from the cookie when the `BindData` method of the physical renderer is invoked (which happens when the user navigates to a different view).

As mentioned earlier, the restoration of the tab sequence from the cookie demands that we insert screen tabs at a certain index position. As this functionality is not fully available in jQuery, we have to write a custom jQuery extension function as follows.

3. After the `BindData` method, add the following code:

```
$.fn.insertAt = function(index, $parent) {
  return this.each(function() {
    if (index === 0) { $parent.prepend(this); }
    else { $parent.children().eq(index - 1).after(this); }
  });
}
```

> Note: The previous code is sourced from a contribution to the *stackoverflow* forum and can be found here:
> http://stackoverflow.com/questions/391314/jquery-insertat.

The jQuery extension function implements the following:

- The function takes two parameters. The first is an index number and the second is a jQuery object representing the parent container of elements to be arranged.

- When the index equals zero (`0`), the jQuery `prepend` method is used to insert the current element at the beginning of the list.
- For indexes other than zero, the child element before the current index number is selected and the current element is inserted after it.

With the previous code changes, we can test our implementation again.

4. Save the file.
5. Empty the browser cache and reload the current page in the Siebel Open UI client.
6. If necessary, use the Behavior view in the User Preferences screen to switch to a theme that supports tab navigation.
7. Arrange screen tabs using drag and drop.
8. Navigate to a different view and observe that the order of screen tabs remains unchanged due to restoration from the cookie.

A video demonstrating the arrangement of screen tabs via drag and drop in Siebel Open UI is available at `https://www.youtube.com/watch?v=uxF-bftMPjI`.

At this point the implementation ensures that the screen tab sequence is restored from a cookie. However, end users might experience functionality disruptions when the cookie is deleted or when they access the Siebel web client from a different browser or a different device. We will address this in the next part of this case study.

Creating a Business Service Method to Store the Screen Tab Layout

As mentioned earlier, end users can use the Tab Layout view in the User Preferences screen to define the order (and visibility) of screen and view tabs. Our custom physical renderer aims to replace the somewhat lengthy process of entering numbers in a table by a simple drag and drop gesture. However, we should store the screen tab sequence *permanently* in the user's tab layout so it can be retrieved by the application independent of the browser, the presence of a cookie, or the device.

In the final steps of our case study, we implement a custom server-side business service to modify the tab layout data and invoke that business service from the custom code. Using server-side business services or workflow processes to get or manipulate data residing in the Siebel database is a recommended practice. The code archive for this chapter includes a Siebel Tools archive file (`OUIBOOK Tab Layout Service.sif`), which represents the business service described in this chapter and which can be imported into a Siebel database using Siebel Tools.

1. Log in to Siebel Tools.
2. In the Object Explorer, select the Business Service object type.

3. In the Business Services list, create a new record with the following values.

Column	Value
Name	OUIBOOK Tab Layout Service
Project	Select a project from the pick list
External Use	Checked

4. Right-click the record and select Edit Server Scripts.

5. Select the Service_PreInvokeMethod event handler and enter the following code:

```
function Service_PreInvokeMethod(MethodName,Inputs,Outputs){
  try{
    switch(MethodName){
      case "SetTabLayout": SetTabLayout(Inputs, Outputs);
                           break;
      default          : break;
    }
  }
  catch(e){
    TheApplication().RaiseErrorText(e.toString());
  }
  return (CancelOperation);
}
```

The code ensures that when the name of the invoked method is SetTabLayout, the SetTabLayout function will be executed and receives the current input and output property sets as arguments. The try and catch blocks ensure that exceptions in this event handler and in the called functions are handled appropriately. The CancelOperation return code ensures that no other event handlers are invoked.

6. Save your changes.

7. Expand the (general) node in the script editor tree.

8. Select the (declarations) node.

9. Type the following line of code and press *ENTER*.

```
function SetTabLayout(Inputs, Outputs)
```

After pressing the *ENTER* key, a new node is generated in the script editor tree for the SetTabLayout function.

10. Select the SetTabLayout node.

11. Enter the following code:

```
function SetTabLayout(Inputs, Outputs){
  //tab layout must come as comma separated string like
  //"Home,Contacts,Accounts"
  var sTabs : String = Inputs.GetProperty("sTabs");
  //convert to array
  var arrTabs : Array = sTabs.split(",");
  //get BO and BC
  var oBO : BusObject = TheApplication()
  .GetBusObject("Page Tab Layout");
  var oBC : BusComp = oBO.GetBusComp("Page Tab Layout VBC");
  var tab : String = "";

  //when not repeated twice,
  //some misalignments can occur due to alphabetic sorting
  //running the loop twice ensures correctness
  //this code should only run before logoff or on button click
  //to limit performance impact
  for (var r = 0; r < 2; r++){
    //loop through array
    for(var i = 0; i < arrTabs.length; i++){
      tab = arrTabs[i]; //get current tab caption
      //prepare BC and find the tab by name
      oBC.ClearToQuery();
      oBC.ActivateField("Sequence");
      oBC.ActivateField("Caption");
      oBC.SetSearchSpec("Caption",tab);
      oBC.ExecuteQuery(ForwardOnly);
      //check record set and only alter sequence
      //if it's different
      if(oBC.FirstRecord()
      && oBC.GetFieldValue("Sequence") != i+1){
        oBC.SetFieldValue("Sequence", i);
      }
      //save
      oBC.WriteRecord();
    }
  }
}
```

The functionality implemented by the previous function is as follows:

- Read the property sTabs from the input property set and store it as a variable.

- Split the value of the sTabs variable into an array named arrTabs.

- Instantiate the Page Tab Layout business object.

- Instantiate the Page Tab Layout VBC business component.

- Implement a for loop that is executed twice. Executing the code that follows twice is necessary to ensure that the business component stores the sequence of tabs correctly.

- Iterate through the array of screen tabs.
  - o For each tab, use the tab text stored in the array item to query the business component.
  - o When the query returns a record and the sequence number is different, set the `Sequence` field to the current index.
  - o Save the record.
12. Save your work.
13. Compile the `OUIBOOK Tab Layout Service` business service.

For more information on business services and eScript in Siebel CRM, refer to the Oracle Siebel documentation or the book 'Oracle Siebel CRM 8 Developer's Handbook' by Alexander Hansal.

In Siebel CRM, each server-side business service that we wish to invoke from a browser script or other external programs has to be registered with the application by means of defining an **application user property**. The following steps illustrate this process.

14. In the Object Explorer, select the Application object type.
15. Query for the application that you are customizing, for example 'Siebel Universal Agent'.
16. In the Object Explorer, select the Application User Prop child type.
17. In the Application User Props list, locate the record starting with `ClientBusinessService` that has the highest sequence number. For example you might find `ClientBusinessService10`.
18. Create a new record and set the Name value to `ClientBusinessService` and append a number that is an increment of 1 of the number you found in the previous step. For example, name the new user property `ClientBusinessService11`.
19. Set the value of the user property to the name of the business service, for example `OUIBOOK Tab Layout Service`.
20. Compile the application object to the SRF file.

These steps complete the work in Siebel Tools to create and register a server-side business service method that is capable of modifying the tab layout data. The previous example code is provided for educational purposes and - in a real-life implementation - the code will likely differ.

Invoking the Custom Business Service Method

The final procedure of this case study describes the steps required to invoke the server-side business service method from our custom JavaScript class.

1. In the `CustomNavigationPR.js` file, locate the last line of code within the `sortstop` event handler and add a new line.

2. Add the following code:

```
var oSvc = SiebelApp.S_App
    .GetService("OUIBOOK Tab Layout Service");
var iPS = SiebelApp.S_App.NewPropertySet();
iPS.SetProperty("sTabs", arrTabs.toString());
if(oSvc){
    var config = {async:true,scope:this,selfbusy:true};
    oSvc.InvokeMethod("SetTabLayout", iPS, config);
}
```

The code does the following.

- Instantiate the `OUIBOOK Tab Layout Service` business service as the `oSvc` variable.

- Instantiate a new property set as the `iPS` variable.

- Set the `sTabs` property of the property set to the string representation of the `arrTabs` array.

- Verify that the `oSvc` object has been successfully instantiated.

- Declare the `config` variable as an object carrying the runtime information for the business service. Note the `async` property is set to `true`, which defines an asynchronous call, allowing the end user to continue working with the client while the business service method is executed on the server.

- Invoke the `SetTabLayout` method of the business service, passing the input property set and the `config` object.

The final test is accomplished as follows.

3. Save the file.

4. Empty the browser cache and reload the current page in the Siebel Open UI client.

5. Navigate to Tools > User Preferences > Tab Layout.

6. Rearrange the screen tabs using drag and drop.

7. Click anywhere in the Screen Tab Layout list applet.

8. Press *ALT+ENTER* to refresh the list.

9. Observe that the data in the list now represents the current tab layout.

Congratulations! You have completed a real-life case study during which you implemented a solution that allows end users to arrange screen tabs with simple drag and drop gestures.

What we learn from the case study is that while the initial solution might be simplistic and often contains only a few lines of code to enable the functionality on the browser side, the imperative for consistency and server-side storage of enterprise grade applications such as Siebel CRM requires that we design our solutions thoroughly from end to end.

This often involves resorting to server-side functionality in the form of custom business services such as in the example, or workflow processes.

Customizing Views

Some customization requirements in Siebel Open UI affect the behaviour of an entire view instead of individual applets. To accomplish such customizations, the Siebel Open UI API offers the possibility of creating custom extension classes for the presentation model and physical renderer for view objects.

In this section, we will learn how to create a custom physical renderer for views in the following case studies:

- Creating extension classes for views
- Displaying form applets in a floating dialog

As with the previous section, we start with a template for a custom extension class.

Case Study: Creating Extension Classes for Views

The following procedure guides us through the steps necessary to create and register a primordial physical renderer for a view using a template:

1. Copy the physical renderer template file provided with this book (ViewPRTemplate.js) and save it in the /siebel/custom folder using a convenient name, for example ParentListViewPR.js.
2. Open the new file with a suitable editor.
3. Replace all occurrences of ViewPRTemplate with the name of the new custom class, for example ParentListViewPR.
4. Ensure that the define method is implemented as follows:

```
define ("siebel/custom/ParentListViewPR", ["siebel/viewpr"],
function () {
```

If you use the template code provided with this book, no changes should be necessary. The previous code line defines the dependency of the new extension class to the as-delivered viewpr.js file, which implements the view physical renderer class.

5. Ensure that the line calling the SiebelJS.Extend method reads like this.

```
SiebelJS.Extend(ParentListViewPR, SiebelAppFacade.ViewPR);
```

This line defines the `ParentListViewPR` class as an extension class of the
`SiebelAppFacade.ViewPR` class. If you use the template provided with this book, ensure
that all other calls to `SiebelJS.Extend` are removed or commented out.

6. Save the file and compare your work with the following screenshot.

```
if(typeof(SiebelAppFacade.ParentListViewPR) === "undefined"){
    SiebelJS.Namespace("SiebelAppFacade.ParentListViewPR");
    define("siebel/custom/ParentListViewPR", ["siebel/viewpr"], function(){
        SiebelAppFacade.ParentListViewPR = (function(){
            var PM;
            var PRName = "ParentListViewPR";
            function ParentListViewPR(){
                SiebelAppFacade.ParentListViewPR.superclass.constructor.apply(this,arguments);}
            //Extend view renderer
            SiebelJS.Extend(ParentListViewPR, SiebelAppFacade.ViewPR);

            ParentListViewPR.prototype.Init = function() {
                SiebelAppFacade.ParentListViewPR.superclass.Init.apply(this,arguments);
                PM = this.GetPM();
                PRName = PM.GetName() + "_ParentListViewPR";
                SiebelJS.Log("Custom PR " + PRName + ": Init method reached.");
            };
            ParentListViewPR.prototype.Setup = function(){
                SiebelJS.Log("Custom PR " + PRName + ": Setup method reached.");
                //implement Setup method here
            };
            ParentListViewPR.prototype.SetRenderer = function(){
                SiebelJS.Log("Custom PR " + PRName + ": SetRenderer method reached.");
                //implement SetRenderer method here
            };
            ParentListViewPR.prototype.EndLife = function(){
                SiebelJS.Log("Custom PR " + PRName + ": EndLife method reached.");
                //implement EndLife method here
            };
            //implement custom functions here
            return ParentListViewPR;
        }());
        return "SiebelAppFacade.ParentListViewPR";
    });
}
```

The screenshot shows the `ParentListViewPR.js` file after the modifications described
so far. The following steps describe how to register the new custom file with a test view
in the manifest. For educational purposes we will use the as-delivered Account List View
as the test object.

7. Log in to the Siebel Developer Web Client with an administrative user
account.

8. Navigate to the Administration - Application screen, Manifest Files view.

9. In the Files list, create a new record.

10. Enter the relative path to the new file, for example:
    `siebel/custom/ParentListViewPR.js`

11. Navigate to the Manifest Administration view.

12. In the UI Objects list, create a new record with the following field values:

Column	Value
Type	View
Usage Type	Physical Renderer
Name	Account List View

13. In the Object Expression list, create a new record with the following values:

Column	Value
Expression	Desktop (use the Pick List)
Level	1

14. In the Files list, click the Add button and associate the file you registered in step 10.

15. Log out of the application.

16. Log in to the application again.

17. Open the browser's JavaScript console.

18. Verify that log messages appear in the console similar to Custom PR Account List View_ParentListViewPR: SetRenderer method reached.

This completes the process of creating and registering a custom extension class for a view renderer. In the following case study we will add code to this class to implement custom behaviour.

Case Study: Displaying Form Applets in a Floating Dialog

The fictitious requirement for this case study is that end users navigate to parent list views (views that display a list of primary records and a form below) in order to compare and inspect records. They often use the Show More functionality to extend the height of the list applet. With the form applet on the bottom of the view, end users need to scroll down, which they consider cumbersome and time-consuming.

As a possible solution, we will implement a floating form applet that end users can move across the browser window to accommodate their viewing habits. The high-level design for the solution is as follows:

- Identify the applets and their business components in the current view.

- Verify that the view contains only a single list and a single form applet and these applets use the same business component (this is the definition of a parent list view).

- If the view is a parent list view as per the previous definition, create a jQuery dialog that displays the contents of the form applet.

- Ensure that the dialog is refreshed when the end user selects a different record in the list applet.

The following procedure describes how to accomplish this task using a custom physical renderer for parent list views. A complete example file (ParentListViewPR.js) is available with this chapter's code archive.

1. If necessary, open the ParentListViewPR.js file with a suitable editor.

2. Add a new line at the end of the SetRenderer method and add the following code:

```
var oAppletMap = PM.GetAppletMap();  //get applet map
var oApplet, sAppletName, oFormAppletPM;
var sFormAppletId, detailForm;
var oControlSet, sControlName, oControl;
var sFieldValue, sElemId, elem;
var aBC = new Array(); //to store buscomp names
var i = 0; //applet counter
var lc = 0; //list applet counter
var fc = 0; //form applet counter
for (var applet in oAppletMap){
  //loop through applet map
  oApplet = oAppletMap[applet]; //get current applet object
  aBC[i] = oApplet.GetBusComp().GetName(); //store BC name
  i++; //increase applet counter
  sAppletName = oApplet.GetName(); //get applet name
  if (typeof(oApplet.GetListCol) === "function"){
    //check if current applet is a list applet
    lc++;  //increase list applet counter
  }
  else //current applet is not a list applet
  {
    fc++; //increase form applet counter
    oFormAppletPM = oApplet.GetPModel(); //get form PM
    sFormAppletId = oApplet.GetFullId();
  }
}
```

This code forms the first part of the implementation and accomplishes the following:

- Instantiate the oAppletMap variable with the object representing the applets in the current view.

- Instantiate several variables to be used later in the code.

245

- Iterate through the applet list.
    - Store the name of the business component for each applet in an array.
    - Check for the availability of the `GetListCol` function for the current applet. This is a workaround to identify a list applet as only list applets expose the `GetListCol` function.
    - Count the list and form applets separately.
    - Obtain the presentation model and element id for the form applet.

3. Continue by adding the following code:

```
if ((lc == 1 && fc == 1) && (aBC[0] == aBC[1])){
  detailForm = "<div id='detailFormDiv' align='left'"
      + "style='width:100%'>" + $("#" + sFormAppletId
      + " table.GridBack").parent().html() + "</div>";

  oDialog = $(detailForm).dialog({
    title:"More Info",
    position:[300,300],
    autoOpen:true,
    show:true,
    hide:true,
    width:'auto',
    height:'auto'
  });

  //attach to ShowSelection function
  oFormAppletPM.AttachPMBinding("ShowSelection",function(){
    if (!oDialog.dialog("isOpen")){  //if dialog is not open
      oDialog.dialog("open");        //open it
    }
    //loop through form applet controls
    //and copy values to dialog
    oControlSet = oFormAppletPM.Get("GetControls");
    for(sControlName in oControlSet){
      if( oControlSet.hasOwnProperty(sControlName) ){
        oControl = oControlSet[sControlName];
        sFieldValue = oFormAppletPM.ExecuteMethod
        ("GetFormattedFieldValue",oControl);
        sElemId = oControl.GetInputName();
        elem = $("#detailFormDiv [name=" + sElemId + "]");
        elem.val(sFieldValue); //set the value
        elem.attr("readonly","readonly");  //make it read-only
      }
    }
  });
  //finally, hide the form applet
  $("#" + sFormAppletId).hide();
}
```

```
else{ //current view is not supported
  SiebelJS.Log("Current view is not a parent list view.");
}
```

The previous code is the second part of this case study's code example and implements the following functionality:

- Verify that the view contains only one list applet and only one form applet and that both applets use the same business component.

- If this is the case, create an HTML string representing a `<div>` element that wraps the entire HTML content of the form applet. To achieve this, we create a jQuery selector using the form applet's element id and locate the `<table>` element within the applet that is associated with the `GridBack` class. At the time of writing, this part of the document object model (DOM) represents the content of a form applet but not the title or buttons.

- With the previous HTML string generated, as the selection, we apply the jQuery UI **dialog** widget providing parameters to control the title of the dialog, its initial position in the browser window, and the automatic adjustment to its content's dimensions.

> More information about the jQuery UI dialog widget can be found at
> `http://jqueryui.com/dialog`.

- Use the `AttachPMBinding` method to implement a function that is invoked every time the `ShowSelection` method is triggered (which happens when the end user changes the record selection).
- Open the dialog if it is not already open.
- Iterate through the form applet's control set.
  - Get the formatted field value of each control.
  - Get the value of the control element's name attribute.
  - Address the corresponding copy of the control in the jQuery dialog.
  - Set the value of the 'twin' control.
  - Make the 'twin' control read only.
- Hide the form applet.

Because the custom dialog will remain open unless the end user closes it manually, we should consider adding code to the physical renderer's `EndLife` method as follows.

4. Locate the `EndLife` function in the `ParentListViewPR.js` file.
5. If the `EndLife` function is not present, add it. The following example code shows the full implementation of the `EndLife` function:

```
ParentListViewPR.prototype.EndLife = function(){
  SiebelJS.Log("Custom PR " + PRName
      + ": EndLife method reached.");
  //implement EndLife method here
  if (oDialog.dialog("isOpen")){
    oDialog.dialog("close");
  }
};
```

The example code shows how to use the EndLife function of a physical renderer to add code that is executed when the object's life cycle is ended by the Open UI framework. The code simply verifies if the custom dialog is currently open and if that is the case, it closes it.

The following procedure illustrates some steps to test the custom physical renderer.

6. Save the file.

7. Empty the browser cache and reload the current page in the Siebel Open UI client.

8. Navigate to the My Accounts view.

9. Observe that the form applet content is displayed in a floating dialog box that can be easily moved across the browser window. Compare with the following screenshot.

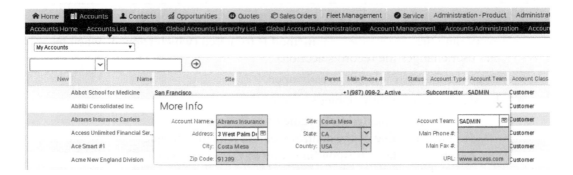

10. Select a different record in the list applet.

11. Observe that the dialog is updated with the current record.

12. Navigate to a different screen, for example the Contacts screen.

13. Observe that the dialog disappears.

Congratulations! You have successfully implemented a custom physical renderer for a view.

Summary

The Siebel Open UI JavaScript API exposes various presentation model and physical renderer classes for all aspects of the client user interface. While applets cover most of the Siebel user's interface estate, several other UI objects exist that we might want to modify to suit end user requirements.

In this chapter, we learned how to create custom physical renderer extensions for navigation elements such as screen tabs and views.

In the next chapter, we will learn how to create custom event listeners to apply customizations independent of individual UI objects.

10
Using Event Listeners

This chapter describes how to apply Open UI customizations outside of applets on a more global level. It introduces the **postload** and **preload** events, which allow for the injection of user interface customizations and logic after (post) or before (pre) a view is rendered. Creating listeners for these events is a powerful alternative to custom presentation models or physical renderers for specific user interface objects. But with power comes responsibility, so we will also discuss points to consider when using event listeners in Siebel Open UI.

The chapter is structured as follows:

- Introduction to the *postload* and *preload* event
- Case Study: Registering a custom postload event listener
- Case Study: Using a custom postload event listener
- Recommended practices and considerations

Introduction to the postload and preload Event

The previous chapters covered, in detail, how Siebel Open UI enhances the user experience by allowing for the customization of individual user interface objects such as applets, views, or screen tabs. However, a change to other UI objects or the enforcement of consistent behavior across the entire application sometimes requires other mechanisms. To address these kinds of requirements, the Open UI API offers two events:

- preload
- postload

Both events are triggered every time a new view is loaded or reloaded. The preload event is triggered after applets are rendered but before any data for applets is loaded. The postload event is triggered after the Open UI framework finishes loading all files and data, and the view is fully rendered.

As the postload event is called after the view is fully loaded, code in this event listener has access to all UI elements and can apply changes and inject logic into every element in the Document Object Model (DOM).

In a standard Siebel CRM installation, Oracle delivers simple subscribers to the postload and preload event. The files are named postload.js and preload.js and are located in the PUBLIC/<Language>/<Build>/SCRIPTS folder on the web server. These files provide very simple functionality. The code in the preload.js file prints the text Loading... and the code in the postload.js file prints Loaded on the browser's console as shown in the following screenshot.

In the screenshot, we see the output of the JavaScript functions in the as-delivered preload.js and postload.js files in the browser console.

The following listing shows the complete code found in the as-delivered postload.js file.

```
if (typeof (SiebelAppFacade.Postload) == "undefined") {
  Namespace('SiebelAppFacade.Postload');
  (function(){
    SiebelApp.EventManager.addListner("postload",OnPostload,
    this);
    function OnPostload(){
      try{
        console.log("Loaded");
      }
      catch(error){
        //No-Op
      }
    }
  }());
}
```

The script registers a new class named Postload. In the function body, the addListner (sic!) method of the EventManager class is used to specify a function (OnPostload), which will be invoked every time the Open UI framework executes the postload event. The OnPostload function contains a single line that uses the JavaScript console.log function to print the text Loaded on the browser console. The preload.js file contains similar code.

Oracle provides the postload.js and preload.js files as a template for custom postload and preload event listener functions. As previously discussed in this book, customers must not modify any standard files but create custom files. Therefore, we should consider implementing a custom postload or preload event listener function by simply copying and pasting the as-delivered code into a custom JavaScript file.

In this chapter's case studies, we will explore some real-life examples for custom postload event listener functions.

The `Siebel Application Context` class is responsible for 'firing' the preload and postload events. Using the browser developer tool to set a breakpoint on the line `SiebelApp.EventManager.fireEvent("preload");` in `applicationcontext.js` reveals the activities that have already been performed before the preload event is triggered. The following screenshot shows the Siebel Call Center application in Google Chrome paused at the breakpoint in the debugger.

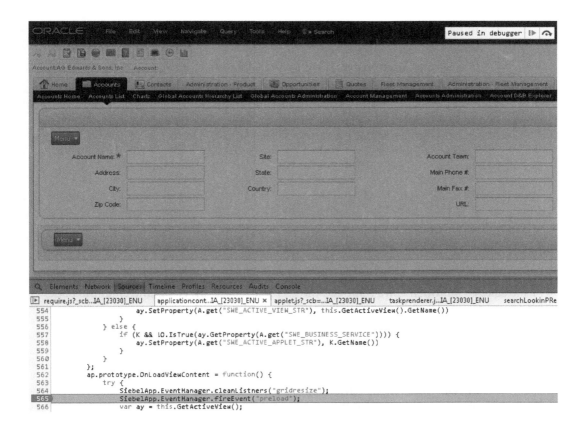

As can be seen in the screenshot, the form applet is already rendered but no data has yet been bound. A list applet header is visible but neither the body of the applet nor the content has been rendered before the preload event is fired.

Case Study: Registering a Custom postload Event Listener

Because the manipulation of as-delivered files is not supported by Oracle, developers who want to execute custom code either at the preload or postload event must implement a custom JavaScript function and register it with the event.

The following steps describe how to register a simple custom postload event listener:

1. Open the as-delivered `postload.js` file from the `/SCRIPTS` folder.

2. Copy the entire file's content to the clipboard.

3. Create a new file in the `/siebel/custom` folder and give it a meaningful name, for example `custompl.js`.

4. In the new file, replace each occurrence of `SiebelAppFacade.Postload` with `SiebelAppFacade.CustomPostload`.

5. Change the input to the `console.log` function call to `'Custom postload event listener loaded'`.

6. Compare your code with the following example:

```
if (typeof (SiebelAppFacade.CustomPostload) == "undefined"){
  Namespace('SiebelAppFacade.CustomPostload');
  (function(){
    SiebelApp.EventManager.addListner("postload",
        OnPostload, this);
    function OnPostload(){
      console.log("Custom postload event listener loaded");
    }
  }());
}
```

For the sake of simplicity, we removed the `try` and `catch` blocks in the example code. This chapter's code archive includes a complete `custompl.js` file.

7. In the Siebel Web Client, navigate to the Administration - Application screen, Manifest Files view.

8. Create a new record in the Files list.

9. Provide the file path, for example `siebel/custom/custompl.js`, obeying exact typing. Preferably, copy and paste the path.

10. Navigate to the Manifest Administration view.

11. In the UI Objects list, **query** for a record with the following values:

Column	Value
Type	Application
Usage Type	Common
Name	PLATFORM DEPENDENT

If the query returns only one record, use the Copy Record command - or press *CTRL+B* - to create a custom override of the existing seed record. Continue with step 12.

If the query returns two records, select the one which is not write protected, as this is the custom record that has been created during previous customizations. Continue with step 14.

12. If you just copied the seed record in step 11, select the new copy.

13. In the Object Expression list, create a new record with the following values:

Column	Value
Expression	Desktop (Use the pick list)
Level	1

14. In the Object Expression list, select the record that uses the *Desktop* expression.

15. In the Files list, click the Add button and select the file you registered in step 9.

16. Log off and log on again to the application.

17. Open the browser's JavaScript console.

18. Navigate to a new view and verify that the text Custom postload event listener loaded appears in the console.

In a similar manner as described in the previous procedure, we could create a preload event listener if needed.

Case Study: Using a Custom postload Event Listener

In the following case study, we will extend the simple custom postload event listener we created in the previous section with some more meaningful capabilities and discuss some challenges along the way.

The following scenarios will be covered by this case study:

- Hiding unwanted tool tips
- Forcing all applets to be collapsible
- Implementing view-specific behavior
- Displaying contextual information

The example file (`custompl.js`) provided with this chapter's code archive contains the full code presented in this case study.

Hiding Unwanted Tool Tips

End users sometimes get annoyed by the appearance of arbitrary tool tips when hovering the mouse cursor over an applet. This is due to the fact that most browsers display the `title` attribute of a `<div>` element as a tool tip. The following screenshot illustrates this behavior.

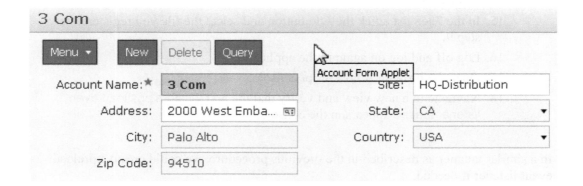

As seen in the screenshot, the browser displays the text Account Form Applet as a tool tip when hovering over the form applet. This behavior - albeit with a different text - applies to all other applets.

To eliminate these tool tips, we can use the custom postload event listener we created in the previous case study and add a single line of jQuery code that effectively removes the `title` attribute from selected `<div>` elements.

The following procedure illustrates how to accomplish this:

1. Open the custom JavaScript file that contains the custom postload event listener class.

2. Locate the `try` block in the `OnPostLoad` function.

3. Add the following code at the end of the `try` block (but within the `try` block):

```
$("[title]").not("[role=grid] td, #s_toolbar, "
    + "#s_toolbar li").removeAttr("title");
```

For an explanation of this code, refer to the information after the steps.

4. Save the file.

5. Clear the browser cache and reload the current page by pressing *F5*.

6. Navigate to an arbitrary view and verify that the tool tips on applets are no longer displayed.

The single line of code in the example uses several jQuery functions. The first (`$("[title]")`) is the jQuery core function and returns a collection object that contains all elements that have a `title` attribute.

The `not()` function of jQuery is used to remove certain elements from the current collection. In the example, we exclude the following elements:

`[role=grid] td`: refers to all table data cell elements (`<td>`) within an element that has an attribute named `role` with a value of `grid`. This represents individual data cells in list applets. The tool tip on these elements shows the value even if the column width currently prohibits the full display of longer text. We want to keep these tool tips.

`#s_toolbar` and `#s_toolbar li`: The application toolbar uses the `title` attribute to display a description for each individual toolbar button. These tooltips are very helpful and need to be included.

Finally, we use the jQuery `removeAttr()` function to actually remove all `title` attributes from the set of elements returned by the `not()` function.

More information about jQuery functions can be found in the jQuery API documentation at `http://api.jquery.com`.

It should be noted that removing attributes from the DOM can result in disruptions with regards to the user experience. For example, screen readers rely on these attributes to support impaired users in navigating the application. So we should use caution when implementing requirements like the one in the previous case study.

Forcing all Applets to be Collapsible

In the following example, we use a postload event listener to make applets collapsible. Siebel Innovation Pack 2013 introduced a new applet user property called **Default Applet Display Mode**. If this user property is set for an applet, an arrow icon is displayed on the upper right corner of the applet header allowing the user to collapse the applet.

The following screenshot shows the *Contact Form Applet* in its normal expanded state with the arrow button in the top right corner.

When the user clicks the arrow button, the applet will collapse so that only the applet header remains visible. Clicking the arrow button again will expand the applet.

The *Default Applet Display Mode* applet's user property can have one of the following values.

- **Expanded**: The applet header and content is visible by default
- **Collapsed**: Only the applet header is visible by default

The standard means of implementing the collapse/expand behavior for an applet would be to use **Siebel Tools** to add a record for the new applet user property for each individual applet - as has been done by Oracle for several standard applets.

However, if it is required to implement the behavior on a large number of applets, a developer would have to modify, compile and test probably hundreds of applets in the Siebel repository. To avoid this time-consuming configuration effort, we can use a custom postload event listener to add the user property to each applet at runtime.

The important trick is that the Open UI framework stores the value of the *Default Applet Display Mode* applet user property in a property named `defaultAppletDisplayMode` so that it is accessible by the applet's presentation model. The default physical renderer evaluates this property and injects the necessary code into the DOM. This functionality is provided by the core framework and does not require any additional configuration.

The following procedure describes how to add the `defaultAppletDisplayMode` property to every applet by adding code to a custom postload event listener function:

1. Open the custom JavaScript file that contains the custom postload event listener class.
2. Locate the `try` block in the `OnPostLoad` function.
3. Add the following code at the end of the `try` block (but within the `try` block):

```
//Making Applets Collapsible
var aApplets = SiebelApp.S_App.GetActiveView().GetAppletMap();
for (var applet in aApplets){
  var oAppletPModel = aApplets[applet].GetPModel();
  if (!oAppletPModel.Get("defaultAppletDisplayMode")) {
    oAppletPModel.SetProperty("defaultAppletDisplayMode",
        "expanded"); //or "collapsed"
    var oRenderer = oAppletPModel.GetRenderer();
    if (oRenderer &&
        typeof(oRenderer.ShowCollapseExpand) === 'function'){
          oAppletPModel.GetRenderer().ShowCollapseExpand();
    }
  }
}
```

The example code accomplishes the following:

- Retrieve an array of all applets - the 'applet map' - in the current view and iterate through it.

- For every applet, obtain a handle to its presentation model instance using the GetPModel function.

- Check whether the defaultAppletDisplayMode property is not already set. In case the property is defined via Siebel Tools, or somewhere else in Open UI, we do not want to override the existing value, which would result in multiple arrow buttons being displayed in the applet header.

- Set the defaultAppletDisplayMode property. In the previous example, we set the default state to expanded but could also use collapsed.

- Get the physical renderer for the current applet using the GetRenderer function.

- Call the ShowCollapseExpand method of the physical renderer to inject the necessary code in the DOM. Because not all applet physical renderers support this method, we have to check if the method is actually available.

  4. Save the file.

  5. Clear the browser cache and reload the current page by pressing *F5*.

  6. Navigate to an arbitrary view and verify that an arrow button is displayed on each applet header and that it can be used to collapse or expand the applet.

Implementing View-specific Behavior

A typical requirement that comes up frequently is the necessity to provide behavioral logic only for a specific view. As shown in the previous example, the Siebel Open UI API provides a method to retrieve a handle to the currently active view. By using this approach we can fulfill these requirements and implement the behavior using a custom postload event listener function. In other words, we can use the postload event listener as an alternative to the server side `Application_Navigate` event that is called every time a user navigates to a new view.

In this part of the case study, we explore a simple example that hides the Predefined Query (PDQ) dropdown list and the thread bar when a user navigates to the homepage view of the Accounts screen.

The following procedure describes the necessary steps to implement this requirement:

1. Open the custom JavaScript file that contains the custom postload event listener class.

2. Locate the `try` block in the `OnPostLoad` function.

3. Add the following code at the end of the `try` block:

```
//Hide thread bar and PDQ list for a specific view
if (SiebelApp.S_App.GetActiveView().GetName() ==
"Account Screen Homepage View"){
  $(".PDQToolbarContainer").hide();
  $("#_swethreadbar").hide();
}
else if ($(".PDQToolbarContainer").css("display") == "none"){
  $(".PDQToolbarContainer").show();
  $("#_swethreadbar").show();
}
```

The example code accomplishes the following:

- Get the current view name and compare it to `Account Screen Homepage View` (the internal name of the account homepage view).

- If the current view is the homepage view of the Accounts screen, use jQuery functions to select the elements representing the predefined query list and the thread bar and hide them.

- In case the current view is different and the thread bar is hidden - in other words we are leaving the Account Screen Homepage View - the thread bar and the predefined query container will be shown again.

4. Save the file.

5. Clear the browser cache and reload the current page by pressing *F5*.

6. Navigate to the homepage view of the Accounts screen and verify that the predefined query list and the thread bar are not displayed.

7. Navigate to any other view and verify that the predefined query list and the thread bar are visible again.

While the code presented in this case study is valid, we should consider custom physical renderers for views as a potential solution in order to avoid having too much code in postload event listeners. Refer to the "Recommended Practices and Recommendations" section of this chapter for a detailed discussion of alternatives to event listeners.

Displaying Contextual Information

Experienced Siebel CRM users might be aware of the so called **message area** in the top application banner, to the right of the menu. This area is used to display system messages such as CTI (Computer Telephony Integration) related events.

In the following example scenario, we will explore how to use a custom postload event listener to display the technical name of the current view in the message area. Likewise we can display any kind of message text or even custom HTML in that area.

1. If necessary, open the custom JavaScript file that contains the custom postload event listener class.

2. Locate the `try` block in the `OnPostLoad` function.

3. Add the following code at the end of the `try` block:

```
//Show view name in message area
if ($(".customMsg").length == 0){
  $("#MsgLayer").after($("<div>").addClass("customMsg"));
}
$(".customMsg").html("Current View: "
    + SiebelApp.S_App.GetActiveView().GetName());
```

The example code does the following:

- Verify that an element with a class named `customMsg` does not yet exist.

- Create a new `<div>` element after the message layer element (using the jQuery `after` function) and associate it with the `customMsg` class (using the jQuery `addClass` function).

- Insert a concatenated string into the new `<div>` element using the name of the currently active view.

Note: For IP 2014 or higher, implement the jQuery `after` function call like the following:

```
$(".applicationMenu").after($("<div>").addClass("customMsg"));
```

Using the `applicationMenu` class as a selector instead of the `MsgLayer` Id is necessary because the latter is no longer available in IP 2014.

4. Save the file.

5. Clear the browser cache and reload the current page by pressing *F5*.

6. Navigate to an arbitrary view and verify that the name of the view is displayed in the application message area.

The following screenshot shows the result of the customization steps.

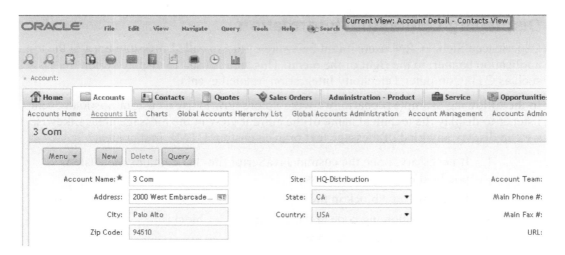

The text Current View: Account Detail - Contacts View is displayed in the application message area (see highlight box at the top right of the screenshot).

As can be seen in the previous screenshot, the text is displayed without any formatting. This can be changed by creating CSS rules for the customMsg class in a custom style sheet such as the custom-global.css file created in Chapter 8.

The following scenario guides us through the steps to enhance the appearance of the message text by adding a CSS rule set to the custom-global.css file. If you need more information on how to create and register this file, refer to Chapter 8.

1. Open the custom-global.css file using a CSS editor.
2. Add the following code to the file.

```
/* Toolbar Info */
.customMsg {
    float: left;
    position: relative;
    top: 5px;
    margin-left: 10px;
    margin-top: 7px;
    padding: 2px;
    background: lightblue;
}
```

The CSS rule implements the correct positioning, margin, and padding for the custom message element and assigns a light blue background color.

3. Save your changes.
4. Reload the browser cache and confirm that the message area is now formatted according to the new CSS rules.

This final code example completes this chapter's case study. This chapter's code archive contains an example CSS file (`custom-global.css`) with the CSS rule described earlier.

Recommended Practices and Considerations

In the previous case study we explored different usage scenarios for a custom postload event listener function. The examples were kept simple for the sake of readability and brevity. While it seems that a custom postload event listener is a great way to handle complex business requirements, it is important to consider the following aspects:

- Maintainability and support
- Interference with other Open UI configurations
- Performance

In the following sections, we will discuss these considerations and present recommended practices that enable us to make educated decisions about when to use custom postload event listener functions or other Open UI customization methods.

In a typical Siebel Open UI project, many requirements will fall into the 'generic' category, which means that they are not specific to a certain user interface object, such as an applet or a view.

If we simply implement all of these non-specific requirements in a single custom postload event listener function, we would do so at the risk of low maintainability. This is because changes to the code will always affect the entire application or at least a great portion of it.

In addition, when we fail to consider alternatives to coding, the amount of code written to implement non-specific requirements might become too high, subsequently slowing down the project.

One might as well consider the performance implications for large amounts of JavaScript code that get executed every time the user navigates to a new view.

Examples for alternatives to writing JavaScript code in a custom postload event listener are the following:

- CSS rules in a custom theme
- Global overrides
- Custom PMs and PRs for non-applet objects

In the following sections, we will use these examples to lay out some recommendations.

CSS Rules in a Custom Theme

Let us consider an end user requirement to increase the readability of list applets by using alternate row colors. In Siebel Open UI we could implement this requirement by writing JavaScript code in a custom postload event listener that iterates through the rows of the list applet and sets the background color. While this solution might sound justified, the requirement can be fulfilled much more easily by writing a CSS rule in a custom style sheet (as demonstrated in Chapter 8).

From a maintenance standpoint, the simplicity of the CSS-based solution is compelling. It follows the principle of 'Keep It Simple' and reduces the amount of code we have to write, test, debug and maintain.

Global Overrides

In previous chapters of this book, we have discussed the concept of using the Manifest Administration view to associate custom JavaScript files with a specific user interface object such as an applet or view.

In case of general - or 'global' - customizations, it would be meaningless to associate a custom JavaScript file with dozens or even hundreds of applets. Of course - as discussed in this chapter - we could use a custom postload event listener to accomplish this.

Let us consider an example where custom functionality should be added across the entire application but is only applicable to form applets. For instance, end users could express the need to rearrange or resize controls on a form applet by double-clicking on the applet.

Again, there are many roads which lead to Rome. One possible solution would be to implement a custom postload event listener, but we would have to take care of additional logic to apply the desired behavior only to form applets. In addition, we would violate the principle of separating the user interface from the application logic that is implemented in Siebel Open UI in the form of presentation models and physical renderers.

The alternative to a custom postload event listener in this case would be to create custom **Default Form Applet** entries in the manifest administration view and associate one or more custom presentation models and one or more separate custom physical renderers with all form applets at once by using this 'default' entry.

This technique is also known as **global override** and while it comes with the risk of rendering all form applets unusable in the case of erroneous code, it is a welcome alternative to the somewhat bulky postload event listener.

The default entries in the manifest administration view have been explained in previous chapters of this book.

Custom PMs and PRs for Non-applet Objects

Another alternative to ending up with a huge amount of code in a custom postload event listener is to consider the possibility of writing custom presentation models and physical renderers not only for applets but also for user interface objects such as views or screen bars.

For example, we could implement the 'View-specific Behavior' example presented in the previous case study using a custom physical renderer for views. While the approach described in this chapter is perfectly viable, a view PR is a more elegant solution. Following the general procedure of creating a View PR - as explained in Chapter 9 - we could create a `SimplifiedViewPR.js` file in the `siebel/custom` folder, adding the following code and registering the file as a view PR for the view Account Screen Homepage View.

```javascript
if(typeof(SiebelAppFacade.SimplifiedViewPR) === "undefined"){
  SiebelJS.Namespace('SiebelAppFacade.SimplifiedViewPR');
  define( "siebel/custom/SimplifiedViewPR", ["siebel/viewpr"],
  function(){
    SiebelAppFacade.SimplifiedViewPR = (function(){
      function SimplifiedViewPR(){
        SiebelAppFacade.ViewPR.superclass.constructor
            .apply(this, arguments);
      }
      SiebelJS.Extend(SimplifiedViewPR,
          SiebelAppFacade.ViewPR);
      SimplifiedViewPR.prototype.Init = function(){
        SiebelAppFacade.ViewPR.superclass.Init
            .apply(this,arguments);
        $(".PDQToolbarContainer").hide();
        $("#_swethreadbar").hide();
      }
      SimplifiedViewPR.prototype.Setup = function(){};
      SimplifiedViewPR.prototype.SetRenderer = function(){};
      SimplifiedViewPR.prototype.EndLife = function(){
        $(".PDQToolbarContainer").show();
        $("#_swethreadbar").show();
      };
      return SimplifiedViewPR;
    }());
    return SiebelAppFacade.SimplifiedViewPR;
  });
}
```

The example code implements the following:

- Register a custom physical renderer extension class named `SimplifiedViewPR`.

- Extend the as-delivered `ViewPR` class.

- In the `Init` method, use the jQuery `hide` function to hide the Predefined Query drop-down list and the threadbar.

- In the `EndLife` method, show the hidden elements.

265

This chapter's code archive includes an example file (`SimplifiedViewPR.js`) with the complete code. Please refer to Chapter 9 for a more detailed description on how to implement and register custom extension classes for non-applet objects.

Summary

The *postload* and *preload* events are powerful tools to apply globally available customizations in Siebel Open UI. When used with care, they allow us to address specific requirements with minimal effort. However, they have to be used carefully as global changes often have unwanted side effects.

In this chapter's case studies, we provided simple but effective scenarios for a custom postload event listener and also discussed the alternatives that the Open UI framework provides.

In the next chapter, we will explore special visualization techniques.

11

Special Visualizations

The Siebel Open UI JavaScript API provides a lot of opportunities for developers to implement end user requirements. Sometimes, these requirements are quite complex and can result in similarly complex code - with all the problems caused by having to maintain large amounts of code. It is therefore advisable to resort to out-of-the-box functionality such as **Tile (Card) Layout** or other specialized renderers provided by Oracle. In addition, the world-wide JavaScript community produces a rich and colorful collection of libraries, most of which are open-source.

By understanding and mastering preconfigured functionality as well as some open-source or commercial JavaScript libraries, we can get the most out of Siebel Open UI and provide a rich user experience. In this chapter, we provide real-life case studies on the following topics:

- Enabling and customizing tile layout
- Providing business data in popup dialogs
- Defining custom transitions
- Visualizing data with third party JavaScript libraries
- Creating custom visualizations
- Achieving custom layout with Nested

Each case study is accompanied by detailed explanations and full example code files that are available with this chapter's code archive.

Case Study: Enabling and Customizing Tile Layout

In this book we have already introduced and discussed the as-delivered **Tile Layout** (renamed **Card Layout** in IP 2014) on several occasions. As a matter of fact, we can enable Tile Layout for any list applet. The Siebel Open UI framework provides developers with pre-built web templates as well as options to customize the control buttons that the end user can use to toggle between visualization modes.

First, we will learn how to enable Tile Layout for a list applet and then move on to customizing it.

Enabling Tile Layout

For demonstration purposes, we will enable Tile Layout for the list applet that displays service requests for a given account. The applet is named *Service Request List Applet (Account)*.

The high-level process of enabling Tile Layout is as follows:

- Add the Applet Tile web template to the applet.
- Administer the manifest.

The following procedure describes how to add the Applet Tile web template to the Service Request List Applet (Account) applet.

1. Log in to Siebel Tools.
2. Locate the applet named Service Request List Applet (Account).
3. Check out the applet.
4. Navigate to the list of Applet Web Templates.
5. In the Applet Web Templates list, create a new record with the following values.

Column	Value
Name	Edit Tile Custom
Sequence	1001
Type	Edit List
Web Template	Applet Tile

Note that the sequence number must be 1000 or higher for special visualization modes because the as-delivered renderer will only generate toggle buttons for applet modes that meet this criterion.

6. Right-click the new applet web template record and select Edit Web Layout.
7. Drag the following list columns (in the sequence indicated) from the Controls/Columns window to the placeholders on the web layout, as indicated in the following table.

List Column	Placeholder
SR Number	First placeholder in topmost group
Priority	First placeholder in first bulleted group
Status	Second placeholder in first bulleted group
Abstract	Third placeholder in first bulleted group
Owner	First placeholder in second bulleted group

The Applet Tile template has four groups of placeholders:

1. The topmost group defines the content of the tile's title bar.

2. The second group (first bulleted) defines content to be displayed on the left side of the tile.

3. The third group is reserved for image fields.

4. The fourth group (second bulleted) defines content to be displayed on the right side of the tile, below the images.

8. Compare your work with the next screenshot.

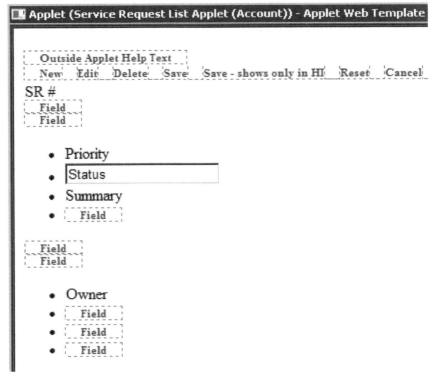

9. Save your changes.

10. Compile the applet.

The next procedure guides us through the steps necessary for administering the manifest information for the Tile Layout.

1. If necessary, log in to the Siebel Web Client using an administrator account.

2. Navigate to the Administration - Application screen, Manifest Administration view.

3. In the UI Objects list, create a new record with the following values.

Column	Value
Type	Applet
Usage Type	Web Template
Name	Service Request List Applet (Account)

4. In the Object Expression list, create a new record with the following values.

Column	Value
Expression	Grid (use the pick list)
Level	1
Web Template Name	Edit List

5. Create another record with the following values.

Column	Value
Expression	Tile (use the pick list)
Level	2
Web Template Name	Edit Tile Custom

Note that the name of the web template must match the value of the Name column in the applet web template list in the Siebel Repository exactly.

6. In the UI Objects list, copy the current record.

7. In the new copy, set the Usage Type field to `Physical Renderer`.

8. In the Object Expression list, create a new record with the following values.

Column	Value
Expression	`Grid` (use the pick list)
Level	`1`

9. In the Files list, click the Add button and select the `siebel/jqgridrenderer.js` file.

10. In the Object Expression list, create a second record with the following values.

Column	Value
Expression	`Tile` (use the pick list)
Level	`2`

11. In the Files list, click the Add button and select one of the following files depending on your Siebel version:
    o   For IP 2013, add the `siebel/Tilescrollcontainer.js` file.
    o   For IP 2014, add the `siebel/TileLayoutPR.js` file.

12. Log out of the application and log back in.

13. Navigate to the Accounts screen, Service Requests view.

14. Locate an account record with two or more service request records (alternatively, use the list applet to create test service request records).

15. Confirm that the Service Requests list applet now has two new buttons that allow for toggling between 'Grid' and 'Tile' modes.

16. Click the Tile (Card in IP 2014) button and confirm that the service request records are displayed as tiles.

17. Compare your work with the following screenshot.

The screenshot shows the `Service Request List Applet (Account)` applet in tile mode as it would appear in IP 2013 (the layout of IP 2014 is slightly different). We can see that a placeholder icon for images is displayed. We will take care of the placeholder icon and the style of the tiles in the next part of this case study.

18. Select one of the tiles and edit some fields. Verify that the tile layout allows for record editing.

19. Drill down on one of the service request numbers on the tile headers to verify that drilldown functionality is preserved.

20. Use the browser back button to navigate back to the Account Service Requests view.

In this part of the case study we learned how to enable the Tile Layout for a list applet. In the next part we will learn how to apply customizations to the Tile Layout.

Customizing Tile Layout

In this part of the case study we will learn how to create a custom physical renderer extension for the out-of-the-box class that implements Tile or Card Layout. As of IP 2013, this class is the `Tilescrollcontainer` class. In IP 2014, the class to extend is `TileLayoutPR`. The latter is an extension of the former, and both serve to implement the as-delivered tile renderer. Before we start, let us have a look at some example requirements.

- The font size of the tile header text should be increased.

- The background colour of each tile should change dynamically based on the priority of the service request.

- Instead of the default contact icon, the service request priority (1 to 4) should be displayed as a big number.

- The misalignment of the pick icon should be fixed.

A (fictitious) friend of ours works as a business analyst in the project and has created the following mock-up as a guideline.

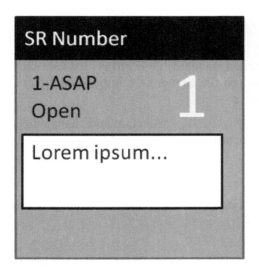 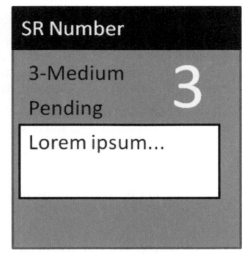

The previous diagram shows the mock-up design for the custom service request tiles. The most prominent features are the conditional background color as well as the 'number icon' in the top right corner representing the priority of the service request.

The following procedure guides us through the steps to create a custom physical renderer extension for the as-delivered class. As usual, we will start with a template file. This chapter's code archive includes a complete example file (SRScrollPR.js).

1. Using a suitable JavaScript editor, open the file that contains the physical renderer template delivered with this chapter's code archive (PRTemplate.js).

2. Use the editor's Save As... functionality to save the file under a new name to the /siebel/custom folder of the Siebel Developer Web Client. For example, use SRScrollPR.js as the file name.

3. In the new file, replace all occurrences of PRTemplate with SRScrollPR (the same string you used as the file name, without the .js extension).

4. Locate the line that calls the define function and change the code depending on your Siebel version as follows:

   o For IP 2013, ensure that the define function is implemented as follows:
      ```
      define("siebel/custom/SRScrollPR",
      ["siebel/Tilescrollcontainer"], function(){
      ```
      Note that in IP 2013, we define the dependency to the Tilescrollcontainer.js file.

   o For IP 2014, the define function must look like this:
      ```
      define("siebel/custom/SRScrollPR", ["siebel/
      TileLayoutPR"], function(){
      ```

> Note that in IP 2014, the `TileLayoutPR.js` file replaces the
> `Tilescrollcontainer.js` file.

The previous line of code ensures that the correct standard file is always loaded before
the `SRScrollPR.js` file is executed. The standard file contains the implementation of the
class that supports the out-of-the-box tile layout.

5. Locate the line that calls the `SiebelJS.Extend` function and change the
   line to look like the following, depending on your Siebel version:
   - For IP 2013, extend the `Tilescrollcontainer` class as follows:
     ```
     SiebelJS.Extend(SRScrollPR,
     SiebelAppFacade.Tilescrollcontainer);
     ```
   - For IP 2014, we must extend the `TileLayoutPR` class:
     ```
     SiebelJS.Extend(SRScrollPR, SiebelAppFacade.
     TileLayoutPR);
     ```

The previous line of code defines our new class as an extension of the standard class that
implements the physical renderer for a tile layout. Again, there are differences between
IP 2013 and 2014.

6. Save the file.
7. Log in to the Siebel Developer Web Client with an administrative user
   account.
8. Navigate to the Administration - Application screen, Manifest Files view.
9. In the Files list, create a new record.
10. Enter the relative path to the new file, for example:
    `siebel/custom/SRScrollPR.js`.
11. Navigate to the Manifest Administration view.
12. In the UI Objects list, query for the Physical Renderer type record for the
    `Service Request List Applet (Account)` applet (this entry has been
    created in the first part of this case study).
13. If your Siebel version is IP 2013, follow the steps below:
    - In the Object Expression list, delete the record with the `Tile`
      expression.
    - Create a new record in the Object Expression list with the
      following values.

Column	Value
Expression	`Tile` (use the Pick List)
Level	`2`

Note: In IP 2013, it is necessary to delete and re-create the expression record because at the time of writing it is not possible to modify records in the Files list that represent seed data.

14. If your Siebel version is IP 2014, select the record with the `Tile` expression.

15. In the Files list, click the Add button and associate the file you registered in step 10.

16. Log out of the application and log in again.

17. Navigate to the Accounts screen, Service Requests view.

18. Locate an account record that has at least two service requests associated.

19. In the Service Requests applet, click the Tile or Card button to switch to tile layout if necessary.

20. Verify that the service request records are displayed as tiles (without any customization so far).

21. Open the browser's JavaScript console.

22. Verify that messages appear in the console, similar to the following.

```
Custom PR Service Request List Applet (Account)_SRScrollPR:
Init method reached.
```

The previous procedure completes the initial setup of our new physical renderer extension class (`SRScrollPR`). Now we can start implementing the requirements. In the solution presented in the following case study we will use custom style sheets and JavaScript together.

The following requirements will be implemented with a custom style sheet:

- Fix the location of the pick icon.
- Remove the contact placeholder image.
- Set the background color of the tile container.
- Increase the font size of the tile header text.
- Create a custom class for the 'priority icon'.

To implement the style sheet changes, we decide to use the `custom-global.css` file, which has been introduced in Chapter 8. An example copy of this file is provided with this chapter's code archive.

The following CSS rules must be added to the custom style sheet.

```css
/* Custom class for SR priority 'icon' in tile layout */
.oui-sr-priority{
    font-family: fantasy;
    font-size: 32pt;
    font-weight: bold;
```

```
        color: rgba(255, 255, 255, 0.5);
        margin-left: 40px;
}

/*fix pick icon for tiles */
.siebui-tile .applet-form-pick{
        padding-left: 30px!important;
}

/* remove placeholder image*/
.siebui-tile-image,
.siebui-tile-container .siebui-tile .siebui-tile-image{
        background: transparent;
}

.siebui-tile-container .siebui-tile .siebui-tile-image::before
{
        content: "";
}

/*set tile container background*/
.siebui-tile-container{
        background: gainsboro;
}

/*move row2*/
.siebui-tile-details-row2{
        right: 100px;
}

/*tile header*/
.siebui-tile-name{
        font-size: 1.3em;
        font-weight: bold;
}
```

Some of these example CSS rules override standard classes, which will affect the look and feel of all tiles. If you have already registered the custom-global.css file (as described in Chapter 8), you can test the changes in the Siebel client. If you need more information on registering custom style sheets, refer to Chapter 8.

To test our new style rules we navigate to the Accounts screen, Service Requests view. After clearing and reloading the browser cache, we should be able to verify that the tile layout has changed according to the CSS rules in the custom-global.css file.

Compare your work with the following screenshot.

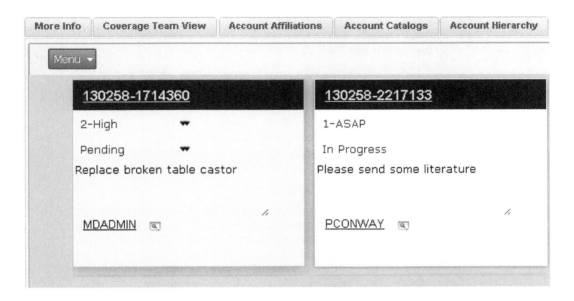

As we can see from the previous screenshot, the header text is larger. In addition, the tile container background is now a slate gray and the pick icon position no longer overlaps with the service request owner name. The default contact image placeholder is no longer visible.

In the next section of this case study, we will implement the necessary JavaScript code in the BindData method of our custom physical renderer extension. The BindData method is the perfect place for code that works with the current data set as the applet is in a fully rendered state when the BindData method of the parent class has executed. In addition, the Open UI framework will call the BindData method when the end user scrolls through the records. This ensures that the custom logic will be applied when the record set of the applet changes.

The following procedure describes the necessary code changes in the SRScrollPR.js file. As mentioned above, a complete example file is available with this chapter's code archive.

1. Open the SRScrollPR.js file.
2. Implement the BindData method as follows.

```
SRScrollPR.prototype.BindData = function(bRefresh){
    SiebelAppFacade.SRScrollPR.superclass.BindData.call(this,
        bRefresh);
    SiebelJS.Log("Custom PR " + PRName
        + ": BindData method reached.");
    var sPriority = "4";
    var sStatus = "Closed";
    //conditional tile background color collection
    //(should be externalized to CSS)
    var oColors = {
```

```
        "1":"coral",
        "2":"sandybrown",
        "3":"lightseagreen",
        "4":"lightgrey"};
    var oRecordSet = PM.Get("GetRecordSet");
    var currentTile;
    var n = 0;
    for (var i = 0; i < oRecordSet.length; i++){
        //get first character of priority
        sPriority = oRecordSet[i].Priority.substring(0,1);
        sStatus = oRecordSet[i].Status; //get SR status
        n = i + 1;
        if (sStatus != "Closed"){
            //get current tile as nth child of tile container
            currentTile = $(".siebui-tile-list"
                + ".siebui-tile:nth-child(" + n + ")");
            //set bg color according to priority
            currentTile.css("background",oColors[sPriority]);
            //set text for 'priority icon'
            currentTile.find(".siebui-tile-image").html(
                "<div class='oui-sr-priority'>" + sPriority
                + "</div>");
        }
        else{//do nothing
        }
    }
};
```

The code accomplishes the following:

- Call the BindData method of the super class to ensure that the applet is completely rendered.

- Declare and initialize the following variables:

    - sPriority: a string representing the priority of a service request. The code assumes that the list of values for the Priority field uses strings like 1-ASAP or 2-High. These strings all start with a single-digit number. The sPriority variable will carry the first character (1, 2 and so forth) of the priority value.

    - sStatus: the status of the service request.

    - oColors: an object which maps color codes to each priority. For example, the color associated with priority 1 is coral in the code example.

    - oRecordSet: an array representing the current record set for the list applet. The value of this variable is obtained by getting the value of the GetRecordSet property from the presentation model instance.

    - currentTile: will be initialized later as a jQuery collection representing the tile for the current record in a loop.

- o `n`: a counter to determine the correct tile for an individual record.
- The code implements a `for` loop to iterate through the record set. For each record we do the following:
  - o Get the value of the `Priority` field and extract the first character using the substring function.
  - o Get the value of the `Status` field.
  - o Calculate the `n` variable as the current index plus one.
  - o Determine whether the status of the current record is not `Closed`.
  - o Select the tile representing the current record using the `nth-child` selector. The argument passed to the selector is the variable `n`, so, for example, for the second record (index 1) in the record set we select the second tile (n is calculated as index plus 1, which is 2 in this example). More information about the `nth-child` selector can be found at `http://api.jquery.com/nth-child-selector`.
  - o Set the background color of the current tile using the jQuery `css` function. The value of the background attribute is chosen from the `oColors` object, so the color will vary according to the priority value.
  - o Insert a `<div>` element into the tile image placeholder. The new element has the class `oui-sr-priority` and contains the current priority value (`1`, `2` and so forth) as text.

3. Save the changes.

4. In the Siebel web client, clear the browser cache and reload the page.

5. In the Service Requests applet, click the Tile button to switch to tile layout if necessary.

6. Verify that the tile background color and the 'priority icon' are applied dynamically.

7. Compare your work with the following screenshot.

The screenshot shows the result of the previous case study. The background color for each tile is set according to the priority, and the priority number is displayed in the upper right corner.

As mentioned earlier, the example code in this case study assumes that the list of values for the Priority field includes display values that start with a single digit. To successfully test the code, you must either use the Siebel sample database (which contains a list of values entries) or add entries like the ones shown in the screenshot to the SR_PRIORITY type in the List of Values administration view.

In the previous case study, we demonstrated that the as-delivered Tile Layout option can be easily applied to any list applet and is, like many other parts of the Siebel Open UI framework, highly customizable.

Case Study: Providing Business Data in Popup Dialogs

End users of enterprise information systems such as Siebel CRM often require access to customer or other data 'on demand', which means that on some occasions additional information is required but is not displayed by the application until the user requests it.

In the next case study we will learn how to implement the following hypothetical requirement:

"When working with opportunities, end users often need ad-hoc information about the account such as the main address (ideally displayed on a map), location, and a link to the corporate home page. This additional information should be accessible from the opportunity form applet by clicking on the account field label."

The Siebel architect analyzed the above requirement and jotted down the following high level solution:

- Implement a click event handler on the account field label in the physical renderer.
- Invoke a workflow process to get data that is not currently available. According to the Open UI architecture, this 'logical' aspect shall be implemented in the presentation model.
- Display the account data and map in a popup dialog in the physical renderer.

The architect pointed out that there is already a custom presentation model and physical renderer for the opportunity form applet (as implemented in Chapter 7) that can be extended to accommodate the requirements.

The following case study scenarios will guide us through the implementation. Complete example code files (OpptyFormPM.js and OpptyFormPR.js) are provided with this chapter's code archive.

Implementing a Click Event Handler

As per the previous requirement, we must capture a click (or 'tap') event on the label for the Account field in the opportunity form applet. While this can be simply accomplished with a few lines of JavaScript code, we must also obey the rules of the Siebel Open UI framework and forward the request to the applet's presentation model.

In the following scenario, we will learn how to implement a click event handler by adding code to a custom presentation model and physical renderer extension.

1. Open the OpptyFormPM.js file with a suitable editor. Note that this file has been created in Chapter 6 and already implements the support logic for the jQuery progressbar widget for the Opportunity Form Applet - Child applet.

2. Add the following code to the Init method of the presentation model:

```
//Account Info Dialog
this.AddProperty("C_AccountData","");
this.AddMethod("GetAccountData",GetAccountData,
    {sequence:false, override:false, scope:this});
this.AttachEventHandler("GET_ACCT_DATA","GetAccountData");
```

The example code implements the following:

- Add a property named C_AccountData to the presentation model and assign an empty string as the default value. We will use this property to hold account data retrieved from the server.

- Register a custom method named GetAccountData (to be implemented later).

- Use the AttachEventHandler method to attach the custom GetAccountData function to a custom event named GET_ACCT_DATA. Whenever this event is called from the physical renderer, the GetAccountData function will be executed.

3. Create a placeholder for the custom GetAccountData function before the return OpptyFormPM; clause as follows:

```
function GetAccountData(){
    //implement custom function here
}
```

Note: We will implement the custom function in the next case study.

4. Save your changes.

5. Open the OpptyFormPR.js file. This file has been created in Chapter 7 and already implements the jQuery progressbar widget functionality on the Opportunity Form Applet - Child applet.

6. Add the following code to the ShowUI method:

```
//Account Info Popup Dialog
var accControl = oControlSet["Account2"];
var sAccountName = "";
var accLabel = $("#Account2_Label");
var mapURL =
http://maps.google.com/maps? "
    + "z=14&ie=UTF8&hl=en&output=embed&q=";
var sDialogHTML = "";
accLabel.addClass("oui-infoButton");
accLabel.click(function(e){
  PM.OnControlEvent("GET_ACCT_DATA");
  //implement popup dialog here
});
```

The code example implements the following:

- The `accControl` variable is assigned the applet control instance of the `Account` control (using the repository name `Account2`). The `oControlSet` object has already been instantiated during the `progressbar` implementation similar to the following code line.
  ```
  var oControlSet = this.GetPM().Get("GetControls");
  ```
- The `sAccountName` variable will hold the name of the account.
- The `accLabel` variable is instantiated as a jQuery selection addressing any element with an `id` value of `Account2_Label`. Note that labels, in the form of applets, use the control name suffixed with `_Label`. As usual, we can find this information by inspecting the HTML elements with the browser's developer tool.
- the `mapURL` variable is initialized with the static parts of a Google Maps URL. The parameters passed in the URL are as follows.
    - `z`: The default zoom factor is set to `14`.
    - `ie`: the character encoding is set to `UTF8`.
    - `hl`: the language is set to `en` (English).
    - `output`: this parameter must be present and set to `embed` when we wish to embed the Google Maps user interface in an iFrame.
    - `q`: the query string. Here we will append the account address later in the code.

Note that we use Google Maps for educational purposes. If your Siebel CRM implementation uses Google Maps or other commercial map providers, you must contact the provider regarding the licensing strategy.

- The `sDialogHTML` variable will carry the custom HTML for the popup dialog.
- Use the `addClass` jQuery function to assign a custom class named `oui-infoButton` to the account label. This allows us to apply CSS rules in a

custom style sheet.

Use the jQuery `click` method to attach a click event handler to the account label. The function receives an event object (`e`) which contains the current state of the user interface such as the click position on the x and y axis.

- Use the presentation model's `OnControlEvent` method to broadcast the `GET_ACCT_DATA` event. Recall that this event is registered with a function in the presentation model code.

The comment indicates that we will have to add more code. We will discuss this in the part of this case study titled "Displaying Account Data in a Popup Dialog".

Implementing a Workflow Process to Retrieve Account Data

As indicated earlier, we need to display the account address on a map along with other account data fields. This data is not available in the context of the opportunity form applet. It would be a viable solution to include these fields in the form applet, but the requirement is to display account data only when the end user deliberately clicks on the account label.

Our imaginary architect decides to implement the process of collecting account data for a given opportunity record with **Siebel Workflow**. He concludes that we must implement one workflow process to collect fields from the `Account` business component and use it as a sub-process in another workflow process that passes the account's `ROW_ID` to the sub-process.

The following scenario guides us through the steps of creating these workflow processes in Siebel Tools. This chapter's code archive provides you with a Siebel Tools archive file (`OUIBOOK Workflows.sif`) with the complete definition of the workflow processes created in this case study.

1. Log in to Siebel Tools
2. If necessary, check out a project.
3. Create a new workflow process definition with the following values:

Column	Value
Name	OUIBOOK Get Oppty Account Sub WF
Business Object	Account

4. Open the new workflow process in the editor.
5. Arrange a *Start* step, a *Business Service* step and an *End* step in the canvas and connect them. Change the names of the steps according to the screenshot below.

The screenshot shows the three steps connected. The names of the steps have been set to Start (default), Get Fields (business service) and End.

6. Save your work.
7. Click the canvas to select the workflow process.
8. In the Multi Value Property Window, select the Process Properties tab.
9. Create three properties with the following names:
   o D_FullAddress
   o D_Location
   o D_URL

By default, the properties will be of type In/Out and the data type will be String, which is suitable for our project.

10. Select the business service step.
11. Right-click the business service step and select View Properties Window.
12. In the Properties window, make the following settings:

Property	Value
Business Service Name	Workflow Utilities
Business Service Method	Echo

13. In the Multi Value Property Window, select the Output Arguments tab.
14. Create three records according to the following list:

Property Name	Type	Business Component Name	Business Component Field
D_Location	Business Component	Account	Location
D_URL	Business Component	Account	Home Page
D_FullAddress	Business Component	Account	Full Address

The Echo method of the Workflow Utilities business service is used in the previous example to assign field values of the current account record to workflow process properties. The account record will be identified by the `Object Id` property, which will be populated by calling the 'master' workflow process.

15. Save your work.

16. Simulate the workflow process with a valid account `ROW_ID` to ensure that it works as expected and the three properties are populated with the values of the test account record.

17. When the workflow process is successfully tested, publish and activate it using the Publish/Activate button in the toolbar.

18. Create a second workflow process for the **Opportunity** business object and name it `OUIBOOK Get Oppty Account Master WF`.

19. In the editor, arrange the workflow steps according to the following screenshot.

As indicated in the screenshot, we use a **Sub Process** step after the Start step and name it Get Account Data.

20. Create three process properties with the following names:
    o D_FullAddress
    o D_Location
    o D_URL

21. Select the sub process step.

22. Set the `Subprocess Name` **property** to `OUIBOOK Get Oppty Account Sub WF` (the name of the first workflow process).

23. In the Multi Value Property Window, select the Input Arguments tab.

24. Create a new record with the following values:

Column	Value
Subprocess Input	Object Id
Type	Business Component
Business Component Name	Opportunity
Business Component Field	Account Id

25. In the Output Arguments tab, create three records according to the table below.

Property Name	Type	Subprocess_Output
D_Location	Output Argument	D_Location
D_URL	Output Argument	D_URL
D_FullAddress	Output Argument	D_FullAddress

These settings for the subprocess step pass the account's ROW_ID to the OUIBOOK Get Oppty Account Sub WF workflow process and collect the output properties from the subprocess into the master workflow's property set.

26. Save your work.
27. Simulate the workflow process with a valid ROW_ID of a test opportunity to ensure that it works as expected and the three properties are populated with the values of the account associated with the opportunity.
28. Once the workflow process is tested, publish and activate it.

Because we will need to invoke the **Workflow Process Manager** business service in order to run the master workflow process and its sub process created in the above procedure, it is important to verify that the *Workflow Process Manager* business service is registered with our application. To do so, we open the respective application definition in Siebel Tools (for example Siebel Universal Agent) and navigate to the Application User Props list for the application. In the list of application user properties, we should find an entry similar to the following screenshot.

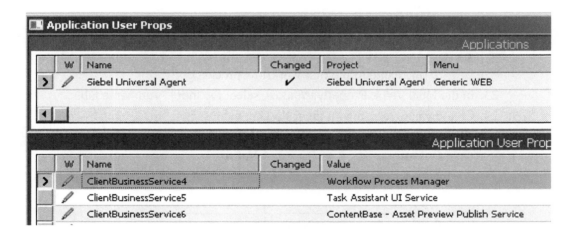

The highlighted record in the screenshot is the out-of-the-box ClientBusinessService4 user property that makes the Workflow Process Manager business service available for external calls such as from browser JavaScript with the Siebel Universal Agent application.

In the unlikely case of the Workflow Process Manager business service not being already registered, we would have to create a new application user property entry - obeying the exact sequencing of the ClientBusinessServiceN user property - and compile the application definition.

We have now created the necessary server-side structures to retrieve account data for a given opportunity ROW_ID. The next step is to modify the presentation model code so that the master workflow process is invoked when a user requests account data via the click on the account label.

The following procedure guides us through this implementation.

1. Open the OpptyFormPM.js file.

2. Locate the GetAccountData function that you created in an earlier step.

3. Implement the GetAccountData function as follows:

```
function GetAccountData(){
  var oRaw = this.Get("GetRawRecordSet");
  var opptyId = oRaw[0].Id;
  var oAccountData = {};
  var oSvc = SiebelApp.S_App.GetService(
      "Workflow Process Manager");
  var inPS = SiebelApp.S_App.NewPropertySet();
  inPS.SetProperty("ProcessName",
      "OUIBOOK Get Oppty Account Master WF");
  inPS.SetProperty("RowId",opptyId);
  var outPS = oSvc.InvokeMethod("RunProcess", inPS);
  //retrieve data from outPS
  oAccountData.URL = outPS.GetChild(0).GetProperty("D_URL");
  oAccountData.FullAddress =
      outPS.GetChild(0).GetProperty("D_FullAddress");
  oAccountData.Location =
      outPS.GetChild(0).GetProperty("D_Location");
  this.SetProperty("C_AccountData",oAccountData);
}
```

The code accomplishes the following:

- Get the raw record set (containing the Id field).

- Get the opportunity ROW_ID value from the Id field.

- Initialize the oAccountData object, which we will use later to hold the account data.

- Create the oSvc variable as an instance of the Workflow Process Manager business service.

- Create the inPS variable for the input property set.

- Set the ProcessName input property set to OUIBOOK Get Oppty Account Master WF (the name of the master workflow process created earlier).

- Set the `RowId` input property to the opportunity's `ROW_ID` value. `RowId` is the internal name of the `Object Id` process property.

- Invoke the `RunProcess` method of the Workflow Process Manager business service, passing the input property set. Because we do not specify a configuration object, the default synchronous execution mode will be used.

- Retrieve the three data field values from the output property set and store them in the account data object.

- Set the `C_AccountData` property to the account data object.

  4. Save your changes

As a result of the previous example code, the `C_AccountData` property of the presentation model carries the account information. We can now use this property in the physical renderer.

Displaying Account Data in a Popup Dialog

In the final part of this case study, we will complete the physical renderer code. The instructions below guide us through the implementation process.

  1. Open the `OpptyFormPR.js` file.
  2. Locate the `accLabel.click` function in the `ShowUI` method block.
  3. Implement the function as follows:

```
accLabel.click(function(e){
  PM.OnControlEvent("GET_ACCT_DATA");
  var oAccountData = PM.Get("C_AccountData");
  sAccountName = PM.ExecuteMethod("GetFieldValue",accControl);
  mapURL += oAccountData.FullAddress;
  sDialogHTML = "<div id='AccountInfo' class='oui-acc-info'>";
  sDialogHTML += "<div id='AccountMap'"
      + "class='oui-acc-map'><iframe src='"
      + mapURL + "'></iframe></div>";
  sDialogHTML += "<div id='Address' class='oui-acc-addr'>"
      + oAccountData.FullAddress + "</div>";
  sDialogHTML += "<div id='Location' class='oui-acc-loc'>"
      + oAccountData.Location + "</div>";
  sDialogHTML += "<div id='URL' class='oui-acc-url'>";
  sDialogHTML += "<a href='http://" + oAccountData.URL
      + "'target='_blank'>" + oAccountData.URL;
  sDialogHTML += "</a></div></div>";
  $(sDialogHTML).dialog({
    title:sAccountName,
    position:[e.pageX,e.pageY + 15],
    show:true,
    hide:true,
    minWidth:400,
    minHeight:600});
});
```

The example code does the following:

- Use the presentation model's OnControlEvent method to invoke the GET_ACCT_DATA event. This triggers the execution of the GetAccountData method in the PM.

- Get the value of the C_AccountData property. The oAccountData variable now represents the account data object that has been populated by the PM.

- Get the current account name.

- Append the account address to the map URL.

- Construct the HTML for the dialog by concatenating plain HTML code with properties of the oAccountData object. The general idea is to wrap the IFrame displaying the map and the other account data fields into <div> elements and assign individual custom class names to allow styling via CSS.

- Use the jQuery dialog widget to display the HTML. The dialog has the following options settings:
  - The title will display the current account name.
  - The position of the dialog will be 15 pixels below the current click position.
  - The show and hide attributes are set to true to achieve a default fade in and fade out effect.
  - The minimum width and height are set to 400 by 600 pixels.

4. Save your changes.

In addition to the JavaScript code, we must take care of the CSS classes defined in the dialog HTML. We can use the custom-global.css file introduced earlier in this book to hold the style rules for these classes.

By putting the following code in the custom-global.css file (or any other custom CSS file) we apply basic formatting to the elements of the popup dialog:

```css
/* Account Info Dialog */
.oui-infoButton,
 .siebui-label .oui-infoButton{
    border-radius: 0px;
    color: #ff5839!important;
    cursor: pointer;
    font-weight: bold!important;
    text-decoration: underline;
}
.oui-acc-map iframe{
    position: relative;
    width: 380px;
    height: 300px;
}
.oui-acc-addr{
```

```
    position: relative;
    height: auto;
    font-size: 1.2em;
    font-weight: bold;
}
 .oui-acc-loc, .oui-acc-url{
    position: relative;
    height: auto;
    font-size: 1.1em;
    font-weight: bold;
}
.oui-acc-url a{
    color: steelblue;
    text-decoration: underline;
}
```

Once all files have been changed and the browser cache is reloaded, we can navigate to the My Opportunities view to test the popup dialog. The Account label should appear as a clickable link with amber-colored text. A click on the label should produce a dialog as shown in the following screenshot.

In the screenshot we can see that the Account label is clickable. The user has clicked the link and the dialog is opened, displaying the account name in its title. The Google map, as well as the account's address, location and URL, are displayed in the dialog according to the CSS rules.

Congratulations! You have successfully implemented a custom visualization of business data that has been fetched by a workflow process.

Implementing a Click Event Handler using the Event Helper Class in Innovation Pack 2014

At the time of writing, the code shown in the previous case study will work as expected in any version of Siebel Open UI; however, the **Event Helper** class that was introduced in IP 2014 allows developers to use a different approach for defining event handlers.

For an implementation of the previous case study example in IP 2014 or beyond, we can use code similar to the following to define the event handler in the BindEvents method of the custom physical renderer.

```
OpptyFormPR.prototype.BindEvents = function(){
  //get the Account Label
  var accLabel = $("#Account2_Label");
  //get the Event Helper
  var eventHelper =
  SiebelApp.S_App.PluginBuilder.GetHoByName("EventHelper");
  if (eventHelper && accLabel.length) { //if they exist
    eventHelper.Manage(accLabel, "click", { ctx:this },
        OnClickMoreInfo); //call EH Manage for click event
  }
  SiebelAppFacade.OpptyFormPR.superclass.BindEvents
      .call(this);
};
```

For a complete description of the example code, refer to Chapter 7 of this book. The Manage method of the event helper object takes four arguments:

- The jQuery representation of the DOM element
- The name of the event to handle, such as click
- The context
- The name of a function that will be invoked when the event occurs (OnClickMoreInfo)

The previous case study described the code necessary to implement the jQuery dialog to show the account data and the map. This code will have to be moved to the OnClickMoreInfo function. For the sake of brevity we do not repeat this code here.

This chapter's code archive provides a .zip archive (`OpptFormProgressBar_Dialog_IP2014.zip`) that contains the presentation model and physical renderer code with the modifications indicated in this section.

Case Study: Defining Custom Transitions

As demonstrated in Chapter 1, transition settings allow end users to select pre-defined transitions such as 'Flip' or 'Slide In'. As a result, Open UI will show a view - after rendering is complete - using a visual effect rather than just drawing it on the screen.

In the following case study we will learn how to create a custom transition effect. As a working example, we choose a 'Fade' transition. The high-level implementation process is as follows:

- Register a List of Values entry for the custom transition.
- Create CSS rules to define the transition.

The next procedure guides us through the implementation steps for a custom transition:

1. In the Siebel client, navigate to the Administration - Data screen, List of Values view.
2. Create a new record with the following values:

Column	Value
Type	PAGE_TRANSITION
Display Value	Custom Fade In
Language-Independent Code	OUIBOOK_FADE
Language Name	English-American
Parent LIC (IP 2013 only)	Desktop

3. Click the Clear Cache button
4. Open the `custom-global.css` file (or any custom style sheet that should hold the CSS rules for the transition effects).
5. In the CSS file, add four new rules as follows:

```
.siebui-prev-ouibook_fade-begin
.siebui-prev- ouibook_fade -end
.siebui-next- ouibook_fade -begin
.siebui-next- ouibook_fade -end
```

The transition logic of the Open UI framework is based on separate `<div>` elements - one that contains the previous view and one that contains the new (next) view. The framework applies CSS classes to the `<div>` elements that represent both views at the beginning or the end of the transition. The naming convention for these classes is `.siebui-<prev or next>-<LIC of transition in lowercase>-<begin or end>`, resulting in the four class names shown above for our custom transition.

6. In order to define the visual appearance of a view in the respective state of transition, we can implement the four CSS rules like in the following code example:

```
/* Custom Fade Transition*/
.siebui-prev-ouibook_fade-begin {
    width: 100%;
    height: 100%;
    opacity: 1;
    position: absolute;
    visibility:visible;
}
.siebui-prev-ouibook_fade-end {
    width: 100%;
    height: 100%;
    opacity: 0;
    transition: opacity 0.5s ease-out, visibility 0.01s
linear;
    visibility: hidden;
}
.siebui-next-ouibook_fade-begin {
    width: 100%;
    height: 100%;
    opacity: 0;
    position: absolute;
}
.siebui-next-ouibook_fade-end {
    width: 100%;
    height: 100%;
    opacity: 1;
    transition: opacity 1s ease-in;
}
```

The example CSS rules use `opacity` and `transition` properties to define a smooth fade-in or fade-out effect by changing the opacity of the element from non-transparent to transparent and vice versa.

Now we are ready to test the new transition.

7. Save your changes and clear the browser cache.
8. Navigate to the User Preferences screen - Behavior view.
9. Set the Transition field to `Custom Fade In`.
10. Click the Save button.
11. Press *F5* to reload the page.
12. Navigate from one view to another and observe that the new view appears with a fade-in effect.

As shown in the previous case study, transition effects can be easily customized by defining CSS rules in a custom style sheet.

Visualizing Data with Third Party JavaScript Libraries

When it comes to implementing advanced requirements for visualizing data, web developers can resort to a vast array of open source and commercial JavaScript libraries. With Siebel Open UI, we can obtain and use these libraries to suit our needs.

The following list describes some of the more popular JavaScript data visualization libraries. The list sorting does not convey any ranking and the authors do not explicitly recommend one library over another.

Library	Description	URL
D3.js	Uses Scalable Vector Graphics (SVG) to apply visualization to data. Highly extensible.	d3js.org
Dygraphs.js	Charting library.	dygraphs.com
InfoVis	Interactive data visualizations.	thejit.org
Springy.js	Force directed graph engine. Applies real world physics to create highly interactive animations.	getspringy.com
dimple	Based on D3. Aimed at analysts with minimal coding requirements.	dimplejs.org
Leaflet	Focuses on mobile-friendly interactive maps.	leafletjs.com
Ember Charts	Based on the ember.js framework.	addepar.github.io/#/ember-charts/
Arbor.js	Force-directed graphs.	arborjs.org
Paper.js	Vector graphics scripting framework.	paperjs.org
Masonry	Cascading grid layout.	masonry.desandro.com
Nested	Multi column grid layout	suprb.com/apps/nested/
Chart.js	Simple HTML5 charting.	chartjs.org
FusionCharts	jQuery based charts with focus on enterprise web applications and mobile support.	fusioncharts.com

No matter which library we choose, we must download the source files and make them available in the siebel/custom directory in order to be able to use them in our custom

JavaScript files. Preferably, we should use the minified versions that are usually available in the download archive for the respective library.

Case Study: Using D3 to Visualize Data in List Applets

In the following case study, we will use the `radialProgress` extension of the D3 library to visualize opportunity revenue data in list applets.

The following screenshot shows the effect we want to achieve.

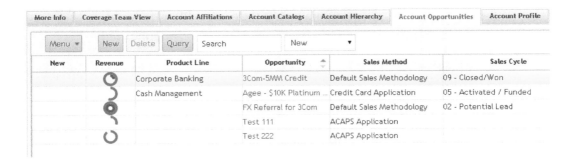

The screenshot shows a list applet that displays opportunities for a selected account (not visible in the screenshot). The Revenue column has been customized to show the opportunity's revenue in a radial progress chart. A full outer circle means that the revenue quota has been reached. The inner circle conveys the amount that exceeds the quota. What cannot be shown in the screenshot is that the diagram is animated.

The following procedure describes the high-level steps to achieve this data visualization using a third-party JavaScript library:

1. Go to `https://github.com/mbostock/d3` and download the D3 master library.

2. Open the downloaded archive and extract the `d3.min.js` file to the `siebel/custom/d3` folder (create the `d3` sub-folder).

3. Go to `http://www.brightpointinc.com/clients/brightpointinc.com/library/radialProgress/download.html` and download the source archive for the radial progress D3 plug-in created by BrightPoint Consulting Inc.

4. Extract the file `radialProgress.js` from the archive and store it in the `siebel/custom/d3` folder.

5. Create a custom physical renderer that extends the `JQGridRenderer` class. As recommended in previous chapters, use a template. This chapter's code archive contains a complete solution file (`ListProgressIndicatorPR.js`).

6. Register the physical renderer file with the FINCORP Client Opportunity List Applet - Basic applet.

7. Implement the define function in the custom PR as follows:

```
define("siebel/custom/ListProgressIndicatorPR",
["siebel/jqgridrenderer", "siebel/custom/d3/d3.min",
"siebel/custom/d3/radialProgress"]
```

The define function resolves the dependencies of the PR code to the as-delivered jqgridrenderer.js file, the D3 library and the radialProgress.js file.

8. Implement the BindData method of the custom PR as follows:

```
ListProgressIndicatorPR.prototype.BindData = function
(bRefresh) {
  SiebelAppFacade.ListProgressIndicatorPR.superclass.BindData
      .apply(this, arguments);
  var pm = this.GetPM();
  var recordSet = pm.Get("GetRawRecordSet");
  var field = "Primary Revenue Amount";
  var minVal = 0;
  var maxVal = 10000000;
  //get field/column map (not documented!)
  var oColumns = this.GetColumnHelper().GetColField();
  if (field) {
    var sColumnName = oColumns[field];
    for (var i=0; i<recordSet.length; i++){
      curVal = parseFloat(recordSet[i][field]);
      //apply D3 plugin
      radialProgress($("#" + (i+1) + sColumnName).empty()[0])
          .diameter(50) // max row height
          .value(curVal)
          .minValue(minVal)
          .maxValue(maxVal)
          .render();
}}};
```

The example code accomplishes the following:

- Get the 'raw' record set from the applet's presentation model. The GetRawRecordSet property contains unformatted data, making it easier to pass the revenue amount to the D3 extension.

- Initialize the field, minVal and maxVal variables. The example code uses hard-coded values for these variables. In a real-life scenario, applet user properties should be used to store these values for each applet individually.

- Use the GetColField method of the GetColumnHelper class to retrieve an array that maps business component field names to column names. The column name is used to identify the DOM element. The GetColumnHelper class is not documented at the time of writing and we should be aware that using it comes with a certain risk that our code might not work as expected in future versions.

- Get the column name for the field.
- Iterate through the record set. For each record, do the following.
  - Get the current field value (revenue in our example).
  - Call the radialProgress function. We must pass a jQuery selector to this function. The selector is constructed using the 'pseudo' row id (starting at 1) for data cells in list applets. The jQuery empty method is used to remove all content from the data cell.
  - The values passed to the radialProgress function are the diameter of the graph (adjusted to the row height of list applets), the current field value and the minimum and maximum value (i.e. the 'quota').

9. Add the following CSS rules to a custom style sheet:

```
/* Radial Progress Styles */
.background {
    fill: #FFFFFF;
    fill-opacity: 0.01;
}

.component {
    fill: whitesmoke;
}
.arc {
    stroke-width: 2;
    fill: #4e8fff;
}

.arc2 {
    stroke-width: 2;
    fill: seagreen;
}

.radial-svg {
    display: block;
    margin: 0 auto;
    height: 20px;
}
```

To test the changes, we should log out of the application, clear the browser cache, then log in again. Compare your work with the screenshot at the beginning of this case study.

The previous case study demonstrated how to use a third-party JavaScript library to create sophisticated data visualizations with a minimum of coding. In a similar manner as shown earlier, we can retrieve data from an applet's record set and pass it to other third-party libraries.

Case Study: Creating Custom Visualizations

If the vast array of third-party libraries does not suit our needs, we can of course go our own way for visualizing data. The following case study will guide us through the process of creating a custom visualization for contact data.

The requirement for this case study is that end users want to sort their contacts by the 'time since their last interaction' so they can plan whom to contact next. In Siebel CRM, we use activities to log contact calls or visits, so we have records in the database that allow us to discern when the last contact occurred.

To visualize this data, our imaginary chief architect designed the following prototype.

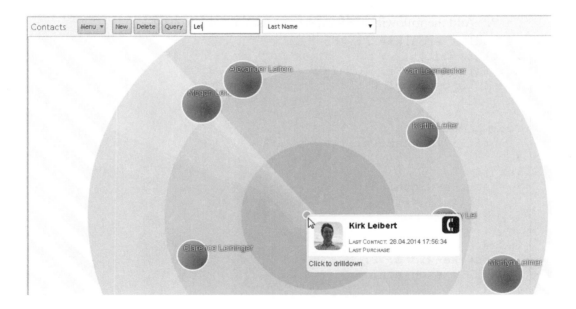

The screenshot shows a prototype for a "contact radar" applet which visualizes contact records in the following ways:

- Each contact is represented by a circle.
- The color of the circle is driven by the contact status (for example, green means the contact is 'active').
- Contacts that are closer to the central circle have been contacted more recently.
- Hovering over a contact circle opens a tool box with information about the contact and a drilldown link which navigates to a detailed view.

- A phone icon in the tool box provides the ability to initiate a call with a click or tap (when the Siebel application is running on a device that is able to initiate phone calls).

To implement this prototype, we must accomplish the following high-level steps:

- Extend the `Contact` business component with custom fields.
- Create a custom applet with applet user properties and expose that applet in a view.
- Implement a custom presentation model to retrieve the applet user properties.
- Create a custom physical renderer to implement the custom visualization.
- Define CSS rules for the new elements.

For the sake of brevity, the following section is limited to a verbal description of the solution. For full code examples, refer to this chapter's code archive as indicated in this section.

Extending the Contact Business Component

In the first procedure, we create repository objects as follows:

1. In Siebel Tools, navigate to the `Contact` business component and add a **new multi-value field** with the following properties.

Name	Multivalue Link	Field
OUIBOOK Action Date	Action	Creation Date

The new `OUIBOOK Action Date` field exposes the `Creation Date` field of the `Action` business component (representing activity records associated with the current contact).

2. Create two **new calculated fields** for the `Contact` business component as follows.

Name	Calculated	Calculated Value
ContactRadarMostRecentAction	checked	max([OUIBOOK Action Date])
ContactRadarJulianDate	checked	JulianDay(max([OUIBOOK Action Date]))

The first field will display the most recent creation date of activities for a given contact. It uses the `max` function of the Siebel Query Language and the previously created `OUIBOOK Action Date` multi-value field as the argument.

The second field contains the **Julian** day number of the most recent activity creation date. Using Julian functions is a common practice for date calculations.

Creating a Custom List Applet and Exposing it in a New View

1. Create a new list applet referencing the `Contact` business component that exposes the following fields as list columns in the Edit List mode. Give the applet a meaningful name such as `OUIBOOK Contact Radar Applet`.

   o   Full Name
   o   Job Title
   o   Status
   o   Image Source Path
   o   ContactRadarMostRecentAction
   o   ContactRadarJulianDate
   o   Created

2. Define the following applet user properties for the new list applet:

Name	Value
ClientPMUserProp	CRFullName, CRTitle, CRStatus, CRImage, CRDateSinceLastContact, CRContactRadarJulianDate, CRCreated
CRFullName	Full Name
CRTitle	Job Title
CRStatus	Status
CRImage	Image Source Path
CRDateSinceLastContact	ContactRadarMostRecentAction
CRContactRadarJulianDate	ContactRadarJulianDate
CRCreated	Created

3. Create a new view with the list applet on top and the as-delivered Contact Form Applet on the bottom of the view.

4. Add the new view to the Contacts screen and register the view with a test responsibility.

5. Compile all new and modified objects.

This concludes the work in Siebel Tools. In the next part of this case study, we will implement the necessary custom JavaScript files.

Implementing a Custom Presentation Model

The following outline describes the major steps of implementing a custom presentation model and physical renderer for the contact radar.

- Create a new presentation model (PM) file with a custom class that extends the `ListPresentationModel` class.

- In the `Setup` method of the presentation model, retrieve the values of the applet user properties of the new list applet and store them as PM properties. Refer to the example code file (`ListContactRadarPM.js`) or Chapter 7 for details on how to retrieve applet user properties in a custom PM.

Creating a Custom Physical Renderer and Implementing the Custom Visualization

Implement the custom physical renderer for this case study using the directions in the following section. For the complete code, refer to the example code file (`ListContactRadarPR.js`) delivered with this chapter's code archive.

1. In the `ShowUI` method, use the jQuery `after` function to add a `<div>` element after the list applet grid (using the `.ui-jqgrid-view` class).

2. In the `BindData` method, retrieve the PM properties and the current record set.

3. Iterate through the record set and create an array of objects representing the contact records. Each object will hold the values for the fields exposed as applet user properties. If the contact has no activity record associated, use the contact creation date instead of the date of the most recent activity.

4. Call a custom 'Refresh' function (to be implemented later) that handles the re-draw of the chart.

5. Hide the original grid using the jQuery `css` function. Set the visibility property to hidden and the height property to 0px.

6. In the `ShowUI` function, create the placeholder HTML container for the radar chart.

7. Implement the 'Refresh' function. In the example code (see the `ListContactRadarPR.js` file), we pass the contact object to the rendering function (another custom function) along with additional parameters such as the zoom level.

8. In the main rendering function, we create the HTML for the popup and render a `<div>` element for each contact. The visual appearance of the `<div>` element (a colored circle) is completely driven by CSS.

9. Associate the custom PM and PR with the custom list applet in the manifest administration.

At runtime, each contact record is transformed visually and placed on the radar graphic in its unique position. The next section describes the rendering logic in more detail.

- A new `<div>` element is created for each contact record and is added to the visualization container. This element is transformed into a circle via the jQuery `css` method.
- The color of the circle is also chosen via the jQuery `css` method.
- HTML that reveals a business card upon `mouseover` is appended to the contact circle.
- Click events are bound to the contact circle triggering row selection in the grid and record drilldown.
- Additionally, a `mouseover` event handler is implemented to enable the hide and show functionality of the business card.
- The coordinates for the contact circle are calculated using the formulas outlined below.

  $$x = r \ * \ \cos (\theta)$$
  $$y = r \ * \ \sin (\theta)$$

  Note: r is calculated by taking the difference between the current date and the last contact date, and dividing by the number of days. θ is calculated using the record set item position to equally distribute each contact circle around the perimeter of the radar graphic.
- Finally, the contact circle is placed onto the radar graphic using an animated effect. The `animate` function, included in jQuery, provides a fly-in effect where each circle glides gracefully onto the screen to its proper location.

This concludes the discussion of the major steps to implement a custom visualization in the form of a 'Contact Radar'. As a final step we have to take care of the CSS rules so that the visualization fulfills our style requirements.

Define CSS Rules for the Custom Visualization

Implement the CSS rules for the custom visualization as needed. Please refer to the `ContactRadar.css` file for a complete set of example rules. Add the CSS code to a custom style sheet or register the entire CSS file with the list applet (only applicable to IP 2014 or higher). In the previous case study, we described the main implementation steps for custom data visualization. While writing our own code allows for greater flexibility, the amount of code to write, debug and maintain is much higher than when using third-party libraries.

Case Study: Achieving Custom Layout with Nested

In this chapter so far we have seen how Open UI provides a solid foundation for building brand new visualizations from scratch. Our next case study takes us further down that exciting path. This time we will employ a third party library called **Nested** to generate a 'nested' visualization of list applet records.

In this scenario, end users work in a customer support center, and have requested a new way to visualize the priority of their assigned issues. Our team of developers came up with a prototype as shown in the following screenshot.

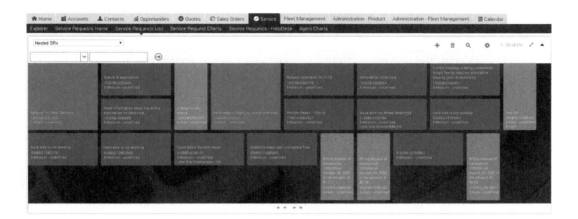

The prototype is built on the standard service request list applet and visualizes data as follows:

- Each service request is displayed as a block of varying size based on data driven attributes.
- The sizes of the blocks are determined by the value of the Priority field.
- Tiles for service requests that are of low importance are smaller, while those for service requests that are higher in importance are larger.
- The color of each service request block is determined by priority, and the border color is determined by the status.
- Service requests that are both 'Open' and 'Urgent' are highlighted by a red frame.

To implement this prototype, we must accomplish the following high-level steps:

- Create a new applet with the correct fields and assign it to a view.
- Create a custom physical renderer to implement the custom visualization.
- Define CSS rules for the new elements.

As in the previous case study, the provided description outlines an overview of the renderer solution. For more details, please refer to the code archive that accompanies this chapter.

Creating a Custom List Applet and Assigning it in to a View

The following procedure describes the major steps to create a new list applet for service requests and assign it to a view. For details on configuration in Siebel Tools, refer to the Oracle Siebel documentation or the Oracle Siebel CRM Developer's Handbook by Alexander Hansal.

1. Create a copy of the `Service Request List Applet`. Give the applet a useful name such as `OUIBOOK Service Request Nested Applet`. Verify the following fields are contained in the applet and are visible to the user when the applet is in *Edit List* mode.
   - Priority
   - Status
   - SR Number
   - Abstract
   - Account

2. Create a new view with the list applet on top and the as-delivered `Service Request Detail Applet` on the bottom of the view.

3. Add the new view to the `Service Request` screen and register the view with a test responsibility.

4. Compile all new and modified objects.

This completes our work in Siebel Tools. In the next part of this case study, we will implement the necessary custom JavaScript files.

Creating a Custom Physical Renderer to Implement the Custom Visualization

Implement the custom physical renderer for this case study using the directions in the following section. For the complete code, refer to the example code file (`ServiceRequestNestedPR.js`) delivered with this chapter's code archive.

1. Go to `https://github.com/suprb/nested` and download the `Nested.js` library.

2. Open the downloaded archive and extract the `jquery.nested.js` file to the `siebel/custom/nested` folder (create the `nested` sub-folder).

3. Create a custom physical renderer that extends the `JQGridRenderer` class. As recommended in previous chapters, use a template.

4. In the `ShowUI` method, use the jQuery `after` function to add a `<div>` element after the list applet grid (using the `.ui-jqgrid-view` class as the selector). The new `<div>` element will serve as the container where the visualization will reside.

5. In the `BindData` method, retrieve the current record set.

6. For each record in the record set, create a local object variable called `ServiceRequest` containing attributes that match each of the fields we are using from the record set.

7. Invoke a new method called `createServiceRequestElement` (to be implemented later) and pass the local `ServiceRequest` variable as an argument. This function will return a `<div>` element which will be appended to the container.

8. Hide the original grid using the jQuery `css` function. Set the `visibility` property to `hidden` and the `height` property to `0px`.

9. Implement the `createServiceRequestElement` function. The goal for this function is to create a new service request block and set its visual attributes. The following code shows the implementation in detail.

10. Using jQuery, append the element that is returned by the `createServiceRequestElement` function to the container `div`.

```
ServiceRequestNestedPR.prototype.createServiceRequestElement =
function(SR) {
  var that = this;
  var classes = "box " + getSizeAndColor(SR);
  var elem = $("<div class='" + classes + "'>")
  .append('<span class="itemtext1">' + SR.Account + '</span>')
  .append('<span class="itemtext2">' + SR.Priority + " - "
      + SR.Status + '</span>')
  .append('<span class="itemtext3">' + SR.SRNumber
      + '</span>')
  .append('<span class="itemtext4">' + SR.Abstract
      + '</span>')
  .on("click", function() {
    var gridlocal = that.GetGrid();
    //trigger row selection
    gridlocal.setSelection(SR.RowCount + 1, true);
  })[0];
  return elem;
}
```

The example code accomplishes the following:

- Save a reference to `this` in a private variable called `that` which we refer to later in the example.

- Call a function named `getSizeAndColor` to determine block size and block color. Refer to this chapter's code archive to view this function in more detail.

- Create a new `<div>` element using jQuery
- Use jQuery to add descriptive text to the `<div>` element.
- Use jQuery to attach a click event handler to the container. This event triggers the `setSelection` event whenever the user clicks a block.
- Return the `<div>` element.

In a final step before testing, we need to associate the custom PR with the custom list applet in the manifest administration.

This concludes the steps required to build a new custom renderer using the third party Nested library. In the following section, we will implement our design by adding a few CSS customizations to the application.

Define CSS Rules for the Custom Visualization

Implement the CSS rules for the custom visualization as needed. Please refer to the `ServiceRequestNested.css` file for a complete set of example rules. Add the CSS code to a custom style sheet or register the entire CSS file with the list applet (only applicable to IP 2014 or higher).

Summary

When it comes to visualizing data in browser clients, developers today can refer to a vast array of third party libraries, many of which are available under an open source license.

Siebel Open UI provides built-in visualizations such as Tile Layout. In an extended case study, we learned how to implement tile layout for an arbitrary list applet and apply customization.

In the next case study, we learned how to apply common JavaScript techniques to create an on-demand information dialog that displays account data for an opportunity. The case study also reinforced the concept of fetching data from the server using a business service or workflow process.

Customizing the transition effects when users navigate between views is an example of applying visual styles without referring to individual records and was demonstrated in a separate case study in this chapter.

Two case studies in this chapter helped us understand how to incorporate third-party libraries into Siebel Open UI to achieve sophisticated data visualization. The D3 library is a popular example for rich data-visualization while the Nested library focuses on achieving a responsive grid layout of elements on the screen.

This chapter also included a full example of a custom visualization (Contact Radar), which does not rely on any third-party code.

In the next chapter, we will stay in 'challenge' mode and explore advanced scripting concepts for Siebel Open UI.

12

Advanced Scripting Scenarios

In this chapter, we will introduce several 'challenge' scenarios that demonstrate advanced scripting concepts in Siebel Open UI. You will find the following case studies in this chapter:

- Display custom tooltips
- Get and set user preferences
- Implement a slider widget
- Use a Plug-in Wrapper to implement a slider widget in IP 2014
- Use applet labels to display metadata
- Enable list applet scrolling
- Collect performance measures

You will notice that some of the scenarios are shortened and do not include complete code listings. This has been done to add a 'challenge' flavor to this chapter and to keep the chapter's content within meaningful boundaries. Please refer to this chapter's code archive for complete and working code examples.

Case Study: Displaying Custom Tooltips

Tooltips are a well-established mechanism for conveying additional information about fields and data to end users. End users are usually well-accustomed to the concept. In the following case study, we will learn how to display custom tooltips in Siebel Open UI. The example also demonstrates a possible approach to storing tooltip content in a central location.

The example code in this case study is provided by Siebel bloggers Neelmani Gautam (siebelunleashed.com) and Jason Le (www.impossiblesiebel.com).

Let's begin the case study with a screenshot of the final solution.

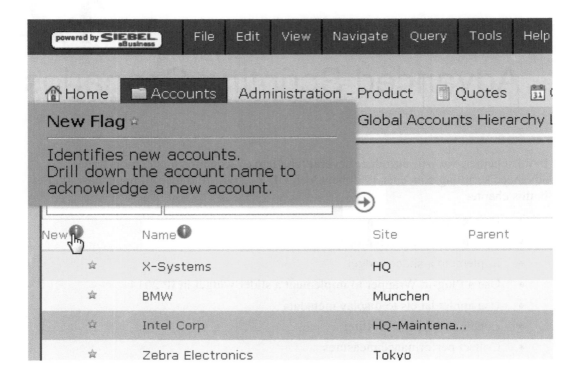

In the screenshot, we can see that a formatted tooltip is displayed whilst the mouse cursor hovers over an 'information' icon in the header of the New column in the account list applet. The tooltip text conveys additional information about the column to the end user.

The following procedures will guide us through the implementation steps for these high-level requirements:

- Store tooltip messages in a central location
- Create a custom view renderer
- Create custom CSS rules

Storing Tooltip Messages in a Central Location

In the first procedure of this case study, we will implement the central storage for tooltip messages. As usual, this chapter's code archive contains complete solution files for all case studies.

1. Create a new text file and save it in the `PUBLIC/<Language>/FILES/custom` folder. For example, name the file `tooltips.txt`.

2. In the new file we will use JSON (JavaScript Object Notation) to store tooltip messages for each applet within a view. For example, the following string will provide example messages for the `SIS Account List Applet` and the `SIS Account Entry Applet` in the `All Account List View`:

```
{
  "All Account List View": {
    "SIS Account List Applet": {
      "Row Status": "<b>New Flag <img
          src=images/asterisk.gif></b><hr>Identifies new
          accounts.<br>Drill down the account name
          to acknowledge a new account.",
      "Name": "<b>Name</b><hr>The account&apos;s name.",
      "Type": "<b>Account Type</b><hr>The type of
          account.<br>Use <i>Residential</i>
          for consumer accounts."
    },
    "SIS Account Entry Applet": {
      "Name": "<b>Name</b><hr>The account&apos;s name.",
      "SalesRep": "<b>Account Team</b><hr>
          The sales team for the account.<br>Assign one or
          more positions."
    }
  }
}
```

To identify the individual views, applets and controls we must use the names of the respective objects as stored in the Siebel repository. It will be necessary to use Siebel Tools to retrieve the field names. For example, `Row Status` is the value of the Name property of a list column in the `SIS Account List Applet` (and not the display name).

As we can see, HTML tags are used to apply some basic formatting to the messages.

The JSON notation is one possible approach for storing tooltip data. Depending on your project preferences, you might want to consider other solutions, such as using a custom administration view to store messages in the Siebel database. The remainder of the case study is built upon the text file we just created.

Creating a Custom View Renderer

In the next part of this case study, we will implement an extension of the physical renderer class for views (`ViewPR`). The new physical renderer will have to accomplish the following:

- Retrieve the message strings from the `tooltips.txt` file.

- Insert an information icon next to each list column or form applet control and set the icon's title property using the message text.

- Apply the jQuery UI tooltip widget to display customizable tooltips when the cursor is hovering over the icon.

This chapter's code archive contains a complete example file (`ToolTipViewPR.js`). For the sake of brevity, the following procedure generalizes some of the implementation steps that you have already learned in previous chapters of this book. If you need more information about the details of the implementation, refer to the respective chapter.

1. Create a new physical renderer file for a view (preferably using a template). Save the file to the `siebel/custom` folder as `ToolTipViewPR.js`.

2. Implement a new function for the custom PR that reads the `tooltips.txt` file and extracts the messages for a given view. We will invoke this function later in the `SetRenderer` method. For example, the new function might be implemented as follows:

```
ToolTipViewPR.prototype.readTips = function(viewName){
  var msgData = "";
  $.ajax({
    url: "files/custom/tooltips.txt", dataType:'json',
    success: function(data){
      msgData = data[viewName];
    },
    async: false
  });
  return msgData;
}
```

The example code implements the `readTips` function, which takes the name of a view as the only input parameter. The function uses the jQuery `ajax` method to perform an HTTP request to get the `tooltips.txt` file. Upon successful retrieval, the function extracts the message object for the given view and returns it.

3. The next helper function that we add, below the one we just created, is needed to determine whether a given applet is actually a list applet or not, and also returns the jQuery selector prefix if the applet is a list applet. The following example code shows a possible implementation of this function:

```
ToolTipViewPR.prototype.getAppletProp = function (sAppletId){
  //get the list applet grid id
  var oGridId=$("#"+sAppletId+" .ui-jqgrid-view");
  var sDataTablePrefix="";
  //if gridid not blank means list applet
  if(oGridId.length>0){
    sGridId=oGridId.attr("id").replace("gview_","");
    //column headers are prefixed with
```

```
    //'jqgh_' plus the table id
    sDataTablePrefix="jqgh_"+sGridId;
    var isListApplet=true;
  }
  else{
    var isListApplet=false;
  }
  return
   {"isListApplet":isListApplet,
    "sDataTablePrefix":sDataTablePrefix}
  }
```

The `getAppletProp` function takes the applet's element id as an input parameter. Using the element id, we try to instantiate a jQuery collection, adding the class used for list applets (`ui-jqgrid-view`). If that is successful, we have identified a list applet and can extract the data table prefix that we will later use to address the list column header. The object returned by the `getAppletProp` function contains the data table prefix and a property that identifies the applet as a list applet or not.

4. The final helper function allows us to retrieve the jQuery selector for a list column header or form applet label. The following example code shows a possible implementation:

```
ToolTipViewPR.prototype.getControlListColSelector =
function(oAppletProp,sControlName){
  var sControlNameUnd = sControlName.replace(/\s/g,"_");
  var sIdSelector = ( oAppletProp.isListApplet ) ? "#"
      + oAppletProp.sDataTablePrefix + "_"
      + sControlNameUnd : "#" +
  sControlNameUnd + "_Label";
  return sIdSelector;
}
```

The `getControlListColSelector` function takes the applet properties produced by the `getAppletProp` function and the name of an applet control as input parameters. It then replaces spaces with underscores in the control name string. In the case of a list applet, the function returns the jQuery selector string for the list column header. In the case of a form applet, the return value is the selector string for the control label.

5. After putting the helper functions in place, we can set out to implement the `SetRenderer` method of our custom physical renderer. The following example code implements the requirements described earlier:

```
ToolTipViewPR.prototype.SetRenderer = function () {
  var viewName = this.GetPM().GetName();
  //retrieve tooltip data for the view
  var tipsObject = this.readTips(viewName);
  var appletTipsObj = "", strTip = "", ctrlName = "",
      ctrlSelector = "", oCtrl = "";
  //get applets in current view
```

311

```
  var oApplets = this.GetPM().GetAppletMap();
  for(var oApplet in oApplets){  //for each applet...
    //retrieve tooltip data for this applet
    appletTipsObj = tipsObject[oApplet];
    if(typeof(appletTipsObj) === "object"){
      //if there is tooltip data
      //get applet properties
      var appletProp =
          this.getAppletProp(oApplets[oApplet].GetFullId());
      var oControls = oApplets[oApplet].GetControls();
      for(var tip in appletTipsObj){
        //for each tooltip definition
        //get the tooltip text
        strTip = appletTipsObj[tip];
        //get the control from the applet
        oCtrl = oControls[tip];
        if(typeof(oCtrl) === "object"){
          // make sure specified control is found
          //get the label selector
          ctrlSelector =
              this.getControlListColSelector(appletProp,
              oCtrl.GetName());
          //append an image to control
          //and add tooltip text as title of image
          $(ctrlSelector).append("<img title='" + strTip
              + "' class='help-icon' height='16px'"
              + "width='16px' src='images/infocenter.png'"
              + "true=''/>");
        }//end of if
      }//end of for
    }//end of if
    else{
      SiebelJS.Log("No tips found for applet: " + oApplet);
    }
  }//end of for loop of applets
  //initialize tooltip
  $("img.help-icon").tooltip({
    //content needed for basic HTML support in tooltips
    content: function() {return $(this).attr('title');},
    position: {my:"center bottom-20",at: "center top"}
  });
};
```

The example code implements the following functionality:

- Get the name of the current view.
- Retrieve the tooltip data for the view from the `tooltips.txt` file.
- Get the current view's applet map.
- Iterate through the applets in the current view. For each applet we do the following.

- o Retrieve the tooltip data for the applet.
- o Invoke the `getAppletProp` function to retrieve the applet type and prefix.
- o Get the controls array for the applet.
- o For each tooltip defined for the current applet, retrieve the selector for the respective control's label (or column header) and append an `<img>` element. The `title` attribute of the image element will be set to the tooltip text.
- Using the class of the new image element, we can then apply the `tooltip` widget of jQuery UI, specifying the content and the position of the tooltip. The `tooltip` widget uses the `title` attribute of the elements specified in the selector and generates customizable tooltip containers.

Creating Custom CSS Rules

To finalize this case study example, we have to specify a CSS rule to apply the desired style to the tooltips. The following example code can be placed in a custom CSS file that is already registered:

```css
/* Custom Tooltips*/
.ui-tooltip {
    padding: 10px 20px;
    color: black;
    background: deepskyblue;
    font-size: 1.1em;
    position: absolute;
    max-width: 300px;
    -webkit-box-shadow: 0 0 7px darkgrey;
    box-shadow: 0 0 7px darkgrey;
    border-width: 2px;
    z-index: 9999;
}
```

The example CSS rule defines the visual appearance of the tooltips.

Testing Considerations for Custom Tooltips

To test the case study scenario, we should register the custom physical renderer file with a test view such as the `All Account List View`, using the manifest administration view. For more information on registering a physical renderer for a view, refer to Chapter 9.

To test the functionality, navigate to the test view and observe that the information icon appears with the controls specified in the text file. Hovering over the icon should result in a tooltip display.

In case you have implemented customizations that remove or modify the `title` attribute of DOM elements - such as in the 'Hiding unwanted tooltips' case study in Chapter 10 -

you must amend the respective code so that the `title` attribute of elements within the `help-icon` class are not affected. For example, you might want to use the following code in the custom `postload` event listener introduced in Chapter 10:

```
//Hiding Unwanted Tool Tips
$("[title]").not("[role=grid] td, #s_toolbar, #s_toolbar li,
    .help-icon").removeAttr("title");
```

In the example code, the `help-icon` class is added to the list of selectors that will be exempt from the `removeAttr` function. Changes to the code that was introduced in Chapter 10 are in **bold** font.

In the previous case study we learned how to store, retrieve and display tooltip messages for list columns and controls on list or form applets. The custom physical renderer can be applied to any view or the `DEFAULT VIEW` object.

Case Study: Getting and Setting User Preferences

Occasionally developers will need to store user-related information, such as the size of applets that have been made resizable through customization, and retrieve this information in future sessions. At first, one would assume that browser cookies would be an ideal medium to store and retrieve this kind of information. In Siebel CRM, however, we should have the big picture in mind and support a solution that is independent of the browser. For example, the user could use a different browser or device for subsequent sessions and will expect the changes she applied in previous sessions to carry through.

In this case study we will learn how the Siebel Open UI API supports getting and setting user preferences for the purpose of retrieving and storing user-specific attributes. The simplistic example scenario is that we would like to support storing and retrieving applet personalization information such as the size of an applet. The high-level requirements would be as follows:

- Retrieve any existing user preference and apply them to applets
- Make applets resizable
- Store the applet size in a user preference when the size is changed
- Ensure that the same applet can have a different size in different views

For educational purposes, we will implement a custom `postload` event listener to accomplish these requirements. The next procedure will guide us through the high-level implementation steps. For details, refer to the previous chapters of this book.

1. In a custom postload event listener (for example the `custompl.js` file created in Chapter 10), add the following code:

```
//Resizable Applets with user preference storage
var siebConsts = SiebelJS.Dependency("SiebelApp.Constants");
var oActiveView = SiebelApp.S_App.GetActiveView();
var oAppletMap = oActiveView.GetAppletMap();
```

```
var sViewName =  oActiveView.GetName();
var sValue,sAppletPref,prefArr,prefWidth,prefHeight;
var sKey = sViewName + "__size"; //create key
//property set for writing user prefs
var prefPS = SiebelApp.S_App.NewPropertySet();
//helper array with applet ids
var arrAppletIds = new Array;
//helper array with applet names
var arrAppletNames = new Array;
var i = 0;
var j = 0;
```

The example code represents the first part of the implementation and declares or initializes the following variables:

- **siebConsts**: References the `SiebelApp.Constants` class to retrieve constant values.

- **oActiveView**: The currently active view.

- **oAppletMap**: An array of all applets within the current view.

- **sViewName**: The name of the current view as in the Siebel repository.

- **sKey**: The soon-to-be user preference to store the applet width. The user preference name is constructed by concatenating the view name and the string `__size`. As user preferences are stored for each applet, the meaning of this key is that the applet can store different-sized information for different views.

- **prefPS**: Needed to store the user preference key.

- **arrAppletIds** and **arrAppletNames**: Helper arrays for easier identification of an applet.

2. In the next part of the case study, we implement a `for` loop that iterates over all applets in the current view. Add the following code below the last line of the first part:

```
for (var theApplet in oAppletMap){
  //get current PM
  var oAppletPM = oAppletMap[theApplet].GetPModel();
  var sAppletId = oAppletPM.Get("GetFullId");
  var oApplet = $("#" + sAppletId); //select applet
  //store applet id in helper array
  arrAppletIds[i] = sAppletId;
  //store applet name in helper array
  arrAppletNames[i] = theApplet;
  i++;
  //try to retrieve user preference
  sAppletPref = oAppletPM.Get(sKey);
  if (!SiebelApp.Utils.IsEmpty(sAppletPref)) {
    //if user preference found
```

```
        SiebelJS.Log("Retrieved user preference '" + sKey
            + "' for applet '" + theApplet + "': " + sAppletPref);
        prefArr = sAppletPref.split("x"); //get width and height
        prefWidth = prefArr[0];
        prefHeight = prefArr[1];
        oApplet.width(prefWidth);  //set applet width
        oApplet.height(prefHeight);  //set applet height
    }
}
```

In the `for` loop we do the following for each applet in the current view:

- Get the applet's presentation model.
- Get the `id` attribute value of the DOM element for the applet.
- Use jQuery to select the applet via the `id` attribute.
- Store the applet id and the name in the helper arrays.
- Get the user preference that stores the applet's custom size.
- In case the user preference is found, extract the width and height attribute values (separated by the `x` character) and set the applet width and height accordingly. This effectively applies the stored settings.

3. Next, we will implement the jQuery `resizable` method for the applet. In continuation of the previous part, add the following code to the custom postload event listener:

```
oApplet.resizable();  //make applet resizable
oApplet.on("resizestop", function (event,ui) {
//when user finishes resizing
  var thisPM, thisApplet;
  sValue = ui.size.width + "x" + ui.size.height;
  //create "Key" property
  prefPS.SetProperty("Key", sKey);
  //set value for "Key" property
  prefPS.SetProperty(sKey, sValue);
  for (j = 0; j < arrAppletIds.length; j++){
    //parse helper array
    if (arrAppletIds[j] == ui.element[0].id){
      //when applet found
      thisApplet = SiebelAppFacade.ComponentMgr.
      FindComponent(arrAppletNames[j]); //find applet
      thisPM = thisApplet.GetPM(); //get PM of applet
      //set user preference
      thisPM.OnControlEvent(
          siebConsts.get("PHYEVENT_INVOKE_CONTROL"),
          thisPM.Get(siebConsts.get
          ("SWE_MTHD_UPDATE_USER_PREF")), prefPS);
      thisPM.SetProperty(sKey,sValue); //set PM property
    }
  }
```

```
})
}
```

The example code accomplishes the following:

- Call the jQuery `resizable` method for the current applet.
- Define the `resizestop` event handler, which is invoked when the end user finishes a resize operation. In the event handler function we implement the following behavior.
- Get the new width and height and concatenate them with `x`.
- Set the `Key` property in the `prefPS` property set to the current key name (i.e. the view name suffixed with `_size`). This is a prerequisite for storing user preferences. The input property set must contain a `Key` property that defines the name of the user preference.
- Create the second required property in the `prefPS` property set to store the key value pair.
- Iterate over the helper array in order to identify the applet that has been resized. We can use the `ui` object passed to the event handler to obtain the value of the element's `id` attribute. This we can use to look up the applet name in the helper array.
- Use the `FindComponent` method of the `ComponentMgr` class to 'find' the applet in the current hierarchy.
- Get the applet's presentation model (PM) instance.
- Call the PM's `OnControlEvent` method and pass the following parameters:
  - The name of the method to invoke: this is retrieved from the `Constants` class using the `PHYEVENT_INVOKE_CONTROL` alias. This translates to a generic 'invoke' command that requires the name of another method that is actually invoked by the framework.
  - The first argument is the name of that method. It is retrieved as a PM property using a constant alias that references the method. The name of the method is `UpdateSWEPMUserPreference`.
  - The second argument is the property set that carries the `Key` property and its value.
- Finally we set the property directly through the PM to refresh it.

4. If necessary, register the custom postload event listener file with the `Application` object in the manifest.
5. After reloading the browser cache, all applets should be resizable. To test the behavior, resize some applets in a view, then log out and in again and navigate back to the same view. The applet size should be retained.

The following screenshot shows the Account Summary view (zoomed out for better observing) with applets that have been resized. This view is suitable for testing because it contains seven applets out-of-the-box.

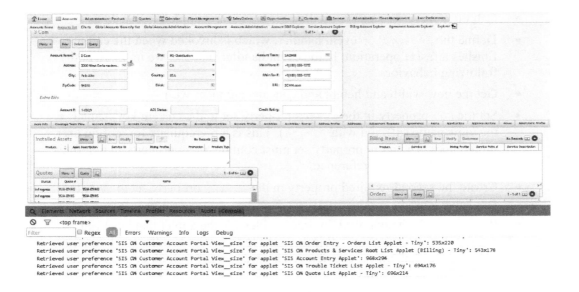

The screenshot also displays the browser's JavaScript console with log messages indicating the retrieval of user preference values for the various applets.

In this case study, we have successfully implemented the storage and retrieval of end user customizations to the user preference file. The nature of the user preference storage in Siebel CRM ensures that the settings can be retrieved independent of the browser or device.

Case Study: Implementing a Slider Widget

With the advent of touch screen devices, developers are challenged with new user experience requirements. Easy-to-use controls such as sliders provide a better user experience than traditional controls in most cases. In our next example case study, we will examine the steps needed to replace a dropdown list (Opportunity Probability) with a jQuery UI slider widget.

The challenge in this case study is not so much in 'drawing' the slider on the screen but in capturing and storing the changes with the current record.

The following screenshot shows the desired result of this case study.

Created Date: *	21.08.2014
Close Date: *	21.08.2014
Probability:	50%

The screenshot shows a portion of the opportunity form applet. The Probability control is implemented as a slider. The user is currently dragging the slider handle and the current value is displayed (50%). The slider's background color changes according to the value. When the user releases the slider handle, the new value is stored with the opportunity record.

The high-level steps to implement the requirement are as follows:

- Implementing a custom PM method that is invoked when the slider value is changed and which applies the changes to the current record.
- In the physical renderer (PR) of the same applet, modify the ShowUI method to create the slider widget.
- Implementing custom PR methods that set the slider value and style (color).

The following procedures guide us through the implementation steps for this case study. The example code is based on the custom presentation model and physical renderer for the applet named Opportunity Form Applet - Child that we created in previous chapters of this book. The full example code files (OpptyFormPM.js and OpptyFormPR.js) are provided with this chapter's code archive. Let's begin with the first step.

> Please note that the example code presented in this case study is based on Innovation Pack 2013. While the same code would be fully operational in IP 2014 and higher, we should consider using a custom plug-in wrapper to implement custom controls beginning with IP 2014. Refer to the next case study for a full example on implementing a custom slider control using a plug-in wrapper.

Implementing a Custom Presentation Model

The code we need to add to the custom presentation model in this case study allows us to capture important UI events such as the user selecting a different record or the slider handle being released. The following procedure describes the implementation steps based on the existing OpptyFormPM.js file:

1. Open the OpptyFormPM.js file and add the following code to the Init method:

```
//probability slider
this.AddProperty("C_ProbValSet",0);
this.AddProperty("C_ProbValNew",0);
this.AddMethod("SetProbability",SetProbability,
    {sequence:false, override:false, scope:this});
this.AttachEventHandler("PROB_SET","SetProbability");
```

The example code implements the following:

- Initialize two PM properties to hold the values of the probability field at different stages.
- Register the custom method SetProbability that implements the business logic.
- Attach the SetProbability method to the PROB_SET event (which will be invoked by the PR).

    2. If the Init method does not include the declaration of the PostShowSelection method, implement it as follows:

```
this.AddMethod("ShowSelection",PostShowSelection,
{sequence:false, scope:this});
```

    3. In the PostShowSelection method, add the following lines of code:

```
//Slider
var arrControls = this.Get("GetControls");
var oControl = arrControls["Probability2"];
var sValue = this.ExecuteMethod("GetFieldValue", oControl);
//set property
//this will trigger PR's update function to set slider
this.SetProperty("C_ProbValNew",sValue);
```

The example code does the following:

- Get the controls array.
- Obtain the instance of the Probability control using the repository name (Probability2).
- Get the current value of the Probability field.
- Set the C_ProbValNew property to the current probability value.

The purpose of this code is to set the C_ProbValNew property to the current probability value each time a new record selection is made. This allows the PR to pick up the value and set the slider control to the value.

4. Implement the `SetProbability` method as follows:

```
function SetProbability(msg){
   //invoked when PR calls event PROB_SET
   var sValue = this.Get("C_ProbValSet");
   var arrControls = this.Get("GetControls");
   var oControl = arrControls["Probability2"];
   this.OnControlEvent(consts.get("PHYEVENT_CONTROL_FOCUS"),
        oControl);
   this.OnControlEvent(consts.get("PHYEVENT_CONTROL_BLUR"),
        oControl, String(sValue));
}
```

The `SetProbability` method will be invoked by the PR through the `PROB_SET` event. It accomplishes the following functionality:

- Get the value of the `C_ProbValSet` property, which is the value that has been set by the slider widget.
- Get the probability control.
- Call the 'focus' event on the control. The correct name of the event should be retrieved from the `PHYEVENT_CONTROL_FOCUS` constant.
- Call the 'blur' event on the control and pass the new value as a string.

The example code illustrates how to trigger the correct framework events ('focus' and 'blur') when we need to update a field value. At the time of writing, the approach presented in the example code can be considered the safest as it does not directly call business component methods (a practice we should avoid in Siebel Open UI).

Implementing the jQuery UI Slider Widget in a Custom Physical Renderer

In the second part of this case study, we take care of the physical renderer as described in the following procedure:

1. Open the `OpptyFormPR.js` file that implements the custom physical renderer for the Opportunity form applet and add the following line of code to the `Init` method of the PR:

```
this.AttachPMBinding("C_ProbValNew",UpdateSlider,
{scope:this});
```

This code attaches the `UpdateSlider` function to the `C_ProbValNew` property. Recall that this property is set by the PM every time the record selection changes. The

UpdateSlider function (implemented later in this section) will take care of setting the slider handle to the correct value for each record.

2. Add the following code to the ShowUI method:

```
//Slider
var cProb = oControlSet["Probability2"];
var curVal = PM.ExecuteMethod("GetFieldValue",cProb);
var cProbID = cProb.GetInputName();
var cProbjq = $("[name='" + cProbID + "']");
var sliderOptions = { //set slider options
  start: function(){ //when slider is initialized
  },
  slide: function(e,ui){ //when user drags the slider handle
    //change the slider background color
    SetSliderStyle(ui.value);
  },
  change: function(e,ui){
    //when user releases the slider handle
    SetSliderStyle(ui.value);
    //set the property
    PM.SetProperty("C_ProbValSet",ui.value);
    PM.OnControlEvent("PROB_SET",ui.value);//wake up the PM
  },
  min:0,max:100,step:10,value:curVal
  //other options for slider
};//end of option settings
cProbjq.parent().hide();  //hide the original control
var mySlider = $("<div id='mySlider'></div>"); //create slider
mySlider.appendTo(cProbjq.parent().parent()); //append slider
mySlider.slider(sliderOptions); //make slider
mySlider.addClass("oui-slider"); //add class
```

The example code accomplishes the following:

- Get the current value of the probability field.
- Get the control's element name.
- Create a jQuery selection for the control, using the element name.
- Set the options for the slider. For more information about the jQuery UI slider widget, refer to http://jqueryui.com/slider.
- The slide event handler function is called when the slider handle position is changed. When this happens, we do the following.
  o Call the SetSliderStyle method that will compute the slider's background color and pass the current slider value.
- The change event handler function is triggered when the user releases the slider handle. Upon this event, we do the following.
  o Call the SetSliderStyle method.
  o Set the C_ProbValSet property to the final slider value.

- o Invoke the PROB_SET event. This will trigger the PM event handler function to save the record changes.
- The remaining slider options control the minimum (0) and maximum (100) values as well as the step increments (10) and the position of the slider handle (the current field value).
- After the slider options have been prepared we hide the original control.
- Next we create the slider container as a <div> element and append it to the original control's parent element.
- Using the jQuery UI slider function, we effectively create the slider.
- Finally we call the jQuery addClass function to add a class reference to the slider (to allow for individual styling in CSS).

3. Now it is time to implement the custom methods in the PR. The UpdateSlider method is attached to the C_ProbValNew property and is invoked every time the PM sets this property. The following is an example implementation of the UpdateSlider method:

```
function UpdateSlider(){
  //will be invoked when needed e.g. at ShowSelection by PM
  var newVal = PM.Get("C_ProbValNew");//get new prob value
  var oldVal = PM.Get("C_ProbValSet");//get old prob value
  if (!isNaN(oldVal) && oldVal != newVal){
    //condition for updating slider
    $(".oui-slider").slider("value",newVal);//set slider value
    SetSliderStyle(newVal);//change slider background color
  }
}
```

The purpose of the UpdateSlider function is the following:

- Get the new probability field value and the current slider value.
- Compare the new and current value and if they are different, set the slider value and call the SetSliderStyle function.

4. Finally, we implement the SetSliderStyle function as follows:

```
function SetSliderStyle(val){
//change the slider background color
  var color;
  //below val = 50, green will be 0-100, above 100
  var g = val <= 50 ? val*2 : 100;
  //below val = 50, red will be 100, above 100 - 0
  var r = val > 50 ? 200 - (val*2) : 100;
  //color in rgb % style e.g. "rgb(40%,100%,0%)"
  color = "rgb(" + r + "%," + g + "%,0%)";
  $(".oui-slider").css("background",color);
}
```

The `SetSliderStyle` function takes a numeric value (`val`) as the input and computes a color according to the value. The algorithm is basically the same as in the conditional formatting case study in Chapter 7 and results in a red-amber-green color scheme where higher values are represented by green.

The jQuery `css` method is used to apply the computed color to the slider.

Creating Custom CSS Rules

Use a custom CSS file such as the `custom-global.css` file that was introduced in Chapter 8 to pass the following styling rules to the browser:

```css
/*Slider and slider tooltip*/
.ui-slider-horizontal {
    height: .8em;
}
.ui-slider {
    position: relative;
    text-align: left;
}
.ui-widget-content {
    border: 1px solid #a6c9e2;
    background: #fcfdfd;
    color: #222222;
}
.ui-slider-horizontal .ui-slider-handle {
    top: -.3em;
    margin-left: -.6em;
}
.ui-slider .ui-slider-handle {
    border: 1px solid #a6c9e2;
    position: absolute;
    z-index: 2;
    width: 1.2em;
    height: 1.2em;
    cursor: default;
}
#tip{
    width: 30px;
    background: whitesmoke;
    color: black;
}
```

The CSS rules ensure that slider widgets appear consistent across all applets. The `#tip` rule at the end of the example code controls the look and feel of the slider tooltip. Note that as an alternative to providing CSS rules for the widget, we could also register the complete **jQuery UI CSS file,** which can be downloaded from `jqueryui.com` with our Open UI theme.

As usual, we have to save all modified files and test against an empty browser cache. In this case study, we have successfully replaced the original dropdown element to set an opportunity's probability value with a fully functional jQuery UI slider widget.

Case Study: Using a Plug-in Wrapper to Implement a Slider Widget (IP 2014 or higher)

In the previous case study we learned how to implement a custom slider control. As indicated at the beginning of the previous section, the example code applies to IP 2013 and IP 2014 alike, but we should consider using a custom plug-in wrapper in IP 2014 and beyond to implement custom controls. As discussed in Chapter 7, a plug-in wrapper can be understood as a physical renderer for controls and as such has an API similar to a physical renderer for an applet.

The following case study will have a similar result to the previous one - a custom slider control that allows one to set an opportunity's probability - but the code will be very different. Actually we will see that the amount of custom code is greatly reduced when we use the plug-in wrapper architecture introduced with IP 2014.

The high-level steps to implement a custom slider as a plug-in wrapper are as follows.

- Create a preliminary plug-in wrapper file and register it in the manifest
- Implement the ShowUI method of the custom plug-in wrapper
- Implement the BindEvents method of the custom plug-in wrapper
- Implement the SetValue method of the custom plug-in wrapper
- Attach the custom plug-in wrapper to control objects
- Create custom CSS rules

The following sections will guide us through this process.

Creating a Preliminary Plug-in Wrapper File and Registering it in the Manifest

As with any other custom JavaScript file in Siebel Open UI, we begin with a preliminary scaffold and register it in the manifest. Thus we ensure we have a simple but working starting point for our implementation.

The following procedure guides us through the process of creating a new custom plug-in wrapper file from a template and registering it in the manifest administration views.

1. Create a new JavaScript file in the siebel/custom folder and give it a meaningful name, such as SliderPW.js. Note the naming convention of using PW as the suffix to identify the file as a Plug-in Wrapper implementation.

2. To save time, we could use a template file to produce the preliminary code. For example, we can peruse Duncan Ford's Open UI PW Template Generator online at http://tiny.cc/pw-code-generator to create the code shown in the screenshot below.

```
if (typeof (SiebelAppFacade.SliderTemplatePW) === "undefined") {

    SiebelJS.Namespace("SiebelAppFacade.SliderTemplatePW");
    define("siebel/custom/SliderTemplatePW", [],
        function () {
            SiebelAppFacade.SliderTemplatePW = (function () {

                function SliderTemplatePW(pm) {
                    SiebelAppFacade.SliderTemplatePW.superclass.constructor.apply(this, arguments);
                }

                SiebelJS.Extend(SliderTemplatePW, SiebelAppFacade.DropDownPW);

                SliderTemplatePW.prototype.ShowUI = function () {
                    SiebelAppFacade.SliderTemplatePW.superclass.ShowUI.apply(this, arguments);
                };

                SliderTemplatePW.prototype.BindEvents = function () {
                    SiebelAppFacade.SliderTemplatePW.superclass.BindEvents.apply(this, arguments);
                };

                SliderTemplatePW.prototype.SetValue = function (value, index) {
                    SiebelAppFacade.SliderTemplatePW.superclass.SetValue.apply(this, arguments);
                };

                return SliderTemplatePW;
            }()
            );

            SiebelApp.S_App.PluginBuilder.AttachPW(consts.get("SWE_CTRL_COMBOBOX"),
                SiebelAppFacade.SliderTemplatePW,
                function (control, objName) {
                    return true;
                });

            return "SiebelAppFacade.SliderTemplatePW";
        })
}
```

The screenshot shows a template file for a custom plug-in wrapper. An example template file (SliderTemplatePW.js) is included in this chapter's code archive.

The following lines in the template need our special attention:

```
SiebelJS.Extend(SliderTemplatePW, SiebelAppFacade.DropDownPW);
```

We recognize this line as it defines the base class for our custom class using the SiebelJS.Extend method. For plug-in wrappers, we must extend the correct base class depending on the type of control we wish to customize. For example, the above code refers to the DropDownPW class which is the base class for drop down fields. Refer to Chapter 7 for a list of control types and their respective base classes.

```
SiebelApp.S_App.PluginBuilder.AttachPW(
    consts.get("SWE_CTRL_COMBOBOX"),
    SiebelAppFacade.SliderTemplatePW,
    function (control, objName) {
       return true;
    }
});
```

In a plug-in wrapper file, we must implement the AttachPW method of the PluginBuilder class as shown in the code example. As discussed in Chapter 7, the 'evaluation function', passed as the third argument, allows us to evaluate conditions for when to attach the plug-in wrapper to a control. In our example code, the return value of the 'evaluation function' is always true, so that the custom plug-in wrapper would be attached to any drop down control in the current view. For a real-life implementation, we will likely have to modify the template code at this line. Please refer to the respective section in this case study for details on using the AttachPW method.

In continuation of this first part of the case study, we will now register the custom file in the manifest.

3. If you used a template, ensure that the class name in the file is correct. If necessary, replace all occurrences of SliderTemplatePW with the correct class name, such as SliderPW and save the file.

4. In the Siebel Web Client, navigate to the Administration - Application screen and register the new file as usual in the Manifest Files view.

5. In the Manifest Administration view, use a custom entry for the Common usage type of the Application UI object named PLATFORM DEPENDENT to register the file. Choose a suitable expression (or none).

6. Log off and on again and verify that the custom plug-in wrapper file is loaded.

This completes the process of creating a preliminary plug-in wrapper file and registering it in the manifest.

Implementing the ShowUI Method of the Custom Plug-in Wrapper

As we recall, the ShowUI method is the place to define the physical appearance of a UI object. The following example code shows how to define a jQuery UI slider widget and append it to an existing control.

```
SliderPW.prototype.ShowUI = function(){
   SiebelAppFacade.SliderPW.superclass.ShowUI
       .apply(this,arguments);
   //get the jQuery object for the control
   var pwEl = this.GetEl();
   //create a slider, using the control name to make it unique
   var mySlider = $("<div id='slider"
```

```
        + pwEl.attr("name") + "'></div>");
    var sliderOptions = { min:0, max:100, step:10, value:0 };
    mySlider.appendTo(pwEl.parent().parent());
    mySlider.slider(sliderOptions);   //make slider
    mySlider.addClass("ouib-slider");  //add class for style
};
```

The example implementation of the ShowUI method for a custom plug-in wrapper accomplishes the following.

- Instantiate the pwEl variable with the jQuery object representation of the control using the GetEl method.

- Instantiate a jQuery object for the slider, using the name attribute of the control to make it unique.

- Set default slider options. In a more sophisticated implementation, we could read these values from control user properties. Refer to this chapter's code archive for a file (SliderPW.js) that uses (and relies upon) control user properties.

- Use the jQuery appendTo method to append the new slider widget to the control.

- Set the slider options and add a class attribute to facilitate CSS styling.

As a result of the above code, a jQuery UI slider widget will be shown below the control that the plug-in wrapper is attached to.

Implementing the BindEvents Method of the Custom Plug-in Wrapper

In the BindEvents method, we define the event handling for the custom control. The following example code shows a simple implementation for the slider control.

```
SliderPW.prototype.BindEvents = function(){
  SiebelAppFacade.SliderPW.superclass.BindEvents.call(this);
  var that = this;
  //define slider events
  $("#slider" + this.GetEl().attr("name")).slider({
    change: function(e,ui){
      //when user releases the slide handle
      //call focus and blur events to trigger event handling
      that.OnControlEvent(
      consts.get("PHYEVENT_CONTROL_FOCUS"),that.control);
      that.OnControlEvent(consts.get("PHYEVENT_CONTROL_BLUR"),
      that.control, String(ui.value));
      },
    slide: function(e,ui){
      //while user slides, show the value
      that.GetEl().val(ui.value);
```

```
    }
  });
};
```

The example code implements the following.

- Pass the current context (this) to the that variable, so we can refer to it in the event handler functions.

- Define the change event handler for the slider, so that when the user releases the slider handle, the current slider value will be passed to the Open UI framework. This is accomplished by calling the 'focus' and 'blur' control events. Using these control events ensures that the chain of events in the Open UI framework is executed correctly.

- Define the slide event handler. The example code updates the control value with the current slider value so that the end user has visual feedback.

As you can probably already tell, the plug-in wrapper architecture that was introduced in IP 2014 allows us to achieve control-specific requirements with much less coding effort than for previous releases.

Implementing the SetValue Method of the Custom Plug-in Wrapper

As described in Chapter 7, the SetValue method is invoked when the Open UI framework changes the control's value. We must override this method to notify our custom control (the slider widget) of these changes.

The following example code shows an implementation of the SetValue method.

```
SliderPW.prototype.SetValue = function(value, index){
  SiebelAppFacade.SliderPW.superclass.SetValue
      .call(this, value, index);
  //set the slider value
  $("#slider" +  this.GetEl().attr("name"))
      .slider('value',Number(value));
};
```

The example code accomplishes the following.

- Call the superclass' SetValue method.
- Set the value of the slider widget to the value passed to the SetValue method.

As a result of the example code, the slider's value will adjust automatically to the control's value - independent of the source of change.

Attaching the Custom Plug-in Wrapper to Control Objects

As discussed above, we want to define precisely which control should be enhanced with our custom plug-in wrapper. The place to do this is the `AttachPW` method of the `PluginBuilder` class.

The following example code shows how to use the `AttachPW` method for our slider scenario.

```
SiebelApp.S_App.PluginBuilder.AttachPW(
  consts.get("SWE_CTRL_COMBOBOX"),
  SiebelAppFacade.SliderPW,
    function (control) {
      if (control.GetName() == "Probability2") {
        return true;   //make it so
      }
      else {return false};
});
```

The example implementation above attaches the custom `SliderPW` class to drop-down controls only if the name of the control is `Probability2` (for demonstration purposes, we use the same control on the *Opportunity Form Applet - Child* applet as in the previous case study). The drop down control type is identified by the `SWE_CTRL_COMBOBOX` constant value.

It must be noted that the example code is kept simple for the sake of brevity. We could implement much higher levels of sophistication when it comes to evaluating the conditions for attaching a PW to a control. For example we could evaluate whether the current device is touch-enabled or use a control user property as a kind of 'switch' to use the custom PW or not.

Creating Custom CSS Rules

To finalize our custom plug-in wrapper, we should take care of its physical appearance by adding CSS rules to a custom style sheet.

The following CSS rules serve as a simple example and can, of course, be adjusted to your needs.

```css
.ui-slider-horizontal .ui-slider-handle {
    top: -.3em;
    margin-left: -.6em;
}
.ui-slider .ui-slider-handle {
    position: absolute;
    z-index: 2;
    width: 1.2em;
    height: 1.2em;
    cursor: default;
    -ms-touch-action: none;
    touch-action: none;
```

```
}
.ui-slider-horizontal {
    height: .8em;
    border: 1px solid #aaaaaa;
    position: relative;
}
.ui-state-default, .ui-widget-content .ui-state-default, .ui-
widget-header .ui-state-default {
    border: 1px solid #d3d3d3;
    background: #e6e6e6;
    font-weight: normal;
    color: #555555;
}
```

You can find these CSS rules in the `SliderPW.css` file that is delivered with this chapter's code archive.

The following screenshot shows the slider widget as rendered by the custom plug-in wrapper that we created in the previous case study.

During testing, you will observe that the value of the probability field changes as soon as you move the slider handle. When you release the handle, the value will be set in the field. This can be observed nicely in a parent list view where you can see the current record in both the parent list applet and the form applet. Using the slider in the form applet will set the field value in the list applet and vice-versa.

This concludes our case study for implementing a custom plug-in wrapper.

In this chapter's code archive you will also find a file named `ListSliderPW.js` which is an extended variant of the previous case study example. The code in the `ListSliderPW.js` file serves as an example for defining user properties on the Control or List Column object level to define the behavior of the slider widget. In addition, the code has been extended to work with form applets and list applets.

Case Study: Using Applet Labels to Display Metadata

The following case study implements a requirement that is not related to typical end users but rather administrators and analysts. Many times, in a Siebel implementation project, there is need to identify the business component field and physical table or column information for a given applet control quickly. The process of finding this information in the traditional way requires familiarity (and access to) Siebel Tools, both of which are often not immediately available to the person who has to find this key information.

In this case study, we will look at a new way - facilitated by the Open UI JavaScript API - to display the business layer and physical layer metadata for every control on a form applet with a simple mouse gesture such as a double click. This functionality is, of course, not intended to be available for end users - it would just confuse or even scare them.

The following screen shot sequence illustrates the outcome of this case study.

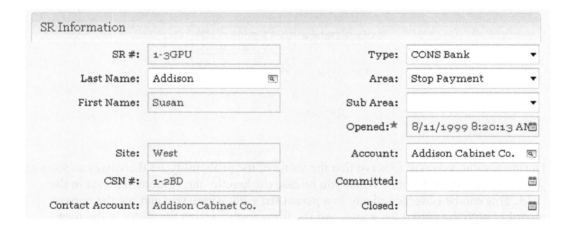

The screenshot shows a portion of a service request form applet in its original state. Note that the labels are displayed as per their definition in the Siebel repository.

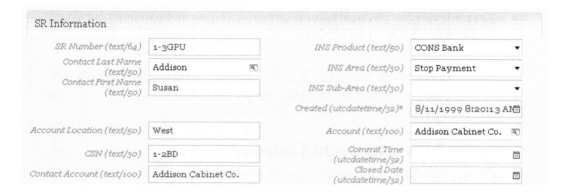

The second screenshot shows the same applet after the user has double clicked anywhere in the applet. The labels are replaced with metadata information from the business layer (BC field name, data type, and length of the respective control).

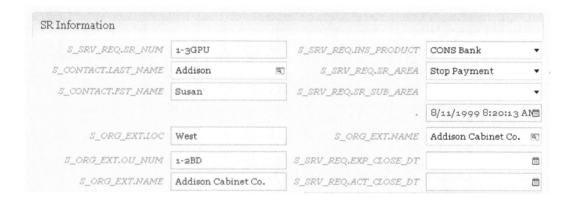

The third and final screenshot shows the same applet after another double click. The labels now convey the name of the physical table and column where the data for the respective control is stored in the Siebel database.

Such insight into repository metadata is very valuable during almost every phase of a Siebel CRM implementation project and quick access to metadata (as demonstrated earlier) is a plausible requirement for technically-oriented users and analysts.

The following are the high-level process steps to accomplish the metadata display for form applets:

- Create a `postload` event listener to add a double click event handler to any form applet within the current view.
- Implement a custom utility method that handles the double click event, retrieves the metadata and toggles the label text.

- For retrieving the physical layer information (tables and columns), a custom business service must be implemented.

As usual, this chapter's code archive contains a complete example. For the sake of brevity, some of the code is not shown in this chapter. Refer to the `custompl.js` and `custom_utils.js` files in the code archive for the complete code.

Creating a Postload Event Listener

The following procedure guides us through the implementation of a custom `postload` event listener to capture and process the double click event on form applets:

1. Create a `postload` event listener file (or open an existing one) and add the following code inside the event handler function:

```
/*Display Metadata on double click*/
var view = SiebelApp.S_App.GetActiveView();
var arrApplets = view.GetAppletMap();
var target; //the future jQuery target
var myPM; //the presentation model object
var theApplet; //the applet object
var isForm = true; //is it a form or not
for(var a in arrApplets){
  theApplet = arrApplets[a];
  target = $("#"+ theApplet.GetFullId());
  //get applet type via list-only function GetListCol
  if (typeof(theApplet.GetListCol) === "function"){
    isForm = false;  }
    else { isForm = true; }
    if (isForm){
      target.dblclick(function(){
      theApplet = view.GetActiveApplet();
      myPM = theApplet.GetPModel(); //the active applet's PM
      var cycle; //the toggle cycle
      switch (myPM.Get("C_ToggleCycle")){
        case "ShowBCFields"    : cycle = "ShowTableColumns";
                                 break;
        case "ShowTableColumns" : cycle = "Reset";
                                 break;
        case "Reset"           : cycle = "ShowBCFields";
                                 break;
        default                : cycle = "ShowBCFields";
                                 break;
      }
    myPM.SetProperty("C_ToggleCycle",cycle);
    SiebelApp.CustomUtils.ToggleLabels(cycle, myPM);
    });
  }
}
```

The example code implements the following:

- Get the current view object.
- Get the applet map for the current view.
- Iterate through the applets. For each applet we do the following.
  - Create a jQuery object for the current applet.
  - Determine whether the applet is a form applet or not by probing for the presence of the `GetListCol` method, which would mean that the applet is a list applet.
  - If the applet is a form applet, apply the jQuery `dblclick` event handler method.
- In the event handler function, set the `cycle` variable according to the current value of the `C_ToggleCycle` property. Basically, the `switch` block assigns one of three string values in the following sequence:
  - ShowBCFields (the default)
  - ShowTableColumns
  - Reset

  The value of the `cycle` variable will therefore always be set forward at each double click event.
- Finally, we call the `ToggleLabels` method of a custom class named `CustomUtils`. As parameters we pass the `cycle` variable and the current presentation model instance. We will yet have to create the custom class (see next section).

This concludes the work on the `postload` event listener. In this case study, we use a custom utility class (`CustomUtils`), which we will implement in the next step.

Implementing a Custom Utility Class

Using a globally available class rather than implementing private functions is a recommended practice to avoid code duplication. The following procedure guides us through the steps needed to create a custom utility class that implements the `ToggleLabels` method that we call from the `postload` event listener:

1. Create a new JavaScript file. For example, name the file `custom_utils.js` and store it in the `siebel/custom` folder as usual.

2. At the beginning of the file, add the following code:

```
if(typeof (SiebelApp.CustomUtils) === "undefined"){
    Namespace("SiebelApp.CustomUtils");
}
```

The code adds the `CustomUtils` class to the `SiebelApp` namespace if it is not already defined.

3. Add the following code to implement the ToggleLabels method:

```
SiebelApp.CustomUtils.ToggleLabels = function(cycle, myPM){
  //some "global" variables
  var target; //the jQuery target
  var sControlName; //the current control name
  var oControl; //the control object
  var sNewLabel; //the replacement label display value
  var sLabelName; //the name (Id) of the control label
  var sLabelHTML; //the replacement HTML
  var arrControls = myPM.Get("GetControls"); //controls
  switch (cycle){
    case "ShowBCFields"     : ShowBCFields();
                              break;
    case "ShowTableColumns" : ShowTableColumns();
                              break;
    case "Reset"            : LabelReset();
                              break;
    default                 : ShowBCFields();
                              break;
  }
}
```

The code listing is the first part of the ToggleLabels method and implements the following:

- Declare various variables for future use.
- Get the controls array from the presentation model instance.
- Depending on the value of the cycle variable, invoke different functions such as ShowBCFields.

4. The following code must be added below the previous example code and implements the ShowBCFields function:

```
function ShowBCFields(){
  var oBC = myPM.Get("GetBusComp"); //get applet's BC object
  var oBCFieldMap = oBC.GetFieldMap(); //get "field map"
  var sDataType; //data type
  var sLength; //field length
  var sReq; //Required flag
  var sCalc; //Calculated flag
  var oField; //the field object itself
  //parse array of applet controls
  for(sControlName in arrControls){
    if(arrControls.hasOwnProperty(sControlName)){
      oControl = arrControls[sControlName];
      sNewLabel = oControl.GetFieldName();
      if (sNewLabel != ""){
        //control has a field, i.e. is not a button etc...
        //get field properties from field map
```

```
            oField = oBCFieldMap[sNewLabel]; //the field object
            sDataType = oField.GetDataType();
            sLength = oField.GetLength();
            sReq = oField.IsRequired() ? "*" : "";
            sCalc = oField.IsCalc() ? "C" : "";
            //create the Open UI label name
            sLabelName = sControlName.replace(/ /g,"_")
                + "_Label";
            sLabelHTML = "<span id='" + sLabelName + "'>"
                + sNewLabel + " (" + sDataType + "/" + sLength
                + ")" + sReq + sCalc + "</span>";
            //alter the target
            target = $("span#" + sLabelName).parent();
            target.html(sLabelHTML); //replace the HTML
            //apply some style, should be done with proper CSS
            target.css({'font-style': 'italic',
                'color': '#FF0000'});
        }
    }
  } //end of loop
}
```

The ShowBCFields function implements the following:

- Get the business component (BC) instance using the GetBusComp PM property.
- Get the field map for the business component.
- Iterate through the applet controls. For each control we do the following.
  - Get the BC field name.
  - Instantiate the BC field as the oField variable.
  - Invoke methods such as GetDataType on the field instance to obtain the field data type, the length, and determine whether it is a required or a calculated field. As we can see, all this metadata is available within the Open UI framework, so no server roundtrip is needed to get this information.
  - Create a new HTML string that will replace the current label by concatenating the string values obtained in the previous step.
  - Use the jQuery html method to effectively replace the current label with the new text.

The ShowTableColumns function is invoked next in the double click cycle. It invokes a server side business service method and passes a property set with field names. The business service queries the business components that represent the repository data for business components and returns an enriched property set with a string denoting the table and column name for the respective field.

For the sake of brevity, we do not discuss the code of the ShowTableColumns function nor the custom business service in this chapter. However, you might want to refer to this chapter's code archive for the full solution.

The LabelReset function is the third in the double click sequence and uses the following code to reset the label captions to their original values:

```
function LabelReset(){
  for(sControlName in arrControls){
    if(arrControls.hasOwnProperty(sControlName)){
      oControl = arrControls[sControlName];
      sNewLabel = oControl.GetDisplayName();
      if (sNewLabel != ""){
        sLabelName = sControlName.replace(/ /g,"_")
            + "_Label";
        sLabelHTML = "<span id='" + sLabelName + "'>"
            + sNewLabel + ":</span>";
        target = $("span#" + sLabelName).parent();
        target.html(sLabelHTML);
        target.css({'font-style': 'inherit',
            'color': '#000000'});
      }
    }
  }
}
```

The example code accomplishes the following:

- For each control in the current controls array, do the following.
    o Use the GetDisplayName method of the control object to obtain the control's original caption text.
    o Generate a new HTML string using the caption text.
    o Replace the current label HTML with the new string.

Do not forget to import the business service provided with this chapter's code archive in Siebel Tools. It is mandatory to register the business service with the application you are using in your implementation and to compile both the business service and the application object to the SRF file.

Register the custom utility file with the PLATFORM DEPENDENT entry that we already used to register custom files that should always be loaded such as the file containing the custom postload event listener or the custom plug-in wrapper.

To test the implementation, make sure to reload the browser cache. Then navigate to a view that has at least one form applet. Double clicking the form applet should toggle the label text for each control to display the business layer metadata. Double clicking again should result in the display of physical layer metadata. Compare your results with the screenshots shown at the beginning of this case study.

In this case study, we learned how to implement a double click event handler for all form applets within the application. The example code demonstrates the use of API methods to retrieve business layer metadata.

Restricting Functionality to Certain User Groups

As indicated earlier in the previous case study, the functionality of displaying field metadata might not be intended for all end users. One possible approach to restrict the functionality would be by creating a **custom manifest expression** similar to the following example:

```
GetProfileAttrAsList('Me.Position') LIKE "*Admin*"
```

A21   The expression uses the `GetProfileAttrAsList` function. This function returns all values of a multi-value field as a comma separated string. The `Position` field of the `Me` profile contains all positions that are assigned to the employee. We compare the result string with the pattern defined by the string `*Admin*` (any string that contains the sub-string 'Admin') using the `LIKE` operator. As a result, the expression will evaluate to `TRUE` when one of the current user's position names contains the text 'Admin'. Otherwise it will evaluate to `FALSE`.

We can now use this manifest expression in the Manifest Administration view to control which JavaScript files are loaded for individuals who hold at least one 'Admin' position.

In your project implementation, the logic to restrict functionality based on user profile information might differ from the approach presented here.

Case Study: List Applet Scrolling

The following case study example is provided by Siebel blogger Neelmani Gautam (`http://siebelunleashed.com`) and demonstrates how to implement mouse wheel support for list applets.

The high-level steps for the implementation are as follows:

- Download the jQuery `mousewheel` plug-in.
- Create a physical renderer extension for list applets to capture the `mousewheel` event and invoke the correct physical events such as 'next record' or 'previous record'.

For the sake of demonstration, we will implement a `mousewheel` event handler that triggers the physical events under the following conditions:

- When the *CTRL* key is pressed during the wheel rotation, go to the next or previous record.
- When the *CTRL* and *SHIFT* keys are pressed during the wheel rotation, go to the next or previous record set (page).

The following scenario guides us through the implementation:

1. Go to `https://github.com/brandonaaron/jquery-mousewheel` and download the jQuery `mousewheel` plug-in.

2. Extract the archive to the `siebel/custom` folder.

3. Create a new physical renderer file (using a template) and save it in the `siebel/custom` folder. For example, name the file `ListWheelScrollPR.js`.

4. Implement the `define` function as follows.

```
define("siebel/custom/ListWheelScrollPR",
["siebel/jqgridrenderer","siebel/custom/jquery-mousewheel-
master/jquery.mousewheel.min"]
```

The list of file dependencies must include the `jquery.mousewheel.min.js` file of the jQuery `mousewheel` plug-in.

5. Implement the `ShowUI` method of the PR as follows:

```
ListWheelScrollPR.prototype.ShowUI = function () {
    SiebelAppFacade.ListWheelScrollPR.superclass.ShowUI
        .call(this);
    var pHolder = this.GetPM().Get("GetFullId");
    var siebConsts=SiebelJS.Dependency("SiebelApp.Constants");
    //code to add mouse scrolling to list applets
    $('#'+pHolder).on('mousewheel',
        {ctx:this,consts:siebConsts},
        function(event){
          var that = event.data.ctx; //get 'this' instance
          var directionNext = "", directionPrev = "";
          if(!(event.ctrlKey) && !(event.shiftKey)){
            //if neither CTRL or SHIFT is pressed do nothing
            return true;
          }
          if(event.ctrlKey && !(event.shiftKey)){
            //in case of CTRL Key but no SHIFT
            //get the constants for Next Record
            //and Previous Record
            directionNext =
                event.data.consts.get("PAG_NEXT_RECORD");
            directionPrev =
                event.data.consts.get("PAG_PREV_RECORD");
          }
          if(event.ctrlKey && event.shiftKey){
            //if both keys are pressed
            //get constants for next and previous set
            directionNext =
                event.data.consts.get("PAG_NEXT_SET");
            directionPrev =
                event.data.consts.get("PAG_PREV_SET");
          }
```

```
      if(event.deltaY <= -1 || event.deltaX >= 1){
        //scroll down detected
        //invoke the physical action
        that.GetPM().OnControlEvent(event.data.consts.get(
            "PHYEVENT_VSCROLL_LIST"), directionNext);
        //stop default action (page scrolling)
        event.preventDefault();
      }
      if(event.deltaY >= 1 || event.deltaX <= -1){
        //scroll up detected
        //invoke the physical action
        that.GetPM().OnControlEvent( event.data.consts.get(
            "PHYEVENT_VSCROLL_LIST" ), directionPrev );
        event.preventDefault();
      }
    });
  };
```

The example code accomplishes the following:

- Get the placeholder id for the list applet container element.

- Get the `Constants` class reference.

- Use the jQuery `on` function to attach the `mousewheel` event handler to the list applet.

- Pass the current PR instance (`ctx:this`) and the constants reference (`consts:siebConsts`) to the event handler.

- In the event handler function, we evaluate which keys have been pressed while the mouse wheel was used.

- The `event.ctrlKey` attribute is `true` when the *CTRL* key was pressed. In a similar fashion, the `event.shiftKey` attribute is `true` when the *SHIFT* key was pressed.

- If only the *CTRL* key was pressed but not the *SHIFT* key, we assign the value of the `PAG_NEXT_RECORD` constant to the `directionNext` variable and the value of the `PAG_PREV_RECORD` constant to the `directionPrev` variable to determine record by record navigation.

- When both keys have been pressed, we use the `PAG_NEXT_SET` and `PAG_PREV_SET` accordingly to navigate by record set (page).

- The next step is to evaluate the `deltaY` (vertical axis) and `deltaX` (horizontal axis) attributes of the event object.

- When the `deltaY` attribute is negative, the mouse wheel direction was down. In combination with the *SHIFT* key, the `deltaX` attribute is typically used to define sideways navigation, but in our case we wish to apply up and down navigation as well. Therefore we interpret a positive `deltaX` value as 'down'. The opposite - positive `deltaY` and negative `deltaX` values - is interpreted as 'up'.

- In both cases we invoke the PM event represented by the `PHYEVENT_SCROLL_LIST` constant. In the 'down' case, we pass the `directionNext` variable, in the 'up' scenario, the `directionPrev` variable is used.

6. Register the PR file in the manifest against a test list applet, then log off and on again and clear the browser cache.
7. Navigate to the view that contains the test applet, hold the *CTRL* key and use the mouse scroll wheel to move from one record to the other.
8. Hold the *CTRL* and the *SHIFT* key at the same time and operate the scroll wheel again. Observe that the list applet now displays the next or previous record set.

Once you have successfully verified that the list applet reacts to the mouse wheel as expected, you might want to register the PR with the `DEFAULT LIST APPLET` entry for an applet's physical renderer.

In this case study, we learned how to use a jQuery plug-in and Open UI constants to implement mouse wheel scrolling for list applets. As always, this chapter's code archive contains complete solution files for this case study.

Case Study: Collecting Performance Measures

When investigating the performance of an enterprise application as perceived by the end user, we not only have to take into consideration server-side processing and network latency but also the effort of the browser to render the user interface.

Of course, there are various products available from different vendors that would offer us great insight into the end-to-end performance and click stream of an application such as Siebel CRM. However, these tools are costly and if it is just a specific measure we need, implementing a custom solution is substantially cheaper.

In this case study we will explore one approach to measure the browser-side performance of Siebel Open UI in terms of view rendering. Let us assume the following requirement:

- The (fictitious) Siebel testing team wants to establish clear and objective measurements for browser performance. One key performance measure is the time the browser takes to render a new view in Siebel Open UI.

Our similarly fictitious chief engineer has come up with an elegant solution that is comprised of the following steps:

- Create a `preload` event listener to capture the start timestamp of a view navigation event.

- Implement a `postload` event listener to capture the stop timestamp when the new view is fully rendered.
- Provide a menu item that allows the user to display a dialog that conveys the measurements for each view.

The following screenshot shows this dialog.

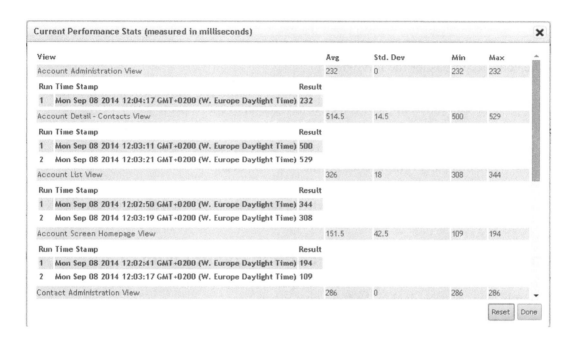

View	Avg	Std. Dev	Min	Max
Account Administration View	232	0	232	232

Run Time Stamp		Result
1	Mon Sep 08 2014 12:04:17 GMT+0200 (W. Europe Daylight Time)	232

View	Avg	Std. Dev	Min	Max
Account Detail - Contacts View	514.5	14.5	500	529

Run Time Stamp		Result
1	Mon Sep 08 2014 12:03:11 GMT+0200 (W. Europe Daylight Time)	500
2	Mon Sep 08 2014 12:03:21 GMT+0200 (W. Europe Daylight Time)	529

View	Avg	Std. Dev	Min	Max
Account List View	326	18	308	344

Run Time Stamp		Result
1	Mon Sep 08 2014 12:02:50 GMT+0200 (W. Europe Daylight Time)	344
2	Mon Sep 08 2014 12:03:19 GMT+0200 (W. Europe Daylight Time)	308

View	Avg	Std. Dev	Min	Max
Account Screen Homepage View	151.5	42.5	109	194

Run Time Stamp		Result
1	Mon Sep 08 2014 12:02:41 GMT+0200 (W. Europe Daylight Time)	194
2	Mon Sep 08 2014 12:03:17 GMT+0200 (W. Europe Daylight Time)	109

View	Avg	Std. Dev	Min	Max
Contact Administration View	286	0	286	286

As can be seen in the screenshot, the performance statistics (in milliseconds) are shown for each view and consist of the individual results as well as aggregates such as average, standard deviation, minimum and maximum runtime.

The following procedures guide us through the implementation of this feature. This chapter's code archive contains the full example files (`timerpre.js` and `timerpost.js`) for your convenience.

Implementing a Custom Preload Event Listener

In this first step of the case study, we implement a new `preload` event listener to capture the timestamp when the user navigates to a new view.

1. Create a new custom JavaScript file named `timerpre.js` and add the following code:

```
var timerStart;
var timerStop;
```

```
var timerResults = {viewtested: [], result: [], times: []};
if (typeof(SiebelAppFacade.TimerPreload) == "undefined") {
   Namespace('SiebelAppFacade.TimerPreload');
   (function () {
      SiebelApp.EventManager.addListner("preload",
         OnPreload, this);
      function OnPreload() {
         timerStart = new Date();
      }
   }());
}
```

The code accomplishes the following:

- Initialize the `timerStart` and `timerStop` variables, which will hold the start and stop timestamps of the view navigation event respectively.
- Initialize the `timerResults` variable as an object that will contain the array of visited views as well as the results and timings.
- Establish an event listener for the `preload` event.
- In the event handler function, assign the current timestamp to the `timerStart` variable, effectively capturing the beginning of the rendering process.

Implementing a Custom Postload Event Listener

To capture the end timestamp of view navigation, we implement a custom `postload` event listener as described in the following procedure:

1. Create a new custom JavaScript file named `timerpost.js` and implement a `postload` event handler function as follows:

```
function OnPostload() {
//create 'fake' menu item
//that shows results dialog when clicked
   if ($(".PerfReview").length == 0) {
     $(".applicationMenu")
     .after($('<div class="PerfReview">')
     .append(
     $('<a href="javascript:void(0)">PerfReview</a></div>')
     .on("click", function() {
       displayPerfStats();
       $("td.viewName").on("click", function (){
         $(this)
         .parent().next().find("table")
         .toggleClass("detailShow")});
     })
     .hover(function() {
       $(this).addClass("PerfHighlight")
     },
     function() {
```

```
      $(this).removeClass("PerfHighlight")
    }))))
  }
  //view is loaded
  //now capture stop timestamp, view name and results
  timerStop = new Date();
  timerResults.viewtested.push(SiebelApp.S_App.GetActiveView()
    .GetName())
  timerResults.result.push(timerStop - timerStart);
  timerResults.times.push(timerStart);
}
```

The function accomplishes the following:

- Append a link after the application menu.
- In the `click` event handler of the link, call the custom `displayPerfStats` function (to be implemented).
- Assign the current timestamp to the `timerStop` variable value. This captures the time at the end of the rendering process.
- Retrieve the current view name and push it to the `viewtested` array of the `timerResults` object.
- Calculate the results as the difference between the stop and start timestamp and push it to the `result` array.
- Save the start timestamp in the array as well.

2. Implement the `displayPerfStats` function as follows:

```
function displayPerfStats() {
  $("<div></div>").dialog({
    title: "Current Performance Stats (measured in
        milliseconds)",
    modal: true,
    width: "800px",
    buttons: {
      "Reset": function () {
        timerResults = {viewtested:[],result:[],times:[]};
        $(".perfTable").find("tr:gt(0)").remove()},
      "Done": function () {
        $(this).dialog("close")}
    },
    open: function () {
     $(this).html(processPerfData())
    }
  })
}
```

The purpose of this function is to display a jQuery dialog with the results that have been collected in the `timerResults` object so far. The main HTML content of the dialog is the return value of the `processPerfData` function which must be implemented next.

For the sake of brevity, we do not print the code of the `processPerfData` function here. Please refer to the `timerpost.js` file in this chapter's code archive for the full code example. However we would like to point out the key functionality of the `processPerfData` function in the following list:

- Create an HTML table for displaying the results.
- Retrieve a distinct sorted list of views from the `timerResults` object.
- For each individual view, create a detail table and fill it with the individual results.

To finish the implementation, we must register the `timerpre.js` and `timerpost.js` files with the `PLATFORM DEPENDENT` entry for the `Application` object type in the Manifest Administration view.

Testing the Collection of Performance Data

To prepare for a test of the new performance measurement feature, we restart the application and clear the browser cache (as usual).

Then, we navigate between views, ensuring that some of the views are visited more than just once. Of course, it is beneficial to have a test script (or even an automated test suite) at hand to ensure consistency.

To open the performance display, click the PerfReview link in the application menu. Observe that the dialog displays performance statistics for all views that have been opened in the current session. Compare the dialog to the screenshot shown at the beginning of this case study.

Summary

In this chapter we presented advanced scripting concepts using case study scenarios.

In the first case study we learned how to implement custom tooltips for arbitrary list columns and controls while the concept of storing and retrieving individual user preferences on the applet level was the topic of the second case study.

Using jQuery widgets, such as the slider, was demonstrated in the third case study.

We also demonstrated the benefits of the plug-in wrapper architecture that was introduced with IP 2014. We investigated a scenario of creating a fully functional slider for Innovation Pack 2013 and did the same using a custom plug-in wrapper (which only applies to Innovation Pack 2014).

Analysts, super users and administrators will benefit from the implementation of displaying metadata in form applet labels, whereas end users would certainly benefit from scroll wheel navigation in list applets which we implemented in a separate case study.

To assist with basic research requirements, the final case study in this chapter demonstrated the collection of performance statistics for view rendering in the browser.

In the next chapter, we will explore browser-side and server-side debugging tools and techniques.

13

Open UI Development and Debugging

Besides understanding the programming interface to an enterprise application such as Siebel CRM, it is paramount for a developer to have a solid grasp of the functionality that is provided in terms of debugging and troubleshooting. With Siebel Open UI, the browser implements much of this functionality. This chapter describes general approaches to developing and debugging Open UI components with the help of the browser's built-in or plugged-in developer tools.

The following topics will be discussed in this chapter:

- Open UI development overview
- Development tools for Siebel Open UI
- Inspecting DOM elements
- Script debugging
- Browser side performance measurement
- Server side debugging
- Case Study: Debugging a physical renderer

Open UI Development Overview

Prior to Open UI, Siebel configuration, development, and debugging were primarily performed via Siebel Tools – Siebel's proprietary metadata driven integrated development environment (IDE). While some administration and configuration tasks were performed through the application, work items like debugging browser scripts or updating web templates required some special tools. The vast majority of configuration tasks involved Siebel Tools and made it a single workspace for all development work.

Open UI significantly changes the way we work from a UI configuration and development perspective. While Siebel Tools is still the primary IDE for configuring metadata objects such as business components or applets, various tasks at the UI level are now performed outside Siebel Tools.

Before discussing these tasks, it is important to mention that the metadata configuration of UI components, such as defining applets and views, and positioning controls on an applet via edit web layout functionality, remain unchanged with the introduction of Open UI. All Open UI configurations are applied on top of the existing metadata definition of UI components. In other words, Open UI configuration is just an option in case the capabilities provided by Siebel Tools are not sufficient to meet the customer's UI requirements.

Development Tools for Siebel Open UI

When it comes to describing the duty of a Siebel Open UI developer, modifying text files such as JavaScript or CSS documents comprises most of the daily routine.

These files cannot be modified with Siebel Tools, and Oracle does not recommend a specific set of tools for Open UI development. As a matter of fact, any development tool (be it a simple text editor or a sophisticated IDE) can be used as long as it supports the minimum standards for web development. These standards - HTML, CSS and JavaScript - were described in Chapter 1. At first, this seems to be rather unspecific, but the flexibility to employ a variety of tools makes a lot of sense for Oracle and its customers.

It is very unlikely that Oracle will provide a specific tool for Siebel Open UI developers. There are a multitude of web development tools available - both open-source and commercial - that provide sophisticated and comprehensive capabilities. Web development has a long history, and every enterprise customer has some in-house or outsourced capabilities and tools in this area, so it would unnecessarily constrain customers if Oracle recommended or supported one tool over another.

The following types of tools are usually used by web developers:

- Text editors or Integrated Development Environments (IDEs)
- Minification tools
- Browser developer tools

The following is a brief description of tools that could be used for development work in Siebel Open UI. The list of tools is by no means complete and should not be interpreted as a recommendation of any sort.

Text Editors or Integrated Development Environments (IDEs)

In general, every text editor can be used to write JavaScript and CSS code. Even Notepad - the simple text editor delivered with Microsoft Windows - would be sufficient. But of course, more advanced text editors such as Notepad++, TextPad or UltraEdit could serve the task as well and usually provide more support and validation for the specific needs of writing code.

More sophisticated IDEs such as Eclipse (open source), Oracle NetBeans, JetBrains WebStorm or Microsoft VisualStudio are most probably better suited to the task of developing custom code in a medium-sized or large team.

The following screenshot shows Oracle NetBeans as an example of an integrated development environment.

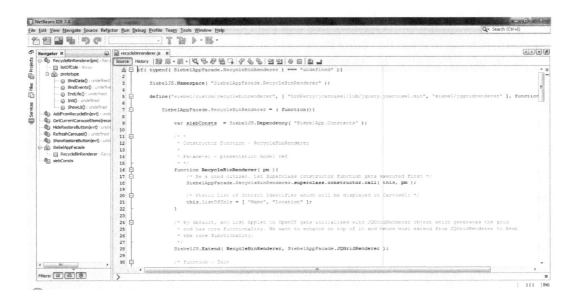

For illustration purposes, an example Open UI JavaScript file has been opened in the NetBeans IDE.

Minification Tools

Minification of JavaScript and CSS files (the removal of all unnecessary characters and thus minimizing the size of files) has already been described in previous chapters. A variety of tools and web sites exist to allow us to minify, un-minify and beautify JavaScript files. A quick web search lists dozens of tools such as Google's Closure Tools (https://developers.google.com/closure) or JS Beautifier (http://jsbeautifier.org).

Browser Developer Tools

All modern browsers, including Microsoft Internet Explorer, Mozilla Firefox and Google Chrome provide sophisticated web development and debugging capabilities such as the following:

- Debugging and modifying the document object model (DOM)
- Comprehensive CSS development functionality

- Built-in JavaScript debugger
- Performance measurement tools

While the built-in web development and debugging capabilities of modern browsers are already impressive, a variety of plug-ins exist that further enhance these capabilities.

In the next sections we will discuss in greater detail how these capabilities can be leveraged for working with Open UI. We will use Google Chrome for demonstration purposes, bearing in mind that other browsers likely provide the same capabilities either out-of-the-box or via plug-ins. Two popular Chrome extensions for developers shall serve as examples of the vast array of productivity-enhancing plug-ins for Google Chrome:

- **Clear Cache**: Provides shortcut functionality to clear the browser cache.
- **User-Agent Switcher for Chrome**: Allows us to 'spoof' various user agents to emulate different browser/device combinations.

The Chrome Web Store
(`https://chrome.google.com/webstore/category/extensions`) is provided by Google to locate and install Chrome extensions. After installing the extension we can navigate to `chrome://extensions` to list and configure all installed plug-ins.

The following screenshot shows the Clear Cache extension installed in Google Chrome.

As can be seen in the screenshot, the Clear Cache extension also provides a toolbar icon (in the upper right corner of the browser). Visiting the Options page (via the link provided below the extension object) allows us to define the desired behavior of the extension's functionality. For the Clear Cache extension, the settings include what part of the cache to clear. In addition, a keyboard shortcut can be defined to trigger the cache purge even faster.

User-Agent Switcher for Chrome allows us to change the user agent string that Chrome sends to the web server. This is most often used to emulate a different browser or device and is particularly helpful during the customization of Siebel Mobile Applications as the plug-in allows for the emulation of most mobile browsers and devices. While in-browser device emulation is good for quick verification of results, we should always apply thorough testing of our customizations using the real browser and device combinations used by our end users.

It should be noted here that Google Chrome - and most other modern browsers - also have built-in device emulation functionality that can be used to verify the rendering of Siebel applications on different browser/device combinations.

Inspecting DOM Elements

In the following section we will introduce the various debugging capabilities that are provided by modern browsers. As announced in the previous section, we will use Google Chrome for demonstration purposes, realizing that all modern browsers have comparable capabilities. For the sake of brevity, we will only introduce the most important features. For a complete reference of the development capabilities of your favorite browser, consult the documentation provided by the browser vendor.

The most important feature to debugging a web application in the browser is most likely Inspect Element. By right-clicking anywhere in the application, the browser displays a context menu that includes an Inspect Element option. Selecting this option for the first time opens the browser's developer tool, which is also accessible via *F12* or other shortcuts, and presents the DOM hierarchy of the current page as shown in the following screenshot.

In the next screenshot, we see the result of positioning the mouse on the first column of a list applet and selecting Inspect Element in the context menu.

```
▼<table id="s_1_1" tabindex="0" cellspacing="0" cellpadding="0" border="0" role="grid" aria-
multiselectable="true" aria-labelledby class="ui-jqgrid-btable" summary="Credit Alert Attachments List"
datatable="1" style="width: 1154px;">
  ▼<tbody>
    ▶<tr class="jqgfirstrow" role="row" style="height:auto">…</tr>
    ▼<tr role="row" id="1" tabindex="0" class="ui-widget-content jqgrow ui-row-ltr ui-state-highlight"
    aria-selected="true" style="height: 20px;">
      ▶<td role="gridcell" style="text-align:center;display:none;" aria-describedby="s_1_1_cb">…</td>
      ▶<td role="gridcell" style="text-align:center;" title="Unchecked" aria-describedby="1Name
      s_1_1_Row_Status s_1_1_altCheckBox" id="1Row_Status">…</td>
      ▶<td role="gridcell" style="text-align:left;" title="3 Com" aria-describedby="s_1_1_Name
      s_1_1_altLink" id="1Name">…</td>
```

In the screenshot, the Elements tab reveals that Open UI uses HTML tables to represent a list applet where the column header is represented by a table row (`<tr>`) with a class of `jqgfirstrow`. Every record in a list applet is represented as a row with a `role` attribute (value: `row`), with each column based on a table cell (`<td>`). Chrome's Development Tools are smart enough to highlight the element that is selected in the DOM viewer on the actual web page. In addition, Chrome allows us to manipulate the DOM directly by right-clicking any element in the DOM-viewer by selecting one of the Edit or Add options or simply double-clicking any of the entries. For example, double-clicking on the `style` attribute of the `td` element with the title `3 Com` and changing it from `style="text-align:left;"` to `style="text-align:right;"` results in a change of text alignment - as shown in the next screenshot.

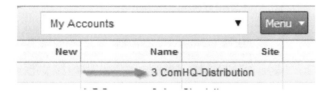

Chrome also allows us to reposition elements in the DOM by dragging and dropping them.

> It is important to understand that none of these changes are persistent as the changes are essentially done in memory and do not modify the underlying HTML, CSS and JavaScript files. Reloading the view or logging off and on again will undo these changes.

There are several good reasons to familiarize ourselves with the browser's DOM elements viewer:

- It provides developers with the necessary insight required for implementing custom JavaScript code and/or custom CSS rules. This includes identifying the correct CSS selectors used in physical renderers and getting an understanding of the HTML code 'injected' via a PR.
- It provides a very quick and agile way for developers to test changes.

- As no additional software has to be installed, it is an essential debugging tool when working on a different client machine such as an end user's PC.

The aforementioned CSS capabilities of the DOM editor allow us to introspect the current style (and the files it originates from) of the selected element. We have discussed the process of 're-engineering' an element's style in Chapter 8. From a debugging perspective, let's look at a simple scenario for using the Styles inspector.

Upon selecting the New column of a list applet in the DOM editor, we can see that various CSS statements are applied to this column. The following screenshot provides an example.

The selected element matches the .ui-jqrid tr.ui-row-ltr td selector, which defines the border color and (foreground) color of this element. We can also see that the CSS rule is stored in line 40 in the file theme-gray.css. The file-name is a hyperlink that allows us to drill to the actual file.

Google Chrome allows us to update the CSS rules in real time as well. Clicking on the current border-color value of #e2e2e2 and replacing it with blue updates the border color of all matching elements in the list applet. However, as is the case with DOM manipulation, these changes are not persistent and will be lost after a page reload.

The Styles tab allows developers to understand why DOM elements are rendered in a specific style and to debug and test custom themes and JavaScript code quickly.

What we can also see in the previous screenshot is that Google Chrome displays an element.style section for the selected DOM element. This section shows CSS rules that were applied implicitly to the element - usually via JavaScript.

> In general web development, it is considered a questionable technique to apply CSS rules by means of JavaScript code, as it unnecessarily hides the source of the style rule. Developers are encouraged to use file-based CSS rules whenever possible. When they believe they have to resort to JavaScript, developers should use jQuery functions like addClass or removeClass to define the class attribute of DOM elements at runtime.

When different CSS rules apply to the same DOM element at the same time, they can override each other. During debugging, it might be difficult to discern why a specific

CSS property is not applied to an element because one has overridden the other. Chrome's Developer Tools help in this case by providing a Computed tab next to the Styles tab. This tab shows all CSS properties that are applied to the currently selected DOM element as depicted in the following screenshot.

As we can see in the screenshot, the `border-bottom-color` property is set by two different selectors in the first line of `ui.jqgrid.css` and in line 40 of `theme-gray.css`. By striking out the values that do not apply (for `ui.jqgrid.css` in the previous example), the developer tool allows us to identify the source of the style rules as `theme-gray.css`.

Script Debugging

While the focus of the previous section was on DOM elements, we also have to understand, in the context of Siebel Open UI, how a browser's developer tools support JavaScript debugging concepts. These include the following:

- Print debug messages on the console
- Verify loaded files
- Set breakpoints and inspect variables

Printing Debug Messages on the Console

A standard requirement in every development environment is to print debug messages. While JavaScript offers a `console` object, it is recommended to use the specific Open UI `SiebelJS.Log` command, which eliminates issues that could arise when the browser does not support the console object (such as older versions of Internet Explorer when not in debug mode). The output of `SiebelJS.Log` is visible in the Console tab of Chrome's Developer Tools window.

In general, most browsers allow for the execution, or 'injection', of JavaScript into a web page via the development console. Prior to the IP 2013 release, the Open UI framework did not prevent this, resulting in full access to the Open UI API at runtime in the browser. As this is a potential security risk, direct JavaScript execution in the browser's console is prohibited by the Open UI framework in IP 2013 and later.

Verifying Loaded Files

Another helpful capability of the developer tool is to browse through the list of loaded files. The Sources tab shows all files that are currently loaded and presents them in the 'Navigator,' a tree structure reflecting the folder hierarchy on the web server as shown in the following screenshot.

In the screenshot we can see that `chrometablefix.js` is the only file stored in the `23030/scripts/siebel/custom` folder that is currently loaded. Selecting the file displays the actual content of the file in a tab to the right of the Navigator.

This functionality is helpful to understand which files are actually used by the application and the dependencies, as defined in the manifest or the `define` function, on different views and applets. In addition, it allows us to quickly check if a (custom) file was actually loaded.

Setting Breakpoints and Inspecting Variables

The Sources tab provides other critical debugging tools such as setting breakpoints and inspecting variables. The following scenario guides us through the process of setting a breakpoint in the as-delivered `preload.js` file (which implements a preload event listener as discussed in Chapter 10) and introduces us to the Google Chrome debugger:

1. If necessary, open the browser developer tool and navigate to the Sources tab.

2. Locate the `preload.js` file in the `scripts` folder and click it to open it in the debugger.

3. Click the line number next to the code line that calls the `console.log` function to set a breakpoint.

4. Compare your work with the following screenshot.

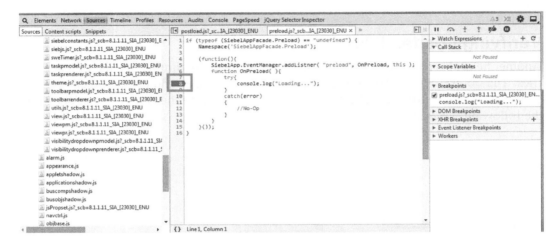

5. Press *F5* to reload the current page.

6. Observe that the browser stops the code execution at the breakpoint.

7. Hover over the `console` object to open an inspection window that displays the current state of the object.

8. Click the Step over... button (second button in the toolbar) or press *F10* to execute the line of code and step to the next line.

9. Navigate to the Console tab and verify that the message Loading... appears.

10. Click the Resume... button or press *F8* to continue to the next break point or - if there are no more breakpoints - leave the debug mode.

In addition to the basic breakpoint navigation shown in the previous procedure, we should familiarize ourselves with the following features of Google's Chrome Developer Tools:

- **Watch Expressions**: Use this section in the debugger to define short code snippets ('expressions') that you want to 'watch' during code debugging. For example, you can add the name of an object or variable to the list and the debugger will show the return value in the current script context.

- **Call Stack**: Useful for discerning the flow of JavaScript code execution.

- **Scope Variables**: Displays all local and global variables and their current values.

For further information, documentation, and training available for Google Chrome Developer Tools go to `https://developer.chrome.com/devtools`.

Browser Side Performance Measurement

As responsible Siebel developers, we should always design and implement with performance in mind. Siebel CRM is a complex application framework with processing taking place on multiple machines such as the database server, Siebel server, web server and the client's browser.

Measuring the end-to-end performance of an enterprise application is a complex endeavor and discussing server-side tools such as Siebel Application Response Measurement (SARM) is outside the scope of this book.

In this section we focus on the tools that modern browsers provide to measure the performance of a web application. As has been laid out in previous chapters of this book, Siebel Open UI relies heavily on JavaScript. On some occasions we might find that the application performance in the browser does not meet our requirements, so we have to identify the JavaScript code that pushes the browser to its limits.

Three of the Chrome Development Tools tabs are focused on performance measurement:

- The Timeline tab provides insight into the different events (such as *Paint*, *Layout* or *Receive Data*) of the application over time and is often the best place to start investigating performance problems.
- The Network tab allows us to investigate which files are loaded, the size of the files, the time it took to load any file and, most importantly, a timeline displaying when a file was loaded and in which sequence.
- The Profile tab allows us to measure the execution time and memory usage of the application during a specific timeframe.

As with the other capabilities of Chrome's Development Tools, a comprehensive presentation of all functionality in this area is beyond the scope of this book. In addition to built-in features of the browser, we can find a multitude of plug-ins that serve the purpose of tracing and interpreting performance measures on the client-side.

As an example, we mention the **Google PageSpeed** plug-in for Chrome that generates suggestions on how to optimize page load and performance.

Server Side Debugging

While the majority of development and debugging in Siebel Open UI happens on the client side, there are some server related items that we might want to debug, such as settings in the manifest views. Prior to IP 2013 it could be tedious to determine why a custom JavaScript or CSS file was not loaded. Luckily, starting with IP 2013, Oracle introduced additional log information that simplifies the debugging process significantly.

The depth of this log information is determined by the log level of the **General Events** property of the corresponding object manager. By default the value is set to 1. Setting it to 3 provides details of which JavaScript files are loaded while a value of 4 will include information about web templates.

> For more information about setting event log levels for server components, refer to the Oracle Siebel documentation or the book "Oracle Siebel CRM 8 Installation and Management" by Alexander Hansal.

After setting the value of the **General Events** event type to 3 or higher, additional information is written to the object manager log file, including tracing messages regarding the evaluation of expressions in the manifest. The following screenshot shows a portion of an object manager log file after the setting has been applied.

In the server log, the lines that include the text MANIFEST_LOG provide information about the decision logic applied by the Siebel Web Engine for a given user interface object. In the previous screenshot we can see that the log file includes information about the Contact List Applet.

In addition to browser-side debugging and troubleshooting efforts, server event logging of manifest data can prove useful to track down erroneous configurations.

Case Study: Debugging a Physical Renderer

To summarize the discussion of browser-side debugging patterns, the following case study guides us through a real life scenario.

In this case study we provide example code for a custom physical renderer for the **Contact Form Applet** that renders a 'speech to text' button for the Job Title field, allowing end users to enter a contact's job title by speaking into the microphone (if the device has one). The ability to use the device microphone and convert speech to text is limited to Google Chrome at the time of writing.

The actual code for the custom physical renderer is available in the file ContactSpeech2TextPR.js that comes with this chapter's code archive.

The following example code is an excerpt of the file and shows the implementation of the physical renderer's ShowUI method:

```
ContactSpeech2TextPR.prototype.ShowUI = function(){
   //get font awesome (for prototype only)
   $("head").append(
      '<link href="//maxcdn.bootstrapcdn.com/font-'
      + 'awesome/4.2.0/css/font-awesome.min.css"'
      + 'rel="stylesheet">');

   SiebelAppFacade.ContactSpeech2TextPR.superclass.ShowUI
      .call(this);
   var controls = this.GetPM().Get("GetControls");
   var JobTitleControl = controls["Job Title"];
   if(JobTitleControl && 'webkitSpeechRecognition' in window){
     //we have a control and support for speech recognition
     var JobTitleInput =  $("input[name='"
        + JobTitleControl.GetInputName() + "']");
     var btn = $("<div id='s2tbutton'"
        + "class='s2tbutton fa fa-microphone'></div>");
     //mic button (uses font awesome)
     var transcript = ""; //recognized text will be here
     var recognition = new webkitSpeechRecognition();
     //http://updates.html5rocks.com/tag/voice
     var that = this; //context, context, context...
     recognition.lang="en-GB"; //language to be recognized
     recognition.onresult = function(event) {
       //callback when recognition stops
       btn.toggleClass("active"); //stop animation on mic icon
       transcript = event.results[0][0].transcript;
       //retrieve awesome speech transcript
       that.GetPM().OnControlEvent(
          consts.get("PHYEVENT_CONTROL_FOCUS"),
          JobTitleControl);
       that.GetPM().OnControlEvent(
          consts.get("PHYEVENT_CONTROL_BLUR"),
          JobTitleControl, transcript);
       //playback ;-) (because we can)
```

361

```
        var msg = new SpeechSynthesisUtterance(
            "Did you just say: " + transcript + "?");
        window.speechSynthesis.speak(msg);
    }
    JobTitleInput.addClass("s2tinput");
    JobTitleInput.parent().append(btn); //add button
    btn.click(function() { //button clicked
        recognition.start(); //start listening
        btn.toggleClass("active"); //animate mic icon
    });
    }
};
```

The example code accomplishes the following:

- Append a style sheet reference to the HTML header of the current page to retrieve the `Font Awesome` CSS file from a public web server.

The example code uses the `Font Awesome` font library to display the microphone icon. In a real life scenario, we would download the CSS and font files and make them available on the Siebel web server rather than rely on the availability of a public version. For more information about `Font Awesome`, go to `http://fortawesome.github.io/Font-Awesome`.

- Retrieve the `Job Title` control from the applet's controls array.
- Get the `Job Title` control instance.
- Verify that the `Job Title` control is available and the browser supports the Speech Recognition API.
- Select the `Job Title` input element via jQuery.
- Create a `<div>` element to represent the microphone button. The `fa` and `fa-microphone` class definitions refer to Font Awesome.
- Instantiate the `recognition` object using the HTML5 Speech Recognition API and set the language for speech interpretation to British English (`en-GB`).
- Define the `onresult` event handler to implement the actions that occur when spoken text has been recognized as follows:
    - Toggle the button class to stop the animation.
    - Retrieve the transcript (the recognized text).
    - Set the field to the transcript value.
    - Play back the recognized text using the HTML5 Speech Synthesis API.

- Add the `s2tinput` class to the `Job Title` control.
- Append the microphone button to the `Job Title` control's parent element.
- Implement a `click` event handler for the button that effectively starts the recognition and toggles the class so that the appearance of the button can indicate the recognition process.

> Note that the example code presented earlier includes a subtle error (on purpose!). Can you spot it? The solution is below…

The example code references classes for the microphone button and the `Job Title` control. Refer to the `Speech2Text.css` file in this chapter's code archive for the CSS rules. Add these rules to a custom style sheet of your choice when you plan to implement this case study. The following screenshot shows a portion of the `Contact Form Applet` with the **correct** example PR code applied.

The microphone icon is displayed in the Job Title field. Upon clicking the icon and acknowledging the use of the device microphone we can speak (in English). When we stop speaking, the field will be updated after a few moments with the recognized text and the text will be replayed using a default speech synthesizer (female voice).

Note that only a few browsers support the HTML5 Speech Recognition and Speech Synthesis API at the time of writing. This case study has been verified against Google Chrome.

In order to debug the erroneous code delivered with the example file, we have to follow this procedure:

1. Save the `ContactSpeech2TextPR.js` file to the `siebel/custom` folder.

2. Register the file as a physical renderer with the **Contact Form Applet** in the manifest.

3. Add the style rules from the `Speech2Text.css` file to a custom style sheet that is already registered or register a new custom style sheet.

4. Empty and reload the browser cache.

5. Login to the application and navigate to the Contact List view.

6. You will notice that the file is loaded but no microphone icon is displayed in the Contact Form Applet due to the error in the example code.

The following checklist guides us through the primary process to isolate the error:

- **Check for JavaScript errors**: Press *F12* to open Chrome's Developer Tools and navigate to the Console tab. It is a recommended practice to verify that the code does not produce any runtime errors as a first step. The browser would report any runtime error in the JavaScript console. However, for our example code, no runtime error occurs.

- **Verify that the file was actually loaded**: Navigate to the Sources tab and try to locate the file in question. For our case study example, the file is loaded properly. Reasons for a file not being loaded can be the following:

  - **Manifest expression evaluated to false**: An expression in the manifest views was evaluated to `false` and hence the file was not loaded. In this case the next step would be to enable server side logging as explained in the previous section.

  - **File not found**: The file path in the manifest is incorrect or the file is not present in the `custom` folder.

  - **Invalid JavaScript code**: Many browsers check the syntax of code before they load it. For example an unclosed block (missing " }") would result in the browser refusing to load the file.

- **Set breakpoints**: As the file is loaded but the desired behavior is missing, there seems to be a logical problem within the code. For further analysis we set a breakpoint in the browser developer tool as shown in the following screenshot.

```
29   ContactSpeech2TextPR.prototype.ShowUI = function () {
30       $("head").append('<link href="//maxcdn.bootstrapcdn.com/font-awesome/4.2.0/css/font-
31       SiebelAppFacade.ContactSpeech2TextPR.superclass.ShowUI.call(this);
32
33       var controls = this.GetPM().Get("GetControls");
34       var JobTitleControl = controls["Job Title"];
35       if (JobTitleControl && 'webkitSpeechRecognition' in window) { //we have a control an
36           var JobTitleInput = $("input[name='" + JobTitleControl.GetInputName() + "']");
```

The breakpoint has been set at the line before the `if` block. We chose this breakpoint location because the applet is rendered correctly, but the customizations within the `if` block (microphone button, etc.) are not applied; hence we believe that the `if` block is never reached.

The following procedure describes the debugging steps after setting the breakpoint:

1. Press *F5* to reload the page. The debugger stops the execution of the file at the breakpoint. For our example, this means that the constructor is called correctly.

2. Press *F10* to continue and confirm that the next line is reached.

3. Continue further by pressing *F10* and observe that the debugger does not step into the `if` block, indicating that its condition does not evaluate to `true`.

4. Hover over the `JobTitleControl` variable and observe that its current value is `undefined`.

5. Hover over the `controls` variable and try to locate the `Job Title` control in the list of controls. Compare your screen with the next screenshot.

6. Compare the name of the `JobTitle` control with the string `Job Title` used to reference the control in the code. Note that the spelling of the latter is incorrect, as it contains a space between the words.

7. Open the `ContactSpeech2TextPR.js` file in an editor and correct the line `var JobTitleControl = controls[ "Job Title" ]` to `var JobTitleControl = controls[ "JobTitle" ]` (remove the space between `Job` and `Title`.

8. Save the file, reload the browser cache, and verify that the speech to text input for the job title now works as expected.

In the previous case study we used an example physical renderer with a subtle spelling mistake in order to demonstrate the steps required for successful debugging and troubleshooting.

Summary

Modern browsers provide a rich toolset and plug-ins for web developers. In this chapter, we explored the functionality of Google Chrome's Developer Tools, which is similar to the development and debugging functionality provided by other browsers.

The chapter also introduced us to performance measurement and logging facilities on both the browser and the server side.

In this chapter's case study we reproduced the process of debugging a custom JavaScript file.

In the next chapter we shall explore Siebel Mobile Applications.

14

Siebel Mobile Applications

With the arrival of Siebel Open UI in version 8.1.1.9 / 8.2.2.2, Oracle shipped a new family of mobile applications with the Siebel Repository. These applications are browser-based just like any other Siebel application but are the first to be built exclusively for modern-day portable devices such as tablets or smartphones. In this chapter, we will introduce the architecture and features of Siebel Mobile Applications.

The chapter is structured as follows:

- Introduction to Siebel Mobile Applications
- Setup and administration
- Disconnected Mobile Applications
- The role of jQuery Mobile in Siebel Mobile Applications

Because of the shift from the jQuery Mobile library to native Responsive Web Design (RWD) that occurred between IP 2013 and IP 2014, the information provided in some sections of this chapter applies only to IP 2013. Please refer to the notes and information boxes in this chapter for clarification.

Introduction to Siebel Mobile Applications

As mentioned earlier, a Siebel Mobile Application can be understood as 'yet another' Siebel web application. As such, it shares common Siebel web architecture and application elements such as screens, views, applets, and so forth with all other applications.

What makes Siebel Mobile Applications interesting is how they differ from traditional Siebel applications. The following list explains those differences:

- Siebel Mobile Applications are built from the ground up to be used on modern touch-screen devices such as tablets or smartphones.
- They are built exclusively using the Siebel Open UI framework.
- Specialized web templates (.swt) have been introduced by Oracle to support mobile applications.

- The jQuery Mobile framework is used to provide a consistent user experience across all devices and browsers (until Innovation Pack 2013).
- The Responsive Web Design (RWD) paradigm introduced in Innovation Pack 2014 enables Siebel customers to use *all* applications on any browser/device combination. However, there will still be a necessity to cater to smaller screen sizes in terms of limiting the number of applets and controls when the application is rendered on a device with a smaller viewport.

The new family of mobile applications introduced with version 8.1.1.9/8.2.2.2 has the following members:

- Siebel Sales Enterprise Mobile
- Siebel Service for Mobile
- Siebel ePharma Mobile
- Siebel CG Sales Enterprise Mobile (CG = Consumer Goods)

The following screenshot shows the four new applications in Siebel Tools.

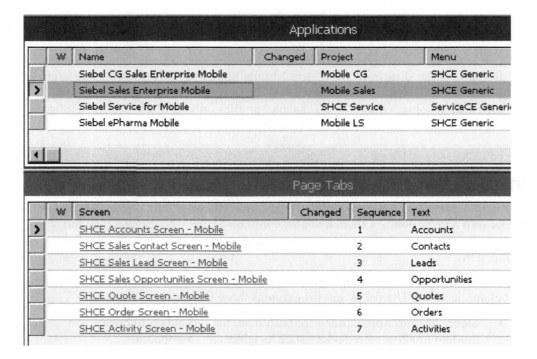

The screenshot shows the applications list in Siebel Tools displaying four mobile application definitions. The Siebel Sales Enterprise Mobile application is selected in the upper applet and the list of page tabs (screens) for this application is visible below.

With Innovation Pack 2014, Oracle added a new mobile application, namely **Siebel Financial Services Mobile**, which is intended for mobile access to Siebel Financial Services data.

Of the aforementioned mobile applications, the **Service** and **ePharma** applications support **disconnected operation** out of the box. This means they are preconfigured by Oracle to store data and metadata on the device in order to make it available when the device has no network connectivity and to synchronize any changes when the network connection is established again.

The next screenshot shows the mobile Service application in Innovation Pack 2013.

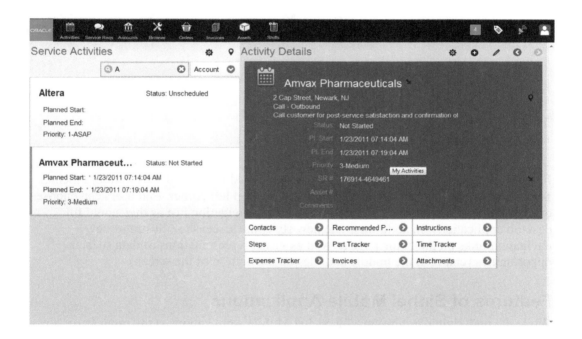

As can be seen in the screenshot, the application offers several screens such as Activities or Accounts. The current view shows activities. On the upper right corner, an icon depicting a transmitting satellite dish indicates that the application is currently in online (connected) mode.

The following screenshot shows the new Financial Services Mobile application as an example for the layout changes that come with the single unified renderer paradigm introduced with Innovation Pack 2014.

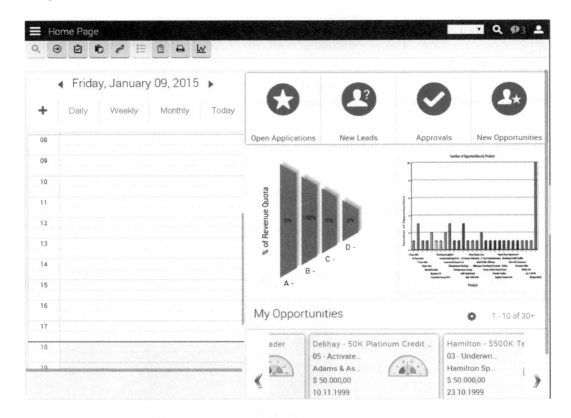

In the screenshot we can see the new layout introduced with the IP 2014 Aurora theme. Screens are available from the sidebar menu in the top left corner. End users can choose other navigation options such as tab- or tree-based navigation just as they could for desktop applications. In addition to the new style, the screenshot illustrates new navigation links on the home page as well as visual representations of data such as opportunities (charts in the middle and tiles on the bottom of the screen).

Features of Siebel Mobile Applications

While the underlying architecture for Siebel Mobile Applications is the same as for any other Siebel application, the user interface provides more flexibility for mobile users than traditional desktop applications. The following list describes the most important features of Siebel Mobile Applications for end users and developers:

- **Responsive Design**: The Siebel mobile user interface adapts to a device's form factor and orientation (landscape or portrait) seamlessly.

- **Infinite Scrolling**: List applets in Siebel Mobile Applications are rendered using JavaScript libraries and plug-ins that provide infinite scrolling through a list of records using swipe gestures on the touch screen.

- **Device Integration**: The features and applications of the device such as telephone, GPS or camera are reachable from the mobile application.

- **Styles and Custom Themes**: In Innovation Pack 2013, Siebel Mobile Applications provide full support for the jQuery Mobile ThemeRoller, which allows developers to quickly modify and create themes. As of IP 2014, the new Aurora theme supports rendering all Siebel applications on any browser and device combination.

- **Business and Development Continuity**: Because Siebel Mobile Applications are built on top of the existing Siebel framework, the 'classic' patterns of customizing and configuration do not change. Traditional user interface elements such as screens, views and applets are the building blocks of Siebel applications and Siebel Mobile Applications are no exception.

In this chapter, we will explore the as-delivered features and possibilities of Siebel Mobile Applications. The next chapter will focus on customization tasks.

Technical Requirements for Siebel Mobile Applications

To run Siebel Mobile Applications, the following components are necessary:

- An object manager on a Siebel server
- A web server that can be reached from the mobile device
- An HTML5 compliant browser on the mobile device
- Server components that handle data extraction and synchronization as well as additional administrative settings if we need to support disconnected operation.

A separate object manager for mobile applications is a necessity because of the different application definition and specific parameter settings.

Because mobile users are usually outside the corporate firewall, access to the web server that hosts the virtual directory for the Siebel mobile application is often a security concern. In most cases, a virtual private network (VPN) connection needs to be established on the device before the mobile application can be accessed.

HTML5-based JavaScript libraries provide much of the application functionality in order to render a rich user experience. The browser on the mobile device must therefore support HTML5 and JavaScript.

To enable offline operation and data synchronization, additional server components are needed. It is also necessary to register mobile users, administer settings such as data filters, and monitor the synchronization activity. More information on disconnected mobile applications is provided later in this chapter.

Setup and Administration

As indicated in the previous section, a separate object manager is required for each mobile application. In this section we will learn how to set up object managers and execute the necessary administrative tasks to successfully deploy Siebel Mobile Applications.

The following list describes the high-level process of setting up a Siebel CRM environment for mobile applications:

- Set up the object manager
- Enable component groups
- Set parameters for mobile applications
- Set up the web server
- Understand mobile application security
- Administer user accounts
- Test mobile client access

In the following sections we will delve into each of these steps in detail.

Setting up an Object Manager for Siebel Mobile Applications

Depending on whether your Siebel environment is the result of a fresh installation or an upgrade from an earlier version, object manager definitions for mobile applications might already exist in your configuration. During a fresh installation of a current version of Siebel CRM, the following default component definitions for mobile applications are created automatically:

- eConsumer Goods Sales Mobile (CGMObjMgr_enu)
- Sales Mobile (SalesmObjMgr_enu)
- ePharma Mobile (ePharmaMObjMgr_enu)
- Service Mobile (ServicemObjMgr_enu)
- FINS Mobile (FINSMObjMgr_enu) (IP 2014 or higher)

If your application has been upgraded from a previous version, such as Siebel 8.0, you must create these component definitions manually using a script provided by Oracle. The following procedure describes the steps needed to create object managers for mobile applications if they are not already defined:

1. On a machine that has a Siebel Server installed, open a command shell and log in to the Siebel server manager command line utility as follows:

```
<SIEBEL_INSTALL_DIR>/siebsrvr/bin/srvrmgr /g localhost /e Siebel
/u SADMIN /p bank49v
```

This command line connects to the **Siebel Gateway Name Server** on the local machine (localhost), opens the configuration for the Siebel enterprise, and authenticates as the SADMIN user.

2. At the prompt, enter the following command:

```
backup namesrvr
```

The command instructs the Siebel Gateway Name Server to create a persistent backup copy of the siebns.dat file. Taking a backup of the siebns.dat file before applying changes is a recommended practice. The backup file will be written to the ADMIN subdirectory of the gateway server installation folder. The name of the file will convey the date and time of its creation.

3. Verify that the prompt returns Command completed successfully

4. Enter the exit command to leave the srvrmgr prompt.

5. Navigate to the subdirectory for the language you want to create the new object managers for. For example enter the following command to access the language specific subdirectory for American English (ENU):

```
cd ENU
```

6. Set the SIEBEL_HOME environment variable value to the root installation folder of the Siebel server. For example on a Microsoft Windows server, enter a command similar to the following:

```
set SIEBEL_HOME=D:\sia\ses\siebsrvr
```

7. Run the script provided by Oracle to generate new component definitions. For example, to generate Siebel mobile application object managers for American English (ENU) enter a command similar to the following:

```
new_compdef_sia localhost Siebel SADMIN bank49v ENU
```

The parameters required by the new_compdef_sia utility are:

- Hostname and port number of the Siebel Gateway Name Server. They must be separated by a colon. The port number can be omitted if the standard port 2320 is used. The previous example uses localhost to specify the local machine as the one that hosts the Siebel Gateway Name Server.

- The name of the Siebel Enterprise, for example Siebel

- Username, for example SADMIN

- Password, for example bank49v

- Language, for example ENU

8. The parameters are prompted for verification. If you are sure they are correct, press *ENTER* to run the script.

9. Log in to the `srvrmgr` command line utility again.

10. Execute the following command to display a list of component definitions for the enterprise:

```
list compdefs
```

11. Verify that the following component definitions exist:

   o `CGMObjMgr_ENU` (eConsumer Goods Sales Mobile)

   o `SalesmObjMgr_enu` (Sales Mobile)

   o `ePharmaMObjMgr_ENU` (ePharma Mobile)

   o `ServicemObjMgr_enu` (Service Mobile)

   o `FinsmObjMgr_enu` (Financial Services Mobile) (IP 2014 or higher)

Note that the language suffix (`enu` in the previous example) is dependent on the language parameter specified during the script execution.

Enabling Component Groups for Siebel Mobile Applications

Depending on which mobile application you intend to use, you have to assign and enable one or more of the following component groups on at least one Siebel server.

Mobile Application	Component Group Name	Component Group Alias
Sales Mobile Service Mobile	Handheld Synchronization	HandheldSync
eConsumer Goods Sales Mobile ePharma Mobile Financial Services Mobile	Handheld Synchronization SIA	HandheldSyncSIS

Note that additional component groups must be enabled for disconnected mobile applications. The setup procedure for disconnected mobile applications will be laid out later in this chapter.

The server manager commands to assign and enable component groups are shown in the following example:

```
assign compgrp handheldsync to server server01
enable compgrp handheldsync for server server01
```

The two commands assign and enable the **Handheld Synchronization** component group - with an alias name of handheldsync - on the Siebel server named server01. An alternative way to accomplish this and other server configuration tasks is the graphical user interface provided by the Administration - Server Configuration screen in the Siebel web client.

After modifying or creating component definitions, we must stop and restart all affected Siebel servers in the enterprise.

Setting parameters for Mobile Applications

To ensure flawless operation, system administrators should understand the component parameters for Siebel Mobile Applications. The following table describes these parameters at the object manager level.

Parameter (Alias)	Value	Description
EnableOpenUI	TRUE	Enables Siebel Open UI
HighInteractivity	TRUE	Enables High Interactivity. Must be always set to TRUE if EnableOpenUI is set to TRUE.
AppletSelectStyle	Applet Select	Must be set to avoid rendering issues with MVG applets.
EnableInlineForList	Never	Disables inline editing in list applets.
ShowWriteRecord	TRUE	Displays the Save button even when HighInteractivity is set to TRUE.
EnableSIFocusTracking	TRUE	Enables the application to control which applet has focus after opening a view.
MobileApplication	TRUE	Applicable in IP 2013 or earlier: Defines a mobile application (as opposed to a desktop application).
SupportedMobileBrowser	See below	Applicable in IP 2013 or earlier: See description below

Additional parameters are necessary for disconnected mobile applications and will be described in the respective section later in this chapter.

The following is an example server manager command to set a parameter for an object manager:

```
change param mobileapplication=TRUE for comp salesmobjmgr_enu
```

The command sets the MobileApplication parameter to TRUE for the English-American Mobile Sales application object manager (salesmobjmgr_enu). Alternatively, system administrators can use administrative views in the Siebel web client to inspect and modify component parameters.

> For more information on Siebel server administration and parameters, refer to the Oracle Siebel documentation or the book "Oracle Siebel 8 Installation and Management" by Alexander Hansal.

Enabling Browser Support for Siebel Mobile Applications in Innovation Pack 2013 and earlier

For Siebel Mobile applications in Innovation Pack 2013 or earlier, the `SupportedMobileBrowser` parameter controls which browser/device combinations are supported by the application. In this context, 'supported' means that the mobile application will render in the browser using the physical renderers and style sheets for mobile applications rather than for desktop applications. It does *not* mean that the application will not be available on non-supported browsers or devices; it would just be displayed in desktop style when accessed from a non-supported browser/device combination.

The value of the `SupportedMobileBrowser` parameter is a string that identifies different device types such as 'Tablet' or 'Phone' and the browsers supported on each device. To identify the browsers, a unique sub-string of the 'user agent string' must be used.

> The **user agent string** defines the version and vendor of the browser and the client's operating system at each request to a web server. A typical user agent string looks like the following:
>
> ```
> Mozilla/5.0 (Windows NT 6.1; WOW64) AppleWebKit/537.36 (KHTML,
> like Gecko) Chrome/35.0.1916.114 Safari/537.36
> ```
>
> This identifies the user agent as Google Chrome version 35 on Windows 7 64 bit.
>
> You can find out more about your browser's user agent string at
> `http://www.whatsmyuseragent.com`.

The following is the default value for the `SupportedMobileBrowser` parameter in IP 2013:

```
Tablet:iPad,Android-Chrome-GT-P7510,Android-ChromeNexus,Android-Chrome-
Micromax P500(Funbook),webOS,MSIE-Windows NT-Touch,MSIEWindows NT-
ARM|Phone:iPhone,iPod,Android-Chrome-Mobile,MSIE-Windows Phone,BB10-
Mobile
```

The string defines the supported browsers for tablets and phones by using sub-strings of the user agent string. For example the entry `Android-ChromeNexus` in the `Tablet` section adds support for the Chrome browser on Nexus tablets.

The `Tablet` and `Phone` sections are separated by the pipe (|) character.

Case Study: Adding Support for Browsers or Devices (IP 2013)

In order to add support for additional browsers or devices, we have to follow the procedure below:

1. On the device, open the browser you want to support.

2. Navigate to `http://www.whatsmyuseragent.com` (or a similar web site)

The following screenshot shows a typical result page of `whatsmyuseragent.com`.

3. Inspect the user agent string returned on the website. For example if the device is an Amazon **Kindle Fire** tablet, the string would look similar to the following:

```
Mozilla/5.0 (Linux; U; Android 2.3.4; en-us; Kindle Fire
Build/GINGERBREAD) AppleWebKit/533.1 (KHTML, like Gecko) Version/4.0
Mobile Safari/533.1
```

4. Locate a substring that uniquely identifies the browser and device combination. For example, you might choose `Kindle Fire` to support all browsers on the Kindle Fire device. If you want to use two different substrings, separate them with a dash (-).

5. Get the current value of the `SupportedMobileBrowser` parameter and copy it into a text editor.

6. Edit the copied string to include the substring you determined previously in the correct device section, separating entries with a comma. For example, the resulting string could be like the following:

```
Tablet:iPad,Android-Chrome-GT-P7510,Android-ChromeNexus,Android-Chrome-
Micromax P500(Funbook),webOS,MSIE-Windows NT-Touch,MSIEWindows NT-
ARM,Kindle Fire|Phone:iPhone,iPod,Android-Chrome-Mobile,MSIE-Windows
Phone,BB10-Mobile
```

The previous string is the default value of the `SupportedMobileBrowser` parameter with the substring `,Kindle Fire` inserted at the end of the `Tablet` section, using a comma as the separator. Changes are highlighted in `bold` text.

7. Copy the edited string to the clipboard and use it to change the `SupportedMobileBrowser` parameter to the new value.

8. Restart the object manager.

9. Access the application from a test device to ensure it is rendered using the mobile renderers.

By setting the `SupportedMobileBrowser` parameter as described in the previous case study, administrators can control which rendering mode (desktop or mobile) is used on which browser and device combination.

Setting up the Web Server

Similar to object manager definitions for mobile applications, virtual directories on the Siebel web server might already exist depending on whether or not we are looking at a fresh installation of a current Siebel version.

The following are examples for default virtual directories for Siebel Mobile Applications for American English (enu):

- salesm_enu (Sales)
- servicem_enu (Service)
- epharmam_enu (Pharma)
- cgm_enu (Consumer Goods)
- finsm_enu (Financial Services Mobile) (IP 2014 or higher)

If the above virtual directories are not present on the Siebel web server, we must generate them by executing a script provided by Oracle.

The following procedure guides us through the process of creating new virtual directories for Siebel Mobile Applications. The process must be repeated for each web server in each Siebel environment.

1. Stop the web server.

2. On the machine that hosts the Siebel Web Server Extension (SWSE), navigate to the `BIN` subdirectory of the SWSE installation folder.

3. Create a backup copy of the `eapps.cfg` and `eapps_sia.cfg` files.

4. In a command shell, navigate to the `config` directory within the `SWSE` installation folder.

5. Execute the following command (example for American English on Microsoft Windows):

```
new_virdirs ENU
```

6. Verify that the script executed successfully.

7. Restart the web server.

After running the `new_virdirs` script, we should find the new virtual directories registered with the web server. We can now access the Siebel Mobile application of our choice from any device that can establish a network connection to the Siebel web server.

Understanding Mobile Application Security

End users will typically access the mobile application from their mobile devices while they are on the road and connected to cellular or Wi-Fi networks external to the company's private network. Administrators must ensure connectivity from the device to the Siebel web server while considering the security risks that come from exposing a web server to external networks.

While it is not within the scope of this book to discuss all aspects of web server security and access from external networks in detail, we shall list some important points as a high-level introduction.

Virtual Private Network (VPN): Most companies provide VPN clients for laptops and mobile devices that allow end users to connect to the corporate network. Siebel Mobile Applications can be used in conjunction with VPN solutions.

Encryption: Siebel Applications often expose sensitive business data. The communication between browser and web server should therefore be encrypted to ensure high levels of data security.

Mobile Device Management: Mobile devices such as smartphones and tablets are often subject to loss or theft. Companies providing corporate data on such devices are advised to allow the devices to be controlled and disabled if necessary using mobile device management software.

Siebel Mobile App: Siebel Mobile Applications can be used in conjunction with a container app that allows secure access to the device's native storage and components such as the camera, microphone or GPS sensors. With Innovation Pack 2014, Oracle provides the *Siebel Mobile App* that can be downloaded from the Apple App Store for iPad and iPhone devices.

The following screenshot shows the Siebel app in the Apple iTunes store.

The predefined Siebel app allows users to connect to an existing Siebel application with the benefit of enhanced security. For example, downloaded attachments can be automatically deleted from the device when the application is closed. In addition to using the app provided by Oracle, customers can download the Siebel mobile archive file (.maa) from Oracle's Software Delivery Cloud and use it to create a custom mobile application using the Oracle Mobile Application Framework (MAF).

Administering User Accounts

To enable users to work with the new mobile applications, we must create and assign new **Responsibilities** to the user accounts.

The document titled *Siebel Mobile Guide: Connected* included in the Oracle Siebel documentation (also known as "Siebel Bookshelf") lists all as-delivered views for each mobile application.

These views are pre-registered in the Siebel database by Oracle as part of the seed data import. However, it is a mandatory administrative task to create new responsibility records (as appropriate to suit the company's business processes) and add the necessary views.

The next screenshot shows the Responsibilities view in the Administration - Application screen with an example responsibility.

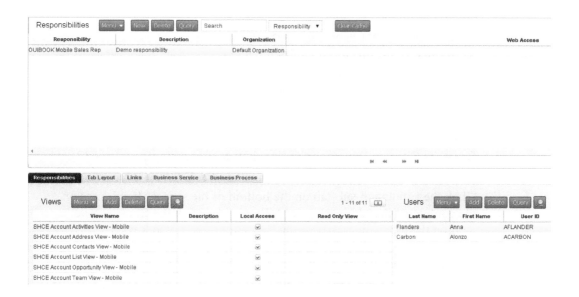

In the screenshot we can see a custom responsibility named OUIBOOK Mobile Sales Rep in the upper list applet. The list of views in the lower left corner of the view displays some of the views of the *Siebel Mobile Sales* application associated to the responsibility. Also visible in the lower right corner is the Users list with two sample user accounts associated to the responsibility.

For more information about Siebel application administration tasks, refer to the Oracle Siebel documentation.

The steps discussed in the previous sections conclude the setup process for Siebel Mobile Applications.

Testing Mobile Clients

While the final connection test should always be carried out using the device type, operating system and browser that will be distributed to end users, administrative staff might not always have access to mobile devices.

To facilitate development and testing for Siebel Mobile Applications, technicians can use a standard desktop browser such as Google Chrome or Mozilla Firefox. When a developer wants to test the application's behavior on a different browser or device, he or she can use the device emulation facilities that come with modern browsers.

The following procedure describes how to access a Siebel Mobile Application for testing purposes using the device emulator of Google Chrome:

1. Launch a new window or tab of Google Chrome.

2. Navigate to the URL of the mobile application, for example
   `http://webserver/finsm_enu` for Siebel Financial Services Mobile in
   American English (`enu`).

3. Provide a valid user name and password to log in.

4. Verify that the application is fully rendered. If you are using IP 2013 or
   earlier, the application might render in desktop mode with the same look
   and feel as, for example, Siebel Call Center. Recall that the
   `SupportedMobileBrowser` parameter can be modified to specify
   browser/device combinations on which the application renders in mobile
   mode.

5. Open the Chrome Developer Tools window (for example, press *F12*).

6. In the Developer Tools window, navigate to the Console tab.

7. Click the Emulation sub-tab on the bottom of the screen. If sub-tabs or
   the content of the 'drawer' is not fully visible, click the Show Drawer
   icon on the top right corner of the Developer Tools window.

8. Click the Toggle icon (depicting a smartphone) on the top left corner of
   the Developer Tools window.

9. In the Emulation sub-tab, navigate to the Device list and select a suitable
   device, for example Apple iPad 3 / 4.

10. Press *F5* to reload the page.

11. Observe that the application now renders in tablet mode.

12. Compare your work with the following screenshot.

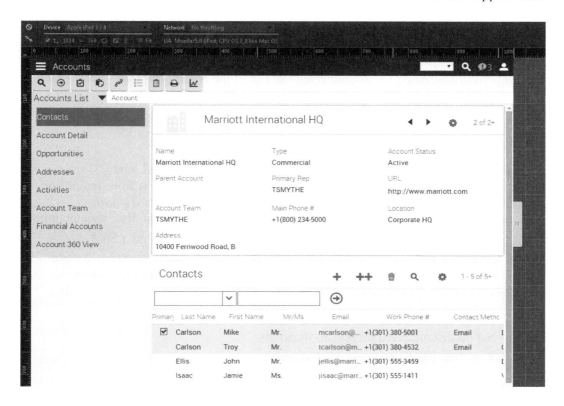

The screenshot shows the Financial Services Mobile application in Google Chrome's emulation mode for an Apple iPad in landscape mode. Depending on the version of Google Chrome you are using, the screenshot may differ from what you see on your screen.

Depending on the browser vendor and version, the steps needed to enable device emulation might differ. We must also be aware that using browser or device spoofing cannot replace testing on the actual device/browser combinations that are, or will be, deployed in your project.

Disconnected Mobile Applications

Siebel has a solid track record in mobile computing, with its **Siebel Remote** technology providing mobile workers with offline data since its first versions. Continuous and ubiquitous mobile connectivity to the internet or corporate data at the end of the nineties was scarce and expensive, if not completely out of reach for the majority of computer users.

Even in today's world of 'always connected' mobile devices, we often find ourselves in situations without a data signal or other limitations such as the prohibition of cell phone use on airplanes or in hospitals.

If constant availability of business data is a requirement, Siebel CRM continues to provide mobile users with solutions. Starting with Innovation Pack 2013, Oracle supports disconnected mobile applications. At the time of writing, the following mobile applications are prepared for disconnected use out of the box:

- Siebel ePharma Mobile
- Siebel Service Mobile

We can use these applications in connected mode or in disconnected mode. However, a network connection is required to log into the application for the first time and during synchronization. Developers refer to this type of connectivity as *occasionally disconnected*, which stresses the fact that end users will only use the disconnected mode under certain circumstances and not for longer periods such as days or weeks.

In this section we will focus on the *additional* administrative tasks needed to enable disconnected mode for mobile applications, and we will also shed some light on functionality. The following topics will be discussed in the remainder of this section:

- Technical requirements
- Set up disconnected mobile applications
- Test disconnected mobile applications

Technical Requirements

As indicated earlier, a disconnected mobile application is a plain mobile application with some additional 'preparation'. In order to store data and metadata on the mobile device and to enable synchronization with the server database, the following minimum requirements must be met:

- The mobile device must be able to establish a network connection to the Siebel web server.

- The browser on the mobile device must support HTML5 - along with JavaScript and CSS 3 - and allow local storage of at least 50 megabytes (MB). See below for more information on local browser storage technologies.

- The application object manager must be enabled for offline mode.

- The Siebel application version must be IP 2013 Patchset 7 (8.1.1.11.7 or 8.2.2.4.7) or higher.

- Server components for data extraction and synchronization must be available on the Siebel enterprise.

- Mobile applications and users must be properly registered.

> The **HTML5 storage** specification - also known as 'Web Storage' or 'Local Storage' - defines a technique to store key value pairs of data locally and is built into most modern browsers. In addition to this standard, Siebel Disconnected Mobile Applications use the **Web SQL** technology that allows developers to create, update and read data tables using simple SQL statements.
>
> More information about HTML5 storage can be found at `http://www.w3.org/TR/webstorage`.
>
> More information about Web SQL (or rather its successor, *Indexed DB*) can be found at `http://www.w3.org/TR/IndexedDB`.

For Innovation Pack 2013, object managers supporting disconnected mobile applications must run on Microsoft Windows server operating systems. This limitation is not present for IP 2014 or higher.

Setting up disconnected mobile applications

Administrators must execute additional tasks to enable disconnected operation for mobile applications. The following section describes the extra steps that have to be carried out in addition to the mobile application setup procedures discussed earlier in this chapter:

- Enable object managers for offline mode
- Enable component groups
- Configure mobile application settings
- Register mobile clients
- Run the database extract batch component
- Configure the web server

Enabling Object Managers for Offline Mode

There is only one component parameter that defines the difference between an object manager for a connected mobile application and a disconnected mobile application. In order to support disconnected - or 'offline' - mode, we must set the `EnableOfflineMode` parameter to `TRUE` for each object manager we intend to use for disconnected mode.

For the two preconfigured disconnected mobile applications, namely *ePharma Mobile* and *Service Mobile*, this setting is already done by Oracle.

In addition, we should verify that the path to the **Siebel File System** is reachable from the server that the object manager resides on.

Enabling Component Groups

Several server components are necessary for extracting data and handling synchronization for disconnected mobile applications. In addition to the component groups discussed in the previous section, we must also enable the following component groups on at least Siebel server in the enterprise to support disconnected functionality.

- Siebel Remote (IP 2013)
- Disconnected Mobile Synchronization (IP 2014 or higher)

With Innovation Pack 2014, a new component group (*Disconnected Mobile Synchronization*, alias MobileSync) is provided as part of the standard enterprise definition. This component group contains the new *Mobile Data Extraction* (MobileDbXtract) as well as the original *Database Extract* (DbXtract) and other 'traditional' components that formerly resided in the *Siebel Remote* component group. The *Siebel Remote* group is no longer needed in IP 2014 or later.

The new *Mobile Data Extraction* component is preconfigured for the *Siebel ePharma Mobile* application. To support other disconnected mobile applications, customers must copy the existing component definition and modify the Application Name parameter for the new component definition to represent another application such as Siebel Service for Mobile.

Configuring Mobile Application Settings

Apart from setting the correct parameters and enabling the correct component group, disconnected mobile applications require additional administrative data to enable offline functionality. Oracle provides initial settings for the *Siebel Service Mobile* and *Siebel ePharma Mobile* applications as seed data.

This data is administered in the Siebel Mobile Setup view of the Administration - Siebel Remote screen in Innovation Pack 2013. This view is depicted in the next screenshot.

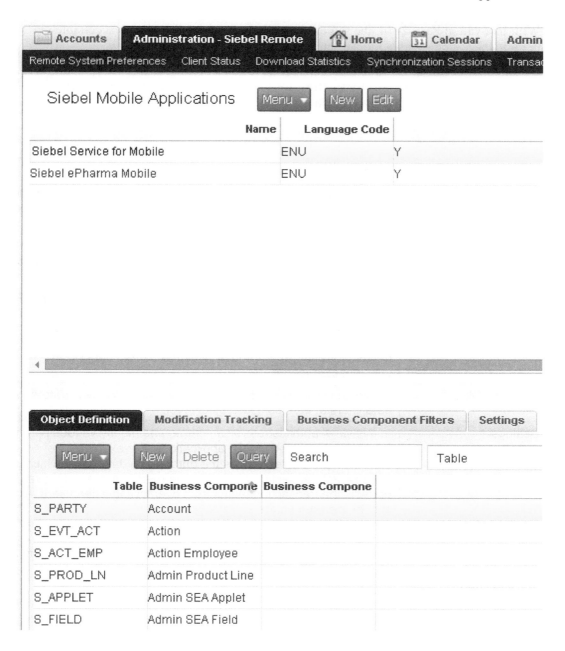

The screenshot shows the seed data entries for the two preconfigured disconnected mobile applications provided by Oracle. The Siebel Service for Mobile application is selected in the upper list applet. The lower list applet allows administrators to inspect and modify the object definitions (base tables and business components) that the mobile application supports for offline mode.

With Innovation Pack 2014, the same data as shown in the screenshot is accessible via the Administration - Siebel Mobile screen, Application Administration view.

Detail views in this screen allow administrators to track modifications, set up data filters and define additional settings (properties) for the selected mobile application. The following table describes the administrative data for disconnected mobile applications in greater detail.

View	Description
Object Definition	The records in this view use table to business component mappings to define the data objects to be synchronized. Administrators must provide the base table names and - if necessary - mappings to intersection tables or tables supporting pick lists.
Modification Tracking	Allows administrators to inspect transaction events for the selected mobile application. This view is read-only.
Business Component Filters	In this view, administrators can inspect and define data filters. For each business component, a search expression can be defined using Siebel Query Language. Only records that match the search expression will be synchronized. Business component filters must be defined carefully in order to provide the correct data set in disconnected mode.
Business Object Filters	Available in IP 2014 or higher, this view allows administrators to set data filters at the business object level.
Settings	In this view, administrators can create and modify various parameters for the disconnected mobile applications. For example, the `Purge Interval` parameter defines the duration (in days) after which incremental transaction data will be purged from the database. This protects the transaction tables from overflowing when users fail to synchronize during the specified period.

For more information about the administrative data for disconnected mobile applications, refer to the document titled *Siebel Mobile Guide: Disconnected* in the Oracle Siebel documentation.

Registering Mobile Clients

In a similar manner to registering mobile client accounts for the traditional Siebel Mobile Web Client, every user account for disconnected mobile applications must have a corresponding entry in the Mobile Clients view.

The following example procedure describes the necessary steps to register a mobile client:

1. In IP 2013, navigate to the Administration - Siebel Remote screen, Mobile Clients view. In IP 2014, use the Administration - Siebel Mobile screen.

2. In the Mobile Clients list, create a new record with the following values (the following are example values).

Column	Description	Example Value
User ID	The login ID of the user.	DSMITH
Mobile Client	The registered name for the mobile client. Suffixed with "-MOBILE" automatically.	DSMITH-MOBILE
Routing Module	The name of the routing module.	MOBILE CLIENT - STANDARD
Mobile Application	The name of the mobile application	Siebel Service for Mobile
Mobile Client Type	IP 2013 only: Identifies the mobile client as a disconnected mobile application client. Must be set to **Siebel Mobile**.	Siebel Mobile

If you are familiar with Siebel Remote technology, you will find that for Siebel Disconnected Mobile Applications, new columns have been introduced to the mobile clients list. The Mobile Client Type (for IP 2013 only) and Mobile Application columns must be set correctly to ensure that the user is registered as a disconnected mobile application client.

Running Database Extract

A familiar task for seasoned Siebel Remote administrators is **Database Extract**. It is mandatory to run this task for each mobile client to finish the setup steps.

The following example scenario explains how to run the *Database Extract* task for mobile clients at the `srvrmgr` command line:

1. On a machine that has a Siebel Server installed, open a command shell and log in to the Siebel server manager command line utility as follows:

```
<SIEBEL_INSTALL_DIR>/siebsrvr/bin/srvrmgr /g localhost
/e Siebel /u SADMIN /p bank49v
```

The command line connects to the Siebel Gateway Name Server on the local machine (`localhost`), opens the configuration for the `Siebel` enterprise and authenticates as the `SADMIN` user.

2. At the prompt, enter the following command:

```
start task for comp dbxtract with client="*-MOBILE"
```

The command initiates the Database Extract (`dbxtract`) task for all mobile clients that have names ending with "`-MOBILE`". The `client` parameter accepts wildcards such as the asterisk (`*`) to broaden the search specification. Alternatively, we can enter the exact name of the mobile client account.

3. It is advisable to monitor the task using a command similar to the following:

```
list tasks for comp dbxtract
```

The command lists all tasks for the *Database Extract* component.

4. Inspect the list and verify that the task executed successfully.

Configuring the Web Server

Siebel Disconnected Mobile Applications use specific filename extensions that must be properly registered as **MIME** (Multipurpose Internet Mail Extension) types in the Siebel web server.

The following filename extensions must be registered for Siebel Disconnected Mobile Applications so that the browser can successfully download the files related to local data and metadata:

- .appcache
- .manifest

The procedure to register MIME types differs between web server vendors and versions. The following procedure describes the process of registering MIME types for Microsoft Internet Information Services (IIS) 7:

1. Open the Internet Information Services (IIS) Manager.
2. In the Connections panel, select the server machine.
3. Double-click the MIME Types icon in the right panel.
4. Right-click in the list of MIME types and select Add...
5. In the Add MIME Type dialog enter the following information.

Field	Value
File name extension	.appcache
MIME type	text/cache-manifest

Note the dot (.) at the beginning of the file name extension.

The following screenshot shows the Add MIME Type dialog with the previous settings.

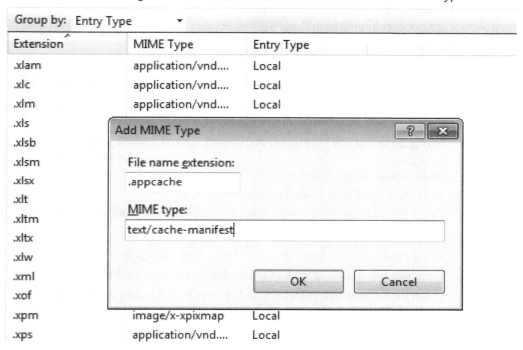

6. Click OK.
7. Repeat steps 4 to 6 to create another MIME type as follows.

Field	Value
File name extension	.manifest
MIME type	text/cache-manifest

8. Restart the web server.

For information on how to register MIME types for web servers on Linux, UNIX or Solaris operating systems, refer to the document titled *Siebel Mobile Guide: Disconnected* in the Oracle Siebel documentation.

Testing Disconnected Mobile Applications

To verify whether the setup steps were successful, we should test the synchronization process. To do so we can either use a mobile device or use a desktop browser and emulate the device as described earlier in this chapter.

Using a desktop browser allows administrators to run a quick test of functionality. However, the final tests (before rolling out the disconnected mobile applications to end users) must include process and functionality tests on exactly the same hardware/software combinations and network connectivity that the end users will be using in the field.

The following procedure describes how to test offline functionality and data synchronization in Innovation Pack 2013 using an emulated mobile device on Google Chrome:

1. Launch a new window or tab of Google Chrome.

2. Navigate to the URL of the disconnected mobile application, for example, `http://webserver/epharmam_enu` for Siebel ePharma Mobile in American English (enu).

3. Provide a valid user name and password to log in.

4. Open the Chrome developer tools (for example, press *F12*).

5. In the developer tools, navigate to the Console tab.

6. Click the Emulation sub-tab on the bottom of the screen.

7. Drag the sub-tab up to make the emulation settings visible.

8. From the Device list, select a suitable device, for example Apple iPad 3 / 4.

9. Click the Emulate button.

10. Right-click the Refresh icon to the left of the address bar and select Empty Cache and Hard Reload. This will clear the cache and reload the page to avoid issues with cached data.

11. Click the Go Offline button (a transmitting satellite dish) in the top right corner.

12. Enter the password for the mobile user and click Ok.

13. Wait for the download process to finish (a progress bar is displayed). The first time synchronization can take a few minutes and might require a page refresh and new log in. Subsequent synchronizations are incremental and therefore much faster.

14. Observe that the satellite dish icon has changed and is now labelled Go Online. The application is now in offline mode.

15. Navigate to the Contacts screen and create a new test contact (Click the plus (+) icon to create a new record). The next screenshot shows an example contact record created in offline mode.

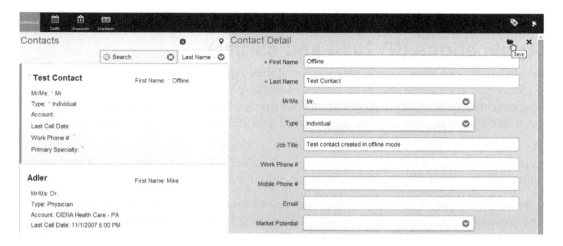

16. Click the Save icon.

17. Observe that the satellite dish icon now displays with a clock symbol. This indicates that local data is available for synchronization.

18. Click the Go Online button.

19. Enter the mobile user password and click Ok.

20. If necessary, log in again to the application. You are now in online mode again.

21. Open another browser window or tab and log in to a desktop application (for example, *Siebel Call Center*).

22. In the desktop application, navigate to the Contacts screen and locate the test record created in step 15.

23. If the test record is visible, the synchronization was successful.

The previous procedure is applicable to Innovation Pack 2014 as well, although IP 2014 provides slightly different navigation patterns, icons, and synchronization processes. For example, an airplane icon replaces the satellite dish icon and there is no need to provide a synchronization password.

In IP 2014 or higher it is possible to enable client-side logging for various events that occur with disconnected operations. To enable logging, go to the Settings/Behavior view and set the desired value in the Log Events field. Once logging is enabled, a bug icon is displayed in the menu bar. When we click this icon, log messages are displayed. We can clear the log, upload it to the server, or make a local copy.

This concludes the setup and simple testing procedures for Siebel Disconnected Mobile Applications.

The Role of jQuery Mobile in Siebel Mobile Applications (IP 2013 and earlier)

As discussed earlier in this chapter, Siebel Mobile Applications are built on top of the Siebel Open UI framework. In addition to JavaScript libraries created by Oracle engineering, Siebel Mobile Applications use much of the features and functionality provided by the **jQuery Mobile** project until and including Innovation Pack 2013.

As stated on the jQuery Mobile web site (`http://jquerymobile.com`), *"jQuery Mobile is a touch-optimized HTML5 UI framework designed to make responsive web sites and apps that are accessible on all smartphone, tablet and desktop devices"*.

The basic concept of jQuery Mobile is tagging elements - typically `<div>` elements - in the browser's document object model (DOM) using HTML5 'data attributes'. The following example HTML code illustrates this concept:

```html
<ul data-role="listview">
    <li><a href="#">First Item</a></li>
    <li><a href="#">Second Item</a></li>
    <li><a href="#">Third Item</a></li>
</ul>
```

The HTML code snippet defines an unordered list (`ul`) with three list items (`li`). The `<ul>` element has the `data-role` attribute set to `listview`, which results in a scrollable list display - using the '*Listview*' widget - when the jQuery Mobile JavaScript libraries are loaded.

The next screenshot shows the previous code as part of a `simple .html` test file without any additional scripts or style sheets loaded in a browser.

The list items are shown as a bulleted list, which is the default browser behavior.

The next screenshot shows the same HTML code snippet in a browser but, this time, the jQuery Mobile libraries and default style sheets are loaded.

The list display has changed dramatically. Each list item is an element in a formatted list, which will appear in the same way on any device or browser.

Siebel Mobile Applications use the *Listview* widget to render list applets. The following screenshot shows a typical list applet in a mobile application.

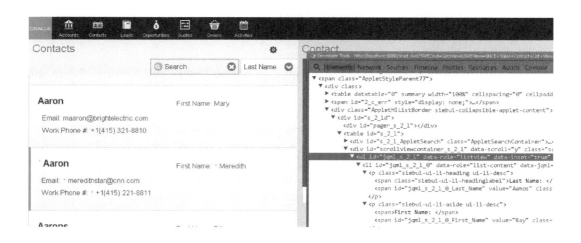

In the screenshot, we can see the contact list applet on the left of the screen. The Google Chrome Developer Tools window is open and highlights the `<ul>` element with the `data-role` attribute set to `listview` in order to demonstrate the use of jQuery Mobile in Siebel Mobile Applications.

Apart from the *Listview* widget, which we discussed in the previous example, jQuery Mobile has numerous other features and visualization options. The following (incomplete) list gives us a general idea of the possibilities of jQuery Mobile:

- **Paging, navigation and transitions**: The jQuery Mobile library provides methods that allow developers to focus on the look and feel of the application without having to write code that handles the navigation between pages or the transitions.

- **Widgets**: A variety of widgets such as the *Listview* widget, demonstrated above, are available. Examples include collapsible sections, tabs, popup dialogs, toggles and filter widgets.

- **Form controls**: In order to provide easy handling for touch screen devices, many of the traditional form controls such as checkboxes, radio groups, flip switches or sliders are available in enhanced versions.

- **Themes**: jQuery Mobile uses CSS in a consistent manner, allowing developers to create custom style sheets using the jQuery Mobile ThemeRoller web application, which we will demonstrate in the next chapter.

More information about jQuery Mobile can be found at `http://jquerymobile.com`.

Summary

Built from scratch using the Siebel Open UI framework, Siebel Mobile Applications are the latest addition to the large family of Siebel Applications.

Siebel Mobile Applications are optimized for touch-enabled mobile devices and ensure that end users can access Siebel CRM data regardless of their location or the device or browser manufacturer.

At the time of writing, two mobile applications, *ePharma Mobile* and *Service Mobile*, are prepared to operate in disconnected mode, using the browser's local storage to hold data while the device has no network connection.

The jQuery Mobile library was used to accomplish the rendering of applets until and including Innovation Pack 2013, providing a consistent look and feel across devices and browsers. As of Innovation Pack 2014, Oracle delivers a common theme (Aurora) for all applications, which is based on Responsive Web Design (RWD) patterns and allows all Siebel applications to be used on any browser and device combinations.

In this chapter we discussed the technical setup steps required to run Siebel Mobile Applications successfully in a Siebel enterprise.

In the next chapter, we will learn how to customize Siebel Mobile Applications.

15

Customizing Siebel Mobile Applications

Providing mobile access to enterprise applications such as Siebel CRM introduces several challenges for developers. In this chapter we will discuss these challenges and provide case studies to explore customization scenarios.

The following topics will be discussed in this chapter:

- Customization challenges for mobile web applications
- Siebel web templates for mobile applications
- Case Study: Create views and applets for mobile deployment
- CSS rules for mobile applications
- Case Study: Use jQuery Mobile ThemeRoller to create custom themes (IP 2013)
- Case Study: Apply Responsive Web Design patterns to traditional Siebel web applications

Because of the differences between Innovation Pack 2013 and 2014, some of this chapter's content does not apply to all Siebel versions covered by this book. Please refer to the notes and information boxes within the chapter to identify the applicable version.

Customization Challenges for Mobile Web Applications

'Mobile First' and 'Responsive Web Design' (RWD) are two modern paradigms for developing web applications. Mobile First involves directly designing a web application for mobile devices rather than modifying an existing web application. RWD creates a web application that has the ability to adapt to different platforms by changing the amount of information displayed based on available screen estate. Whether dealing with back-office-style ERP or front-office-style CRM, when the traditional world of desktop- or laptop-based enterprise applications meets the world of modern web design for mobile devices, several points have to be considered in order to avoid a 'clash of cultures'.

Among these points are the following:

- Which user groups need mobile access, and what business processes will they execute?
- Is there already a mobile user community with the existing application?
- What data objects need to be accessible to mobile users?
- What device type (Laptop, Convertible, Tablet, Phablet, Smartphone, Wearable, etc.) will be used, and what is the available screen size?
- Does the application require access to the device camera, GPS, or other sensors?
- What functionality and data should be available when the device has no network connection?
- What are the security measures (VPN, Container app)?

While this list is not intended to be complete, we can see that analyzing the current situation and devising a mobile strategy is a good idea when it comes to bringing applications that have been designed for desktop or laptop use to modern mobile devices.

With Siebel CRM and its legacy in mobile computing, Oracle has taken the decision to provide completely new applications (as described in Chapter 14) that fulfil the requirements of both 'Mobile First' and 'Responsive Web Design' patterns.

Customers with an existing investment in Siebel CRM can choose to adopt these new mobile applications as they are delivered by Oracle, or they can decide to apply customizations to tailor the applications to their needs.

As we will see in the remainder of this chapter, some aspects of customizing Siebel mobile applications remain unchanged with regards to the tasks that a developer has to accomplish. For example, the process of creating a new applet, or view, still requires work in Siebel Tools, and administrative views in the client, just as for any earlier Siebel version.

However, Siebel Open UI provides developers with a much broader tool set such as CSS and custom JavaScript that can be applied to mobile applications in the same fashion as desktop applications, as we discussed in earlier chapters.

As the field of mobile web development is still young and ever-evolving, we also have to keep in mind that (sometimes) we have to rid ourselves of old ballast and start from scratch. For example, it is paramount for the ambitious developer to stay up-to-date with the latest technologies and libraries in the world of mobile web applications.

In the following case studies we will explore traditional and modern ways of customizing Siebel applications for mobile use.

Siebel Web Templates for Mobile Applications

To support specific layout requirements for mobile applications, Oracle provides several web templates for form applets, list applets, and views. In the following section, we will give a short description of the most prominent web templates.

Web Templates for Mobile Form Applets

The following table describes the most commonly used web templates for form applets that have been introduced in 8.1.1.9 / 8.2.2.2:

Web Template Name	Description
Form Applet Mobile	Basic form applet template, used for Base and Edit/New mode. File Name: CCAppletFormMobile.swt Example Applet: SHCE Contact Form Applet Mobile
Form Applet Mobile - Icon	Extension of the basic form applet template that displays an icon (uses the icon map object named *Mobile Icon Map*). File Name: CCAppletFormMobile_Icon.swt Example Applet: SHCE Account Entry Applet - Mobile
Form Applet Mobile - Icon-NoMenu	Extension of the previous web template, but without the applet menu. File Name: CCAppletFormMobile_Icon_NoMenu.swt Example Applet: Mobile Pharma Contact Form Applet

The next table provides information about form applet web templates introduced with Innovation Pack 2014.

Web Template Name	Description
Form Applet 1 Column Mobile (Edit/New) - NoMenu	Used for Edit/New modes, provides a single column layout for data entry. File Name: AppletForm_NoMenu.swt Example Applet: Mobile Pharma Contact Form Applet Default
Form Applet 2 Column Mobile (Edit/New) Form Applet 2 Column Mobile (Edit/New) - NoMenu	Rarely used 2-column variant (with and without menu) of the previous web template. File Name: AppletForm.swt Example Applet: CG Contact Entry Applet - Mobile

Web Templates for Mobile List Applets

Apart from highly specialized web templates such as the **Mobile Calendar List** template, which supports calendar applets, list applets in Base or Edit List mode do not use specific web templates for mobile applications. The following standard list applet web templates that are also used for desktop applications are also frequently utilized for mobile list applets:

- Applet List (Base/EditList)
- Applet List Edit (Edit/New/Query)

When we intend to create new applets for mobile applications, it is highly recommended to search for a standard applet that matches our requirements and copy it instead of developing an applet from scratch. Copying an existing mobile applet ensures that the correct web templates are used.

As far as applet layout is concerned, we should ensure that only the minimum number of fields are exposed in order to maintain a highly satisfying user experience and to avoid overloading the mobile UI with too much information.

Considerations for Popup Applets in Siebel Mobile Applications

Popup applets such as Pick applets do not use any specialized mobile web templates. The same holds true for MVG and Associate applets, but these are only supported in mobile applications beginning with IP 2014.

From a design perspective, it might also be worthwhile creating mobile variants of popup applets (with a limited number of columns displayed) in order to provide a leaner user interface on mobile devices.

Web Templates for Mobile Views

Oracle provides the following web templates for views in Siebel Mobile Applications.

Web Template Name	Description
View Detail Mobile	The main template for parent list views that typically have a list applet on top and a form applet below where both applets usually represent the same business component. **File Name:** CCViewDetail_Mobile.swt **Example View:** SHCE Account List View - Mobile
View Detail Mobile Related Items	The main template for detail views with a form applet on top and a list applet. The business components for these applets are typically in a parent/child relationship. **File Name:** CCViewDetail_Mobile_RelatedItems.swt **Example View:** SHCE Account Contacts View - Mobile

If we need to create custom views for mobile applications, we should copy an existing mobile view to ensure that the correct web template is referenced - as we do with applets. In the following case study we will explore this safe path to a new view for a mobile application.

Case Study: Creating Views and Applets for Mobile Deployment

The following case study demonstrates how to create a new view for a Siebel Mobile Application in Innovation Pack 2014. The same process applies to IP 2013.

For this case study we assume that we want to display an existing applet that is used in the desktop version of Siebel Call Center in a mobile application. While that could be any standard or custom applet, we decide to use the applet named Account Revenue Schedule List Applet DC which is used to display the Revenues Spreadsheet in the Account Revenues view. The following screenshot shows this view in Siebel's Call Center desktop application.

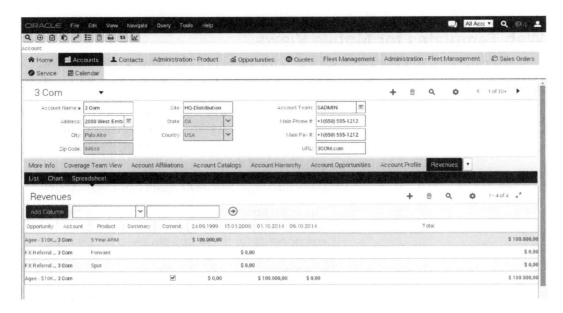

The Spreadsheet applet allows the end user to verify, alter, and add revenue items for the parent account.

In order to carry out the task of 'migrating' the view presented in the previous screenshot to the Siebel Sales Mobile application, we should follow the procedure described below. As most of the steps should be very familiar to our readers, we are focusing on high-level instructions only.

1. Open Siebel Tools.

2. Copy the applet named `Account Revenue Schedule List Applet DC` and rename the copy to `OUIBOOK Account Revenue Schedule List Applet DC - Mobile`. Note that it is a recommended practice to create a mobile version of the applet in case you want to adapt to the available screen estate on a mobile device. If you want to follow a 'define once, deploy everywhere' approach, omit this step and use the original applet instead.

3. Copy `SHCE Account Activities View - Mobile` and rename the copy `OUIBOOK Account Revenue View - Mobile`. In this step, we copy a standard view that is already exposed in the Siebel Sales Mobile application. By doing so, we ensure that the correct view web template is used.

4. Navigate to the list of view web template items for the new view and replace the activities list applet at **Item Identifier 4** with the new `OUIBOOK Account Revenue Schedule List Applet DC - Mobile` applet.

5. Edit the screen named `SHCE Accounts Screen - Mobile` and add the new view, using the following field values.

Column	Value
View	OUIBOOK Account Revenue View - Mobile
Type	Detail View
Parent Category	Account List
Sequence	7 (next in list)
Viewbar Text	Revenue (select Symbolic String)
Menu Text	Revenue (select Symbolic String)

6. Compile all new and modified objects and register the new view with a test responsibility.

7. Log in to the Siebel Sales mobile application and verify that a new detail view is available.

8. Compare your work with the following screenshot.

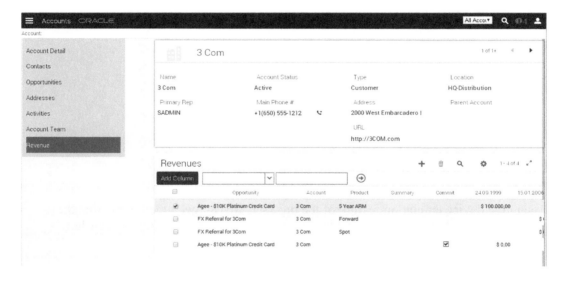

The screenshot shows the new Account Revenue view in the Siebel Sales mobile application.

CSS Rules for Mobile Applications

As discussed in previous chapters of this book, one of the big differences between Innovation Pack 2013 and Innovation Pack 2014 is the shift to a single theme for all applications.

Recall that in IP 2013 we have separate themes for desktop and mobile applications while in IP 2014, the Aurora theme is used across all applications, somehow blurring the lines between classic desktop and modern mobile applications. This section focuses on IP 2014 and the implications of the single theme approach.

With IP 2014 it is possible to use any Siebel application on any device with the limitation that very small screen sizes, such as with smartphones, might cause usability issues due to the number of controls exposed by the applets.

To illustrate the 'define once, use everywhere' approach, we can compare how a traditional desktop-style application is rendered on different screen sizes. The following screenshot shows the Siebel Call Center application on a laptop screen with a resolution of 1600 by 900 pixels.

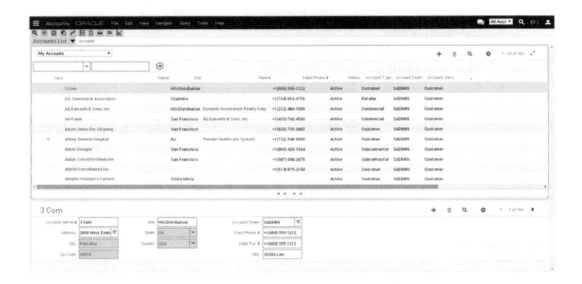

Using the device emulation feature of the browser, we can get a feeling of what the application would look like on a tablet device, as displayed in the next screenshot.

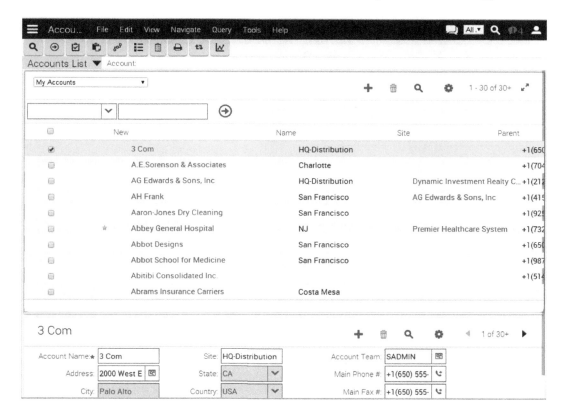

The previous screenshot shows Siebel Call Center on an emulated screen size of 1024 by 768 pixels and a device pixel ratio of 2, which is typical for the Apple iPad in landscape orientation.

The next screenshot shows the effect of putting the tablet in portrait orientation so that the width of the screen is now 768 pixels.

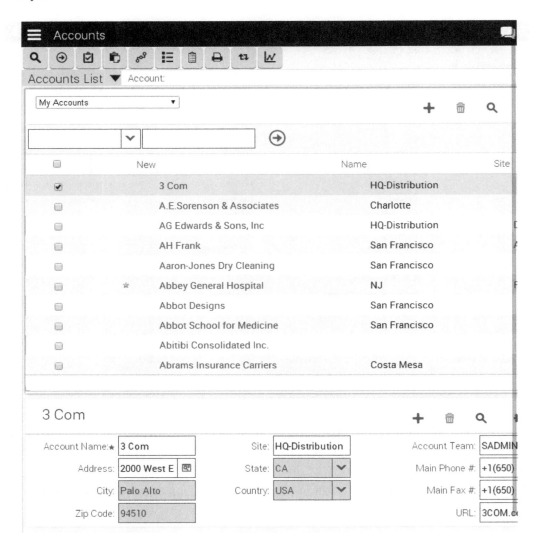

By comparing the three screenshots, we notice several differences…

Feature	Desktop/Laptop	Tablet (Landscape)	Tablet (Portrait)
Menu	Displayed		Not displayed
Logo	Displayed	Not displayed	
Font Size	Small	Large	
Toolbar	Small icons	Large icons	
List Applet	Record navigation buttons	Scroll by touch/swipe gesture	
List Applet	Select multiple records with mouse and keyboard	Select multiple records using check boxes	

We notice that changes produce a slightly different look and feel to the application depending on the screen size. However, we also note that the list and form applets do not adapt to the screen resolution.

Let's dig a little deeper and use the browser's style inspector to investigate the CSS rules for the application logo in desktop mode. The following CSS rule applies to the logo when the application is rendered on a large screen:

```
#_sweclient #_sweappmenu .siebui-logo {
  float: left;
  height: 40px!important;
  line-height: 40px;
  background-image: url("../images/ebus.gif");
  background-repeat: no-repeat;
  background-origin: content-box;
  background-position: 4px 12px;
  width: 106px;
  white-space: nowrap;
}
```

After toggling the emulation to a smaller device, the following CSS rule is added to the logo element.

```
@media (max-width: 1199px)
.siebui-navigation-side #_sweappmenu .siebui-logo {
  display: none;
  visibility: hidden;
}
```

The key feature in this example is the `@media` at-rule that sets the `display` property to `none` and the `visibility` property to `hidden`, effectively hiding the logo element.

The 'media query' in the CSS rule is the maximum available window width (`max-width`), such that the additional CSS properties only apply when the window size is `1199` pixels or less.

> For more information about CSS media queries, refer to the Mozilla Developer Network documentation at `https://developer.mozilla.org/en-US/docs/Web/Guide/CSS/Media_queries`.

CSS media queries are a powerful mechanism to control the visual appearance (or the presence) of elements on a web page depending on factors such as the screen size. The out-of-the-box Aurora theme makes ample use of media queries, as we have demonstrated in this section.

From a customization perspective, we can use CSS media queries in custom style sheets to further optimize the appearance of Siebel web applications on different devices. For example, we could display only the first column in a list applet and hide the form applet of a parent list view when rendered on a smartphone by simply creating a custom style sheet. Later in this chapter, we will look at a case study during which we use CSS media queries.

CSS media queries can also be used in customization scenarios for IP 2013 and earlier, even though they were first introduced in IP 2014. However, we must be aware that we will most likely have to repeat our efforts for custom themes when we migrate to IP 2014 or later and adopt the single-theme approach.

Case Study: Using jQuery Mobile ThemeRoller to Create a Custom Mobile Theme (IP 2013 only)

Siebel customers can use the **jQuery Mobile ThemeRoller** web application to create custom themes for Siebel Mobile Applications, albeit only in Innovation Pack 2013. Following the principle of separating web layout from style, the ThemeRoller web application allows mobile application developers to create so-called **swatches**, which are groups of CSS rules regulating the colors, fonts and icons used in certain areas of the mobile application.

Siebel Mobile Applications for Innovation Pack 2013 uses six swatches, as described in the *Configuring Siebel Open UI* guide of the Oracle Siebel documentation library. The following table describes these swatches:

Swatch	Description
A	Application-level navigation bar
B	List applets
C	Popup applets
D	Grid items
E	Third-level view area
F	Second-level form applets

Source: Configuring Siebel Open UI Guide, Version 8.1/8.2

The following procedure describes the steps needed to create and apply a custom mobile theme using jQuery Mobile ThemeRoller. Please note that this procedure only applies to IP 2013 and is not applicable to IP 2014 or later because those versions no longer use the jQuery Mobile framework.

1. Go to http://themeroller.jquerymobile.com.
2. Use the dropdown list in the Version number field to select version 1.3.2., which is the version used to build Siebel Mobile Applications in IP 2013.
3. Create six swatches ('A' to 'F'), using the ThemeRoller UI. You might want to start in the Global tab, specifying generic settings such as font

size. A good way to achieve a consistent look and feel is to delete all default swatches except 'A'. Then modify the 'A' swatch using drag and drop or Theme settings. Use Duplicate functionality to create five additional swatches ('B' to 'F'). Finally modify the new swatches to suit your needs.

The following screenshot shows the jQuery Mobile ThemeRoller web application with example swatches.

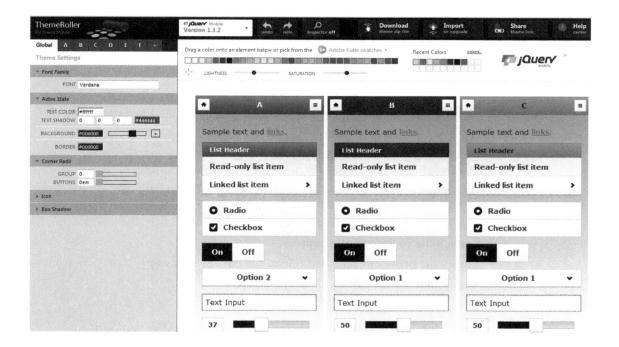

4. Click the Download button and provide a name (for example oui-book) for the theme to download.
5. Extract the downloaded .zip archive.
6. Open the themes folder in the extracted folder.
7. Copy the .css files from the themes folder to the PUBLIC/<Language>/files/custom folder of the Siebel Developer Web Client and/or Siebel Web Server Extension installation directory.
8. Open the images subfolder in the extracted archive.
9. Copy all files from the images subfolder to the PUBLIC/<Language>/images/custom folder of the Siebel instance. (Create the custom folder if necessary).

10. Navigate to the PUBLIC/<LANGUAGE>/files/custom folder and open the file with the *.min.css* extension using a suitable editor.

11. Replace all occurrences of images/ with ../../images/custom/

12. Save the file.

13. Open the custom mobiletheme.js file that should already exist in the siebel/custom scripts folder (if not, create it).

14. Add the following code to the file:

```
SiebelApp.ThemeManager.addResource(
  "SBL-MOBILE",
  {
    css: {
       custom: "files/custom/oui-book.min.css"
}});
```

The code uses the addResource method of the ThemeManager class to add the oui-book.min.css file to the existing SBL-MOBILE theme. Note that the file name could be different, depending on the name you chose in step 4.

15. If not already done, register the custom/mobiletheme.js file in the Manifest Files view of the Administration - Application screen.

16. If necessary, add the custom/mobiletheme.js file to the custom PLATFORM DEPENDENT entry in the Manifest Administration view, providing a valid object expression such as 'Mobile'.

17. Launch the mobile application.

18. Empty the browser cache and reload the page if necessary.

19. Verify that the custom style sheet is loaded.

Using the jQuery Mobile ThemeRoller web application is a plausible approach for quickly creating custom mobile themes for Siebel Mobile Applications in IP 2013. However, the style sheet produced by ThemeRoller does not cover all aspects of Siebel Mobile Applications such as icons and buttons. The appearance of these artefacts usually requires manual fine-tuning.

Case Study: Applying Responsive Web Design Patterns to Traditional Siebel Web Applications

The following case study guides us through the procedure of 'modernizing' a traditional Siebel web application such as **Siebel eEvents**. The goal is to use Siebel Open UI to render the application and adapt to different devices and screen sizes dynamically using responsive web design patterns, thus making the application ready for mobile or desktop use. The scenario for this case study is as follows:

- Enable the application for Siebel Open UI
- Create a custom application container web page
- Create a custom web template for the home page view
- Use CSS media queries to achieve responsive web design

> The authors wish to thank Jake Patterson and Andy Stevens of Boxfusion Consulting (www.boxfusionconsulting.com) for providing us with this example configuration and the code files.

Enabling the Application for Siebel Open UI

Siebel eEvents is a traditional Standard-Interactivity (SI) customer-facing application. We chose Siebel eEvents for this case study because it provides a simple base for experiments and education. The configuration steps shown in the following case study are applicable to all Siebel web applications.

The following screenshot shows the out-of-the-box appearance of Siebel eEvents.

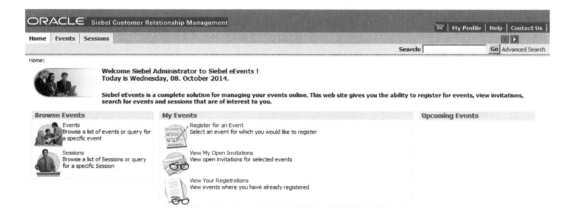

The Siebel eEvents application displays the home page that allows customers to browse and register for events. The application is in Standard Interactivity (SI) mode and does not currently use Siebel Open UI.

The following scenario guides us through the steps for enabling Siebel eEvents for Open UI. As mentioned earlier, this should apply to other Siebel web applications as well. For development purposes, we use the Siebel Developer Web Client.

1. Open the eevents.cfg configuration file in the Developer Web Client's BIN/<Language> folder.

2. Locate the `[InfraUIFramework]` section and ensure that the following parameters are set:

```
EnableOpenUI = TRUE
HighInteractivity = TRUE
AppletSelectStyle = "Applet Select"
```

As discussed in Chapter 3, the combination of setting both the `EnableOpenUI` and the `HighInteractivity` parameter to `TRUE` effectively enables Open UI. The `AppletSelectStyle` parameter must always be set to `"Applet Select"` to avoid issues with the rendering of MVG applets.

3. Save the file and launch the Siebel eEvents application, preferably using the Siebel Sample Database and logging in as the Siebel Administrator (SADMIN).

Observe that the application launches in Open UI mode, but the appearance is less than desirable. Compare your application with the following screenshot.

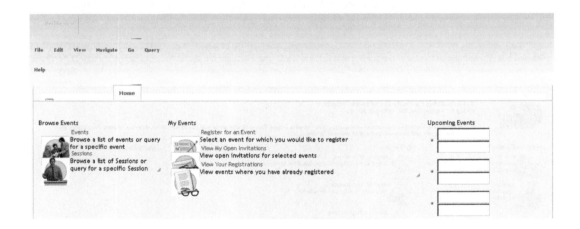

The Siebel eEvents application now uses Siebel Open UI, but the layout is broken.

Boxfusion Consulting has provided us with a prototype of a customer-facing application that we can use as a guideline for our efforts to modernize Siebel eEvents. The following screenshot shows this prototype.

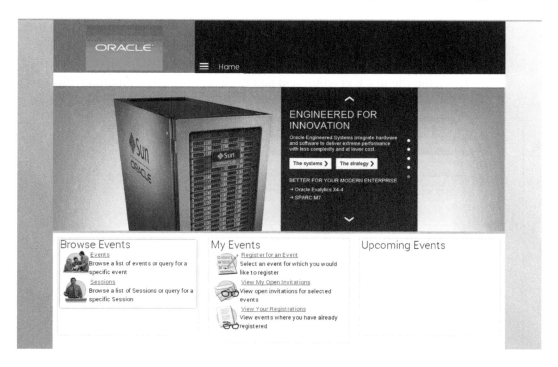

As we can see in the screenshot, the application layout is modern and suitable for use on desktop and mobile devices.

In the following sections of this case study, we will use custom web templates and style sheets to convert Siebel eEvents to a modern web application that uses responsive web design patterns.

Creating a Custom Application Container Web Page

Siebel web applications use a container web page to define the initial HTML framework. Because we want to achieve a completely new look and feel, we decide to replace the existing container web page with a custom version. This process includes the following high level steps:

- Create a custom Siebel Web Template (SWT) file
- Register a new web template in Siebel Tools
- Create a new web page and associate it with the application

Creating a Custom Siebel Web Template (SWT) File

The following scenario guides us through the steps to implement a custom application container web page.

1. Create a new file named OUIBOOKPageContainer.swt in the WEBTEMPL/OUIWEBTEMPL/CUSTOM folder of the Siebel Developer Web Client installation directory.

2. Open the file in a text editor and add the following lines. Alternatively you may want to refer to the example file provided with this chapter's code archive.

```
<!--  Template Start: OUIBOOKPageContainer.swt -->
<html dir="swe:dir">
  <head>
    <meta name="viewport" content="width=device-width">
    <title><swe:this property="Title"/></title>
  </head>
  <body>
    <div id="mobileDebug"></div>
    <div class="siebui-page-container">
     <div class="siebui-app-container">
      <div class="siebui-header">
       <!-- Header Logo Place holder -->
       <div id="bclLogo">
        <a title="Oracle Home Page"
        href="http://www.oracle.com">
         <img src="images/custom/oracle-logo.png"
         height="100px" alt="Placeholder Logo"></a>
       </div>
       <!-- Screen Tab Place holder -->
       <div id="screenTabs" class="siebui-ss-screentabs">
        <swe:nav-control type="Screen With Category"
        style="Tab" indentWidth="8"/>
       </div>
      </div>
      <!-- View Container Place holder -->
      <div class="siebui-view-container">
       <swe:frameset htmlAttr="cols='0%,100%' border='0'
       frameborder='No'">
        <swe:frame type="View" >
         <swe:current-view/>
        </swe:frame>
       </swe:frameset>
      </div>
     </div>
    </div>
    <swe:scripts/>
  </body>
</html>
<!--  Template End: OUIBOOKPageContainer.swt -->
```

The web template code in the example accomplishes the following:

- Define the meta viewport tag in the header to allow the browser to define the virtual viewport it uses for rendering the page.

- Define several nested `<div>` elements as follows:
  - o Class `siebui-page-container`: The overall page container
  - o Class `siebui-app-container`: The application container
  - o Class `siebui-header`: The header/banner section
- In the header section, we add an image reference to define the location of the logo. Note that this example uses a fixed image path. In a real-life scenario, the logo should be defined in a style sheet. You will find the image file `oracle-logo.png` in this chapter's code archive. You must copy that file to the `IMAGES/custom` folder in your client's directory.
- Next, we define a `<div>` element to hold the screen (first level) navigation control. We use the `swe:nav-control` SWE tag to let the Siebel Web Engine know to position the first and second level navigation controls at this point.
- In the following `<div>` element, we use the `swe:frameset` and `swe:frame` tags to define the wrapper for the view content.
- The view content is displayed using the `swe:current-view` tag.

> For more information about SWE tags and how to use them in Siebel web templates, refer to the *Siebel Developer's Reference* book in the Oracle Siebel documentation.

While the previous web template file is kept short for the sake of brevity, we could also refer to existing container files in the `WEBTEMPL` or `OUIWEBTEMPL` folder in order to find useful SWE tags. For example, we could choose to display page items such as a help link or to include other SWT files such as a banner definition.

Registering a new Web Template in Siebel Tools

After saving the file, we must register it as a web template in the Siebel Repository. The following procedure provides the major steps to accomplish this:

1. In Siebel Tools, create a new Web Template object with the following properties.

Property	Value
Name	OUIBOOK Page Container
Type	Web Page Template

2. Expand the Web Template File list for the new Web Template object and add a new record with the following properties.

Property	Value
Name	OUIBOOKPageContainer
Filename	OUIBOOKPageContainer.swt

3. Compare your work with the following screenshot.

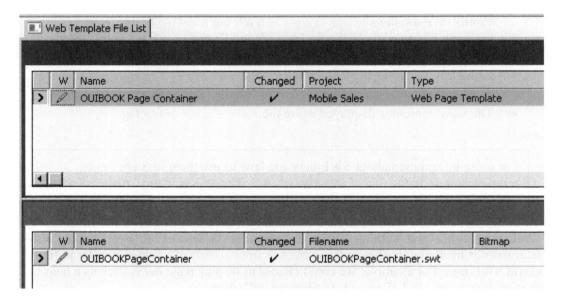

The screenshot shows the new OUIBOOK Page Container web template object and the associated SWT file in Siebel Tools.

Creating a New Web Page and Associating it with the Application

Now we can use the web template object we created in the previous section to define a new web page object, which we then associate with the Siebel eEvents Management application definition. The following procedure guides us through this process:

1. In Siebel Tools, locate the existing Web Page definition named CC Container Page (eEvents). Note that this is the web page currently specified in the Container Web Page property for the Siebel eEvents Management application.

2. Copy the CC Container Page (eEvents) web page definition and rename the copy to OUIBOOK Container Page. Copying an existing web

page rather than creating a new one has the benefit that all child objects such as web page items are present in the copy.

3. Change the Web Template property of the new web page definition to OUIBOOK Page Container.

4. Navigate to the Application object type and locate the Siebel eEvents Management application definition.

5. Change the Container Web Page property of the Siebel eEvents Management application definition to OUIBOOK Container Page.

6. Compile all new and modified object definitions.

This procedure concludes the process of creating and registering a new container web page for a Siebel application. In the next section of this case study, we will create and register a custom web template for the application home page view.

Creating a Custom Web Template for the Home Page View

The following procedure describes how to create a custom view web template and assign it to the eEvents home page view:

1. Create a new file named OUIBOOKHomeView.swt in the WEBTEMPL/OUIWEBTEMPL/CUSTOM folder of the Siebel Developer Web Client installation directory.

2. Open the file in a text editor and add the following lines. Alternatively you may want to refer to the example file provided with this chapter's code archive.

```
<!-- Template Start: OUIBOOKHomeView.swt -->
<div id="bclEventsHomeViewContainer">
 <div id="bclEventsHomeSliderContainer">
  <img src="images/custom/eng-sys-big.png" width="958px"
  height="317px" alt="Placeholder Image">
 </div>
 <div class="bclEventsHomeBoxContainer">
  <div class="bclEventsHomeBox bclEventsHomeBoxLeft">
   <swe:applet hintMapType="Applet" id="103" hintText="Applet"
   property="FormattedHtml" var="Parent" />
  </div>
  <div class="bclEventsHomeBox bclEventsHomeBoxMiddle">
   <swe:applet hintMapType="Applet" id="202" hintText="Applet"
   property="FormattedHtml" var="Parent" />
  </div>
  <div class="bclEventsHomeBox bclEventsHomeBoxRight">
   <swe:applet hintMapType="Applet" id="302" hintText="Applet"
   property="FormattedHtml" var="Parent" />
  </div>
 </div>
</div>
<!-- Template End: OUIBOOKHomeView.swt -->
```

The example web template defines the following elements:

- The overall view container
- A container element for the 'slider'; at the moment we only display a placeholder image here. The `eng-sys-big.png` image file can be found in this chapter's code archive and must be copied to the `IMAGES/custom` folder. In a later stage, this container will harbor an image slider with promotional imagery and text.
- A container for the lower section of the view with three sub-containers, each of which uses the `swe:applet` tag to define an applet placeholder.

For the sake of brevity, we keep the example web template nice and easy. Refer to existing view web templates and the *Siebel Developer's Reference* for more options to create view web templates. For example, we could include code that would only show certain applets depending on whether the current user is authenticated (logged in) or not (browsing anonymously).

After saving the file, we must register it as a web template in the Siebel Repository. The steps described next are basically the same as for registering the container web template we created earlier in this case study:

1. In Siebel Tools, create a new Web Template object with the following properties.

Property	Value
Name	OUIBOOK Home Page View
Type	View Template

2. Expand the Web Template File list for the new Web Template object and add a new record with the following properties.

Property	Value
Name	OUIBOOKHomeView
Filename	OUIBOOKHomeView.swt

Finally, we must assign the new web template with the home page view for the Siebel eEvents application. The following procedure describes the steps to do so:

1. Navigate to the Home Page View (eEvents) view.
2. Open the list of View Web Templates for the view.
3. Set the value of the Web Template property to OUIBOOK Home Page View.

4. Compile all new and modified objects.

This concludes the work on the application container and the home page view. Remember that in this case study we focus on basic steps. Details such as creating alternative applet web templates or images are outside the scope of this chapter. Refer to the *Siebel Developer's Reference* guide in the Siebel bookshelf for details on creating web templates.

In the final section of this case study, we will introduce the CSS rules to apply custom styles to the application as well as define media queries to adapt to different screen sizes.

Using CSS Media Queries to Achieve Responsive Web Design

Designing and implementing the visual appearance of our refurbished eEvents application would certainly fill a whole chapter on its own. For the sake of brevity we focus on the most important CSS rules and pay special attention to CSS media queries to adapt the look and feel to the device screen estate.

In this chapter's code archive, we provide the file `OUIBOOK-eEventsRWD.css` that contains all CSS rules as an educational starting point. This style sheet (or its content) must be included in a custom theme, a procedure we already practiced in Chapter 8.

After registering the `OUIBOOK-eEventsRWD.css` style sheet, the Siebel eEvents Management application appears as shown in the following screenshot.

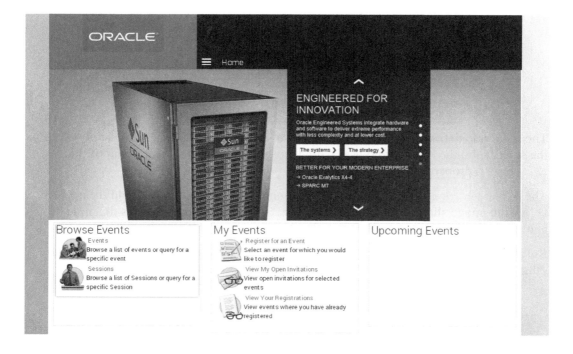

The screenshot shows the result of applying the example CSS file on a laptop screen.

In the following section we will discuss key CSS rules as defined in the example CSS file. We will focus on the following topics:

- Define the layout for large screens
- Define the overall style for smaller screens
- Define styles for tablets and smartphones

Defining the Layout for Large Screens

In order to achieve the look and feel shown in the previous screenshot, the following CSS rules (amongst others) have been put in place:

```
body {
    font-family: "Helvetica Neue", Helvetica, Arial, sans-
    serif;
    line-height: 1.5em;
    color: #333333;
    background: linear-gradient(45deg, #a8a8a8 0%, #f9f9f9
    100%);
    background-attachment: fixed;
    overflow-y: auto;
}
.bclEventsHomeBox {
    margin: 0 10px 10px;
    width: 298px;
    min-height: 205px;
    overflow: hidden;
    float: left;
    padding-bottom: 10px;
    background-color: #fff;
    border: 1px solid #ddd;
}
```

The body rule defines the font and background style of the page. As can be observed in the screenshot, the background uses a gradient gray color pattern as a result of the background property.

The .bclEventsHomeBox class is assigned to the child containers that hold the applets below the image slider. The key property is float: left, which causes the three applets to align in a row from left to right.

Refer to the upper section of the OUIBOOK-eEventsRWD.css style sheet to review the other style rules for the general look and feel of the application on large screens.

Defining the Overall Style for Smaller Screens

For our example, we define a 'smaller screen', as reported by the device, with a width of 1000 pixels or below. For demonstration purposes, we make the following assumptions about the look and feel on smaller screens:

- Set the background color to a solid gray
- Align the content from top to bottom

In addition, we would like to include a debug message on top of the screen that conveys information about the current device size. This debug option will, of course, have to be removed before we deploy the application to end users.

The following CSS rules have been defined to implement the previous requirements:

```css
@media (max-width: 1000px) {
  body, #_sweclient, .siebui-app-container,
  .siebui-view-container, .siebui-header {
    background-color:#a8a8a8;
    background:#a8a8a8;
  }
  .bclEventsHomeBox {
    width:100%;
    min-height:inherit;
    overflow:auto;
    float:none;
    margin:0 0 10px 0;
    padding-bottom:0px;
    background-color:#fff;
  }
  #mobileDebug {
    display:block;
  }
  #mobileDebug:before {
    content: " [Mobile Enabled] ";
  }
}
@media (min-width: 480px) and (max-width: 1000px) {
  #mobileDebug:after {
    content: "Tablet";
  }
}
```

The first rule is a media 'at-rule' and defines a block that will be applied by the browser if the device reports a screen width of 1000 pixels or less.

Within the media rule, we override the background color to a solid gray.

In addition, we override the .bclEventsHomeBox class and set the float property to none. This will cause the browser to align the elements from top to bottom.

If you inspect the page container SWT file (that we implemented at the beginning of this case study) you will notice a `<div>` element with an id of `mobileDebug`. This element is used to display the debug messages. In the previous CSS rule, the message displayed will be `" [Mobile Enabled] "` followed by the type of device. In a separate media query (that is applicable to screen sizes between 480 and 1000 pixels), we define the second part of the debug message as `"Tablet"`.

To test the media queries, we can either resize the browser window or use the browser's emulation features to spoof a tablet device.

The following screenshot shows the example application in Google Chrome while emulating an Apple iPad in portrait mode.

As we can see in the screenshot, the applets are aligned from top to bottom on a gray background. In addition we can see the debug message at the top of the screen indicating that the media query for tablets matches the current screen size.

Defining Styles for Tablets and Smartphones

While the current style works well for desktop/laptop and tablets, we have to implement additional media queries for smaller screen sizes such as on smartphones.

The following CSS rules have been implemented to adapt the application's look and feel to small screens.

```css
/* Larger Mobile Phones */
@media (min-width: 321px) and (max-width: 480px){
  #mobileDebug:after{
    content: "[Phone: Large] ";
  }
  #bclEventsHomeSliderContainer img{
    width: 100%;
    height: auto;
  }
}
/* Small Mobile Phones */
@media (max-width: 320px) {
  #mobileDebug:after {
    content: "[Phone: Small] ";
  }
  #bclEventsHomeSliderContainer {
    display:none;
  }
}
```

The first media query defines the overrides when the screen width, reported by the device, is between 321 and 480 pixels, which is typical for larger smartphones. After setting the debug message to `"[Phone: Large]"`, we set the `width` and `height` properties for the slider image so that the browser can automatically adjust the image size.

In the second media query we define the look and feel for small smartphone screens below a width of 320 pixels. Here we set the `display` property of the slider container to `none`, effectively removing it.

The following screenshot shows the example application on an emulated Samsung Galaxy phone with a large screen.

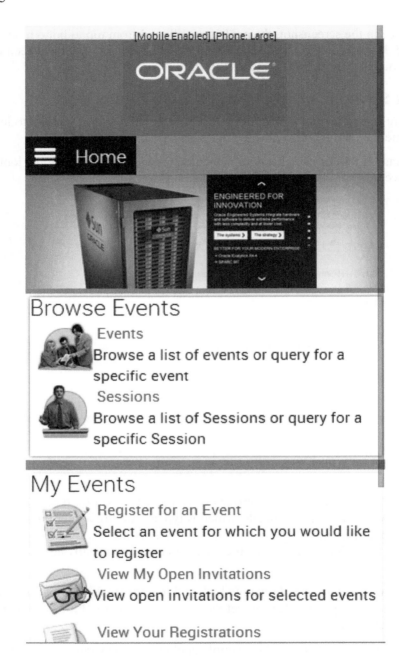

As we can observe in the screenshot, the slider image size has been adjusted to the smaller screen.

In the next screenshot, we see the example application as rendered on an Apple iPhone 5, which reports a 320 pixel screen width to the browser.

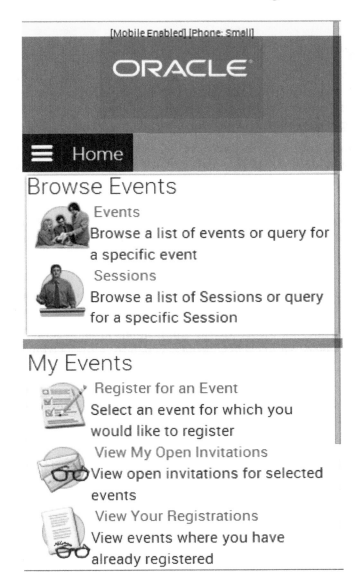

As shown in the screenshot, the slider image no longer appears on small screen devices.

This concludes our case study for using CSS media queries to implement responsive web design patterns for a traditional Siebel application such as Siebel eEvents Management. While our case study focused on the home page only, the techniques demonstrated here would apply to other views and applets as well.

Summary

Siebel CRM was always a pioneer in mobile computing. Starting with the Mobile Web Client almost 20 years ago and extending to browser-based applications with Siebel Web Client and Siebel Wireless Web Client soon after that, Siebel CRM has a solid track record of making enterprise data available on mobile devices.

With Siebel Open UI, we not only have a new family of mobile applications but also new ways of applying modern web design patterns such as responsive web design to the entire Siebel landscape.

In this chapter we learned how to combine traditional Siebel development techniques with modern web design. After discussing the key challenges for mobile access to enterprise applications, we used Siebel Tools - in the same way as for traditional applications - to deploy new views and applets to a mobile application, using new web templates provided by Oracle.

Style sheets play an important role in the customization of Siebel web applications and, as such, we discussed important CSS patterns that apply to mobile browsing.

Creating custom themes for Siebel Mobile Applications in Innovation Pack 2013 is facilitated by the jQuery Mobile ThemeRoller, which we introduced in this chapter as well.

Finally, we navigated through a complete case study of applying modern web design patterns to a traditional Siebel application (Siebel eEvents). In this case study we demonstrated how custom web templates and CSS media queries come together to provide a seamless user experience across all device types and screen sizes.

In the next chapter, we will discuss integration scenarios for Siebel Open UI.

16

Integrating Siebel Open UI

While Siebel CRM traditionally has a large footprint when it comes to integrating with other applications, Siebel Open UI offers us additional ways of creating interfaces, like the new portlet API or using drag and drop for data import in list applets. In this chapter we will discuss the following topics related to integrating Siebel Open UI with other applications:

- The Open UI Portlet API
- Case Study: Displaying a Siebel Open UI applet in Oracle Sales Cloud
- Drag and drop data import
- Symbolic URLs and Open UI
- Case Study: Integrating Oracle BI Mobile Applications with Siebel Open UI
- Case Study: Using the Google Maps API for address auto-complete
- Case Study: Accessing applications on a mobile device
- Case Study: Consuming data from a REST service

The Open UI Portlet API

Siebel CRM traditionally provides an API for the Siebel Web Engine (SWE API) that is a part of the **Siebel Portal Framework**. With the introduction of Siebel Open UI in 2012, this API has been extended with new commands to allow - for the first time – access to individual applets as 'portlets'. In earlier versions of Siebel CRM, the lowest level object to access via the SWE API was a view.

> For more information about the SWE API and the Siebel Portal Framework, refer to the *Siebel Portal Framework Guide* in the Oracle Siebel documentation library.
>
> Please note that the information in this section has been verified against Innovation Pack 2013. While the content should be applicable as well to IP 2014; newer releases of Siebel CRM have several security restrictions that require additional configuration in the applications we wish to integrate.

In this section, we will explore the possibilities of the new portlet API and demonstrate how to use it to display Siebel applets or views within the context of other web applications. We will discuss the following scenarios:

- Build a portlet URL to display a single applet
- Define the business object for an applet
- Display a view in an external application
- Use search criteria

Building a Portlet URL to Display a Single Applet

The SWE API supports so-called SWE commands to be passed as parameters to a Siebel application base URL. In an integration scenario, we want to display an entire view or a single applet in another web application's browser window.

The following example focuses on the single applet scenario and shows a URL that instructs the SWE to return an instance of the Quote List Applet for Siebel CRM Innovation Pack 2013.

```
http://mywebserver/callcenter_enu/start.swe?SWECmd=ExecuteLogin&SWEUserN
ame=SADMIN&SWEPassword=5tzm99vq&SWEAC=SWECmd=GetApplet&SWEApplet=Quote+L
ist+Applet&IsPortlet=1&SWESM=Edit+List&KeepAlive=1&PtId=GRAY_TAB
```

The following screenshot shows the result of calling the example URL in a new browser tab.

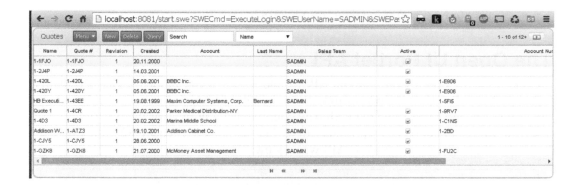

In the screenshot, we can observe that the Quote List Applet is displayed in the browser tab without any surrounding UI elements such as application menu, screen tabs, or view bar. Using a new tab in a browser is a good choice for a quick test. Once you have verified that the URL yields the desired results, you can use it in the external application to display the Siebel applet or view.

The commands that are used to build the previous example URL are described in the following table.

Command	Description and Example
Base URL	The base URL for the Siebel application object manager that will process the request. Example: `http://mywebserver/callcenter_enu/start.swe`
? (question mark)	The question mark separates the base URL from the command sequence.
& (ampersand)	The ampersand character separates individual command/value pairs within the command sequence.
SWECmd	The SWE command to execute. Example: `SWECmd=ExecuteLogin` The `ExecuteLogin` command must be followed by username and password (see below) and is necessary if your integration scenario does not involve Single-Sign-On (SSO) or if the user is not already logged in.
SWEUserName	Used together with `ExecuteLogin` to specify the name of the user account. Example: `SWEUserName=SADMIN` Note: This parameter is no longer supported in IP 2014 and later for security reasons. As an alternative, we have to implement SSO authentication.
SWEPassword	Used together with `ExecuteLogin` to specify the password for the user account. Example: `SWEPassword=5tzm99vq` Note: This parameter is no longer supported in IP 2014 and later for security reasons. As an alternative, we have to implement SSO authentication.
SWEAC	Specifies an additional command (AC) to be executed after the primary command. Example: `SWEAC=SWECmd=GetApplet`
GetApplet	Instructs the SWE to instantiate an individual applet. This SWE command available in IP 2013 and later.
SWEApplet	Used in conjunction with GetApplet to specify the name of the applet to instantiate. Example: `SWEApplet=Quote+List+Applet` Note that spaces in object names must be replaced by plus (+) characters.
IsPortlet	Mandatory command to isolate the object (applet or view) as a portlet. The returned HTML will not contain the application menu, toolbar or other navigation elements. Example: `IsPortlet=1`

(Continued)

SWESM	(Optional) Specifies the applet mode (such as Base, Edit or Edit List). **Example:** SWESM=Edit+List
KeepAlive	(Optional) Keep the session alive to avoid timeout issues. **Example:** KeepAlive=1
PtId	(Optional) Specifies the name of the Open UI theme to use. We must use the internal name as specified in the Language-Independent Code column of the List of Values record for the theme. **Example:** PtId=GRAY_TAB

As described in the table, it is not always necessary to call the ExecuteLogin command. While this might be alright for simple test scenarios, we should resort to a solid Single-Sign-On (SSO) solution for production purposes so that user account names and passwords are not visible in clear text in the URL. Besides, the ExecuteLogin command will result in a new session on the object manager every time it is invoked, causing a significant delay in processing and loss of any context established before.

Defining the Business Object for an Applet

The previous example shows how to retrieve a single applet outside its usual view boundary. Having no surrounding view also means that the applet has no business object context, as the view specifies the business object to be used in the Siebel application architecture.

Therefore, if we intend to use an applet as described earlier, we have to specify the business object to be used for the applet by using the Business Object user property of the applet.

The following screenshot shows the definition of the Quote List Applet in Siebel Tools.

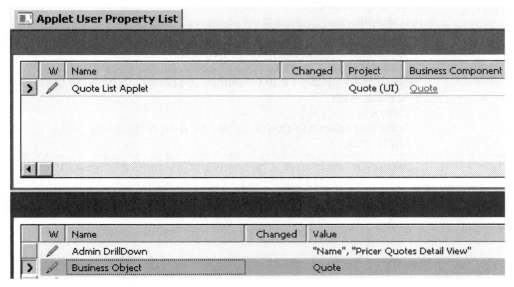

The screenshot shows the list of user properties for the Quote List Applet. The `Business Object` user property is highlighted and its value is `Quote`, specifying that the Quote business object will be used to establish the context for the applet when it is accessed outside of a view.

The `Business Object` user property must be set correctly for each applet that we intend to access using the Open UI Portlet API.

Displaying a View in an External Application

As described in the previous section, the `GetApplet` command drives the SWE to instantiate a single applet. In case we want to display an entire view in a different web application's context, we must build a URL as in the following example:

```
http://mywebserver/callcenter_enu/start.swe?SWECmd=GotoView&SWEView=Quote+Detail+View&IsPortlet=1&KeepAlive=1
```

In the previous example, we omitted the `ExecuteLogin` command and its dependents for the sake of brevity. We have specified the `IsPortlet` parameter similar to the first example to retrieve the view without any surrounding navigation elements. The following table describes the SWE commands that are specifically used to retrieve a view.

Command	Description and Example
GotoView	Instructs the SWE to navigate to a view. The view name must be specified using the SWEView command (see next). Example: `SWECmd=GotoView`
SWEView	Defines the name of the view. Example: `SWEView=Quote+Detail+View`
SWEApplet	(Optional) Can be used in conjunction with GotoView to display only the applet defined with this command. Example: `SWEApplet=Quote+Form+Applet`

The following screenshot shows the result of accessing the example URL in a new browser tab.

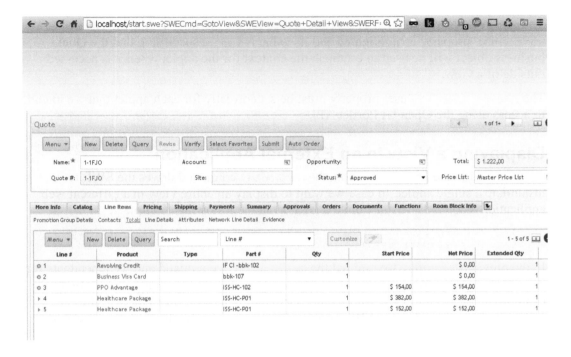

The example screenshot shows a portion of the Quote Detail View as displayed when the example URL is used.

Using Search Criteria

On many occasions it is not enough just to display a view or applet in an external application. Most times, we must establish context with a record that exists in the external application and use the Siebel applet or view to display details about that record.

To accomplish this, the Siebel SWE API allows us to specify search criteria for fields in the business component exposed by the applet as per the following syntax:

```
BCFieldN=field_name&BCFieldValueN=field_value
```

In the previous syntactical example, N represents a sequence number (starting at 0). The BCFieldN parameter is used to specify a business component field name, and the BCFieldValueN parameter is used to define the filter criteria for the field.

If we expose a view, we can address the parent (or primary) business component of the view's business object using the following syntax:

```
PBCFieldN=parent_field&PBCFieldValueN=parent_field_value
```

Again, N represents a sequence number. Note that the difference to the previous example lies within the prefix P used for the parameters.

The following URL is an example to retrieve a list of quotes for the account of Nick Brown with a status of 'Order Placed':

```
http://mywebserver/callcenter_enu/start.swe?SWECmd=ExecuteLogin&SWEUserN
ame=SADMIN&SWEPassword=SADMIN&SWEAC=SWECmd=GetApplet&SWEApplet=Quote+Lis
t+Applet&IsPortlet=1&SWESM=Edit+List&KeepAlive=1&PtId=GRAY_TAB&BCField0=
Status&BCFieldValue0=Order+Placed&BCField1=Account&BCFieldValue1=Brown,+
Nick
```

In the previous example, we have highlighted (in bold font) the SWE commands that have been added to accomplish the data filter. The following table describes these commands.

Command	Description and Example
BCField0	Specifies the first field to query. Example: BCField0=Status
BCFieldValue0	Specifies the filter value for the first field. Example: BCFieldValue0=Order+Placed
BCField1	Specifies the second field to query. Example: BCField1=Account
BCFieldValue1	Specifies the filter value for the second field. Example: BCFieldValue1=Brown,+Nick

The author's tests have shown that it is not possible to use wildcards or query operators in the field values. Instead, the value passed to the BCFieldValueN parameter is used for an exact, case sensitive query.

Case Study: Displaying a Siebel Open UI Applet in Oracle Sales Cloud

In this case study we want to demonstrate the use of the Portlet API to display Siebel data within a cloud application. In our example we will use Oracle Sales Cloud as the external application.

Within Oracle Sales Cloud, end users can manage customer account data and typical sales-related data such as opportunities. Here, we imagine an Oracle customer who has deployed Siebel CRM to capture quotes and orders for customers and who has recently deployed Oracle Sales Cloud. One of the (fictitious) requirements from the sales staff is to be able to view a list of quotes (stored in Siebel CRM) for a sales account in Sales Cloud.

To implement this exemplary requirement we define the following high-level steps:

- Expose the applet as a portlet
- Create a new tree node in Oracle Sales Cloud

In the following sections we will provide step-by-step scenarios for this implementation.

Exposing the Applet as a Portlet

As discussed in the previous section, we must be able to access the Quote List Applet as a standalone applet in order to integrate it into an external application such as Oracle Sales Cloud.

The following procedure describes the steps to expose a Siebel applet as a portlet:

1. In Siebel Tools, navigate to the applet definition (for example the Quote List Applet) and verify that the `Business Object` user property is set correctly. For our example applet, this is the case, and we can skip the next step.

2. If the `Business Object` user property is not set to the applet, create a new user property record, provide the correct business object name as the value, and compile the applet.

3. Log in to the Siebel application.

4. Locate an account record that has associated quotes and note the account name. In the Siebel Sample Database you might find accounts like `BBBC Inc.` or `Brown, Nick`.

5. Open a new browser window or tab and enter a URL similar to the following in the address bar:

```
http://localhost/start.swe?SWECmd=ExecuteLogin&SWEUserName=SADMIN&SWEPas
sword=SADMIN&SWEAC=SWECmd=GetApplet&SWEApplet=Quote+List+Applet&IsPortle
t=1&SWESM=Edit+List&KeepAlive=1&BCField0=Status&BCField0=Account&BCField
Value0=Brown,+Nick
```

In the example URL to be tested against the Siebel Developer Web Client and the Siebel Sample Database, we define one of the test account names (`Brown, Nick`) as the input value for the `BCFieldValue0` parameter. For details on the other parameters, refer to the previous section.

6. Verify that the application returns the standalone applet and that only the records for the test account are displayed. Compare your work with the following screenshot.

434

The screenshot shows the Quote List Applet as returned from the test URL. Only records for the Account Brown, Nick are shown.

The next steps in this process would actually include testing the URL pattern against a Siebel server environment. As Oracle Sales Cloud only supports SSL connections to external applications, the target Siebel environment must be configured to use SSL, and the URL actually starts with https. However, these configuration steps are outside the scope of this book.

Creating a New Tree Node for Sales Accounts in Oracle Sales Cloud

The following procedure describes the high-level configuration steps in Oracle Sales Cloud to create a sub-page that displays the Siebel quote list for a given sales account. For details on the concepts of extending and configuring Oracle Sales Cloud please refer to the Oracle Cloud documentation library.

1. Log in to your Oracle Sales Cloud instance using an account with enough privileges to use the Application Composer.
2. Navigate to the **Application Composer**.
3. Create a new sandbox to isolate your configurations.
4. Open the Customer Center application.
5. Navigate to the Sales Account object.
6. Open the Pages details for the Sales Account object.
7. In the Tree Nodes section, click the Create icon.
8. Select Web Content and click Next.
9. In the Web Content page, set the following values.

Field	Value
Category	Sales
Tree Node Label	Siebel Quotes

10. Click the Expression button below the URL Definition field to open the Groovy Editor.
11. Enter the following code:

```
def url="https://webserver/callcenter_enu/start.swe?"
    + "SWECmd=ExecuteLogin&SWEUserName=SADMIN&SWEPassword=PWD"
    + "&SWEAC=SWECmd=GetApplet&SWEApplet=Quote+List+Applet"
    + "&IsPortlet=1&SWESM=Edit+List&KeepAlive=1"
    + "&BCField0=Status&BCField0=Account&BCFieldValue0="
    + PartyUniqueName
return (url)
```

The `PartyUniqueName` field references the Sales Account's name and is concatenated at the end of the URL, so that the `BCFieldValue0` parameter value is the name of the current account.

For the previous code to work in a real-life environment, we must replace `webserver` with the actual host name or IP address of the Siebel web server. The example in this case study uses the `SWEUserName` and `SWEPassword` parameters for authentication, which is only supported in Innovation Pack 2013 and earlier. For the example to work with Innovation Pack 2014, or later, we would have to implement a Single-Sign-On (SSO) authentication solution, which is outside the scope of this book.

> Depending on the security settings for Oracle Sales Cloud (or any other external application) and Siebel CRM, it might also be necessary to apply additional configuration steps such as setting the `X-Frame-Options` HTTP response header to a correct value. For more information about this configuration, refer to the Oracle Siebel documentation at
> `http://docs.oracle.com/cd/E58886_01/books/config_open_ui/customizing_external_apps6.html`.

In continuation of the case study, we can now test our changes in Oracle Sales Cloud.

12. Click OK to close the Groovy Editor.
13. Click Save and Close.
14. For testing purposes, navigate to the Customer work area and create a customer with the same name as the existing Siebel test account that has quotes attached.
15. In the Customer Center tree, click the Siebel Quotes node and observe that the Siebel quote list is displayed.

Congratulations! You have successfully used the Siebel Open UI Portlet API to integrate a Siebel applet with Oracle Sales Cloud.

Drag and Drop Data Import

One of the new features introduced with Open UI in Innovation Pack 2013 is the ability to create new records by dropping spreadsheet data on list applets. While we have already quickly covered this functionality in Chapter 1, we will provide more detail on this feature in the following section as follows:

- Enable and test drag and drop data import
- Considerations for drag and drop data import

Enabling and Testing Drag and Drop Data Import

As mentioned earlier, the drag and drop data import feature works for list applets. To enable the feature we must modify the applet's user properties. Furthermore, this feature is only available in version 8.1.1.11.4 (patchset 4 for IP 2013) or above.

The following procedure describes how to enable a drag and drop data import for a list applet. In our example, we will use the account list applet:

1. In Siebel Tools, locate the list applet definition, for example the SIS Account List Applet.
2. Add the following two applet user properties.

Name	Value
ClientPMUserProp	EnableDragAndDropInList
EnableDragAndDropInList	TRUE

Note that if the ClientPMUserProp applet user property already exists, you can either add the EnableDragAndDropInList value at the end of the existing value string, using a comma to separate the entries, or you can create a new sequenced user property such as ClientPMUserProp1.

3. Compile the applet.
4. For a first test, use a spreadsheet application such as Microsoft Excel to create a simple list of records to import.
5. In the first row, specify the exact display names as they appear in the web client. The sequence of columns is of no concern and you do not need to include all columns that are currently visible in the applet. However we should avoid placing a column with a pick list as the last column in the spreadsheet.
6. Enter simple test records in the rows of the spreadsheet, paying attention to the values of pick list columns. Compare your work with the following screenshot.

	A	B	C	D	
1	Name	Main Phone #	Status	Account Type	Site
2	Test Account 1	1112223333	Active	Customer	MS Excel
3	Test Account 2	1112223334	Active	Customer	MS Excel
4	Test Account 3	1112223335	Active	Customer	MS Excel
5	Test Account 4	1112223336	Active	Customer	MS Excel
6	Test Account 5	1112223337	Active	Customer	MS Excel

The spreadsheet in the screenshot shows the header row, specifying five columns that are available in the *SIS Account List Applet* by using the exact display name. The screenshot also shows five test records. Note that the Status and Account Type values must match the pick list for those fields.

7. Log in to the Siebel application and navigate to a view that exposes the list applet.

8. Highlight the data area in the spreadsheet application and drag it onto the list applet.

9. Observe that the test records are created. Compare your work with the following screenshot.

New	Name	Site	Main Phone #	Status	Account Type
Test Account 5	MS Excel	1112223337		Active	Customer
Test Account 4	MS Excel	1112223336		Active	Customer
Test Account 3	MS Excel	1112223335		Active	Customer
Test Account 2	MS Excel	1112223334		Active	Customer
Test Account 1	MS Excel	1112223333		Active	Customer

The screenshot shows the five test records in the Siebel web client after importing them using drag and drop.

Considerations for Drag and Drop Data Import

As mentioned earlier, there are several limitations and considerations that apply to the drag and drop data import option.

*   **Picklists**: The values in the data source must match picklist values if the target field uses a picklist. Picklist columns should not be at the end of the source spreadsheet.

*   **Insert Behaviour**: The records are created sequentially just as they would be if you typed them in manually. Hence, there is no rollback of all records when one of them fails. In addition, all record lifecycle events such as NewRecord, SetFieldValue and WriteRecord are triggered for each individual record.

*   **No Updates**: Drag and drop import works for insert operations only; it cannot be used to update existing records. Actually, trying to import a record again would result in a duplicate error message because of a unique index violation.

*   **Performance**: Because of the processing overhead associated with data entry points in the Open UI JavaScript framework, we should not expect

impressive performance. As a rule of thumb it should be okay to import several dozen records at once.

- **Multi-Value Fields**: Importing data into multi-value fields using the drag and drop import feature is not supported at the time of writing.

In summary, the drag and drop import feature introduced with Siebel Open UI in IP 2013 can be helpful to achieve simple but effective alternatives to other types of import. However, we must understand its limitations to put it to good use.

Symbolic URLs and Open UI

If you spent a certain part of your professional career with Siebel CRM, you are most probably familiar with the Symbolic URL functionality of the Siebel Portal Framework. This functionality allows a Siebel administrator to define the construction of dynamic URLs to populate portal applets in the Siebel client with content from external web applications.

While Symbolic URLs have nothing to do with Open UI in a technical sense, we can still leverage this functionality to integrate a Siebel Open UI client with an external web application.

Discussing the Siebel Portal Framework and Symbolic URLs in detail is outside the scope of this book. Please refer to the *Siebel Portal Framework Guide* in the Siebel bookshelf for more information.

However, we want to discuss a few aspects of using Symbolic URLs with Siebel Open UI and provide a case study that demonstrates how easily an external web application's content can be displayed in a Siebel client, no matter the UI or platform.

The following topics are to be considered when you intend to use Symbolic URLs for integration with Siebel Open UI:

- Verifying the Siebel Web Template
- Controlling the iFrame for Symbolic URLs

We will briefly discuss these topics in the following section.

Verifying the Siebel Web Template

Almost all applets that are used to display the content returned from a symbolic URL use the `SAAppletAnalytics.swt` web template file. Depending on your version of Siebel CRM, the Open UI-specific version of this file (in the `OUIWEBTEMPL` folder) could be damaged.

It is, therefore, a good idea to verify that the `SAAppletAnalytics.swt` file in the `OUIWEBTEMPL` folder contains the following SWE tag.

```
<swe:control id="501" property="FormattedHtml"
hintText="Field" hintMapType="ListItem"/>
```

Note that the file might have additional lines, but the SWE tag shown must be present.

If the Open UI version of the `SAAppletAnalytics.swt` file does not contain the previous line, you can copy over the same file from the `WEBTEMPL` folder (used for non-Open UI clients), thus overwriting the damaged file.

In a current version of Siebel CRM, this should not be necessary, as the bug leading to a damaged file has been fixed.

Controlling the iFrame for Symbolic URLs

When we configure symbolic URLs, we can use special commands to define the size and behavior of the iFrame that is generated by the Siebel Portal Framework. The syntax for these commands has changed in Siebel Open UI clients.

The following is an example for a working iFrame command and has been confirmed in current versions of Siebel Open UI at the time of writing:

```
IFrame Height = 750 Width = 1200 Frameborder = Off
```

The command defines the height and width of the iFrame in pixels and turns off any frame border. For an example of how to use this command, refer to the following case study.

Case Study: Integrating Oracle BI Mobile Applications with Siebel Open UI

In the following case study we will examine a scenario of integrating an external web application with Siebel CRM using Symbolic URLs. We chose Oracle BI Mobile Applications, a relatively young offering in the Oracle BI product family, to serve as the external web application for our case study.

> Oracle BI Mobile Applications are built on top of the well-established Oracle BI Publisher foundation (formerly known as XML publisher) and provide business intelligence information in HTML5 format so that it can be consumed easily on mobile devices of any size. For more information (and a trial edition for free download) refer to the Oracle product information at
> `http://www.oracle.com/technetwork/middleware/bi-foundation/bi-mobile-app-designer-1983915.html`.

Before we start with the case study, let us reaffirm that the solution shown next is applicable to any version of Siebel, including non-Open UI clients. However, with Open UI fitting into modern mobile devices, integrating content served by BI Mobile

Applications is ideal to demonstrate the capabilities of the Siebel Portal Framework within Siebel Open UI.

Let us begin with a screenshot of what we intend to achieve.

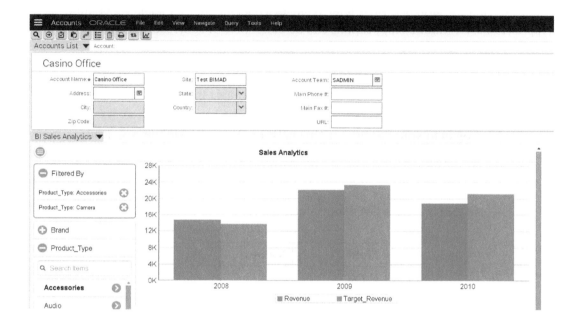

The screenshot shows a new view in Siebel Call Center. The upper form applet shows data about a Siebel account (from the Siebel database), and the lower applet displays a page of an Oracle BI Mobile Application served by an external web server. The information displayed in the chart compares revenue and target revenue figures for the selected account.

To achieve this solution, we need to implement the following:

- Create a data model for BI Mobile Applications
- Create a BI Mobile Application
- Add a calculated field to the Account business component
- Create a portal applet
- Create a new detail view
- Create a symbolic URL definition

The following scenarios will guide us to the individual steps. It should be noted that the first two scenarios require familiarity with Oracle BI Mobile Applications. It is outside the scope of this book to go into greater detail on these steps. Please refer to the documentation and tutorials provided by Oracle for Oracle BI Mobile Applications for more information.

Creating a Data Model for BI Mobile Applications

The following scenario describes how to create a data model for Oracle BI Mobile Applications. BI Mobile Applications can be built upon BI subject areas, data models or Excel Spreadsheets. Using a data model provides us with a greater level of control regarding the query and parameters. This case study assumes that we access data residing in an Oracle BI instance, which is a suitable scenario for many Siebel CRM projects. For educational purposes, we use the **SampleApp** subject area that is provided with Oracle BI out-of-the-box.

1. Log in to your instance of Oracle BI or Oracle BI Mobile Applications.
2. Navigate to New > Data Model.
3. In the Diagram tab, click the New Data Set button and select SQL Query.
4. In the New Data Set dialog, enter the following information.

Field	Value
Name	DataSet1
Data Source	Oracle BI EE

5. Click the Query Builder button.
6. In the Query Builder's Model tab, select the following tables and columns.

Table	Column
Offices	Office
Office	Department
Time	Per Name Year
Products	LOB
Products	Product Type
Base Facts	Revenue
Base Facts	Target Revenue

7. Select the Conditions tab and enter the following condition for the Office column.

```
=:p_office
```

The condition specifies a `WHERE` clause for the Office column to be matched against the value of a parameter named `p_office`.

8. Compare your work with the following screenshot.

9. Navigate to the Results tab.

10. Enter a test value for the `p_office` parameter such as `Casino Office`.

11. Verify that data is returned.

12. Click Save. When prompted for the creation of a new parameter, allow and acknowledge it.

13. Open the Data tab and provide the name of an office such as `Casino Office` in the Parameter field.

14. Set the Rows field to `50` and click the View button.

15. Verify that data is returned.

16. Click the Save As Sample Data button and click OK to acknowledge the sample file generation. Note that a sample data file is required for the work in the report or mobile application editor later.

17. In the Data Model editor, click the Save button.

18. Select or create a shared folder and provide a name for the new data model such as `Sales Analysis DM`.

The previous procedure describes how to create a parameterized data model based on an Oracle BI subject area that can be used for BI Mobile Applications (or BI Publisher reports). Recall that we created a custom parameter to allow passing the name of an office to the query at runtime.

Creating a BI Mobile Application

Now that we have a data model, we can continue to create a new Mobile Application. The following procedure guides us through the implementation steps:

1. In the Oracle BI environment, select New > Mobile App.

2. Choose Tablet as the target device type.

3. Select BI Publisher Data Model as the data source.

4. Browse for the data model you have created in the previous procedure.

5. Click Save and provide a name for the new mobile app, such as `SalesAnalyticsApp`. Note that to avoid issues with automatically generated URLs later, we should avoid spaces and special characters in the name.

6. Click Save. The BI Mobile App Designer is launched.

In the next steps we will create a simple, yet functional, demo application. Your implementation might differ to a great extent.

7. Click New Page and select Exploration as the template.

8. From the Data Source panel, drag the Brand and Product Type columns to the area on the left of the new page.

9. Click the plus (+) icon atop the page and drag the Chart icon to the right half of the page.

10. Drag the Revenue and Target Revenue columns to the Drop Value Here drop target in the chart area.

11. Drag the Per Name Year column to the Drop Label Here drop target in the chart area.

12. Delete the Cover Page item so that only the new page remains.

13. Click the Preview button and verify that the mobile application works correctly. Compare your work with the next screenshot.

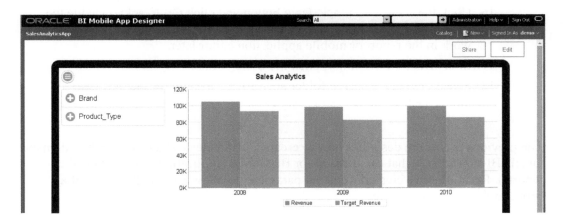

14. Click the Share button and copy the link provided in the dialog to the clipboard.

15. Paste the link URL into a temporary text file to keep it safe for later use when we will define the symbolic URL.

16. Close the Share dialog and click Edit to return to the designer.
17. Save your work in the BI Mobile App Designer.

This scenario completes the work in the Oracle BI environment. Depending on your environment and requirements, you might have to accomplish different tasks. The important output of any third party web application configuration is a URL and the parameters that are usually part of that URL which we can access from within a portal applet. The remaining steps are to be executed in the Siebel CRM environment.

Adding a Calculated Field to the Account Business Component

In order to display the content returned from an external web server via a Symbolic URL, we must create a calculated field in the respective business component. The value of this calculated field is a single string with the name of the Symbolic URL as defined in the Administration - Integration screen.

With regards to the case study scenario, we must add a new calculated field to the **Account** business component. The following procedure describes how to accomplish this:

1. In Siebel Tools, navigate to the Account business component.
2. Create a new field with the following properties.

Property	Value
Name	OUIBOOK BIMAD URL
Calculated	TRUE
Calculated Value	"BIMAD"

3. Compile the Account business component.

Creating a Portal Applet

The next step is to create a new applet that exposes the calculated field we just created. We can accelerate this step by simply copying an existing applet that uses the correct class and property settings. Luckily, the Siebel Repository contains a variety of standard applets that provide symbolic URL functionality.

The following procedure describes how to create the portal applet for our case study scenario:

1. In Siebel Tools, locate the applet named SSO Analytics Profile Applet and copy it.
2. Rename the copy to OUIBOOK BIMAD Applet.

3. Set the Business Component property to Account.

4. Navigate to the list of list columns for the new applet and change the field name for the only list column definition to OUIBOOK BIMAD URL.

5. Compile the OUIBOOK BIMAD Applet.

Creating a New Detail View

To finalize our work in Siebel Tools, we must expose the new applet in the user interface. For testing purposes, we create a new view. Note that the steps in the following procedure are not explicit. If you need more information about Siebel configuration, refer to the Oracle Siebel documentation, available training classes, or the book *Oracle Siebel CRM Developer's Handbook* by Alexander Hansal.

1. Copy the Account Detail - Contacts View to create a new view named OUIBOOK Account BIMAD View.

2. In the new view, set the OUIBOOK BIMAD Applet to occupy Item Identifier 2 in the view web template.

3. Add the new view to the Accounts screen as a detail view using meaningful text for the menu (site map) and view bar.

4. Compile the new view and the Accounts screen.

5. In the web client, register and administer the OUIBOOK Account BIMAD View with a test responsibility and verify that you can access it.

The new view will display an error message indicating that the symbolic URL is not defined. We will take care of this in the next step of this case study.

Creating a Symbolic URL Definition

In Siebel CRM, a Symbolic URL definition captures the logic of creating a URL to be displayed in an HTML iframe (which is generated by means of the portal applet). The following procedure guides us through the steps of setting up a symbolic URL to display the BI Mobile Application defined in previous steps of this case study:

1. In the Siebel web client, navigate to the Administration - Integration screen, Symbolic URL Administration view.

2. In the upper applet, create a new record with the following values

Column	Value
Name	BIMAD
URL	http://biserver:port/mobile/viewer.jsp
Fixup Name	Default
SSO Disposition	IFrame

Note that the value for the URL column must match the beginning of the BI Mobile Application URL captured in a previous section. Replace `biserver` with the correct host name or IP address of the web server that provides access to Oracle BI and `port` with the correct port number used by your implementation.

3. In the Symbolic URL Arguments list applet (at the bottom of the view), create the following records.

Name	Argument Type	Argument Value (Example, see below for details)	Append As Argument	Sequence #
id	Constant	bimaduser01	Y	1
passwd	Constant	trp9zbv	Y	2
_xma	Constant	/OUIBOOK/SalesAnalyticsApp.xma	Y	3
p_office	Field	Name	Y	4
Style	Command	IFrame Height = 750 Width = 1200 Frameborder = Off	N	5
IsRecordSensitive	Command	TRUE	N	6

4. Compare your work with the following screenshot.

Let's see the detailed explanations for the symbolic URL arguments used in this case study.

- The Siebel Portal Framework will append all arguments that have the `Append as Argument` flag set to `Y` in the sequence defined by the `Sequence #` field to the base URL, using ampersand (`&`) as the separator.

- The `id` and `passwd` arguments are BI Mobile Application parameters and allow a username and password combination to pass. We must be aware that this form of authentication is the most insecure with credentials being stored and transmitted as clear text. For real-life production scenarios, more secure authentication options such as Single-Sign-On should be considered.

- The `_xma` argument provides the catalog path to the mobile application. Ensure that you use forward slashes and that the path contains no spaces or special characters.

- The `p_office` parameter is the one we created while setting up the data model. We use it to pass the value of the `Name` field of the current account record, thus displaying BI data only for the selected account.

- The `Style` command is not passed to Oracle BI but is interpreted by the Siebel Portal Framework. We have discussed the syntax of this command briefly in a previous section. This syntax has been verified against IP 2013 and IP 2014 to control the `height`, `width` and `frameborder` attributes of the iframe.

- The `IsRecordSensitive` command should be set to `TRUE` to allow a refresh of the external URL when a different record is selected, for example when a user navigates to the next record.

Testing the Case Study Scenario

If you have followed the case study until this point, you might want to follow the next procedure to test your configuration:

1. Log off and back in to the Siebel application.
2. Ensure that the BI Mobile Application is reachable over the network.
3. Navigate to the Account List view and create several account records that have names which match the names of offices in the BI sample application. Example names are `Blue Bell Office`, `Casino Office` or `Eiffel Office`.
4. Drill down on one of the new test accounts and navigate to the view you created in the case study.
5. Verify that the portal applet displays the BI Mobile Application page.
6. In the form applet, navigate to the next test record and verify that the BI Mobile Application refreshes with data representing the new test account.
7. Compare your screen with the screenshot presented at the beginning of the case study.

Congratulations! You have successfully integrated an Oracle BI Mobile Application with Siebel Open UI using the Siebel Portal Framework. Remember, this configuration is neither limited to Open UI nor desktop applications. This configuration works in the same way whether the (Open UI) application is used on a mobile device or with a dedicated Siebel Mobile Application.

Case Study: Using the Google Maps API for Address Auto-Complete

Some third party service providers such as Google do not allow direct downloads of libraries. Instead we must load these libraries at runtime. The following case study is provided by Siebel blogger Shivakumar Badli from the Siebel & Open UI blog (`siebel-openui.blogspot.com`). It demonstrates how to load the Google Maps JavaScript API using asynchronous JavaScript and XML (AJAX). In the example scenario we will use *Auto-complete for Addresses and Search* functionality to implement type-ahead search behavior when a Siebel user adds a new address.

> For more information about the Google Maps JavaScript API go to `https://developers.google.com/maps/documentation`.

The following screenshot shows the result of this case study.

The screenshot shows the *Account Address Mvg Applet* in New mode. A custom text field on top of the form allows end users to enter an address. In the screenshot, the user has entered "500 oracle" in the field and we can observe that the Google Maps Autocomplete feature displays possible matches in a dropdown list.

When the user selects an address from the dropdown list, the form applet controls will be populated with the address data. The following screenshot shows the form after selecting the first address in the list.

Account Addresses   ✕

500 Oracle Parkway, Redwood City, CA, Uni

Street Address:★	500 Oracle Pkwy
Street Address 2:	
City:★	Redwood City
State:	CA ⌄
Zip Code:	94065
Country:	USA ⌄

In the screenshot, the address returned by the Google Maps API has been used to populate the controls of the Account Address Mvg Applet.

The following high-level steps have to be completed to implement this example scenario:

- Create a custom physical renderer
- Load the Google Maps JavaScript API using AJAX
- Display the address input field
- Map address data to applet controls

As usual we provide example scenarios to guide you through the implementation steps. This chapter's code archive contains a complete example code file (AddressAutoCompletePR.js).

Creating a Custom Physical Renderer

To implement an example scenario, we have to start with a custom physical renderer file. Using the usual techniques (as discussed in previous chapters of this book) we create a new JavaScript file in the siebel/custom folder (preferably using a template) and name it, for example, AddressAutoCompletePR.js.

As we will be extending an MVG applet that is technically a list applet, we have to implement a physical renderer extension for list applets. Therefore we must ensure that the define function has the following signature:

```
define("siebel/custom/AddressAutoCompletePR",
["siebel/jqgridrenderer"], function () {
```

Note that we define a dependency to the `jqgridrenderer.js` file that contains the base renderer for list applets.

In addition, we must extend the `JQGridRenderer` class (the base class for list applets) as follows.

```
SiebelJS.Extend(AddressAutoCompletePR,
SiebelAppFacade.JQGridRenderer);
```

The previous line of code shows the call to the `SiebelJS.Extend` function and correctly specifies the `SiebelAppFacade.JQGridRenderer` class so that our new class will become an extension of that class.

For a test scenario, we register the new custom file as a physical renderer for the `Account Address Mvg Applet` in the manifest administration views (as discussed in previous chapters of this book in detail) and restart the client.

Loading the Google Maps JavaScript API Using AJAX

The following scenario guides us through an example implementation of loading the Google Maps JavaScript API using AJAX. For demonstration purposes, the code shown in the following is implemented directly in the custom physical renderer. For a more generic solution, we should consider placing such code in custom utility classes (as shown in Chapter 12).

In the `AddressAutoCompletePR.js` file add the following code before the define function call:

```
var InitAutoComplete = function () {};
var initialize = function () {};
var autocomplete;
var pm;
var bc;
var googleAPILoaded = false;
var preGoogleLoadAPI = function(){
  googleAPILoaded = false;
  var prevValue = $.ajaxSetup().async;
  $.ajaxSetup({async: false});
  $.getScript(
      "https://www.google.com/jsapi?callback=loadGAPIs",
      function() {});
  $.ajaxSetup({async: prevValue});
}

var loadGAPIs = function () {
  SiebelJS.Log("[LoadGAPIs] Google APIs Loaded...");
  googleAPILoaded = true;
};

var LoadAPI = function (func, retryCount) {
  if (!googleAPILoaded || typeof (google) == "undefined") {
```

```
  if (retryCount < 10) {
    retryCount++;
    setTimeout(LoadAPI(func, retryCount), 1000);
  }
}
else {
  google.load("maps", "3", { other_params:
  'libraries=places,geometry&sensor=false',
      callback: func
  });
  SiebelJS.Log("Google load called");
}
};
```

The example code defines the following functions and behavior:

- Initialize variables for future use.
- Implement the preGoogleLoadAPI function, which does the following.
  - Sets the googleAPILoaded variable to false to indicate that the Google API is not loaded.
  - Captures the current value of the async property of the jQuery ajaxsetup object.
  - Sets the default value for the async property to false to allow asynchronous execution of jQuery AJAX calls.
  - Retrieves the Google API JavaScript and specifies loadGAPIs as the callback function.
  - Resets the async property to its original value.
- The loadGAPIs function sets the googleAPILoaded variable to true, indicating that the Google API has been loaded successfully.
- Implement the LoadAPI function, which accomplishes the following.
  - Create a retry loop using the setTimeout function when the Google API is not loaded.
  - When the Google API is loaded, call the Google load function to load the maps module and specify the function passed to the LoadAPI method (func) as the callback function.

The helper functions implemented in the previous code example will be called from within the physical renderer functions. We will implement these functions in the following scenario.

Displaying the Address Input Field

In order to provide end users with a text field that exposes address autocomplete behavior, we will display a new text field when the MVG applet is in New mode.

The following scenario guides us through the implementation in our custom physical renderer.

Add the following code in the ShowUI method:

```
pm = this.GetPM();
var active_View = SiebelApp.S_App.GetActiveView();
var applet_Map = active_View.GetAppletMap();
var MVGNewRecordApplet = null;
var appletName = pm.Get("GetName");
try {
  if (applet_Map.hasOwnProperty(appletName)) {
      MVGNewRecordApplet = applet_Map[appletName];
      if (MVGNewRecordApplet.GetMode() == "New") {
         var controls = pm.Get("GetControls");
         var staddrctrl = controls["Street Address"];
         var staddripname = staddrctrl.GetInputName();
         var staddrIPHolder = $("[name=" + staddripname + "]");
         var tableHolder = staddrIPHolder.closest("table");
         tableHolder.before('<tr><td colspan=2>'
             + '<input type="text" id="dynamic_addr_ip"'
             + ' style="height: 20px; width: 258px;" '
             + ' maxlength="200" tabindex="0"'
             + 'class="siebui-input-align-left"'
             + ' aria-readonly="false" placeholder="'
             + 'Enter your address here"></td></tr>');
         preGoogleLoadAPI();
         InitAutoComplete = function () {
           initialize();
         };
         var check_mapAPILoaded = function () {
           if (!googleAPILoaded)
           setTimeout(check_mapAPILoaded, 500);
           else {
             SiebelJS.Log("Show UI before initmap");
             LoadAPI("InitAutoComplete", 0);
             SiebelJS.Log("Show UI after initmap");
           }
         }
         $('#dynamic_addr_ip').focus();
         check_mapAPILoaded();
      }
    }
  }
catch (error) {
    SiebelJS.Log(error);
}
```

The example code accomplishes the following:

- Get the current presentation model instance.

- Get the applet map using the active view object.
- Get the applet's repository name from the `GetName` property.
- Instantiate the applet as an object.
- Verify that the applet's current mode is `New`.
- Instantiate the `Street Address` control and get its `name` attribute value.
- Insert a new text input control, setting the `id` attribute to `dynamic_addr_ip`.
- Call the `preGoogleLoadAPI` function.
- Define the `InitAutoComplete` function. This function calls another function named `initialize` (see implementation below).
- Implement the `check_mapAPILoaded` function, which invokes the `LoadAPI` method.
- Set the focus on the new text input control.
- Call the `check_mapAPILoaded` function.

Implement the initialize function after the ShowUI function body as follows:

```
initialize = function () {
  if (typeof (google.maps.places) !== "undefined") {
    var input = $('#dynamic_addr_ip')[0];
    $('#dynamic_addr_ip').focus();
    autocomplete = new google.maps.places.Autocomplete(input);
    google.maps.event.addListener(
        autocomplete, 'place_changed', function () {
            fillInAddress();
    });
  }
};
```

The `initialize` function does the following:

- Verify that the Google Maps Places API is available.
- Create a new `autocomplete` object, passing the new input text control as the argument.
- Add an event listener (`place_changed`) to the `autocomplete` object which invokes the `fillInAddress` function (see next) every time a different address is selected from the dropdown box.

The example code in this section provisions an autocomplete address input control on top of the form layout for the MVG applet's *New* mode. When the end user selects an address from the dropdown box, we can retrieve the address data from the `autocomplete` object. In the final section of this case study, we will discuss how to map the address data from Google to the applet controls.

Mapping Address Data to Applet Controls

After the `initialize` function, we have to implement the `fillInAddress` function. For the sake of readability, we have split the example code in two parts.

The following code listing shows the first part of the example code:

```
function fillInAddress() {
  // Get the place details from the autocomplete object
  var place = autocomplete.getPlace();
  var controls = pm.Get("GetControls");
  var controlsArray = {
    "Street Address": controls["Street Address"],
    "City": controls["City"],
    "Postal Code": controls["Postal Code"],
    "State": controls["State"],
    "Country": controls["Country"]
  };
  var componentForm = {
    street_number: 'empty',
    route: 'empty', //Street Address
    locality: 'empty', // City
    postal_town: 'empty', // City
    administrative_area_level_1: 'empty', //State
    administrative_area_level_2: 'empty', // County
    country: 'empty',
    postal_code: 'empty'
  };
  for (var component in controlsArray){
    $("[name=" + controlsArray[component].GetInputName()
        + "]").val("");
  }
  // Get each component of the address from the place details
  // and fill the corresponding field on the form.
  for (var i = 0; i < place.address_components.length; i++) {
    var addressType = place.address_components[i].types[0];
    if (componentForm[addressType]) {
      componentForm[addressType] =
          place.address_components[i]["short_name"];
    }
  }
}
```

This part of the example code accomplishes the following:

- Get the return data from the Google Maps API using the `getPlace` function. Within the returned object, we can locate the individual data fields.

- Initialize an array with five controls that represent the major address fields in the applet.

- Initialize a temporary object array (`componentForm`) that represents the most important fields in the Google object structure.

- Iterate through the controls array and clear all values (in case they have been previously populated).

- Iterate through the `place` object and retrieve the short string (`short_name`) representation for each address field into the temporary `componentForm` object.

The next code listing shows the continuation of the code example:

```
var streetAddress = "";
var countryCode = "";
var state = "";

if (componentForm["street_number"] != "empty"){
  streetAddress = componentForm["street_number"] + " ";
}
if (componentForm["route"] != "empty") {
  streetAddress += componentForm["route"];
}
countryCode = componentForm["country"] ==
    "US" ? "USA" : componentForm["country"];
state = componentForm["administrative_area_level_1"] !=
    "empty" ? componentForm["administrative_area_level_1"]
    : componentForm["administrative_area_level_2"]!= "empty"
    ? componentForm["administrative_area_level_2"] : "";

SetValue(controlsArray["Street Address"], streetAddress);
if (componentForm["locality"] != "empty"){
  SetValue(controlsArray["City"], componentForm["locality"]);
}
else if(componentForm["postal_town"] != "empty"){
  SetValue(controlsArray["City"],
      componentForm["postal_town"]);
}
if (componentForm["postal_code"] != "emtpy"){
  SetValue(controlsArray["Postal Code"],
      componentForm["postal_code"]);
}
SetValue(controlsArray["State"], state);
SetValue(controlsArray["Country"], countryCode);
```

The example code verifies each object in the temporary array.

- If the data object provides a value, it is either used for concatenation or to derive the final field value.

- The final address field values are then written to the applet controls using the `focus` and `blur` events of the presentation model. The example code refers to a helper function named `SetValue` which is implemented as follows.

```
function SetValue (control, value){
  pm.OnControlEvent(consts.get(
      "PHYEVENT_CONTROL_FOCUS"), control);
  pm.OnControlEvent(consts.get(
      "PHYEVENT_CONTROL_BLUR"), control, String(value));
}
```

The SetValue helper function passes the control object and the new value to the focus and blur events of the presentation model, thus setting the control value and triggering all required framework functions.

With this case study, we demonstrated a use case for integrating Siebel Open UI with the Google Maps API.

In some situations, the address dropdown box is not visible due to a low z-index value (default 1000). If you cannot see the dropdown box on the custom address input control, apply the following CSS rule using a custom style sheet.

```
.pac-container{

    z-index: 10000!important;

}
```

The CSS rule sets the z-index property for the pac-container class (used for the address dropdown box) to 10000.

Case Study: Accessing Applications on a Mobile Device

Today's mobile device users enjoy a wide variety of apps, games, and social media options. Many of these apps such as Maps, SMS, and Video Chat have become so integral to modern existence that it seems a real challenge to live without them.

In this case study we will explore a mobile scenario, demonstrating application integration between Siebel Open UI and **Apple Maps**. In this example, we will learn how to add an icon capable of triggering Apple Maps from the Account Form Applet. The following screenshot shows a preview of this feature.

The screenshot shows the *Account Form Applet* adorned with a new icon resembling a familiar fruit which, when clicked, will trigger the Apple Maps application.

To implement this prototype, we must accomplish the following high-level steps:

- Explore the concept of App URL Schemes
- Create a custom physical renderer
- Define CSS rules for the icon
- Deploy and Test on an iPad

Exploring the Concept of App URL Schemes

Before we start coding, it is necessary to explore the concept of app URL schemes in the Apple iOS operating system. At their most basic level, URL schemes are a supported mechanism providing integration from one app to another via a simple hyperlink. In much the same way as URLs for websites, the URL scheme format is comprised of both an app "domain name" and additional text that may follow. This additional text may include optional arguments that the app may need to use.

Documented below are a few examples of app URL schemes, the last of which is used in the case study example.

URL Scheme Supporting Integration with SMS

The *Apple Messages* app can be easily launched using the SMS URL scheme. The proper usage pattern for SMS URLs is the following: `sms:<phone>`, where `<phone>` is the argument specifying the target phone number for the SMS text message. As expected, the target phone number can contain any digit between 0 and 9. The following is an example of using a SMS URL scheme.

```
<a href="sms:1-919-555-1212">Send Text Message</a>
```

URL Scheme for Integration with Facetime

The *Apple Facetime* app can be invoked using the Facetime URL scheme. Either the user's email address or phone number can be used to initiate the Facetime call. Once the link is clicked, a user prompt is displayed confirming the user wishes to place a Facetime call. The valid usage pattern for Facetime URLs is the following: `facetime:<phone>` or `facetime:<email address>`.

URL Scheme for Integration with Apple Maps

As shown in the case study code that follows, the *Apple Maps* app can be easily triggered using the Apple Maps URL scheme. Unlike in the previous examples, the Apple Maps URL scheme resembles a traditional URL that would normally be used in a web browser. The proper expected pattern for Apple Maps URLs is the following:

```
http://maps.apple.com/?q=<location>
```

In the above URL, `<location>` is the argument specifying the address that is used in the maps query.

Note: there are many additional arguments supported by Apple Maps that are discussed in the Apple iOS Developer Library at `developer.apple.com`.

Creating a Custom Physical Renderer

To implement the example scenario, we will create a custom physical renderer. Using the usual techniques (as discussed in previous chapters of this book), we create a new JavaScript file in the `siebel/custom` folder (preferably using a template) and name it, for example, `FormMobileAddressAppleMapsPR.js`. Please refer to the code archive that accompanies this chapter to retrieve the code and graphic used in this example. You may follow the outlined steps below to build the renderer.

> This case study applies to Siebel Innovation Pack 2013 and therefore references jQuery Mobile. To implement the example in IP 2014 or higher, you would have to implement the example without jQuery Mobile, as this is no longer used for Siebel Mobile Applications.

The following procedure describes the high-level steps for implementing a custom physical renderer for a mobile form applet in IP 2013.

1. Since this physical renderer applies to a form applet on Siebel Mobile Applications 2013, make sure the custom physical renderer extends the `JQMFormRenderer` class. For IP 2014, extend the `PhysicalRenderer` class.

2. Copy the provided `apple.jpg` icon from the chapter's code archive to the `images/custom` folder.

3. In the `ShowUI` method, use the jQuery `append` function to affix the icon (of the apple) to the form applet header. The following code example provides a possible approach.

```
var link = $("<a href='#' id='AppleMapsIntegration'"
    + " class='mapLinkApple'></a>");

$("#"+this.GetPM().Get("GetFullId"))
    .find("#_FormAppletH1").append(link);
```

4. In the `BindData` method, use the jQuery `click` method (or the `on` method) to bind the click event of the icon to the code that we wish to invoke. Inside this code, use the `GetFieldValue` method to get the current record's address value that will be passed to Apple Maps. Store this value in a variable to be used in the next step.

5. Next, in the same `click` method as step 4, use the `window.open` command to trigger the URL Scheme for Apple Maps, making sure to pass the address argument it needs to use. The completed code is shown below.

```
var that = this;
$("#AppleMapsIntegration").on("click", function(){
  var oPM = that.GetPM();
  var controls = oPM.Get("GetControls");
  var Address=oPM.ExecuteMethod("GetFieldValue",
      controls["Primary Account Address Name"]);
  window.open("http://maps.apple.com/?q=" + Address);
});
```

This code will result in the following. When the user clicks the apple icon, a new browser tab will be opened that will trigger the URL Scheme for Apple Maps. At this point, the Applet Maps app will open in the foreground, and the Mobile Safari browser will fall to the background.

6. In the manifest administration views, register the custom physical renderer to the applet named `SHCE Account Entry Applet - Mobile` for testing purposes. Ensure that you use the correct expression such as Mobile, Phone, or Tablet to load the custom PR only on mobile devices.

Defining CSS Rules

Next we need to add styling settings. We are using the `custom-global.css` file which was introduced in Chapter 8. The following CSS rules must be added to the custom style sheet.

```
a.mapLinkApple {
  background:url(../../images/custom/apple.jpg) no-repeat 0 0;
  background-position: center center;
  margin-right: 10px;
  margin-top: 2px;
```

```
    float: left;
    height: 28px;
    width: 28px;
    border-radius: 5px;
}
```

The above CSS rule can be found in the `FormMobileAddressAppleMaps.css` file which is part of this chapter's code archive.

Deploying and Testing on an iPad

In order to achieve the highest level of confidence, we should test the configuration using a physical device. Open a session of Siebel Sales Mobile on your iPad and navigate to the Accounts List View. This view most likely is the default view assigned to the Accounts screen tab in the screen navigation bar.

If the configuration is correct, you will see an apple icon appearing near the top of the account form applet. Tapping the apple icon should result in the display of the account's primary address in Apple Maps as shown in the following screenshot.

This case study demonstrated the integration of a mobile app with Siebel Open UI. As indicated above, the case study is applicable to IP 2013 but works similarly in IP 2014.

Case Study: Consuming Data from a REST Service

Web service integration via SOAP and XML has been the traditional mainstay of Siebel integration in service-oriented architectures (SOA). The benefits of SOA include a loosely coupled architecture with the flexibility of integration with most modern applications. Not surprisingly, however, bright minds have created an even simpler, yet equally flexible, mechanism for integration based on Representational State Transfer (REST) and JavaScript Object Notation (JSON).

The goal of this case study is to provide a working integration demonstrating how to consume data from a REST service. The service we will use in the example is the free Telize service for IP geo-location (www.telize.com) that provides a response encoded in JSON containing the IP address and physical location of the invoking client. After the client receives this information, the JSON message will be parsed, and the data contained will be displayed in the user interface as shown in the screenshot below.

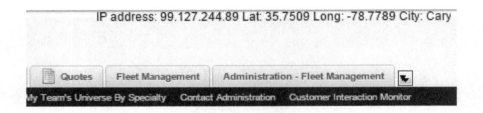

The screenshot shows the Siebel application enhanced with a new scrolling marquee that displays information retrieved from the REST service. To implement this prototype, we must accomplish the following high-level steps:

- Create a view renderer
- Define the CSS rules

Creating a View Renderer

To implement the example scenario, we will create a custom physical renderer for views.

We start by creating a new JavaScript file in the siebel/custom folder (preferably using a template) and name it, for example, JSONServiceViewPR.js. Please refer to this chapter's code archive for the full example code. In the following, we outline the major steps to create the view renderer.

1. Since this is a physical renderer for a view, make sure the custom renderer extends the ViewPR class.

2. In the `Init` method, use the jQuery `append` function to add HTML code for the scrolling marquee. The code below shows an example implementation.

```
var marqueeText;
marqueeText = '<div class="marquee">';
marqueeText +='<div id="marqueetext">';
marqueeText +='<span>In process</span>';
marqueeText +='</div>';
marqueeText +='</div>';
if ($(".marquee").length == 0) {
    $(".siebui-button-toolbar").append(marqueeText);
}
```

3. In the `SetRenderer` method, use the jQuery `getJSON` method to invoke the sample REST service. The URL we are using is `http://www.telize.com/geoip?callback=?`

   Note: If you find the example REST Service is not available, do not despair. You will find many available substitutes on the web that provide similar services.

4. Define the `success` clause as a function. Pass the returned JSON as an argument to the success function so that it can be processed and used.

5. In the success function, process the JSON object. In our case we will be reading the data values for IP address, latitude, longitude, and city. Each value will be concatenated, and the resulting string will be placed in the `marqueeText` element via jQuery.

It is important to observe that the return value comes to us in the form of a JSON object. As such, its data values can be derived very easily via dot notation. For example: `var x = json.property;`

The following example code implements the `SetRenderer` method.

```
$.getJSON("http://www.telize.com/geoip?callback=?",
function(json) {
    var appendtext = "IP address: "+ json.ip;
    appendtext += "  Lat: "+ json.latitude;
    appendtext += "  Long: "+ json.longitude;
    appendtext += "  City: "+ json.city;
    var displaytext = '<span>' + appendtext + '</span>';
    SiebelJS.Log(displaytext);
    $("#marqueetext").html(displaytext);
});
```

6. In the `EndLife` method, use the jQuery `remove` function to remove the custom HTML, such as in the example below.

```
    $(".marquee").remove();
```

In order to assign the new custom JavaScript file to a view for testing purposes, we should follow the steps in the procedure below.

1. If necessary, log in to the Siebel Web Client using an administrator account.
2. Navigate to the Administration - Application screen, Manifest Files view.
3. Create a new record to register the `siebel/custom/JSONServiceViewPR.js` file.
4. Navigate to the Manifest Administration view.
5. In the UI Objects list, create a new record with the following values.

Column	Value
Type	View
Usage Type	Physical Renderer
Name	Contact Screen Homepage View

6. In the Object Expression list, create a new record with the following values.

Column	Value
Expression	Desktop
Level	1

7. In the Files list, click the Add button and select the `siebel/custom/JSONServiceViewPR.js` file.
8. Log off and on again.
9. Navigate to the Contact Home Page view to verify that the custom code is loaded.

At this moment, the information returned by the REST service should be visible on top of the screen but lacks style information. In the next section, we define the style rules for the new element.

Defining the CSS Rules

The following CSS rules can be used to apply a marquee-style animation to the new element.

```
.marquee {
  height: 25px;
  width: 420px;
```

```
    right: 20px;
    overflow: hidden;
    position: absolute;
}

.marquee div {
  display: block;
  width: 200%;
  height: 30px;
  right:20px;
  position: absolute;
  overflow: hidden;
-webkit-animation: marquee 20s linear infinite;
   -moz-animation: marquee 20s linear infinite;
    -ms-animation: marquee 20s linear infinite;
     -o-animation: marquee 20s linear infinite;
}

.marquee span {
  float: right;
  width: 50%;
}

@-webkit-keyframes marquee {
  0% { left: 0; }
  100% { left: -100%; }
}
```

As usual, we must add custom CSS code to a custom style sheet. Refer to Chapter 8 for details on custom themes and style sheets.

After modifying the custom style sheet and reloading the page, we should be able to verify that the IP address, geographical location and city information are now displayed in a scrolling marquee on top of the application window.

Summary

In this chapter we discussed several integration scenarios that are available with Siebel Open UI.

The Portlet API allows us to display fully functional UI objects such as views and applets in external web applications.

Enabling Drag and Drop Data Import functionality for Siebel Open UI allows us to transfer small amounts of data from spreadsheets to Siebel list applets. In this chapter, we provided the exact steps to enable this functionality.

The Symbolic URL functionality of the Siebel Portal Framework is not limited to Siebel Open UI but allows for the easy integration of external web content in a Siebel applet.

We demonstrated this in a case study using Oracle BI Mobile Applications as an example of an external web application.

When we resort to developing custom JavaScript for Siebel Open UI, we can use external systems as the source of data or additional functionality as demonstrated in a case study where we use the Google Maps API to support the user when entering address data. In another case study we demonstrated how to retrieve and display JSON data from an external service provider.

Siebel Mobile Applications can benefit from integration as well, as was demonstrated in the case study on displaying an account's address on Apple Maps.

In the next chapter we will discuss deployment options for Siebel Open UI.

17
Deploying Siebel Open UI Customizations

In this final chapter of our journey across the world of Siebel Open UI, we will discover the scenarios and considerations for deploying customizations from one Siebel environment to another.

Regarding the different areas of customization for Open UI, we will organize the chapter as follows:

- General deployment options
- Deploying administrative data
- Deploying manifest data
- Deploying files for the SWSE
- Managing the browser cache
- Deploying web template files

General Deployment Options

When it comes to migrating customizations, the Siebel CRM framework offers a variety of options, as simple as copying files from one machine to another, or as challenging as migrating an entire repository from development to production.

In general, we can categorize customizations by the location where new or modified object definitions are stored. In Siebel CRM, customizations typically affect objects or data in the following areas:

- Siebel Repository Tables
- Siebel Data (Runtime) Tables
- Files

In the remainder of this section, we will discuss the migration options for each of these areas.

Siebel Repository Tables

Siebel Repository data are defined as all objects stored in Siebel Repository tables. Examples for such objects are applets, business components, or workflow processes. Repository data is usually available for modification within Siebel Tools.

There are also occasions when data can be modified within Siebel Tools but not stored in a repository table (such as *List of Values* (LOV) data), or data is stored in repository tables but cannot be modified using Siebel Tools (such as Open UI manifest data).

Because Siebel Repository and Siebel Tools are the primary means of customizing Siebel CRM, various well-established techniques exist to deploy changes from one environment to another. The following list describes the two most common mechanisms for repository data migration:

- The **Migrate Repository** process supported by the **Siebel Upgrade Wizard** and often referred to as **dev2prod** (development to production). This process automates the export of the *entire repository* from a source environment and the import into a target environment. This includes the content of all repository tables.

- Export and import of individual repository objects or groups using Siebel Tools archive files (`.sif`). Archive files can be used for manual deployment as well as automated deployment using Siebel Tools' command line options.

With regards to Siebel Open UI, we have to consider that **manifest administration data** are stored in repository tables, even if it is accessed and edited via views in the Siebel Web Client and not via Siebel Tools. Because of this fact, the Migrate Repository process is the only official option to transport Open UI manifest data between environments (at least at the time of writing).

Siebel Data (Runtime) Tables

Data that is usually accessed via the Siebel Web Client resides in so-called *data* or *runtime* tables. The term "runtime tables" has been coined because the object manager reads the data at runtime rather than using the repository metadata from the SRF file.

With regards to customizing a Siebel application, the runtime data to be migrated is typically of an administrative nature and includes, for example, the following items:

- List Of Values (LOV)
- Assignment Rules
- Data Validation Rule Sets
- Personalization Rules
- and much more

As far as Open UI is concerned, List of Values (LOV) is most probably the only runtime data object that is subject to customization. As discussed in previous chapters, custom themes and transitions must be registered in the LOV administration views.

The techniques to migrate administrative data from one Siebel environment to another include the following:

- **Application Deployment Manager Screen**: We can deploy administrative data manually by using the Application Deployment Manager screen in the Siebel Web Client. There is also an automation option including the ADM workflow processes available.

- **Pre-built XML export and import**: Many objects such as *Data Validation Rules* are delivered by Oracle along with the necessary metadata to export data to XML files and import them into the target environment. This is typically accomplished manually using the respective menu commands or buttons in the administrative views where these objects can be modified.

- **Custom Interfaces**: By perusing the array of EAI business services such as *EAI Siebel Adapter* or *Read CSV File*, and by creating custom integration objects, customers can build their own interfaces for moving or synchronizing data between Siebel environments.

- **Enterprise Integration Manager (EIM)**: Mainly used to import large volumes of runtime data into a Siebel database, EIM relies on the concept of staging tables, which are known as interface tables to the seasoned administrator. While EIM is capable of exporting and importing data, including administrative data, there is no pre-built process delivered with Siebel CRM, making it a less attractive option when it comes to the effort of deploying customizations.

- **dataexp and dataimp**: These two command line utilities can be used to export and import records from (and into) individual tables, including runtime and repository tables. Similar to EIM, we can consider these utilities as a tool to fulfill our deployment requirements, but Oracle does not deliver any predefined processes out-of-the-box.

- **Drag and drop data import**: As discussed in Chapter 16, the support for drag and drop data import for list applets could serve as a viable, albeit simplistic, transport mechanism for flat data such as List of Values, Manifest Files or Manifest Expressions.

> In the previous list and throughout his chapter, you might notice the absence of the Siebel Management Server architecture that allows for the orchestration of ADM processes. In 2014, Oracle announced that the Siebel Management Server and Agent products will be discontinued in future versions of Siebel CRM; therefore we do not cover them in this book.
>
> What remains of ADM, according to Oracle, is the 'lightweight' option of using the functionality provided by the Application Deployment Manager screen and the workflow processes supporting this functionality. In the remainder of this chapter, any reference to ADM actually means the 'lightweight' option.

Files

The majority of customizations in Siebel Open UI are implemented in files that reside outside the Siebel database. These files can be categorized as:

- **Custom and third party JavaScript (** `.js` **) files** that must be uploaded to custom directories within the `PUBLIC` folder of the Siebel Web Server Extension (SWSE).
- **Cascading Style Sheets (** `.css` **)**, also stored in custom subdirectories of the `PUBLIC` folder of the SWSE.
- **Any other type of supporting files** that the browser must be able to download at runtime from the Siebel web server. This includes image files, HTML files, or media such as audio or video files.
- **Siebel Web Template (** `.swt` **) files**, residing in the `OUIWEBTEMPL/CUSTOM` folder on the Siebel Server.

We can employ the usual file copy mechanisms offered by the operating system to distribute files between source and target environments.

Alternatively, files to be uploaded to a Siebel web server can be copied to the Siebel server's `WEBMASTER` directory. The synchronization of the `WEBMASTER` directory with the SWSE's `PUBLIC` folder is triggered via a special URL command or simply by re-starting the web server.

In the remainder of this chapter, we will discuss example deployment scenarios for each area of customization.

Deploying Administrative Data

As discussed earlier, the data object that is most often affected by customization for Open UI is **List of Values (LOV)**. Nonetheless, the following descriptions would equally apply to any other type of administrative data.

Because List of Values data is among the data types that are supported out-of-the-box by ADM, using the latter to deploy customizations comes as a natural choice, simply because of its cost effectiveness and ease of use.

As indicated earlier, ADM has two ways of operation. The first one, which will be discussed in this chapter, is often referred to as "manual", and utilizes the export and import functionality available in the Application Deployment Manager screen. The second method includes automating workflow processes via the server command line and is beyond the scope of this book. The manual process is a good choice for small volumes of data and 'ad-hoc' deployment scenarios such as hot fixes. Automation should be considered for repeating migrations of data with higher volumes of data.

Case Study: Migrating List of Values Data for a Custom Theme Using the ADM Screen

The following example scenario uses the Application Deployment Manager screen and describes the steps needed to create a deployment project for LOV data and use it in an ADM export session. Deployment projects are defined, once, as a list of data objects and associated filters, and can be reused for multiple export sessions.

1. Log in to the Siebel application for the source environment (for example, the development server) using an administrative account.
2. In the site map, navigate to the Application Deployment Manager screen, Deployment Projects view.
3. Locate and copy the existing project named LOVs. (Tip: use *CTRL+B* to copy records in Siebel CRM).
4. Enter a name for the new deployment project, such as OUI Theme Definitions.
5. Check the Export to File flag.
6. In the lower list applet, modify the Deployment Filter column so that the search string matches the following example:

```
[Value]='OUI_THEME_SELECTION' OR [Value]='NavCtrlPR'
```

Note: This filter ensures that parent and child values for the Open UI theme selection are exported.

7. Click the Validate Filter button in the lower list applet. If no message is displayed, the filter is valid. If an error message appears, correct the syntax of the deployment filter and validate again until no error is displayed.
8. Click the Enable button in the upper list applet. Once a deployment project is enabled, it can no longer be modified.

9. Navigate to the Deployment Sessions view.

> Note: Subsequent deployments of the same data begin at this step.

10. Create a new record in the upper list applet and select the deployment project created before, from the dropdown list in the Project Name field.
11. Press *CTRL+S* to save the record. This populates the lower list applet.
12. Click the Deploy button in the upper list applet.
13. In the Export dialog box, enter a valid path to an existing folder where the export files should be written to.

> Note: We can only use file paths that have been explicitly registered using the EAIFileTransportFolders parameter as described in Chapter 3 of this book.

14. Click the Export button.
15. Verify that the Status column displays a value of Export Completed
16. Open the export folder and verify the existence of three new files. You should see two .xml files and one .ini file. For manual import into the target environment, only the .xml file that does not have _des in the name is needed.

The following screenshot shows the result of the previous procedure.

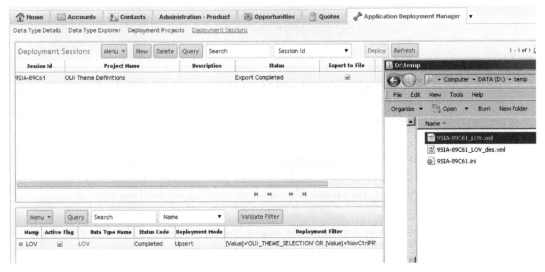

The screenshot shows a completed deployment session of List of Values data for Open UI themes. The Windows Explorer window (visible at the right of the screenshot) shows the content of the export folder, with the .xml file containing the exported LOV data selected.

The exported data can now be imported into the target environment by following the next procedure:

1. Log in to the Siebel Developer Web Client for the *target* environment (for example, the production or test server) using an administrative account.

2. In the site map, navigate to the Application Deployment Manager screen, Deployment Sessions view.

3. In the menu of the upper list applet, select Deploy from File.

4. In the ADM - Deploy from File dialog, enter the full path to the .xml file containing the exported data.

5. Click the Import button.

Note that there is no deployment session record created for an import session. A notification message is generated for each import but might not be immediately visible via the notification icon in the upper left corner of the application.

6. Navigate to the administrative view for the imported data object, for example, the List of Values view in the Administration - Application screen and verify that the data has been successfully imported.

The previous procedures apply to any type of administrative data supported by ADM. We shall also note here that customers can extend the list of data types for ADM by creating additional integration artifacts in the Siebel repository.

Deploying Manifest Data

As discussed earlier, manifest data has a special role in deployment scenarios as it is stored in repository tables but edited via the Siebel Web Client. As a consequence, we cannot - at least at the time of writing - use Siebel Tools' archive files (also known as .sif files) to export and import manifest data.

The only mechanism that can be used as-is to deploy manifest data is the Migrate Repository process. This process is executed by the **Siebel Upgrade Wizard** and exports the entire repository from a source database and imports it as the new "Siebel Repository" into a target database.

As a result, the manifest data is effectively migrated to the target environment.

On a side note, it seems that there is no mechanism for deploying specific manifest records such as files, expressions and objects created during a specific project phase.

> The authors' experiments have shown that the `dataexp` and `dataimp` command line utilities can be used to accomplish a semi-automated deployment, but it seems safer to revert to manual re-entry of the manifest administration data, especially in mission-critical production environments.

Deploying Files for the SWSE

The vast majority of customizations for Siebel Open UI occur in the form of physical files that must be deployed to the correct location on the Siebel web server.

For this purpose we can theoretically use any program that is capable of transferring files from one file system to another. This ranges from simple copy commands to secure FTP tools or similar. However, direct access to web server machines is often restricted for security reasons.

When security constraints such as firewalls and demilitarized zones make it impossible to write to the file system of a web server directly, we can employ the synchronization mechanism built into Siebel application object managers.

This mechanism allows us to copy all files that should be uploaded to the web server into the Siebel server's `WEBMASTER` directory. By simply re-starting the web server or by issuing a SWE request via a specialized URL, we can trigger the synchronization between the `WEBMASTER` directory and the web server's `PUBLIC` directory. We will explore this option in the following case study.

Case Study: Uploading Custom Open UI files to the Siebel Web Server Using the WEBMASTER Directory

In the following scenario we will highlight the steps necessary to deploy Open UI file-based customizations using the `WEBMASTER` folder on a Siebel server.

1. Using a utility of your choice, navigate to the `WEBMASTER` folder that is situated within the Siebel Server installation folder. The following is an example path on a Windows machine:
    `D:\siebel\ses\siebsrvr\WEBMASTER`

2. Open the `siebel_build` sub-folder.

3. Verify that the `siebel_build` folder contains the folders for Open UI customizations. The following is an example for a valid path:
    `D:\siebel\ses\siebsrvr\WEBMASTER\siebel_build\scripts\siebel\custom`

4. If the previous folder structure is not present, create the necessary sub-folders.

5. Copy all custom JavaScript files to the `siebel\custom` folder.

6. For style sheets (CSS files) use the language specific subfolder of the files folder; for example, use `\WEBMASTER\files\ENU` for `.css` files that should be deployed to the `PUBLIC\enu\files` folder on the SWSE.

7. For image files use the language specific subfolder of the `images` folder.

8. To start the synchronization process, we can either re-start the web server or issue a URL similar to the following from a browser:
   ```
   http://webserver/callcenter_enu/start.swe?SWECmd=UpdateWebI
   mages&SWEPassword=supersecret
   ```

The previous URL will invoke the synchronization process between SWSE and the Siebel server's `WEBMASTER` folder via the English-American Call Center object manager (`callcenter_enu`). The password (`supersecret`, in the previous example) must match the unencrypted value of the `SiebEntSecToken` parameter that is specified in the SWSE configuration file (`eapps.cfg`).

> For more information about the `SiebEntSecToken` parameter and password encryption in the `eapps.cfg` file, please refer to the Oracle Siebel Security Guide at
> `http://docs.oracle.com/cd/E14004_01/books/Secur/Secur_ChangePwd12.html`

Managing the Browser Cache

With the techniques discussed in the previous case study, we can upload new and modified files efficiently to the Siebel web server. However, we should also have a good strategy for convincing the browsers on hundreds or thousands of end user devices to load a newer version of the same file.

While one possible approach could simply be to inform end users and have them clear the browser cache manually, this is quite impractical in a real-world production scenario. The main argument against this is that end users are likely to ignore the communication or lack the privileges or skills to clear the browser cache.

The following techniques can be used to automate browser cache management:

- Busting the browser cache via JavaScript
- Expiring content on the web server

'Busting' the browser cache is a technique that relies on the fact that the browser not only requests a file from a folder on the web server but also stores the full path to that file, including any URL arguments. When the path does not change between requests and the file has not expired on the web server, the browser will use the cached version of the file. The 'busting' technique appends and modifies mockup arguments to a file path so that we can control when the URL no longer matches a previously used file path, thus forcing the browser to get the file from the web server instead of the cache.

The 'busting' technique is used by Oracle to force new files to be loaded after applying a patch. Because this technique requires the modification of third-party JavaScript files, it is not recommended for production environments but can prove useful on local developer machines or test environments.

Web server administrators can control the expiry timestamp of files. This technique does not involve custom scripting and is therefore highly recommended for production environments.

Case Study: Busting the Browser Cache via JavaScript

In the following, we will demonstrate a simple, yet effective solution to force the browser to download a file from the web server. The technique demonstrated is informally known as 'cache busting'. This case study demonstrates how to alter file paths using the require.js framework (which is delivered with Siebel Open UI), so that the browser will always download a newer version of custom JavaScript files.

It is important to note that the solution presented in this case study involves changes to a third-party file. We should always consider such changes as a last resort and consult with Oracle if they provide an out-of-the-box solution in future releases.

The following scenario guides us through the implementation steps for cache busting:

1. Create a new text file named customversion.js and store it in the FILES/custom folder.

2. Add the following line of code to the new file:

```
var cv="1.1.0";
```

The example code instantiates the cv variable with a value of 1.1.0. This value serves as the initial version counter and will be subject to modification later on.

3. Open the require.js file in the SCRIPTS/3rdParty folder and add the following code at the *end* of the file:

```
//cache buster
require(["files/custom/customversion.js?bust="
    + (new Date()).getTime()],
    function() {
      originalAttach = require.load;
      require.load = function (context, moduleName, url) {
        if (url.match(/\/custom\//)) {
        url += "&cv=" + cv;
      }
    }
    var node = originalAttach.call(this, context,
        moduleName, url);
```

```
        return node;
    }
})
```

The code accomplishes the following:

- Call the `require` function to load the `customversion.js` file and attach a mockup argument (`bust`) to the file path. The value of the `bust` argument will be the current time stamp, thus creating a unique file path every time the code runs. This will effectively force the browser to load the `customversion.js` file always from the web server and never from the cache.

- Override the `require.load` function. If the URL of any loaded file contains the string `custom`, a mockup argument named `cv` is attached to the original file path. The value of the `cv` argument is the current value of the `cv` variable defined in the `customversion.js` file.

- The return value of the code is a `require.js` node that has a `cv` mockup argument if the file path contains the string `custom`.

After saving the file changes and restarting the application, we can test the solution as follows.

4. In a custom JavaScript file such as a custom physical renderer, add a line of code that is easily traceable. For example, you could add a line like the following:

```
SiebelJS.Log("Version 1");
```

5. Open the `customversion.js` file and change the value of the `cv` variable so that the new value refers to a new version, such as `1.1.1`.

6. Save all modified files.

7. Log in to the Siebel Web Client, but *do not clear the browser cache* as you would normally do.

8. Navigate to the view that uses the custom code and observe that the JavaScript console displays the trace message you added.

9. Modify the custom JavaScript file you use for the test and increase the version test string to `Version 2`.

10. Modify the `customversion.js` file again, this time increase the version string to `1.1.2`.

11. Save both files.

12. In the Siebel Web Client, navigate away from the current view and then back again *without* clearing the cache.

13. Verify that the JavaScript console now displays `Version 2`. Note that you never had to clear the browser cache.

The case study demonstrates that it is possible to override `require.js` functions to add mock-up arguments to file paths. By modifying the values of these arguments, the browser interprets this as a new file path and will subsequently load the respective file from the web server rather than from the cache.

All we have to do is alter the `customversion.js` file for each new minor release.

Case Study: Expiring Content on the Web Server

In the following case study, we will discuss a scenario for setting content expiry on the Siebel web server to force the browser to download a newer version of a file instead of using the cached version. The example demonstrated uses Microsoft Internet Information Services (IIS) but is applicable to other web servers such as Apache-based web servers used for Siebel installations on Linux or UNIX systems.

1. In the Internet Information Services administration console, navigate to the folder you want to control, for example, the `siebel/custom` folder where the custom JavaScript files reside.

2. Open the HTTP Response Headers dialog.

3. In the Actions panel, click Set Common Headers...

4. Check the Expire Web content flag (if not already checked).

5. Select the After option and set the time to a very short duration, such as 1 second.

6. Compare your work with the following screenshot.

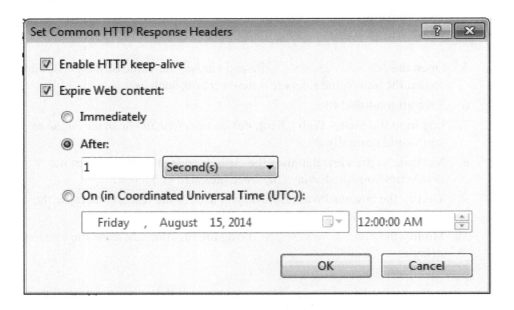

7. Click OK.

8. To test the new setting, log in to the Siebel web client and navigate to a view that references a custom JavaScript file.

9. Use the browser developer tool to inspect the HTTP header properties for the custom file and verify that the `If-Modified-Since` property is set to the current timestamp.

10. Modify the custom JavaScript file and reload the page without clearing the browser cache.

11. Verify that the new version of the file has been loaded.

The previous case study discussed the necessary settings on the web server that allow administrators to control the expiration date of web server content such as JavaScript or CSS files. As indicated earlier, this technique is recommended for production environments as it does not involve the modification of as-delivered files.

Deploying Web Template Files

In case we have custom versions of Siebel Web Template (SWT) files, those must be copied to the respective folder on all Siebel servers of the target environment.

As discussed in previous chapters of this book, we must obey the rules for choosing the correct folder for any custom SWT files for which Open UI is always the `OUIWEBTEMPL/CUSTOM` folder within the Siebel server installation directory.

Any suitable file transport tool can be used to copy the files. There is no utility to accomplish this delivered by Oracle at the time of writing.

Summary

Siebel CRM offers a variety of tools and features for manual, semi-automated, or fully automated customization deployments. In this chapter, we focused on easily accessible tools for each type of customization. We introduced Application Deployment Manager (manual sessions) for migrating administrative data such as List of Values (LOV). In addition, we discussed the *Migrate Repository* process of Siebel Upgrade Wizard for migrating manifest administration data.

The Siebel server `WEBMASTER` directory is a good place for uploading JavaScript files, style sheets or images and synchronizing these items to Siebel web server's `PUBLIC` folder. To control which files the browser downloads from the web server, rather than from its cache, we discussed a simple script-based solution, which we referred to as 'cache busting'. As an example of a script-less cache control solution we demonstrated how to set web content expiration on the Siebel web server. For files such as Siebel Web Templates, we can refer to any suitable file transport mechanism in order to migrate them from one environment to another.

You have now reached the end of this book's final chapter. Please refer to the appendices for even more information on Siebel Open UI.

Installing a Siebel CRM Self-Study Environment

To follow the case study examples in this book, it is recommended to have access to a private Siebel CRM self-study environment. The following Siebel CRM software modules are required to install such an environment:

- Siebel Mobile/Developer Web Client
- Siebel Sample Database
- Siebel Tools

In this appendix, we will briefly outline the steps necessary to download, install and configure a Siebel CRM self-study environment.

In order to support our readers in the best possible manner, we chose to provide this guidance for an installation of Siebel IP 2013 or IP 2014 on the Microsoft Windows 7 64 bit operating system. This combination is very common at the time of writing and can easily be adapted for future versions of Siebel CRM or Microsoft Windows.

The installation can be equally done on physical or virtual machines.

Minimum Hardware Requirements

The following minimum hardware configuration is recommended to complete the installation successfully and allow flawless operation of the self-study environment:

- Memory: 4 GB free RAM
- Processor: 1.5 GHz CPU, dual-core
- Disk space: 15 GB free disk space for installation files and software

Third-Party Software Requirements

The following third-party software should be installed as a prerequisite:

- Microsoft Windows 7 64 bit (or equal)

- Microsoft **Internet Explorer** browser (IE 8 is supported for Siebel High-Interactivity applications, IE 11 Enterprise Mode runs Siebel HI applications as well, but is not supported at the time of writing).

- Current versions of additional browsers such as **Mozilla Firefox** or **Google Chrome** (for testing Siebel Open UI and Standard-Interactivity applications).

- **Java Runtime Environment** (JRE) 1.5 or later

- Download Management Software (optional, for example, **Free Download Manager** available at http://freedownloadmanager.org)

- Archive software (for example **7-Zip** available at http://www.7-zip.org)

Downloading and Extracting Siebel CRM Software Installers

The following list describes the process of downloading and extracting Siebel CRM software installers:

- Register at Oracle's Software Delivery Cloud

- Read and agree the license

- Download the installation archives

- Access Oracle Siebel Documentation

- Extract the Siebel installers

- Adjust browser security settings

In the following section we will discuss these steps in detail.

Registering at Oracle's Software Delivery Cloud

Oracle makes Siebel CRM software available for download on its Software Delivery Cloud web site (formerly known as "E-Delivery") at http://edelivery.oracle.com. Before we can download software from this site, we have to register with our name, company, and e-mail address and accept the trial license terms and export restrictions outlined on the web site. Oracle will send a notification e-mail after approximately one business day.

Understanding the license agreement

Oracle grants an unlimited developer license for its software. The license agreement grants "a nonexclusive, nontransferable limited license to use the programs only for the purpose of developing, testing, prototyping and demonstrating your application, and not for any other purpose."

The full license agreement can be found on the following page on the Oracle Technology Network (OTN):

`http://www.oracle.com/technetwork/licenses/standard-license-152015.html`

It is important that we read and understand the license agreement.

Downloading the installation archives

Because of the size of the `.zip` archives that contain the Siebel CRM installation files, it is highly recommended to use a download management tool such as Free Download Manager.

After logging in to Oracle's Software Delivery Cloud, we choose Siebel CRM in the Select a Product Pack dropdown list and choose Microsoft Windows (64-bit) in the Platform dropdown list. The following screenshot shows this selection.

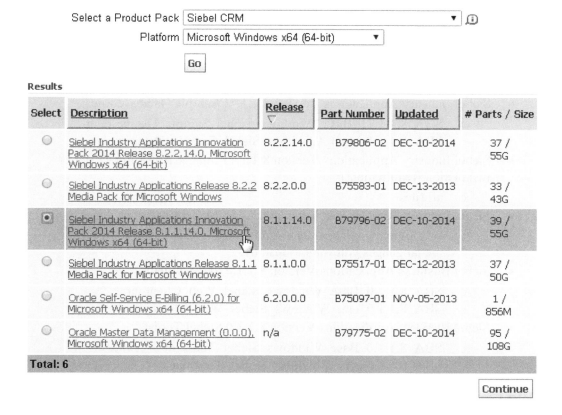

Note that the actual search results may vary in the future.

After clicking the Go button, a list of media packs is displayed. To access the installers for Innovation Pack 2014, click the media pack named Siebel Industry Applications Innovation Pack 2014 Release 8.1.1.14 Media Pack for Microsoft Windows. At the time of writing, the Innovation Pack 2013 (8.1.1.11) release is made available by Oracle on the My Oracle Support portal.

After clicking the media pack link, a list of download archives is displayed. The following .zip archives must be downloaded and extracted to a single folder. The following list also shows the .jar files we need to extract from the .zip archives for a self-study environment, referring only to the English-American (enu) language pack. If we wish to install additional language packs, we must extract the respective language-specific files as identified by the three-letter code in the name of the .jar file (for example: "fra" for French).

File List for Innovation Pack 2013

- Siebel Industry Applications Version 8.1.1.11 Siebel Client (Starter Installation Requirement)
  - SBA_8.1.1.11_Base_Windows_Siebel_Web_Client.jar
  - SBA_8.1.1.11_enu_Windows_Siebel_Web_Client.jar
- Siebel Industry Applications Version 8.1.1.11 Siebel Tools (Starter Installation Requirement):
  - SBA_8.1.1.11_Base_Windows_Siebel_Tools.jar
  - SBA_8.1.1.11_enu_Windows_Siebel_Tools.jar
- Siebel Industry Applications Version 8.1.1.11 Sample Database Files:
  - SBA_8.1.1.11_Base_Windows_Siebel_Sample_Database.jar
  - SBA_8.1.1.11_enu_Windows_Siebel_Sample_Database.jar
- Siebel Industry Applications Version 8.1.1.11 ImageCreator Files (Starter Installation Requirement):
  - all files
- Siebel Industry Applications Version 8.1.1.11 Siebel Repository Files:
  - srf.zip (extract the content of this file and keep only the files for the languages you want to install)
- Siebel Business Applications Version 8.1.1.0 Siebel Client:
  - SBA_8.1.1.0_Base_Windows_Siebel_Web_Client.jar
  - SBA_8.1.1.0_enu_Windows_Siebel_Web_Client.jar
- Siebel Business Applications Version 8.1.1.0 Siebel Tools:
  - SBA_8.1.1.0_Base_Windows_Siebel_Tools.jar
  - SBA_8.1.1.0_enu_Windows_Siebel_Tools.jar

File List for Innovation Pack 2014

- Siebel Industry Applications Version 8.1.1.14 Siebel Client (Starter Installation Requirement):
  - SBA_8.1.1.14_Base_Windows_Siebel_Web_Client.jar

- o SBA_8.1.1.14_enu_Windows_Siebel_Web_Client.jar
- Siebel Industry Applications Version 8.1.1.14 Siebel Tools (Starter Installation Requirement):
  - o SBA_8.1.1.14_Base_Windows_Siebel_Tools.jar
  - o SBA_8.1.1.14_enu_Windows_Siebel_Tools.jar
- Siebel Industry Applications Version 8.1.1.14 Sample Database Files:
  - o SBA_8.1.1.14_Base_Windows_Siebel_Sample_Database.jar
  - o SBA_8.1.1.14_enu_Windows_Siebel_Sample_Database.jar
- Siebel Industry Applications Version 8.1.1.14 ImageCreator Files (Starter Installation Requirement):
  - o all files

The ZIP Preview feature of Free Download Manager can be used to dramatically reduce the download size by only selecting the files we need. With regard to language packs, we should always download the **American-English (enu)** language pack. Other language packs can be downloaded as needed.

Accessing Oracle Siebel Documentation

The Oracle Siebel Documentation (also known as Siebel Bookshelf) can be accessed online and downloaded in various versions from the following Oracle Technology Network web site:

http://www.oracle.com/technetwork/documentation/siebel-087898.html

To support the examples in this book, it is recommended to download the **Siebel Business Applications Innovation Pack 2013 Documentation Library** for IP 2013 or the **Siebel CRM Innovation Pack 2014 Documentation Library** for IP 2014.

Extracting the Siebel Installers for IP 2013

The **Siebel Image Creator** - extracted along with the installation archives - must be used to create the Siebel installation images. For details on this process, please refer to Chapter 3 of this book.

The following procedure describes how to create a Siebel installation image for Siebel Tools, the Siebel Mobile/Developer Web Client, and the Siebel Sample Database, using the Siebel Image Creator in Innovation Pack 2013.

Step	Description	Tasks and Example Values
1	Open a Windows command shell.	• Press WIN+R • Type cmd • Press ENTER
2	Navigate to the folder containing the .jar files and snic.bat	Use the cd command to navigate in the command shell.
3	Set the JAVA_HOME environment variable.	Run a command similar to the following (the path to the JRE on your machine might be different): set JAVA_HOME=C:\Program Files (x86)\Java\jre1.7.0_45
4	Run the Siebel Network Image Creator	At the command prompt, type snic.bat and press ENTER.
5	The Welcome dialog is displayed.	Click Next
6	Select options.	Select the following: • Create a new image or add product(s) to an existing image Click Next
7	Specify a directory path.	Example: C:\Siebel_Install_Image Click Next
8	Select a Siebel version.	Except for base installers for Siebel Developer Web Client and Siebel Tools select: • 8.1.1.11 Click Next
9	Select a platform	Select the following: • Windows Click Next
10	Select products	Select the following: • Siebel Sample Database • Siebel Tools • Siebel Web Client Click Next

(Continued)

11	Specify languages	Select the following: • ENU – English (American) • Any other language(s) needed Click Next
12	Files are extracted	Wait until the file extraction is finished.
13	Extraction summary is displayed	Review the summary information. Click Finish

Repeat the steps in the previous table to extract the base installers (8.1.1.0) for Siebel Tools and the Siebel Web Client.

As a result, the folder specified in step 7 of the previous procedure now contains several subfolders with the installers for the Siebel Mobile or Developer Web Client, Sample Database and Siebel Tools.

Extracting the Siebel Installers for IP 2014

The following procedure describes how to create a Siebel installation image for Siebel Tools, the Siebel Mobile/Developer Web Client, and the Siebel Sample Database, using the Siebel Image Creator in Innovation Pack 2014.

Step	Description	Tasks and Example Values
1	Open a Windows command shell.	• Press WIN+R • Type cmd • Press ENTER
2	Navigate to the folder containing the .jar files and snic.bat	Use the cd command to navigate in the command shell.
3	Set the JAVA_HOME environment variable.	Run a command similar to the following (the path to the JRE on your machine might be different): set JAVA_HOME="C:\Program Files (x86)\Java\jre1.7.0_45"
4	Run the Siebel Network Image Creator	At the command prompt, type snic.bat and press ENTER.
5	The Welcome dialog is displayed.	Click Next

(Continued)

6	Select options.	Select the following: • Create a new image or add product(s) to an existing image Click Next
7	Specify a directory path.	**Example:** "`C:\Siebel_Install_Image`". Click Next
8	Select a platform	Select the following: • Windows Click Next
9	Select products	Select the following: • Siebel Sample Database • Siebel Tools • Siebel Web Client Click Next
10	Specify languages	Select the following: • ENU – English (American) • Any other language(s) needed Click Next
11	Files are extracted	Wait until the file extraction is finished.
12	Extraction summary is displayed	Review the summary information. Click Finish

Adjusting Browser Security Settings

In order to allow the browser to download and install the ActiveX controls for the Siebel High-Interactivity Framework, we must adjust the security settings of Microsoft Internet Explorer as follows:

1. Open Internet Explorer.
2. Navigate to the Tools menu and select Options.
3. In the Options dialog, click the Security tab.
4. Click the Trusted Sites icon.
5. Click the Sites button.
6. Uncheck the flag Require server verification (https:) for all sites in this zone.
7. In the Add this website to the zone field enter `http://localhost`

8. Click the Add button.
9. Repeat steps 7 and 8 and create an entry for your machine's hostname. Hint: You can obtain the hostname of your machine by entering hostname in a command shell window.
10. Click the Close button.
11. Click the Custom Level button in the Security Level area.
12. From the Reset to dropdown list on the bottom of the dialog, select Low.
13. Click Reset...
14. Click Yes.
15. Click OK.
16. Click Apply.
17. Click OK.

Depending on our system settings it might be necessary to make Microsoft Internet Explorer temporarily the default browser, in order to avoid problems during the installation of the Developer Web Client.

Also, we should ensure that pop-ups are always allowed for the same sites we entered in the security administration part of the above.

Installing Siebel CRM Client Software

The installation process for a self-study environment is as follows:

- Change compatibility settings and security privileges
- Install and patch the Siebel Web Client
- Install the Siebel Sample Database
- Install and patch Siebel Tools
- Copy the new SRF File
- Configure Siebel Tools to connect to the sample database
- Enable Open UI
- Use the Demo Users Reference

Changing Compatibility Settings and Security Privileges

The installation of Siebel CRM client software on Windows 7 (and higher) requires the installer software to run in "compatibility mode" and with administrative privileges.

Before we run the installers, we must open the Windows Properties dialog for all of the files shown next and apply the settings as described.

- In the Compatibility tab, check the Run this program in compatibility mode for flag and select Windows XP (Service Pack 3) from the list.
- In the Privilege Level section of the Compatibility tab, check the Run this program as an administrator flag.

Change these settings for the following files (note that the file path is shown relative to the folder containing the installation image):

- ..\Windows\Client\Siebel_Web_Client\Disk1\install\oui.exe
- ..\Windows\Client\Siebel_Tools\Disk1\install\oui.exe
- ..\Windows\Client\Siebel_Web_Client\Disk1\install\module.exe
- ..\Windows\Client\Siebel_Tools\Disk1\install\module.exe
- ..\Windows\Client\Siebel_Sample_Database\install.exe
- ..\Windows\Client\Siebel_Sample_Database\Setup.exe

Installing and Patching the Siebel Web Client (IP 2013)

The following procedure describes how to install and patch the Siebel Developer/Mobile Web Client for Innovation Pack 2013. The Windows user account used during this installation must have administrative privileges.

Step	Description	Tasks and Example Values
1	Start the Oracle Universal Installer.	Double-click the `oui.exe` file in the **8.1.1.0**\Windows\Client\Siebel_Web_Client\Disk1\install folder.
2	The Welcome dialog is displayed.	Click Next
3	Specify the home directory	Example: `C:\Siebel\8.1\Client_1` (default value). Click Next
4	Prerequisite checks	The installer performs prerequisite checks. Verify that all checks are passed successfully. Click Next
5	Select Languages	Select English Click Next
6	Welcome to Siebel Business Applications Client Setup	Click Next

(Continued)

7	Type of Client	Select Mobile Web Client Click Next
8	Siebel Remote Server hostname	Keep the default value Click Next
9	Search Server Information	Keep the default values Click Next
10	Summary	Review the summary information Click Install
11	The installation progress is displayed	
12	Microsoft Internet Explorer is launched	The browser loads the `predeploy.htm` file in the client's `PUBLIC` directory to load the preconfigured ActiveX controls for the High-Interactivity client. When the page displays The download is complete... the browser window must be closed to continue with the installation.
13	The installation process continues	
14	Success Message	Click Exit and Yes to leave the installer.

After installing the base version (8.1.1.0) of the Siebel Web Client, we must apply the patch for Innovation Pack 2013. The following procedure guides us through the patching process.

Step	Description	Tasks and Example Values
1	Start the patch installer.	Double-click the `setup.bat` file in the **8.1.1.11\Windows\Client\Siebel_Web_Client\Disk1\install** folder.
2	The Welcome dialog is displayed.	Click Next
3	Specify the home directory	Specify the same home directory that you used during the base installation. Click Next
4	Install patch	Click Install
5	Wait until patch installation is complete	Exit the installer

Installing the Siebel Web Client (IP 2014)

The following procedure describes how to install the Siebel Developer/Mobile Web Client for Innovation Pack 2014. As of IP 2014, the client installer is similar to the server installer and provides a 'migrate' option to detect and patch existing installations, hence no separate patch installation is required.

Step	Description	Tasks and Example Values
1	Start the Oracle Universal Installer.	Double-click the `setup.bat` file in the **8.1.1.14**\Windows\Client\Siebel_Web_Client\Disk1\install folder.
2	The Welcome dialog is displayed.	Click Next
3	Oracle Configuration Manager	Uncheck the option to receive security updates. Click Next. Click Yes to confirm that you do not wish to receive security updates.
4	Installation Type	Select New Installation if this is the first installation. Select Migrate Installation to patch an existing client installation. Click Next
5	Installation Details	Provide an Oracle Home name (or keep the default) Enter the client installation directory path. Example: `C:\Siebel\8.1\Client_1` (default value). Click Next
6	Language Selection	Choose additional languages. English should be selected by default. Click Next
7	Client Type	Select Mobile Web Client. Keep Yes for the Activate Open UI option. Click Next
8	Siebel Remote Server	Keep the default value Click Next
9	Summary	Review the summary information Click Install
10	The installation progress is displayed	

(Continued)

11	Microsoft Internet Explorer is launched	The browser loads the `predeploy.htm` file in the client's PUBLIC directory to load the preconfigured ActiveX controls for the High-Interactivity client.
		When the page displays The download is complete… the browser window must be closed to continue with the installation.
12	The installation process is displayed	Wait for the installation to finish
13	Success Message is displayed	Click Next
14	Finish	Click Close
		Click Yes to confirm

Installing the Siebel Sample Database

The following procedure describes how to install the Siebel Sample Database. The installation path must be set to the folder where the Siebel Mobile/Developer Web Client has been installed previously.

Step	Description	Tasks and Example Values
1	Start the InstallShield Wizard.	Double-click the `install.exe` file in the Siebel_Sample_Database folder.
2	Choose Setup Language	Example: English
		Click OK
3	The Welcome dialog is displayed	Click Next
4	Setup Type	Select Custom
		In the Destination Folder section, click Browse and navigate to the Siebel client installation directory.
		Click Next
5	Select Components	Keep Sample Files selected
		Unselect Sample Search Index
		Click Next
6	Choose Languages	Select English (American).
		Click Next

(Continued)

7	Select Program Folder	Keep the default. Click Next
8	Installation progress is displayed	Leave the installer window open and wait for the process to finish.
9	Event Log	Summary information is displayed. Click Next
10	The wizard displays successful completion	Click Finish

Installing and Patching Siebel Tools (IP 2013)

The following procedure describes how to install Siebel Tools for Innovation Pack 2013. First, we start with the base version (8.1.1.0).

Step	Description	Tasks and Example Values
1	Start the Oracle Universal Installer.	Double-click the `oui.exe` file in the **8.1.1.0**\Windows\Client\Siebel_Tools\Disk1\install folder.
2	The Welcome dialog is displayed.	Click Next
3	Select a Product to install	Select Siebel Business Application Tools Click Next
4	Specify the home directory	Example: `C:\Siebel\8.1\Tools_1` (default value). Click Next
5	Prerequisite checks	The installer performs checks for prerequisite checks. Verify that all checks are passed successfully. Click Next
6	Select Languages	Select English Click Next
7	Siebel Database Server	Select Oracle Database Server Click Next

(Continued)

8	Database Identification	Database Alias: orcl Table Owner: SIEBEL Click Next
9	File System	Directory Path Example: `C:\Siebel\8.1\Client_1\SAMPLE\FILES` Click Next
10	Siebel Remote Server hostname	Keep the default Click Next
11	Enterprise Server Information	Gateway Name Server address: localhost Enterprise Server: Siebel Click Next
12	Summary	Review the summary information Click Install
13	The installation progress is displayed	
14	Success Message	Click Exit and Yes to leave the installer.

After installing the base version (8.1.1.0) of Siebel Tools, we must apply the patch for Innovation Pack 2013. The following procedure guides us through the patching process:

Step	Description	Tasks and Example Values
1	Start the patch installer.	Double-click the `setup.bat` file in the **8.1.1.11\Windows\Client\Siebel_Tools\Disk1\install** folder.
2	The Welcome dialog is displayed.	Click Next
3	Specify the home directory	Specify the exact home directory that you used during the base installation. Click Next
4	Install patch	Click Install
5	Wait until patch installation is complete	Exit the installer

Installing Siebel Tools (IP 2014)

The following procedure describes how to install Siebel Tools for Innovation Pack 2014. As of IP 2014, the installer is similar to the server installer and provides a 'migrate' option to detect and patch existing installations, hence no separate patch installation is required.

Step	Description	Tasks and Example Values
1	Start the Oracle Universal Installer.	Double-click the `setup.bat` file in the **8.1.1.14**\Windows\Client\Siebel_Tools\Disk1\install folder.
2	The Welcome dialog is displayed.	Click Next
3	Oracle Configuration Manager	Uncheck the option to receive security updates. Click Next. Click Yes to confirm that you do not wish to receive security updates.
4	Installation Type	Select New Installation if this is the first installation. Select Migrate Installation to patch an existing client installation. Click Next
5	Installation Details	Provide an Oracle Home name (or keep the default) Enter the client installation directory path. Example: "`C:\Siebel\8.1\Tools_1`" (default value). Click Next
6	Language Selection	Choose additional languages. English should be selected by default. Click Next
7	Database Server	Keep the default selection. Click Next
8	Database Account	Keep the default selection Click Next
9	File System	Enter the path to the Siebel Web Client's SAMPLE/FILES directory. Click Next
10	Siebel Remote Server	Keep the default value. Click Next

(Continued)

11	Enterprise Server	Keep the default values. Click Next
12	Summary	Click Install
13	The installation process is displayed	Wait for the installation to finish
14	Success Message is displayed	Click Next
15	Finish	Click Close Click Yes to confirm

Copying the New SRF File (IP 2013)

Oracle ships new standard SRF files with each Innovation Pack. It is necessary to copy the `siebel_sia.srf` file that we extracted from the `srf.zip` archive into the `OBJECTS` sub-directories of both Siebel Developer Web Client and Siebel Tools.

Configuring Siebel Tools to Connect to the Sample Database

The following procedure must be followed to allow Siebel Tools to connect to the Siebel Sample Database:

1. Use Windows Explorer to navigate to the Siebel Mobile Web Client installation directory.
2. Open the `uagent.cfg` file in the client's `BIN\ENU` directory with Notepad.
3. Copy the value of the `ConnectString` parameter in the `[Sample]` section of the `uagent.cfg` file to the clipboard.
4. Navigate to the Siebel Tools installation directory.
5. Open the `tools.cfg` file in the Siebel Tools `BIN\ENU` directory with Notepad.
6. Overwrite the value of the `ConnectString` parameter in the `[Sample]` section of the `tools.cfg` file with the value you copied in step 3.
7. Save and close all files.

Enabling Open UI (IP 2013)

For each application we wish to run in Open UI mode, we must locate the client configuration file (`.cfg`) in the language specific `BIN` sub-folder of the installation directory. It is recommended to copy the existing file (e.g. `uagent.cfg` for Siebel Call

Center) and rename the new file (e.g. to `uagent_oui.cfg`). This is necessary only for IP 2013. In IP 2014, we can choose to activate Open UI in the installer. Nonetheless, we can edit the `.cfg` files manually if we need to make any changes.

In the copied file, locate the `[InfraUIFramework]` section and add (or edit) the following line:

```
EnableOpenUI = TRUE
```

If we wish to create Windows shortcuts using the new configuration file, we can use the following example shortcut as a guide:

```
D:\siebel\client\BIN\siebel.exe /c
D:\siebel\client\bin\enu\uagent_oui.cfg /d sample /u SADMIN /p
SADMIN
```

This shortcut will run the application in the system's default browser. In order to open the application in a specific browser (for example Microsoft Internet Explorer), we can add a command similar to the following to any existing shortcut.

```
/b "C:\Program Files (x86)\Internet Explorer\iexplore.exe"
```

The `/b` switch for the `siebel.exe` program must be followed by a valid path to a browser executable.

Using the Demo Users Reference

The **Demo Users Reference** guide in the Siebel Bookshelf can be used to find demo user accounts with different roles that might be useful during exploration of standard Siebel CRM functionality.

Manifest Administration and Migration for Versions Prior to Innovation Pack 2013

If you find yourself having to administer or customize a Siebel Open UI release prior to Innovation Pack 2013, which is either 8.1.1.9 / 8.2.2.2 or 8.1.1.10 / 8.2.2.3, you will find the following information useful.

- Manifest files overview
- Structure of manifest XML files
- Structure of the manifest map file
- Migrating manifest data to Innovation Pack 2013 and later

Manifest Files Overview

One of the major differences between the earlier releases of Siebel Open UI and the current Innovation Pack releases is that manifest data was not captured in administrative tables via the client user interface but had to be manually administered in a set of two XML files and one text file.

These files are located in the OBJECTS sub-directory of the Siebel Server or Developer Web Client installation folders. The following list provides a short description of the files:

- **core_manifest.xml**: This file contains the references to JavaScript files constituting the Siebel Open UI framework as delivered by Oracle. It must not be modified.
- **custom_manifest.xml**: This file is reserved for customer use to reference the JavaScript files created by developers at the customer site.
- **manifest_extensions.map**: This file establishes the mapping between user interface objects (mainly applets) and keys used in the XML files.

Structure of Manifest XML Files

The following screenshot shows a portion of the `core_manifest.xml` file as delivered with Siebel CRM release 8.1.1.10.

```
- <ROOT>
  - <COMMON>
      <FILE_NAME>3rdParty/jquery.cookie.js</FILE_NAME>
      <FILE_NAME>3rdParty/jquery.livequery.js</FILE_NAME>
      <FILE_NAME>preload.js</FILE_NAME>
      <FILE_NAME>postload.js</FILE_NAME>
      <FILE_NAME>siebel/perf.js</FILE_NAME>
    </COMMON>
  - <PLATFORM_COMMON>
    + <PLATFORM Name="Desktop">
    + <PLATFORM Name="Mobile">
    </PLATFORM_COMMON>
  + <KEY_COMMON>
  - <PLATFORM_KEY_SPECIFIC>
    + <PLATFORM Name="Mobile">
    - <PLATFORM Name="Desktop">
      - <KEY Name="AppletPR">
          <FILE_NAME>siebel/phyrenderer.js</FILE_NAME>
        </KEY>
      + <KEY Name="ListPR">
      + <KEY Name="GridPR">
      + <KEY Name="TaskPanePR">
      + <KEY Name="TreePR">
      + <KEY Name="CalPR">
      + <KEY Name="NAVIGATION_TREE">
      + <KEY Name="NAVIGATION_TAB">
      + <KEY Name="RestOfUIPR">
      + <KEY Name="SmartScriptPR">
      + <KEY Name="SearchBarPR">
      + <KEY Name="SearchAllResultsPR">
      + <KEY Name="SignViewPR">
      </PLATFORM>
    </PLATFORM_KEY_SPECIFIC>
  </ROOT>
```

In the following list we provide an explanation for the major elements in the file:

- `<COMMON>`: contains `<FILE_NAME>` elements that carry the relative paths to JavaScript files which should always be loaded.

- <PLATFORM_COMMON>: Allows for a distinguishing list of files that should always be loaded by platform (Desktop or Mobile).

- <KEY_COMMON>: Uses <KEY> elements to provide a grouping mechanism for lists of JavaScript files to be loaded for a certain user interface object. Keys used by customers must be associated with a concrete UI object (i.e. applet) in the manifest_extensions.map file (see below).

- <PLATFORM_KEY_SPECIFIC>: Allows for a distinguishing list of object specific files (identified by a key) on a specific platform (Desktop or Mobile).

The custom_manifest.xml file has the same structure but is empty. Developers at customer sites must register each custom JavaScript file in the correct area of the file.

The following screenshot shows the custom_manifest.xml file with an example entry to illustrate this concept.

```
- <ROOT>
  + <COMMON>
  + <PLATFORM_COMMON>
  - <KEY_COMMON>
    - <KEY Name="SliderPM">
        <FILE_NAME>siebel/applet.js</FILE_NAME>
        <FILE_NAME>siebel/pmodel.js</FILE_NAME>
        <FILE_NAME>siebel/custom/SliderPM.js</FILE_NAME>
      </KEY>
```

The developer has added the <KEY Name="SliderPM"> element to the <KEY_COMMON> section. The three <FILE_NAME> child elements reference two standard JavaScript files and the custom JavaScript file (SliderPM.js),which contains an extension class for a presentation model.

Note that developers have to register not only the custom files they write but also the necessary standard files. To identify the correct standard files, it is recommended to inspect the core_manifest.xml file.

Structure of the Manifest Map File

The manifest_extensions.map file must be used to register dependencies between applets and keys which - as shown in the previous example - are used to group files in the custom_manifest.xml file.

The following screenshot shows how an example manifest_extensions.map file can look.

```
[Presentation_Model]
Opportunity Form Applet - Child=SliderPM

[Physical_Renderer]
Literature List Administration Applet=CBOXPR
Contact Form Applet=PartialRefreshRenderer
```

The map file contains two sections, which can be described as follows:

- `[Presentation_Model]`: Contains a list of applet-key pairs for custom presentation models.

- `[Physical_Renderer]`: Contains a list of applet-key pairs for custom physical renderers.

Each entry for an applet-key pair must use the exact name of the applet as stored in the Siebel Repository followed by an equals sign and the exact name (case sensitive) of the key used in the `custom_manifest.xml` file.

In the previous screenshot we can see that in the `[Presentation_Model]` section, the applet named `Opportunity Form Applet - Child` is associated with the `SliderPM` key which references the JavaScript files as described in the previous section.

> After making modifications to either the `custom_manifest.xml` file or the `manifest_extensions.map` file, we must restart the object manager to make the changes available to end users.

Migrating Manifest Data to Innovation Pack 2013 and Later

Custom manifest administration data from files present in the `OBJECTS` folder of the Siebel Server installation directory is migrated automatically during the "Upgrade Physical Schema (upgphys)" step of the upgrade process to Innovation Pack 2013, or later.

Developers are advised to verify that the migration was successful by inspecting the data using the Manifest Administration views that are included in IP 2013 and later in the Siebel Web Client. Manual re-entry of manifest administration data might become necessary under certain circumstances.

C
Working with Example Code Files

This book contains case study examples that are complemented by code archives. In this appendix, we will briefly review the techniques for importing code files into your self-study environment. The following will be covered:

- Copy example JavaScript files
- Copy example style sheets
- Copy example image files
- Copy example web templates
- Import Siebel Tools archive files

Copying Example JavaScript Files

Most of the code archives contain example JavaScript files that implement custom presentation models or custom physical renderers. To implement the case study, extract the code archive for the chapter and copy the JavaScript files mentioned in the case study to the following folder in your Siebel Developer Web Client installation:

```
<Client Installation
Folder>\PUBLIC\<Language>\<Build>\SCRIPTS\siebel\custom
```

The following is an example of a valid path for custom JavaScript files in Siebel Open UI:

```
D:\Siebel\Client\PUBLIC\enu\23044\SCRIPTS\siebel\custom
```

In the example, `D:\Siebel` is the client installation folder, `enu` (American English) is the language-specific sub-directory of the `PUBLIC` folder and `23044` is the build number (representing IP 2014).

Depending on your installation, Siebel version, and language pack(s), the path on your machine might be different.

After copying the files to the correct location, follow the instructions in the case study to complete the example scenario.

Copying Example Style Sheets

The following is an example of the correct location of example style sheets:

```
D:\Siebel\Client\PUBLIC\enu\FILES\custom
```

Custom style sheets must always be located in the custom sub-folder of the FILES directory. If the code archive contains .css files, copy them to the folder location indicated in the example above. If the custom folder is not present, create it.

After copying the example style sheet files, follow the instructions in the case study scenarios to complete the implementation.

Copying Example Image Files

When the code archive contains image files, copy them to the following folder location:

```
D:\Siebel\Client\PUBLIC\enu\IMAGES\custom
```

The example folder path refers to the custom sub-folder of the IMAGES directory. If the custom folder does not exist, create it before you copy example image files.

Copying Example Web Templates

Siebel Web Template (SWT) files delivered with a chapter's code archive must be placed in the following folder location:

```
D:\Siebel\Client\WEBTEMPL\OUIWEBTEMPL\CUSTOM
```

The example folder path denotes the CUSTOM folder of the OUIWEBTEMPL directory within a Siebel client's WEBTEMPL folder.

Importing Siebel Tools Archive Files

For case studies that use repository object definitions delivered as .sif files, the following procedure describes how to import a Siebel Tools archive file:

1. Log in to Siebel Tools.
2. In the Tools menu, select Import from Archive...
3. In the Select Archive to Import dialog, browse to the .sif file you want to import.
4. Click the Open button.
5. Click Next.
6. Click Next.
7. Click Yes to confirm the summary message.

8. Wait for the import process to finish.
9. On the Summary page, click Finish to close the Import Wizard.
10. Compile all imported object definitions.

After importing and compiling the example repository object definitions, follow the instructions in the case study scenario to complete the implementation.

D
More Information

You have reached the final pages of this book. Congratulations! But even if you are a seasoned Siebel consultant with years of experience, the learning path to master Open UI and Siebel Mobile Applications might be steep. In this appendix, we will have a look at additional training and information available from Oracle and other sources.

Please note that the URLs in this chapter have been verified as accurate at the time of writing this book. Given the nature of the internet, they could have changed in the meantime.

Getting Trained

The success of a Siebel CRM project, or any standard software implementation project in general, is linked to the education of the professionals who undertake it. Complex systems like Siebel CRM will not reveal their intricate patterns to naïve consultants (or their managers) who believe in self study or 'fast track' trainings.

The money saved on training (or no training) will be spent equally fast on project delay. It is paramount for the Siebel professional to expose him- or herself to high quality instructor-led training that is provided, for example, by Oracle University and its training partners throughout the world.

The following websites may serve as an entry point for your personal training plan:

- Oracle University: http://education.oracle.com
- Oracle Partner Network: http://opn.oracle.com
- Oracle Technology Network: http://otn.oracle.com
- Oracle Learning Library: http://oracle.com/goto/oll

In the Oracle Learning Library (OLL) we can find - amongst many other tutorials and videos - highly useful online training material for Siebel CRM in general and Open UI and Siebel Mobile Applications specifically. OLL is a free resource but the training provided is nonetheless high in quality.

Additional Information

Siebel CRM has been developed under the assumption that customers will employ their own technicians or hire external consultants to install, configure and manage the software. Documenting the necessary steps to do so and also providing information about the features of Siebel CRM has evolved into what is known today as the Siebel Bookshelf.

The Siebel Bookshelf

Oracle has made the entire Siebel documentation available online. We can access the documentation library for each supported version from the following internet address: http://www.oracle.com/technetwork/documentation/siebel-087898.html.

Before we start downloading and installing Siebel CRM, we should ensure that we have read and digested the information given to us by the technical writers at Oracle. The following guides in the Siebel Bookshelf are highly recommended to prepare for work with Siebel Open UI and Mobile Applications:

- Configuring Siebel Open UI
- Siebel Fundamentals for Open UI
- Deploying Siebel Open UI
- Siebel Mobile Guide: Connected
- Siebel Mobile Guide: Disconnected

Oracle Community

Not every trick, bug or workaround can be found in the official Siebel documentation. While you are reading these lines, somebody encounters a problem or explores some functionality within Siebel CRM. Many Siebel professionals use the Oracle Community (formerly known as Oracle Forums) to post questions and findings. Experienced consultants pick up the posts and answer them so the community has a great place to search for information outside the official documentation.

We can access the Oracle Community at https://community.oracle.com.

My Oracle Support

Customers, partners and employees of Oracle have access to the Oracle support portal, which not only allows for the creation of service requests but also for searches of the knowledge base of resolved service requests, bulletins and other documents.

My Oracle Support is a centralized portal for all Oracle products and can be accessed via the URL http://support.oracle.com.

The Oracle support team maintains dedicated 'information centers' for certain topics. The information center for Siebel Open UI can be found as document Id 1511846.2.

The My Oracle Support Community (MOSC) is an Oracle Community area for everyone who has access to My Oracle Support. The MOSC space for Siebel Open UI can be found at

`https://community.oracle.com/community/support/siebel/siebel_open_ui`.

The Internet Community

Various channels exist to share findings and knowledge on the internet. Over the past years, many IT professionals decided to create their own websites, weblogs or social network channels to distribute information on Siebel CRM.

A good starting point for research on this vast amount of information might be Google's blog search: `http://blogsearch.google.com`.

Alexander Hansal's blog on Siebel CRM, Oracle BI and Fusion/Cloud Applications can be found at `http://siebelhub.com`.

Index

Index

Index

Index

Index

Other P8 Titles